Can America Govern Itself?

Can America Govern Itself? brings together a diverse group of distinguished scholars to analyze how rising party polarization and economic inequality have affected the performance of American governing institutions. It is organized around two themes: the changing nature of representation in the United States and how changes in the political environment have affected the internal processes of institutions, overall government performance, and policy outcomes. The chapters analyze concerns about power, influence, and representation in American politics, the quality of deliberation and political communications, the management and implementation of public policy, and the performance of an eighteenth-century constitution in today's polarized political environment. These renowned scholars provide a deeper and more systematic grasp of what is new and what is perennial in challenges to democracy at a fraught moment.

FRANCES E. LEE is Professor of Government and Politics at the University of Maryland. She is author of *Insecure Majorities: Congress and the Perpetual Campaign* (2016), *Beyond Ideology: Politics, Principles, and Partisanship in the U.S. Senate* (2009), and coauthor of *Sizing Up the Senate: The Unequal Consequences of Equal Representation* (1999). Her books have received national recognition, including the APSA's Richard F. Fenno Award and the D. B. Hardeman Award presented by the Lyndon Baines Johnson Foundation for the best book on a congressional topic.

NOLAN MCCARTY is the Susan Dod Brown Professor of Politics and Public Affairs at Princeton University. He has co-authored three books: *Political Game Theory* (Cambridge, 2006), *Polarized America: The Dance of Ideology and Unequal Riches* (2006), and *Political Bubbles: Financial Crises and the Failure of American Democracy* (2015). He is an elected member of the American Academy of Arts and Sciences.

SSRC Anxieties of Democracy

Editors

John Ferejohn, *New York University*
Ira Katznelson, *Columbia University*
Deborah J. Yashar, *Princeton University*

With liberal democracies afflicted by doubt and disquiet, this series probes sources of current apprehensions and explores how such regimes might thrive. What array of pressures most stresses democratic ideas and institutions? Which responses might strengthen these regimes and help them flourish?

Embedded in the Social Science Research Council's (SSRC) program on "Anxieties of Democracy," the series focuses on how representative institutions – including elections, legislatures, political parties, the press and mass media, interest groups, social movements, and policy organizations – orient participation, learning, and accountability.

The volumes in the series further ask how particular policy challenges shape the character of democratic institutions and collective actors, and affect their capacity to address large problems in the public interest. These challenges include, but are not limited to: (1) designing democratic institutions to perform successfully under conditions of social and political polarization; (2) managing and orienting contemporary capitalism and alleviating hierarchies of inequality; (3) addressing questions of membership, including population movements and differentiated citizenship; (4) choosing policies to balance national security and civil liberty; (5) exploring the effects of global climate on citizens and the human impact on the environment; (6) managing the development of media and information technologies to ensure they enhance, rather than degrade, robust pluralism and civil political engagement.

Sponsored by the Social Science Research Council

The Social Science Research Council (SSRC) is an independent, international, nonprofit organization driven by its mission to mobilize social science for the public good. Founded in 1923, the SSRC fosters innovative research, nurtures new generations of social scientists, deepens how inquiry is practiced within and across disciplines, and amplifies necessary knowledge on important public issues.

The SSRC is guided by the belief that justice, prosperity, and democracy all require better understanding of complex social, cultural, economic, and political processes. We work with practitioners, policymakers, and academic researchers in the social sciences, related professions, and the humanities and natural sciences. We build interdisciplinary and international networks, working with partners around the world to link research to practice and policy, strengthen individual and institutional capacities for learning, and enhance public access to information.

Can America Govern Itself?

Edited by

FRANCES E. LEE
University of Maryland

NOLAN MCCARTY
Princeton University

CAMBRIDGE
UNIVERSITY PRESS

University Printing House, Cambridge CB2 8BS, United Kingdom

One Liberty Plaza, 20th Floor, New York, NY 10006, USA

477 Williamstown Road, Port Melbourne, VIC 3207, Australia

314–321, 3rd Floor, Plot 3, Splendor Forum, Jasola District Centre, New Delhi – 110025, India

79 Anson Road, #06–04/06, Singapore 079906

Cambridge University Press is part of the University of Cambridge.

It furthers the University's mission by disseminating knowledge in the pursuit of education, learning, and research at the highest international levels of excellence.

www.cambridge.org
Information on this title: www.cambridge.org/9781108497299
DOI: 10.1017/9781108667357

© Cambridge University Press 2019

First published 2019

Printed and bound in Great Britain by Clays Ltd, Elcograf S.p.A.

A catalogue record for this publication is available from the British Library.

ISBN 978-1-108-49729-9 Hardback
ISBN 978-1-108-73972-6 Paperback

Contents

Acknowledgments

This book originated in Ira Katznelson's original vision for the Anxieties of Democracy program that he initiated at the Social Science Research Council (SSRC). We are especially appreciative of his efforts and those of the SSRC and Anxieties of Democracy staff, Anoush Terjanian, Ron Kassimir, and Kris-Stella Trump. We would also like to thank the wonderful scholars who provided guidance through their roles on the Anxieties of Democracy steering committee: John Ferejohn, Deborah Yashar, Stephen Ansolabehere, Nancy Bermeo, Josh Cohen, Claudine Gay, Sam Issacharoff, Uday Mehta, Nate Persily, Nancy Rosenblum, and Frances Rosenbluth.

The planning for this volume was done by the Anxieties of Democracy Institutions Working Group that included Brandice Canes-Wrone, Dan Carpenter, Anthony Chen, Elisabeth Gerber, Daniel Gillion, Matt Grossman, Suzanne Mettler, Gillian Metzger, David Samuels, Eric Schickler, Mark Schmitt, Arthur Spirling, and Charles Stewart. We were delighted that so many of these great scholars agreed not only to help plan the volume but to contribute to it as well.

We would also like to thank the Princeton Department of Politics and the Center for the Study of Democratic Politics for their financial and logistical support for the volume's conference. Michele Epstein did a wonderful job managing the affair. Our chapters benefited greatly from several discussants, including: Doug Arnold, Sarah Binder, Devin Caughey, Henry Farrell, Megan Ming Francis, Cathie Jo Martin, Burt Monroe, and Dara Strolovitch. We thank SoRelle Wyckoff and Michelle Anderson for excellent editorial assistance. Finally, we would like to thank Sara Doskow of Cambridge University Press for all of her support for this project and book.

I

The Anxieties of American Democracy

Frances E. Lee and Nolan McCarty

Since 2006, the American Psychological Association (APA) has conducted an annual *Stress in America* survey to examine the sources of stress and its impact on the health and well-being of Americans. But only in October of 2016 did the APA deem it necessary to include questions about American politics and the upcoming election. Their findings were startling. Fifty-two percent of the respondents said that the 2016 election was a very or somewhat significant source of stress. Moreover, those who reported election-induced stress reported significantly higher overall levels of stress (APA, 2017).

Clearly, the stress of the 2016 election did not end on election night. The APA refielded its study in November of 2017. Not only had overall stress increased, but nearly two-thirds of Americans (63 percent) described the future of the nation as a very or somewhat significant source of stress, and more than half (59 percent) said that they regarded this as the lowest point in U.S. history they could recall. These reported levels of political stress rivaled those of more traditional sources such as personal finances, health, and work. The poll's findings seem to be confirmed by the reports of therapists that more patients are asking for assistance with their "Trump Anxiety Disorder" (Schwartzman, 2016).

While the APA didn't begin polling on political anxiety until 2016, American politics was angst-ridden long before Trump's election. Polls reveal that Americans' trust in political leaders and all federal government institutions has been falling for over 20 years.[1] In 2016, 40 percent of registered voters reported having lost faith in American democracy (Persily and Cohen, 2016).

---

[1] Pew Research Center. 2017. Public Trust in Government: 1958–2017. Retrieved from www.people-press.org/2017/12/14/public-trust-in-government-1958-2017/ (last accessed December 9, 2018).

The reasons for the loss of faith and the concomitant stress and anxieties are many. The first is the well-recognized resurgence of partisanship and ideological polarization among our political elites. The ability and proclivity of Democratic and Republican officeholders to work together has deteriorated. Such trends undermine Americans' faith in the ability of our institutions, especially Congress, to solve pressing social and economic problems. Moreover, the deepening partisan divisions at the elite level have reinvigorated intense partisanship within the electorate. While many democracies can flourish with strong partisanship and little inter-party cooperation, our Madisonian constitutional system, with its separation of powers and checks and balances, has resulted in an unsettling mixture of both gridlock and policy uncertainty.

The rise of dysfunctional government could hardly have come at a worse time. The past four decades have witnessed tremendous changes to the American society and economy. Income and wealth inequality has been a problem since the late 1970s. While the top 1 percent of taxpayers earned 8 percent of national income in 1980, that group has raked in more than 17 percent in recent years (Piketty and Saez, 2003). Although increasing economic inequality is a feature of many advanced democracies, the United States is a clear global leader.

Recent economic performance has not only been unequal, it has been marked by stagnation interrupted only by crisis. By almost all accounts, the wages of the middle class have been flat or falling in the 2000s. Total compensation has risen only when increasingly expensive health-care benefits are factored in. The financial crisis of 2007–2008 hit all Americans hard, but the effects have been the most acute and long-lasting for middle- and lower-income Americans.

Over this period, American society has become much more diverse. Following reforms of immigration law in the 1960s, migration (legal and undocumented) from Latin America, Asia, and Africa increased dramatically. While many Americans have embraced the newcomers, many others view mass immigration as a significant economic and cultural threat. The era is also marked by tremendous social change in the rights and social standing of women, the LGBTQ community, and racial and ethnic minorities. These social changes have provoked fear and anxiety among some Americans, even while these changes have also fallen far short of civil rights reformers' goals.

The pace of social and economic change has clearly fueled political conflicts and deepened polarization. But in turn, polarization has made it more difficult for our political system to address the important policy problems generated by economic and social inequality. Increases in economic inequality translate into growing political inequality. For example, in 1980, the top .001 contributors accounted for 15 percent of the money going into federal campaigns, in 2012 it was 41 percent (Bonica et al., 2013). Shockingly, the magnitude of wealth inequality is so great, the wealthy accomplished this feat while spending a slightly lower share of their wealth on politics (Bonica and Rosenthal, 2015).

It is not surprising that studies routinely show that policymakers are far more responsive to high-income voters than middle-income voters.

It was against the backdrop of these longer-term trends, but well before the election of Donald Trump, that the Social Science Research Council (SSRC) launched its "Anxieties of Democracy Program." This multifaceted program includes working groups on political participation, distribution, climate change, security, and the media. The coeditors and several of this volume's authors headed the working group on American institutions. Our charge was to examine the capacities of our governing institutions for effective, responsive, and accountable governance in the United States. This volume reflects the outcome of those examinations.

As a group, we identified a core set of institutional challenges. The first and most prominent is the consequences of the long-term rise in partisanship and ideological polarization that has transformed American politics over the past three generations. But unlike many other academic interventions, we accept polarization and hyper-partisanship as an inevitable feature of our political life, at least over the short to medium term. Thus, rather than focusing on ways of reducing polarization, our attention is on its effects and how those might be mitigated. We also set out to explore whether there are aspects of our institutions that have continued to function well even in our intensely partisan environment.

Despite the recognition that our Madisonian constitution fits uncomfortably with Westminsterian party discipline, we also eschewed major constitutional reforms. Constitutional amendment and revision – challenging even during consensual eras – seem foreclosed by the persistent divides in American politics. This recognition, however, does not blind us to the fact that constitutional norms and practices are evolving under the stress of the shifts in our party system. The powers and performance of the Congress, the executive, and the judiciary have been profoundly reshaped by the polarized currents of American politics. Our federal balance between the national government and the states is also transforming. At the same time, we are interested in the various resiliencies that have held the system in place.

But an exclusive focus on the changes wrought by polarization and partisanship would be limiting. Americans obviously share many other anxieties about the performance of our institutions. An especially relevant set of anxieties focuses on rising economic inequality and how those inequalities have shaped the political sphere. Money in politics and how it speaks has long concerned us, but the potential scale of political inequality generated by our current economic system has heightened worries about the role of special interest lobbies, corporations, and wealthy individuals. At the other end of the continuum, we worry about the opportunities for the poor and marginalized to have a voice in the system.

The working group on American institutions structured our discussions and subsequent work across three broad themes. The first theme concerned the

changing nature of representation in the United States. Second, we explored
how changes in the political environment have affected the internal performance of institutions with a focus on Congress. Finally, we asked how the effects
of polarization, partisanship, and inequality have manifested themselves in
government performance and policy outcomes.

* * *

Anxieties about representation have clearly increased in recent years. Considerable research has undermined the idea that elective representatives are
highly responsive to the views of the typical voter. The apparent correlations
between representative behavior and voter preferences appear to be largely
driven by responsiveness to the interests of higher-income Americans (Gilens,
2012, Gilens and Page, 2014, Bartels, 2016). Findings about legislative polarization also undermine arguments about electoral responsiveness. For example,
Democratic and Republican legislators represent nearly politically and demographically identical districts in increasingly disparate ways (Bonica et al.,
2013). Together these concerns about "plutocracy" and polarization suggest
a fundamental disconnect between typical voters and their representatives.
Several pieces in our volume take up aspects of these anxieties. The first three
chapters of this volume take up the concerns about the influence of wealth and
political inequality.

In an era where corporate profits are an increasing share of gross domestic
product (GDP) and the market power of large firms has risen dramatically,
the fear that big business will use its economic clout to shape political outcomes
has become central to our constellation of anxieties.[2] In an extensive review of
the academic literatures in political science and sociology in Chapter 2,
Anthony Chen catalogues how the evidence for and scholarly understanding
of "business power" has evolved over time. Despite long-time concerns about
corporate domination, pluralists of the mid-twentieth century were generally
sanguine about the possibilities of democratic checks on corporate political
demands. The rise of the new social movements of the 1970s that pushed back
against business interests appeared to support the case for optimism. Evidence
of intra-business political disputes also was seen as an important constraint on
business power. But in reviewing more recent studies of corporate political
activity and policy success, Chen makes the case that business interests have
clearly reasserted themselves and have been successful in moving policy toward
the preferences of specific firms and industries as well as toward those of the
corporate community at large.

---

[2] On trends in market power and corporate profits, see DeLoecker, Jan and Jan Eeckout. 2017.
"The Rise of Market Power and the Macroeconomic Implications." NBER Working Paper
No. 23687, August.

A major source of the resurgence of business has been its outsized role in the advocacy sector, a fact amply documented in Chapter 3 by Lee Drutman, Matt Grossmann, and Tim LaPira. These authors use longitudinal data on federal lobbying activity to identify the "top tier" of the top 100 entities in the lobbying community. Some of their findings are reassuring. While the lobbying expenditure threshold for inclusion in the top 100 increased 75 percent from 1998 to 2012, the median expenditure rose by the same amount, indicating little increase in cross-sectional lobbying inequality. Moreover, the share of lobbying undertaken by business interests has been stable. But their other findings are more disquieting. In the early 2000s, there was quite a bit of churn in the entities that constituted the top 100. From 1998 to 1999, 24 members of the top 100 business spenders dropped from those ranks. But the persistence of organizations on that list has increased dramatically. From 2011 to 2012, only five business organizations left the list. A similar pattern is evident among nonbusinesses. The result is a very highly stratified lobbying industry. Moreover, elite lobbying organizations have dramatically increased the breadth of their lobbying activities. They increasingly lobby on more issues, contact more agencies, and contact legislators about more bills. Consequently, the likelihood that a member of a persistent lobbying elite will be active on an issue is growing.

While recent concerns about the disproportionate influence of the wealthy have speculated that the source of the problem lies in the campaign finance system, scholarship on the question has produced mixed results. This is especially true of studies that try to link the contributions of groups and political action committees to congressional decisions. In Chapter 4, Brandice Canes-Wrone and Nathan Gibson suggest that scholars may have been looking in the wrong place by focusing on political action committees rather than individual donors. Using data from the American National Election Study (ANES) and the Cooperative Congressional Election Study (CCES), Canes-Wrone and Gibson measure the policy preferences of the national "donorate" of each party as well as the policy preferences of voters in each state. This allows them to estimate the impact of donor preferences on Senate roll call voting behavior. While they find that donor opinion had little effect on Senate votes in early 1990s, they find a substantial impact of national partisan donor opinion over the past decade. Based on their estimates, senators weigh the views of donors at least as much as they weigh the opinions of their constituents. Moreover, their evidence suggests that senators are responsive to donors, not the wealthy per se. This suggests that campaign finance may be an important source of unequal responsiveness. Raising even more anxieties about the functioning of the campaign finance system, Canes-Wrone and Gibson find that it is the least electorally vulnerable senators who are most responsive to donors' interests: the senators who personally need the money the least are the most influenced by it.

In Chapter 5, Daniel Gillion and Patricia Posey come at these questions of unequal representation and responsiveness from the opposite vantage point.

Rather than ask why the wealthy are so powerful, they address how poor and marginalized communities have any political impact at all. A persistent anxiety of democracy is that majoritarian political institutions are unlikely to register the interests and viewpoints of disadvantaged minorities. Although there has been much research on the impact of minority protest on policy outcomes, the precise nature of how that influence arises is an open question. In their piece, Gillion and Posey examine the effect of minority protest on congressional elections from 1960 to 1990. They find that protest activity in a congressional district is associated with changes in vote shares consistent with the ideological leanings of the protest. They argue that protests can serve as a signal of incumbent vulnerability, which can lead to better and more experienced challengers.

While some scholars often argue that polarization and the consequent loss of responsiveness to voters is caused by parties that have become too strong, in Chapter 6, Daniel Schlozman and Sam Rosenfeld argue that the central problem is that parties have "hollowed out" significantly over the past several decades. While partisanship runs high among the voters, parties as organizations are weak. They fail to mobilize voters, control nominations, and develop policy expertise. As weakened institutions, they argue that today's parties facilitate the capture of our democracy by "donors and demagogues." To Schlozman and Rosenfeld, a restoration of an organizationally strong and issue-oriented party system is key to reducing the anxieties of American democracy.

* * *

Part II of the book focuses on the internal dynamics of our representative institutions. These authors address the common lament that the quality of legislative deliberation and debate has deteriorated as Congress has become a more partisan institution. Such concerns are related to broader worries about the general coarseness and dumbing down of political discussion in the United States.

The chapters in this section provide at least some cause for optimism. In Chapter 7, Lee Drutman and Peter Hanson evaluate the common complaint that the Congress of our partisan era has lost its capacity to deliberate effectively. Legislation has increasingly been produced and packaged by leaders who bring bills to the floor under rules that restrict both amendments and debate. Laments about the lack of deliberation are often followed by the recommendation that Congress should return to the procedures of "regular order" that allow robust debates and amendments to committee-produced legislation. Drutman and Hansen, however, show that at least in the important area of appropriations, the norms of regular order are alive and well. They find that on spending bills, members of both the majority and minority parties are able to participate in debate and to offer successful amendments. In fact, despite heightened partisanship, the amendments of the majority party are no less successful than the minority. But despite these bipartisan advantages, they find that extremists are able to exploit the afforded opportunities to engage in ideological messaging and to force divisive votes. This "paradox of regular order" may help to explain why given its apparent virtues it is disappearing on non-spending legislation and why it may eventually be reined in for the appropriations process.

In Chapter 8, James Curry and Frances E. Lee also take up the laments about the erosion of legislative processes. They provide some reassurances that abandonment of regular order has not crippled Congress. They argue that Congress has shown an ability to undertake major actions under both the decentralized, committee-dominated "textbook Congress" and the modern centralized, leader-driven contemporary Congress. In their view centralization is not the cause of congressional dysfunction, but an adaptive response to the highly partisan environment, which would otherwise strangle a decentralized legislature. In their account, centralized negotiating processes are essential for managing crises and logjams, enhancing flexibility in consultations and coalition building, and permitting legislative entrepreneurship. Curry and Lee also provide compelling evidence against claims that centralization is harmful. First, they find that the coalitions backing enacted laws are just as bipartisan in the party era as they were in the decentralized era. While Congress may well produce less legislation, there is no strong evidence that the outputs have become more partisan. Second, they demonstrate, contrary to the conventional wisdom, that committees and their chairs and ranking members continue to play an important part in the policy process. While the number of formal committee reports is down, informal mechanisms of committee consultation have emerged.

Lee and Curry also stress some of the benefits of legislative centralization. They argue that it has worked to the benefit of voters through the clarification of responsibility and the articulation of policy differences. Leader-driven agendas provide voters with significantly more information about where the parties stand on important issues. Centralized procedures are better able to formulate the "Democratic" or "Republican" alternative on issues. At the same time, strong leadership can screen out attempts of individual legislators to message in ways that muddy the water. Together Curry and Lee's arguments imply that the insistence of some observers that congressional dysfunction would be cured by a return to regular order is based on a misdiagnosis of the underlying problems and conflates cause and effect.

As Kenneth Benoit, Kevin Munger, and Arthur Spirling point out in Chapter 9, anxieties that the intellectual level of political discourse in a democracy is invariably regressing to the least common denominator are as old as democracy itself. Clearly concerns about our modern media culture's effect on the attention and informedness of voters have amplified these concerns. Quantitative studies of the reading level of presidential State of the Union (SOTU) addresses have lent support to these concerns. But Benoit, Munger, and Spirling provide assurance that anxieties about the "dumbing down" of American political discourse are overblown. Not only are such worries hard to reconcile with the fact that Americans are increasingly well educated and that our IQs are increasing, they are not born out in direct evidence about the sophistication of political discussion. First, they argue that inferences drawn from the SOTU address are unreliable. The declining trends in the sophistication of the SOTU appear to be outliers as they are not found in any other major political corpus including congressional debate and Supreme Court cases. Second, the changes they do find are relatively inconsequential and mirror broader changes in language patterns generally. Specifically, there are no trends in word complexity, just a broad movement to shorter sentences.

* * *

A considerable amount of our anxiety is rooted in the fact that we face major policy challenges ranging from income inequality and slow economic growth to inadequate health-care coverage and spiraling costs to climate change and environmental degradation at the same time that our government seems so ill-equipped to address them. Thus, Part III of the book addresses the anxieties surrounding the policymaking and governance capacities of our political institutions.

In Chapter 10, Suzanne Mettler and Claire Leavitt focus on how the "policyscape" – the dense constellation of existing programs and policies – structures the opportunities for new policy innovations. As they demonstrate, the policyscape is not a static element confronting policymakers, but one continuously reshaped by the interaction of changing economic and social forces with existing policy designs. They highlight four important ways in which the policyscape shapes contemporary governance. First, the existing constellation of policies helps determine which avenues of policy intervention are open and which are foreclosed. Second, the complexity of the contemporary policyscape makes reform harder and contributes to the gridlock and dysfunction related to excessive partisanship and polarization. This gridlock in turn forecloses the required maintenance and updating of policy regimes causing policy outcomes to drift in unintended ways. Strikingly, they find that among policies related to America's top issue priorities more than half were overdue for reauthorization or were "out of date."[3] Finally, the increased complexity of the policyscape requires much more oversight from Congress at precisely the time that Congress's capacity to perform it effectively has diminished. While Congress remains actively engaged in oversight during divided government, it has been

---

[3] They define "out of date" policies as those for which the elapsed time since the last reform exceeded the typical reform interval for that policy.

focused more on highly salient partisan issues rather than routine policy functions.

In Chapter 11, David Spence continues on the themes of governance in a polarized system by reviewing the potential effects of polarization on the administrative state. Given that administrative and regulatory agencies are central to many partisan fault lines such as health care, financial regulation, and the environment, their performance during our divided era profoundly shapes our governing capacities. Spence's review uncovers some notes of optimism. He notes that there is little evidence that agencies have either been paralyzed by polarized conflicts or have been driven to take extreme policy positions. At the same time, he suggests ample evidence that congressional gridlock and division have placed significant strains on agencies. Ultimately, our ideological divisions have mapped onto divergent views of the administrative state, which range from the impulse for greater insulation from political principals (e.g., the Consumer Financial Protection Bureau) to Steven Bannon's stated desire to "deconstruct the administrative state." These debates will shape the future role of administrative agencies in the constitutional system.

The general question of how polarization is likely to affect our constitutional system is taken up by Nolan McCarty in Chapter 12. Starting with the premise that lawmaking and oversight capacities of Congress have diminished, McCarty considers how the other branches of the federal government and the states are likely to respond. Will the president, judiciary, and the states successfully assert more policymaking authority? How might these assertions impact policy and its responsiveness to voters? Will the new constitutional balance of power lead to better or worse governance outcomes than the congressionally centered Madisonian constitution?

* * *

While no single volume can diagnose and assess all of the causes for the anxieties that Americans share about the future of their democracy, we hope that this one will make a substantial contribution to increasing understanding of the root causes. Like any good diagnosticians, the contributors to this volume have sought to distinguish those causes from mere symptoms.

While, as is usually the case in collective scholarly endeavors, we reach no airtight consensus on root causes, several stand out as especially important. Clearly, the American political system has been stressed by dramatic social and economic changes over the past 40 years, which have increased both economic and social inequalities. These inequalities have not only polarized voters and activists, but have created the conditions for greater political inequalities. At the same time, our party system has become much more competitive with virtually every recent election raising the prospect for a change in party control of one governing institution or another, layering an intense partisanship atop all of the other social and economic cleavages (Lee, 2016, Fiorina, 2017).

Unfortunately, these conditions appeared in a political system that was not designed with political parties in mind. Our constitutional system premised on the consensus of large supermajorities is very vulnerable to intense polarization and deep partisan antagonisms. The results are deep challenges to the capacities of our institutions to govern.

Perhaps the more important contributions of this volume are its more complete accounting of the problems and its rejection of easy fixes. We often hear laments such as democracy has been imperiled because it has been "dumbed down" or that Congress could restore its position in the constitutional system if it would only return to regular order. Clearly, some of these laments are unfounded – political discourse has simply not been declining in sophistication. Others confuse cause for effect. If Congress returned to regular order in the current environment, things would only get worse.

We also hope that this volume inspires more social scientists to take up these sets of questions about the state and future of American politics. These are big, important questions. Research that can further clarify the problems and suggest potential solutions will have great potential to reduce our anxieties and restore our faith in our democratic institutions.

REFERENCES

American Psychological Association. 2017. Stress in America. Retrieved from www.apa.org/news/press/releases/stress/2017/state-nation.pdf (last accessed November 12, 2018).
Bartels, Larry M. 2016. *Unequal Democracy: The Political Economy of the New Gilded Age*. Princeton, NJ: Princeton University Press.
Bonica, Adam, and Howard Rosenthal. 2015. The Wealth Elasticity of Political Contributions by the Forbes 400. Working paper, Stanford University.
Bonica, Adam, Nolan McCarty, Keith T. Poole, and Howard Rosenthal. 2013. "Why Hasn't Democracy Slowed Rising Inequality?" *The Journal of Economic Perspectives* 27(3): 103–123.
Fiorina, Morris P. 2017. *Unstable Majorities: Polarization, Party Sorting, and Political Stalemate*. Stanford, CA: Hoover Institution Press.
Gilens, Martin. 2012. *Affluence and Influence: Economic Inequality and Political Power in America*. Princeton, NJ: Princeton University Press.
Gilens, Martin, and Benjamin I. Page. 2014. "Testing Theories of American Politics: Elites, Interest Groups, and Average Citizens." *Perspectives on Politics* 12(3): 564–581.
Lee, Frances E. 2016. *Insecure Majorities: Congress and the Perpetual Campaign* Chicago, IL: University of Chicago Press.
Persily, Nathaniel and Jon Cohen. 2016. "Americans Are Losing Faith in Democracy – And in Each Other," *Washington Post*, October 14. Retrieved from www.washingtonpost.com/opinions/americans-are-losing-faith-in-democracy–and-in-each-other/2016/10/14/b35234ea-90c6-11e6-9c52-0b10449e33c4_story.html (last accessed November 12, 2018).

Piketty, Thomas, and Emmanuel Saez. 2003. "Income Inequality in the United States, 1913–1998," *The Quarterly Journal of Economics* 118(1): 1–41 and data updates.

Schwartzman, Paul. 2016. "Psychologists and Massage Therapists Are Reporting 'Trump Anxiety' Among Clients," *Washington Post*, March 6. Retrieved from www .washingtonpost.com/local/how-do-we-know-america-is-anxious-about-a-presi dent-trump-shrinks-and-massage-therapists/2016/03/03/e5b55a22-e0bb-11e5-846c-10191d1fc4ec_story.html (last accessed November 12, 2018).

PART I

ANXIETIES OF POWER, INFLUENCE,
AND REPRESENTATION

2

In the Private Interest?

Business Influence and American Democracy

Anthony S. Chen

One of the oldest and most persistent anxieties afflicting American democracy is the worry that it is vulnerable to what Madison (Hamilton, Madison, and Jay, 2008) termed the "mischiefs of faction."* While the phrase has been understandably interpreted in our time as a reference to the perils of excessive partisanship, Madison himself made it clear in Federalist No. 10 that he saw faction more broadly as any "number of citizens" who shared a "common impulse of passion" or "interest" that was adverse to either the "rights of other citizens" or the "permanent and aggregate interests of the community" (p. 49).

There were many sources of faction in Madison's view. But he argued that the "most common and durable source" was the "various and unequal distribution of property," which divided people in "civilized nations" into a "landed interest," a "manufacturing interest," a "mercantile interest," a "moneyed interest," and many other "lesser interests." Indeed, it was the "regulation of these varying and interfering interests" that defined the "principal task of modern legislation" and made the imbrication of "party and faction" and the "operations of government" practically inescapable (p. 50).

Madison believed that a large republic formed out of a union of the states would prove a powerful counterweight to the dangers of faction, which were most threatening in small jurisdictions. A large republic did eventually take root. Indeed, it flourished. But concerns about faction have nevertheless recurred throughout American history. Since the Gilded Age and the advent of the modern, large-scale corporation, Americans have perhaps been most intensely and consistently concerned with the power wielded by one particular

* The author is grateful to Josh Basseches, Lee Drutman, Ira Katznelson, Frances Lee, Nolan McCarty, Devin Wiggins, members of the Social Science Research Council (SSRC) Anxiety of Democracy program's Working Group on Institutions, and two anonymous reviewers for valuable feedback.

faction – business, which may reasonably be defined as groups, associations, or organizations that are formally constituted for the purpose of engaging in for-profit enterprise.

A decade on from the *fin de siècle*, what generalizations may be hazarded about business influence in the American political system? How politically powerful is business? Is it merely one of many interest groups active in American politics, and does it prevail no more frequently or decisively than other interest groups? Or does American business stand apart in the extent and kind of power that it wields? If so, does the political power of business distort the quality of democratic representation? How anxious should we be?

This essay looks broadly at the development of the literature in several disciplines to compose an answer to these questions. It draws some cautious conclusions, makes some tentative suggestions about promising directions for future research, and presents some brief reflections on the political power of business in our time.

———————————

From the postwar period, scholarly perspectives on business power have differed in emphasis from one discipline to another, and views on the nature and magnitude of business power have fluctuated significantly over time. Key's *Politics, Parties, and Pressure Groups* (2nd ed., 1948), Truman's *The Governmental Process* (1955), Dahl's *Who Governs?* (1961), and other classic statements in political science conveyed the distinct impression that business was simply one of several groups in American politics (Vogel, 1989, p. 5). None was powerful enough to prevail on all of the issues all of the time – or even most of the issues most of the time. This image was only reinforced by the publication of Bauer, Pool, and Dexter's *American Business and Public Policy* (1963), which examined the politics of foreign trade from the Reciprocal Trade Agreements Act in 1953 to the passage of the Trade Expansion Act in 1962. Bauer, Pool, and Dexter concluded that their analysis "cast doubt on the stereotype of pressure politics, of special interests effectively expressing themselves and forcing politicians to bow to their dictates or fight back vigorously" (p. 484).[1]

A similar imagery prevailed at roughly the same time in the writing of American history. Hofstadter's *The Age of Reform* (1955), Hartz's *The Liberal Tradition in America* (1955), and even Schlesinger's *The Age of Roosevelt* trilogy (1957, 1958, 1960) were all broadly premised on a vision of American politics in which conflicts over economic issues had never really been fundamental in nature or the excesses of capitalism had been adequately checked by the arrival and triumph of the New Deal. Progressive-era chronicles of the struggle between business and financial elites and "the people" faded in

---

[1] For important exceptions to the postwar pluralist consensus, see Huntington (1952) and Bernstein (1955), as noted in Novak (2014).

influence, and postwar historians worked instead within a kind of "liberal consensus" about what constituted a proper balance between market and state, in Higham's (1959) phrase (Phillips-Fein and Zelizer, 2012, pp. 4–5).

Sociology was a partial exception. Parsons's structural functionalism dominated the discipline, but the insurgent sociology of Mills provided something of a counterweight. Around the time that Truman published his synthesis, Mills (1956) was writing in *The Power Elite* that a small number of top leaders in the federal government, industrial enterprises, and the armed forces dominated the American political system.

Starting in the 1960s, however, there was a convergence toward a shared sense that business wielded more power that other groups, that it occupied a distinctive place in the political system, and that it wielded power for its own private benefit.

The trend was perhaps visible first in history. Kolko's *The Triumph of Conservatism* (1963), Weinstein's *The Corporate Ideal in the Liberal State* (1968), and Sklar's *The Corporate Reconstruction of American Capitalism* (1988) all looked back upon the Progressive Era and glimpsed a time when "corporate liberals" used government action to prop up the interests of big companies and powerful banks by dampening the wild and unpredictable swings of *laissez-faire* capitalism (Phillips-Fein and Zelizer, 2012, p. 5, Novak, 2014, p. 30). Kolko (1963) argued that it was "business control over politics . . . rather than the political regulation of the economy that is the significant phenomenon of the Progressive Era" (p. 3). Sklar sought specifically to explain how American industrial capitalism moved from a "proprietary-competitive" stage to a "corporate-administered" stage, and he argued that the transformation was led by businessmen who were tied to the large corporations that would come to dominate the economy (pp. 4, 13, 15).

The trend appeared fairly quickly within sociology, which quickly trained a critical eye on postwar society itself. A stream of work from Domhoff (1967, 1978) expanded on the "power elite" thesis of Mills, starting with *Who Rules America* and running through *The Powers That Be*. There was a sudden efflorescence of work in political sociology that stressed the special place of business elites in the American political system, including Fred Block's (1977) influential essay on how the "ruling class does not rule."

Change came to political science as well. Casting his eye over the politics of his time and their antecedents in American history, McConnell (1966) wrote in *Private Power and American Democracy* that certain convictions prevalent in our political tradition had made public authority uniquely susceptible to appropriation by private interests. Our tendency to conceive of liberty as the right of individuals and associations to remain free from coercion by government; our commitment to the idea that "small units of association" constituted the "essence of democracy"; our distaste for authority derived from formal or legal sources – these ideas came together over time to facilitate and legitimate the "establishment of varying degrees of control and exercise of public authority by ... private groups within the public areas with which they are concerned" (pp. 7, 89–90).

Among the most successful of such groups was business. McConnell argued that many trade and farm groups along with professional associations unhesitatingly exploited the fragmentation of state government to influence and shape public policy. Among the examples he gave were banking and insurance agencies, which, quoting a mid-century study by James W. Fesler, he characterized as "creatures of the enterprises they regulate" (p. 188). At the federal level, war and depression led to "extensive devolution to private groups in business," while commodity groups enjoyed "extensive powers over public policy affecting public resources of grass and timber." Progressive-era regulatory agencies were given autonomy and discretion as was the wont of their technically minded architects, but without "principled guides to action," regulation became accommodation, and "accommodation slipped imperceptibly into corruption" (pp. 8, 50).

This sentiment in political science only deepened in the next decade. By 1976, Dahl and Lindblom (1976) were arguing in *Politics, Economics, and Welfare* that business enjoyed a "privileged position" because government officials accepted the idea that businessmen shouldered "special responsibilities" and therefore acknowledged their "special claims for indulgences, authority, and other power" (p. xli). In *Politics and Markets*, published a year later, Lindblom (1977) observed that a "large category of decisions" with a clear impact on the economic well-being of the voting public were "turned over to businessmen" in a market economy and "taken off the agenda of government." As a result, "businessmen do not appear simply as representatives of a special interest" to government officials in countries that run a market economy but as "functionaries" with responsibilities affecting the "welfare of the whole society." Government thus exhibits heightened responsiveness to "business demands" by "adapting public policy to the needs of business" (pp. 172–175, 180, 182).[2]

Indeed, business power was seen as extending throughout the political system. In his 1978 presidential address to the Southern Political Science Association, Dye (1978) outlined and sought to substantiate a "model of oligarchy in national policy-making" in which the national policymaking agency is largely set by "policy-planning organizations" (e.g., Council on Foreign Relations) that derive their "initial resources" from "corporate and personal wealth" and that are guided in their priorities by "corporate presidents, directors, and top wealthholders" (pp. 310–311). Focusing on political parties, Ferguson (1983, 1984) offered a distinct alternative to Downsian ideas about parties as teams of politicians interested mainly in achieving election or reelection by catering to the preferences of the median voter. Instead, he proposed that

---

[2] See Vogel (1989) on Lindblom (pp. 5–6).

parties were better conceived as "blocs of major investors who coalesce to advance candidates representing their interests" (Ferguson, 1995, p. 27).

A concern that business held the upper hand in the American political system even emerged in certain precincts of economics. In 1971, Stigler (1971) laid out the theory that economic groups (including industries and occupations) typically sought to influence the political process in order to secure public resources for private benefit. Stigler went on to outline four distinct ways in which industry might "capture" government regulation and increase profitability: by providing direct subsidies, by erecting barriers to entry, by encouraging a pattern of substitutes and complements advantageous to the industry, or by encouraging the government to fix prices. In these respects, he theorized, regulation is generally "acquired by the industry and is designed and operated primarily for its benefit" (Stigler, 1971, pp. 3, 4–6)[3]

But the moment did not last. The sense that business exerted disproportionate power in the American political system began to fade, and scholarly interests started heading in numerous other directions.

Of course, interest in business power did not vanish instantly. Indeed, some of the most important contributions to the literature were made in the decade after the concerns about business power peaked. But the vast majority of scholars adopted a restrained stance, tending on balance to stress the variability, limits, and conditionality of business power.[4]

In *The Inner Circle* (1984), Useem asked whether a small network of influential corporate leaders lent "coherence and direction to the politics of business" and sought to promote the broader common interests of private corporations on a classwide basis. Drawing on interviews conducted with 57 executives and directors of large American companies in 1980, he found evidence that such a group of executives and directors did indeed exist in the United States, and they constituted the "leading edge of business political activity." But political inputs of a more traditional kind still balanced out the rising power of the inner circle. "[V]oter preferences" and "special-interest lobbying" continued to matter, even as a "vastly powerful new institution" had "joined the political fray" (pp. 3, 6–7, 19, 114).

A similar degree of restraint could be seen in Mintz and Schwartz's *The Power Structure of American Business* (1985), which focused on how corporations were networked together. Based on the analysis of data on interlocking corporate directorates (1962–1973) for more than 1,000 firms, along with a set of detailed case studies, Mintz and Schwartz found that commercial banks and insurance companies were situated at the center of the inter-corporate

---

[3] For a set of illuminating essays on regulatory capture, see Carpenter and Moss (2014).
[4] Smith (2010) stresses the theme of conditionality in his survey of the literature.

networks, giving them the capacity to promote a degree of coordination within the business community over the flow of capital as well public institutions implicated by such flows. Nevertheless, they took care to note that the power wielded by financial institutions was limited, and the coordination that they were capable of encouraging within the business community was loose, indirect, and fragile (pp. 249–254).

Vogel (1989) offered an even more qualified portrait of business power in *Fluctuating Fortunes*, which traced out patterns of corporate success and failure in tax policy, industrial relations, energy policy, and health, safety, and environmental regulation from the 1960s to the 1970s. Accepting at "face value" what companies defined as their interest – "as revealed by their actual efforts to influence the terms of political debate and policy" – he observed a major turnaround in corporate outcomes over the course of the 1970s. From 1969 to 1972, business was dealt a number of major policy setbacks in what Vogel describes as a "kind of Great Society for the private economy." Congress passed the progressively tilted Tax Reform Act of 1969, four major environmental laws including the National Environmental Policy Act of 1969 and the Clean Air Act of 1970, the Occupational Safety and Health Act, and a series of consumer protection statutes that included the Consumer Product Safety Act of 1972. The oil industry found itself beleaguered in the middle of the decade, losing the oil-depletion allowance and enduring the extension of price controls. But the political fortunes of the private sector turned around dramatically from 1977 to 1981. Congress rejected common-situs picketing in 1977 and labor law reform in 1978; it declined to establish a Consumer Protection Agency in 1978 and deprived the Federal Trade Commission of the authority to regulate "trade groups that set product and industry standards"; it loosened price controls on oil and gas; and it passed the Revenue Act of 1978, which reduced capital-gains taxation, lowered corporate tax rates, and solidified the investment tax credit. Business won a number of even more valuable tax concessions in the Economic Recovery Tax Act of 1981 (pp. 13–14, 59–61, 122–129, 148, 239, 245).

According to Vogel (1989), what explains the shift is partly the political mobilization of large and small business in the 1970s. However, this was one of several necessary conditions that only together would prove sufficient. As he writes,

business has tended to be politically effective when its resources have been highly mobilized, when companies share similar objectives, when the public is critical of government, when the economy is performing relatively poorly, and when its preferences coincide with those of powerful politicians. (p. 293)

Vogel argued that the ability of business to influence each of these factors is limited – except for the first – and he concluded that "business is more affected by broad political and economic trends than it is able to affect them" (p. 293).

Martin's (1991) analysis of major shifts in postwar paradigms of corporate taxation was similarly circumspect in how it handled business power. In her reckoning, there were three models of corporate taxation that governed fiscal policy after the Second World War, each one tied to a different idea about the best approach to promoting economic growth. The first was a "commercial Keynesianism" strategy in which a progressive individual income tax along with savings- and investment-related incentives (such as accelerated depreciation and the investment tax credit) were meant to encourage reciprocally rising levels of mass consumption and mass industrial production. The second was a "hyper-accumulation" (supply-side) strategy in which regressive cuts to the individual income tax and a reduction in corporate taxation through the expansion of investment incentives would encourage greater capital formation, which adherents believed was languishing. A third and final paradigm was organized around a "postindustrial growth strategy" that sought to promote more efficient allocation of capital by promoting tax neutrality across sectors and industries while at the same time putting into place other incentives that would raise across-the-board investment in human capital as well as research and development. Martin's analysis provides evidence that new directions in fiscal policy were ushered in when presidents – who were motivated by a desire to "secure political advantage and manage economic policy-making" – assembled a coalition of supportive business groups around a new growth strategy. Business groups were a powerful force in shaping fiscal policy, but they took a back seat to presidents and their administrations (pp. 1–2, 9–32, 44, 197).

A number of the most recently published studies continue to thematize limits. In their analysis of how the financial crisis emerged and why it was unsatisfactorily resolved, McCarty, Poole, and Rosenthal (2013) argue that "pressures from organized interests" are inadequate on their own as an explanation (p. 7). In their account, interests intersected with the ideological rigidity of legislators and the constraints of American political institutions to generate a set of "policy biases" (a political bubble) that served to "foster and amplify the market behaviors" responsible for the crisis, rather than counteract them (p. 14). Waterhouse's *Lobbying America* (2013) builds on Vogel to insist on the historical variability of business power. "Although business leaders continued to wield substantial power as individuals," Waterhouse concludes, "the coalition that emerged from the economic crisis of the 1970s did not survive the 1980s with nearly as much collective clout" (pp. 4, 247). In *The Fracturing of the American Corporate Elite*, Mizruchi (2013) argues that the "American corporate elite, since the early 1990s, has become fragmented, without an organized group of pragmatic leaders capable of addressing the issues with which the group has been confronted" (p. 264). It is the weakness of the corporate elite, in Mizruchi's view, which has actually led to polarization and inequality (p. 265). In his look at public affairs consultants in contemporary politics, *Grassroots for Hire*, Walker (2014) finds his subjects deeply involved in the work of framing issues, messaging audiences, and managing the political process. But they did so in the face of constraints, and they found themselves contending with "competing interests and existing preferences in public opinion." Walker concludes that the "efforts of the elite consultants are, to some extent, limited by the independent force of existing preferences and organized interests, thus providing some pluralist counterbalance to elite influence" (pp. 44–45).

The images of business influence that prevail today are a far cry from those that emerged in the work of Sklar (1960), Domhoff (1967), and Lindblom (1977) half a century ago.

Yet a different line of recent scholarship has also begun to breathe new life into the idea that business is "more equal" than other interest groups in the American political system.

In their broad look at the political origins and political perpetuation of contemporary inequality, Hacker and Pierson (2010) carve out a large role for business groups. Hacker and Pierson argue that the political mobilization of organized business in the 1970s began to drown out other voices (notably organized labor) and started to pull both Republicans and Democrats to the right. By the 1990s, Republicans had chosen to form a close alliance with various segments of organized business, and Democrats abandoned opposition to business for accommodation with it. What ultimately resulted was a procession of economic policies – upwardly tilted tax cuts, financial deregulation, lax oversight of corporate governance – which contributed to levels of economic inequality not witnessed since the Gilded Age. Today, "[p]owerful groups defending the winner-take-all economy," including "business coalitions, Wall Street lobbyists, medical industry players," continue to prevail, and Hacker and Pierson (2010) lament that our political system continues to drift further away from the principles of majoritarian representative democracy that inspired the Founding Fathers (pp. 116–135, 170, 177–186, 207, 291, 297–300).

Drutman's (2015) study of corporate lobbying gives further reason for concern. Individual corporations, trade associations, and business-wide associations spent a combined $2.57 billion on lobbying in 2012 – many multiples more than 30 years ago – and their expenditures have brought them into contact with "almost every process of American democratic policymaking." Drutman asks why "large corporations have achieved a pervasive position" in the American political system, and he argues that corporate lobbying began proliferating because lobbying is a "sticky," self-reinforcing activity. Since many corporations are motivated to preserve the status quo, this tendency further reinforces the status quo bias of the policymaking process and makes it less responsive to other inputs. It also increases the complexity of policymaking and makes it more difficult for legislators and their staffs to make sense of it. This, in turn, diminishes responsiveness by making government officials dependent on lobbyists (pp. 1, 3, 8–9, 133–167, 220).

A series of recent papers by Hertel-Fernandez gives further support to the idea that business may be a uniquely powerful political actor. One paper examines why some states adopted more "model bills" proposed by the American Legislative Exchange Council (ALEC) than other states. ALEC is a conservative business group that features a membership consisting of state legislators, private companies, and conservative think tanks. Drawing on a state-level dataset of bill enactments in 1995, Hertel-Fernandez (2014) finds that states with "low policy capacity" were most susceptible to adopting ALEC "model bills." Since it faced few or no rival groups proposing alternatives, ALEC exerted a distinctively powerful source of influence in state politics. ALEC's capacity, in turn, stemmed in large measure from the organizational structures that political entrepreneurs put into place in order to contain and manage otherwise fractious corporate interests (Hertel-Fernandez, 2016). Hertel-Fernandez and Skocpol (2015) explore why Democrats proved unable to take action against the Bush tax cuts. Analyzing votes in 2009 and 2010, they find that pressure from small business – including mobilization by the National Federation of Independent Business (NFIB) – reduced opposition to the cuts on the part of Democrats, even when controlling for legislator ideology.

A literature on interest groups, campaign contributions, and lobbying has developed (somewhat in parallel) in political science and economics, but it has also begun to turn up evidence that is consistent with the idea that business is unusually influential.

A main theory that undergirds the literature, as noted by Ansolabehere, de Figueiredo, and Snyder (2003) is the idea that there is a "market" for public policy. Campaign contributions are payments or investments by interest groups that are made in exchange for subsidies, price regulation, and other types of benefits that policymakers are poised to deliver (e.g., Grossman and Helpman, 1994).[5]

Some evidence of business influence can be glimpsed in studies of interest-group contribution patterns to elected officials, notably members of Congress. A useful point of departure is Snyder, Jr.'s argument that campaign contributions by such groups should be understood as investments – essentially long-term contracts – which are meant to strengthen connections with elected officials, who are uniquely positioned to provide a range of legislative and political services (Snyder, 1990, 1992). Investment-oriented interest groups should hence repeatedly disburse their contributions to the same set of officeholders over time, and they should also steer their contributions toward officeholders who are best positioned to deliver the greatest "lifetime service value." This is indeed how he interprets what he finds when he analyzes the contribution pattern of political action committees (PACs) established by corporations, trade associations,

---

[5] For an incisive anatomization of the literature, including the introduction of a new theoretical framework, see Hall and Deardorff (2006).

farm groups, and labor unions compared to more ideologically motivated PACs (Snyder, 1992).

However, McCarty and Rothenberg (1996) raise important questions about Snyder's interpretation, and they conclude from an analysis of their own data that legislators do not punish PACs that fail to contribute in an investment-oriented manner. Since punishment is the only theoretically validated mechanism capable of overcoming commitment problems when external enforcement mechanisms such as the courts are not an option, McCarty and Rothenberg conclude that either the flow of campaign contributions to officeholders is driven by ideological affinity or that a yet-theorized mechanism is encouraging the fulfillment of long-term contracts.[6]

Kroszner and Stratmann (1998) propose that reputations are the key mechanism by which commitment problems may resolved, and they theorize that the committee system that has taken root in Congress provides a structure for encouraging and staging the kind of repeated and focused interactions between interest groups and officeholders that are integral to the development of reputations. The essence of their theory is that interest groups and officeholders have strong incentives to interact repeatedly in order to form reputations, which can be valuable assets for interest groups and officeholders alike. Interest groups make successive contributions over time in order to observe which officeholders tend to support the same positions, and the resulting reputations enable interest groups to target their contributions more effectively. Officeholders are incentivized to interact repeatedly and develop a clear reputation because doing so presents a compelling way to increase the contributions they receive. This set of incentives can overcome commitment problems and lead to a "high-effort, high-contribution, repeated-play equilibrium" so long as interest groups and officeholders find that acting in ways that protect and promote their reputations yields a net present value to them that exceeds the net present value of acting in ways that undermine their reputations (p. 1166). This set of incentives can also lead lawmakers to develop a system of legislative organization that features standing committees with specialized jurisdiction and stable membership – precisely the form of legislative organization that has developed in Congress over the twentieth century.

Kroszner and Stratmann (2005) report several pieces of empirical evidence that are consistent with the predictions of their framework and inconsistent with the theory that officeholders can maximize their contributions through "strategic ambiguity" instead. Examining contributions to House members from the early 1980s to the early 1990s – years when Congress was the locus of an intense discussion about whether to permit commercial banks to take on financial activities previously limited to investment banks and insurance companies – they find that members of the House Banking Committee took in more

---

[6] This strand of the literature is discussed in Stratmann (2005).

contributions from the financial services industry than nonmembers; that different segments of the financial industry tended to contribute to different members of the committee; that the sources of contributions to members of the committee grew more concentrated as seniority increased; that contributions tended to fall off for older members, retiring members, and members who switched committees; that the reputation of a member (as measured by the frequency of repeat giving) grew stronger as their service time on the committee increased; and that the level of contributions taken in by committee members grew as their reputations strengthened. Kroszner and Stratmann (2000) also find similar patterns when they analyze data on a broader set of committees over a somewhat wider period of time.

Still, it is not entirely clear that it makes sense to think that PAC contributions should influence roll call votes. Hall and Deardorff (2006) point out that the sums of money with which PACs are estimated to buy votes just seem too small to do the trick. The calculations reported in many studies imply that votes go for so little that "even the impoverished reader of political science journals could buy a vote every once in a while" (p. 70).[7]

Indeed, empirical evidence of business influence on roll call voting behavior has been uneven, and there is disagreement about how to interpret it. Ansolabehere, de Figueiredo, and Snyder (2003) represent one widely held viewpoint. Surveying roughly three dozen studies on PAC contributions and voting behavior published from 1976 to 2002, they point out that three out of four coefficients associated with contributions were not statistically significant or incorrectly signed. Moreover, they note that many of the studies do not grapple with the simultaneity of contributions and votes, which potentially biases the estimated coefficients (p. 114).

To illustrate the issues that typically crop up in such studies, they compile a panel of data on members of the House from 1978 to 1994 and estimate the effect of corporate contributions on the voting score assigned to each member by the United States Chamber of Commerce (USCC). These scores essentially amount to the percentage of key votes in which a member voted in accordance with USCC's preferred position (Ansolabehere, de Figueiredo, and Snyder, 2003). To be sure, using such scores or indexes may be problematic for the purposes of detecting influence (Stratmann, 2002, p. 347), and USCC scores in particular may not be sufficiently informative since they are based on a selective subset of broad issues on which members exhibit a high degree of consensus (Smith, 2000). That being said, what Ansolabehere, de Figueiredo, and Snyder (2003) find is that contributions have small effects on voting scores when the party affiliation of the member and district preferences are directly controlled, and these small effects disappear in specifications that include district- or

---

[7] See also Ansolabehere, de Figueiredo, and Snyder (2003, pp. 110–111) and Milyo, Primo, and Groseclose (2000, p. 82).

member-fixed effects – regardless of whether the specifications are estimated with ordinary least squares or instrumental variables. As a result, they conclude that campaign contributions from organized groups generally have a "miniscule" impact on voting behavior, which is "almost entirely" a function of what legislators themselves believe and the "preferences of their voters and their parties" (p. 116).

Stratmann has a different take on the literature. In a 2005 meta-analysis of the studies surveyed by Ansolabehere, de Figueiredo, and Snyder (2003), he makes use of information about the sign and significance level of the key coefficients and considers whether the estimation procedure took steps to reckon with simultaneity. Stratmann (2005) argues that his meta-analysis yields statistical evidence sufficient to reject the hypothesis that contributions have no effect, even when high-quality estimates are given twice the weight of low-quality estimates. As he writes, "money does indeed influence votes," although he does not make a clear claim about the magnitude of the effect, and he cautions that his results may be sensitive to different choices about weighting (pp. 145–146).

If there is uncertainty about what to make of these conflicting perspectives, there can be little question about the relevance of parsing whether and how money influences votes: Business groups are simply more numerous and better resourced than any other type of interest group. Of the nearly 12,000 organizations listed in the *Washington Representatives* directory in 2001, more than 33 percent were corporations and more than 13 percent were trade groups or other business associations (Schlozman, Verba, and Brady, 2012, p. 321). Corporations and trade groups are far more likely than citizen groups to employ hired lobbyists and former government officials, and the average spending of corporations and trade groups on lobbying and campaign contributions routinely exceeds that of citizen groups by several multiples. Data collected from 1999 to 2002 as part of the Advocacy and Public Policy-Making Project show that the average trade association spent $1.2 million on lobbying compared to $177,814 spent by the average citizen group (Baumgartner et al., 2009, p. 199).

But these resources do not readily translate into policy outcomes. Looking over the 1,224 interest groups in their sample, Baumgartner et al. (2009) find a low correlation between the level of resources spent by a group and whether it got what it wanted (p. 212). But they rightly caution against the hasty inference that "resources are unimportant in politics" (p. 212). Instead, they argue that the low correlation may stem from the fact considerable resources are often brought to bear on all sides of a particular issue, partly because resource-rich groups do not consistently align with other resource-rich groups. Moreover, they instructively point to Smith's finding that groups like the USCC were unable to spend their way to policy success since the kinds of issues on which they took positions were partisan, salient, and ideological – and tended to draw a competitive countermobilization (p. 213).

Yet business influence does seem indicated by certain studies that share a particular set of characteristics; namely, studies that analyze roll calls on legislative proposals with clear stakes for well-defined interest groups whose economic prospects are highly sensitive to policy changes. These proposals tend to focus on issues that may be of high salience to the stakeholders but do not seem salient to the mass public. Many of these studies focus on struggles that have taken place in the last 20 years, and the best of them make use of quasi-experimental methods that have been developed to overcome problems of inference that typically plague the empirical analysis of observational data (de Figueiredo and Richter, 2014).[8]

One such study is Stratmann's analysis (2002) of a 1991 vote and 1998 vote in the House on whether to roll back Glass-Steagall's separation of commercial banking and investment banking. This struggle unfolded over the course of the 1990s, and it pitted commercial banks, who wanted to embark on lucrative new lines of business, against investment banks and insurance companies, who wanted to protect their traditional turf. A substantial number of legislators switched their allegiances from one side to the other, and Stratmann uses their two votes to construct a member-level panel dataset that permits him to relate changes in contributions to changes in votes – in a more credible manner than cross-sectional studies, which are more plentiful but more vulnerable to endogeneity and omitted variable bias. The estimates themselves taken on reasonable magnitudes, and they seem fairly robust to a variety of approaches and checks. In a specification that includes legislator-fixed effects, Stratmann reckons that a contribution of $10,000 by the commercial banks (which amounts to two-thirds of a standard deviation) raises a junior member's chances of casting a pro-bank vote by 8 percentage points (Stratmann, 2002, p. 361).

Similar conclusions are yielded by other studies that examine roll call votes on issues of major concern to the financial industry. Nunez and Rosenthal (2004) analyze roll call votes on the Bankruptcy Reform Act of 2001, which changed the treatment of unsecured debt (especially credit card debt) in a way that made it more difficult for individuals to liquidate under Chapter 7 and forced more individuals to restructure their finances under Chapter 13. The legislation was strongly favored by creditor groups, including banks, credit unions, credit card companies, and retailers – who all stood to benefit in various ways from the expansion of consumer credit. The bill passed the House by a veto-proof majority, and the results of their analysis across several key votes

---

[8] The importance of focusing on legislative conflicts in which there are clearly identifiable winners and losers has been stressed by others. For instance, see Peltzman (1984, 1985) and Mian, Sufi, and Trebbi (2013, p. 376).

indicate that PAC contributions exerted an independent and meaningful influence on voting behavior, even controlling for legislator ideology. Nunez and Rosenthal estimate that PAC contributions by creditor groups essentially amounted in aggregate to a difference of about 15 votes, which could have put the veto-proof majority into jeopardy (p. 553).

Another study in the same vein is Mian, Sufi, and Trebbi's analysis (2010) of key House votes on the Emergency Economic Stabilization Act (EESA) of 2008, which gave the US Treasury Department the authority and resources (upward of $700 billion) to shore up the balance sheets of ailing financial institutions. Whether the intervention involved the provision of capital through the acquisition of preferred stock or the purchase of hard-to-value, mortgage-backed securities, it unambiguously represented an "expected net transfer to the financial industry." The authors analyze a member-level dataset and find that PAC contributions from the financial industry increased the chance a member would vote for the passage of EESA, even when controlling for constituent interest and legislator ideology. A one-standard deviation increase in the per-cycle contribution (from 1993 to 1998) increases the probability of a favorable vote by 6 percentage points. The result is robust to multiple checks, and the authors favor a causal interpretation because contributions do not raise the likelihood of a favorable vote by members who know (at the time of the vote) that they intend to retire, suggesting that they no longer require the resources to run for reelection. In another paper, Mian, Sufi, and Trebbi (2013) take a close look at more than 700 mortgage industry...related roll calls that were taken from 1994 to 2008, and they find that the percentage of votes in which campaign contributions from the mortgage industry are a significant explanatory factor begin to tick up sharply in the late 1990s, even when controlling for legislator ideology and constituent interest (and weighted by a measure of significance).

Building on Stratmann's approach, Igan and Mishra (2014) find further evidence of business influence. Looking over activity in Congress from 1999 to 2006, they classify all of the legislative proposals that were made in the area of financial regulation. They find that six major pieces of legislation were passed, and they identify the preceding string of related proposals that ultimately led to each one. For instance, two proposals related to derivatives regulation were introduced and considered in Congress before a third became the Commodities Futures Modernization Act (CFMA) in 2000. This fact enables them to construct a panel of data that tracks whether a member switches to a deregulatory position in particular area of legislation and whether her change in position is related to changes in the level of campaign contributions she received from the financial industry. In a number of fixed-effect models, they find that a one-standard deviation increase in purged PAC contributions raises the probability that a lawmaker switches to a deregulatory position by 6.7 percentage points.

Of course, as many students have long noted, roll calls are only one type of congressional activity that potentially influences the profitability of business, and they occur at a fairly advanced stage of the legislative process. Depending on the circumstances and people involved, members may be able to sponsor or cosponsor legislation, amend the language of a bill during committee markup, share information on what position another member intends to take, convince a colleague to join forces or back off, work behind the scenes to facilitate a compromise, speak up or stay quiet at a committee hearing, develop a legislative strategy, and work to change the content of legislation in conference committee. Outside of the legislative process, members can call a press conference, defend or denounce a company on television, decide how constituent concerns about corporate decisions should be addressed, support or oppose a presidential nominee, and demand oversight hearings – among many other things. Only some of these activities are directly observable to investors trying to form or confirm an opinion about the reputation of a lawmaker, and not all of them happen within the immediate context of standing committees, but it nevertheless stands to reason that investors are interested in observing and influencing the totality of the effort made by lawmakers over time, not just their voting behavior at specific moments.[9]

There is mounting evidence that the investor-legislator exchange delivers value to business groups in terms that they would appreciate. Akey (2015) finds some credible evidence that political connections – as measured by PAC contributions – have a causal effect on equity prices. It was unclear from previous studies whether campaign contributions should be interpreted as evidence of investment behavior on the part of contributing firms or agency problems within the firm. Akey takes a regression-discontinuity approach that essentially compares cumulative abnormal returns (CAR) for firms contributing to candidates who barely won their races with CAR for firms contributing to candidates who barely lost their races. His median estimate is that the "difference between firms connected to a winning politician and a losing politician is 3% of firm equity value over a three- to seven-day window" (p. 3190). Other patterns in his results are also broadly consistent with the investment view. Akey finds that industries that are the most strongly connected also receive the most value on their connections, that indirect contributions (to the leadership PACs of senior politicians) generate higher value than direct contributions (to election PACs), and that connections to certain committees in the House and Senate (banking, appropriation, agricultural, taxation, small business, and armed services) have above-average value (Akey, 2015).

Akey's study is not the only one to present evidence on the value of political connections. Analyzing the effect of James Jefford's surprise switch out of the

---

[9] For a discussion of these and other types of involvement that are not roll calls on the floor, see Schlozman and Tierney (1986), Hall and Wayman (1990, p. 802), Hall (1996), Hall and Deardorff (2006), and Van Houweling (2007).

GOP, which threw control of the Senate into Democratic hands in 2001, Jayachandran (2006) finds that the level of soft-money contributions made by firms in the Forbes 500 was related to changes in their market capitalization. The results of her event study indicate that that the capitalization of a firm dropped 80 basis points for every quarter million dollars that was contributed to the GOP, while it increased to a comparable degree when contributions of the same magnitude were made to the Democratic party. Goldman, Rochell, and So (2009) examine the board of directors for S&P 500 firms in the late 1990s, and they find that the stock of a firm nominating a politically connected individual (e.g., former members of Congress, deputy assistant secretary, mayor, or regulatory commissioner) exhibits a positive CAR in a 2-day window before and after the announcement; they also observe a positive CAR for Republican-connected firms and a negative CAR for Democratic-connected firms after the outcome of the 2000 election was announced, even when controlling for firm characteristics and industry effects.

If roll calls are only one type of activity in which a lawmaker participates, campaign contributions are only one way in which business can seek to influence lawmakers. Such contributions may actually have limited significance in the bigger picture, as they are dwarfed by the amount of money spent on lobbying. Milyo, Primo, and Groseclose (2000) point out that lobbying expenditures for corporations and trade groups in 1997–1998 totaled $2.3 billion, compared to the $140 million spent by corporations and trade groups through PACs (p. 83). Akey (2015) reports that the firms in his sample (S&P 500) spent $4.7 billion on lobbying the federal government versus only $245 million – 19 times less – on campaign contributions to congressional incumbents (p. 3216). Indeed, there is a link between campaign spending and lobbying dollars. Firms and groups that tend to make contributions also tend to lobby heavily, and they account for much of the money in the political system. Drawing on information for groups active in 1997–1998, Tripathi, Ansolabehere, and Snyder (2002) find that groups that have a lobbyist and a PAC comprise only a fifth of all groups but represent "fully 70 percent of all interest group expenditures and 86 percent of all PAC contributions" (p. 131).

There is a growing stock of credible evidence that lobbying is valuable to those who buy it no less than those who sell it. The underlying source of the value is becoming increasingly clear as well. Blanes I Vidal, Draca, and Fons-Rosen (2012) examine a panel of data on commercial lobbyists from 1998 to 2008, and they relate the revenue generated by a lobbyist to the number of active politicians for which he or she once worked. What they find strongly suggests that political connections are a valuable asset. The average lobbyist suffers a drop of $182,000 in annual revenue when a senator for whom he or she once worked exits Congress (p. 3732). The falloff does not track with prior trends; there is a sharp break that coincides with the timing of the exit; and the lower level of revenue persists. Bertrand, Bombardini, and Trebbi (2014) analyze data on lobbyists and legislators from 1999 to 2008 to determine whether connections or expertise accounts for their pattern of association. When the committee assignments of legislators change, do lobbyists follow the legislators or look to peddle their expertise to new legislators on the same committee? Using campaign contributions to measure personal connections, they find evidence that lobbyists generate value primarily because of their connections to lawmakers: Lobbyists do follow lawmakers (p. 3904). There is some evidence that expertise is valued, but their estimates suggest that connections count twice as much as expertise (p. 3910).

The value of lobbying is perhaps most intuitively evident in studies that estimate how it affects policy outcomes. In one such study, Igan and Mishra (2014) not only examine the impact of PAC contributions but also the impact of lobbying expenditures in six areas of legislative conflict of clear interest to the financial industry. Running a series of fixed-effects models, they find that spending on lobbying raises the likelihood that a lawmaker switches to a deregulatory position. A one standard-deviation "increase in spending on lobbying is associated with a 3.7 percentage-point increase in the probability of switching" (p. 1077). Igan, Mishra, and Tressel (2012) compile and analyze data on 250 lending institutions in years before and after the financial crisis, and they find that lobbying institutions (in comparison to nonlobbying institutions) took on riskier loans; securitized them at a faster clip; expanded their portfolio of mortgage loans more quickly; experienced more problems with their loans; saw their cumulative abnormal returns fall with the collapse of Bear Stearns and then rise upon announcement of EESA; and prove more likely to receive bailout money. The overall pattern strongly suggests the lobbying lenders were able to influence public policy in two major ways – first by encouraging lax regulation of mortgage lending and then tapping the federal government as a lender of last resort after capital markets seized up (p. 196). Richter, Samphantharak, and Timmons (2009) compile and examine a dataset on thousands of firms from 1998 to 2005, and they find statistical evidence suggesting that spending on lobbying lowers effective tax rates in the following year. According to their analysis, when lobbying expenditures rise by 1 percent, firms see a 0.5–1.6 percent point drop in their effective tax rate (p. 906). Each additional dollar spent on lobbying yields a $6 to $20 return in terms of tax benefits (p. 907). This estimate may be large; it may reflect bias from omitted variables such as time-varying, firm-level expenses on legal services related to corporate taxation. But it is nevertheless a valuable finding, and it fits readily with pieces of evidence from other studies.[10]

Naturally, lobbying is not only directed toward legislative activity, and there is evidence that lobbying pays dividends for business in other policymaking contexts. One of the most important is the federal bureaucracy, where

---

[10] The literature is still unclear on why connections are valuable. Do they enhance the quality of the information that is transmitted (Groll and Ellis, 2014)? Perhaps by building up a reputation for reliability and accuracy (Groll and Ellis, 2014, 2016)?

administrative agencies promulgate numerous rules and regulations annually to guide the implementation or enforcement of statutory law. Evidence of business influence in rule-making remains inconclusive for now, but Yackee and Yackee (2006) represent an important step forward. They compile a dataset of 1,700 comments that were submitted from 1994 to 2001 in connection with 30 rules issued by the Occupational Safety and Health Administration, the Employment Standards Administration, the Federal Railroad Administration, and the Federal Highway Administration, and they find that agency rule-making strongly tracks business preferences about the degree of government intervention. Moreover, business interests exert a stronger influence over rule-making than competing interests, and they remain influential even when controlling for the preferences of other interests. The influence that business wields appears to derive not from the quality but the quantity of comments that it is able to inject into the rule-making process.[11]

Across "inputs" that range from campaign contributions to lobbying expenses and "outputs" that range from roll calls to administrative regulations, market capitalization, and effective tax rates, evidence is accumulating that business wields substantial influence in the political system. But is it disproportionately influential? If so, disproportionate in what sense? These are essentially questions about representation and responsiveness, and they have always been foremost in the minds of anyone working on the subject. But they have only recently begun to receive systematic and explicit empirical treatment.

One of the most important contributions to the literature is still Smith's *American Business and Political Power* (2000), which asks whether a unified business community dominates policymaking in Congress. Smith's study focuses on the US Chamber of Commerce, which has tended to take positions on issues only when there has been a large supermajority of members in agreement. These issues have tended to be highly ideological, partisan, and salient in character. What is notable is that there has been a great deal of variability from 1953 to 1996 in the degree to which Congress has given the chamber what it wanted. These fluctuations are highly correlated with public opinion about the government and business as well as the partisan composition of Congress. On issues where it was unified, business tended to prevail when the public looked unfavorably upon government and favorably upon business; it also tended to prevail when higher proportions of Republicans held office. Most of these correlations held up even in models controlling for PAC contributions, lobbying capacity, chamber membership, and economic conditions. Smith argued that the patterns were evidence that business – even when it was

---

[11] For an analysis of how the lobbying of administrative agencies is organized among small and large firms, see also de Figueiredo and Tiller (2001).

unified – was not "especially powerful in determining government policies" (p. 3). "The policy preferences and voting choices of the citizenry," he wrote, "determine whether business, when unified, will celebrate victories or absorb defeats" (p. 200). Smith took his findings as a repudiation of the notion that a unified business community tended to prevail unchecked in policymaking, and he concluded that the American political system exhibited a degree of "genuine" responsiveness to public preferences (p. 213).

Hojnacki et al. (2015) approach the same general question by looking at whether business groups tended to prevail over other interest groups in a random sample of 98 issues that were contested from 1999 to 2002. Using data from the Advocacy and Public Policy-Making Project (Baumgartner et al., 2009), they find that business groups – when opposed – rarely realized their policy preferences more frequently than other groups, and especially citizen groups. Only in a small number of cases in which business groups were unopposed by other groups did they tend to prevail (Hojnacki et al., 2015, pp. 216–217). To the extent that mass opinion reflects the preferences of citizen groups, their findings suggest with Smith that there is little representational skew in the American political system.

However, one of the most striking results in recent years points to a different conclusion. Gilens and Page (2014) collect data on the preferences of affluent Americans, ordinary Americans, and business groups on a large number of policy issues that were on the public agenda from 1981 and 2002 – along with information on how those issues were resolved. This enables them to relate the preferences of different groups to policy outcomes. The policy preferences of average Americans (fiftieth income percentile) and affluent Americans (ninetieth income percentile) are measured using 1,779 survey questions that asked whether the respondents favored or opposed a proposed policy change. Business preferences are measured by looking at the position taken by major interest groups and industry associations on each of the proposed policy changes, and then constructing an index that summarizes the "net" alignment of the groups. The outcome variable is measured by scouring a range of primary sources to determine whether the proposed policy change actually occurred within four years of when the question was asked. What their multivariate analysis indicates is that policy change is a function of elite preferences and interest-group preferences but not the preferences of average Americans. When they disaggregate interest groups into mass groups and business groups, they continue to find that policy change is not driven be average Americans but rather by affluent Americans and interest groups. The magnitude of the effect is largest for elites, followed by business groups, and then followed by mass groups. On their evidence, what ordinary people want has little to do with what emerges from the policymaking process, which may be "dominated by powerful business organizations and a small number of affluent Americans" (p. 577). It is not possible from their data to rule out the possibility that elites and interest groups anticipate policy changes rather than give rise to them, but what Gilens and

Page (2014) find certainly heightens long-standing concerns that business influence undermines the quality of democratic representation.

After decades of research and writing, there is still no easy consensus about business influence and whether it distorts American politics and policy. Looking broadly over the literature, one could be forgiven for thinking that meaningful generalizations are still not possible. But some broad points can be made, if cautiously.

One point is that evidence of influence seems more readily detectable in certain types of studies. The evidence is mixed in studies that are pitched at a broad level of analysis where business interests and policy outcomes are highly aggregated (e.g., Smith, 2000, Gilens and Page, 2014). But studies set up at a more granular level of analysis seem to more consistently generate evidence that comports with the idea that business is influential because resources are politically and economic valuable, and businesses are resource-rich enough to outgun other groups. Many of these studies draw on a delimited set of empirical techniques that are increasingly accepted as establishing a basis for credible inference (de Figueiredo and Richter, 2014).

For instance, evidence that resources matter can been seen in studies that relate firm-level lobbying expenditures or firm-level political connections to higher cumulative abnormal returns or lower effective tax rates (Jayachandran, 2006, Goldman, Rochell, and So, 2009, Richter, Samphantharak, and Timmons, 2009, Blanes I Vidal, Dara, and Fons-Rosen, 2012, Bertand, Bombardini, and Trebbi, 2014, Igan and Mishra, 2014, Akey, 2015). Some of the most credible evidence comes from studies of outcomes at the industry level. In studies of roll calls on a range of legislation in which the financial industry (or various segments of it) are clear stakeholders, there is rapidly accumulating evidence that campaign contributions deliver a definite and nontrivial improvement in the probability of obtaining a favorable vote (Stratmann, 2002, Nunez and Rosenthal, 2004, Mian, Sufi, and Trebbi, 2010, Mian, Sufi, and Trebbi, 2013, Igan and Mishra, 2014).[12] Other evidence of influence is also detectable in studies that look outside Congress to specific policymaking institutions within the executive branch (Yackee and Yackee, 2006) as well as state legislatures (Hertel-Fernandez, 2014, 2016).

It should perhaps come as little surprise that evidence of influence seems easier to discern in studies of organized interests at the industry level and studies of outcomes wrought within smaller units of the political system. These units are where Madison (Hamilton, Madison and Jay 2008) believed that the "mischiefs of faction" were prone to run the most rampant because interests would be less heterogeneous and it would easier to form a majority that might

---

[12] For a valuable historical study that illuminates the influence of insurers in shaping the content and design of the American health-care system, see Chapin (2017).

wish to "invade the rights of other citizens" (p. 51). In fact, McConnell's (1966) chief insight into private power and American democracy was Madisonian in nature. McConnell believed that the "capture of government" fairly characterized the biggest risk to American democracy, but "capture" did not take the form of a single, overarching group dominating whole branches of the federal government. Instead, different groups exerted influence over policy through the different institutions of government that mattered the most to them – banks concentrated on shaping the activities of the Senate Banking Committee, insurance companies on the state insurance departments, and corn growers on the Feed Grains Advisory Committee of the Department of Agriculture. The implication of McConnell's insight is worth stating explicitly. If business is indeed influential, then evidence of influence should come out of studies that look at the "fragmentation of rule and the conquest of pieces of governmental authority by different groups" (p. 7).

This idea seems worthy of exploration in future research. While the study of "peak" associations like the USCC and the National Association of Manufacturers remains valuable, concentrating attention on industry and trade groups seems theoretically and empirically warranted. Along with Baumgartner and Leech, David M. Hart (2004) rightly highlights the need for additional work on individual corporations as well. Congress as a whole should remain a focus, but there are sound reasons to look closely at individual committees within Congress and the firms and industries that tend to enter their orbit (Kroszner and Stratman, 1998, 2000). Further research on notice-and-comment rule-making is certainly merited (Yackee and Yackee, 2006) along with work on the activities of individual agencies like the Food and Drug Administration (Carpenter, 2010) and the industries and companies that have them most contact with them. Lastly, it is no accident that the states were a special point of emphasis for McConnell, and additional studies of business-driven groups like the American Legislative Exchange Council (ALEC) and their activities (Hertel-Fernandez, 2014, 2016) should be highly welcome.

A second point is that more granular studies that are narrowly and precisely designed to generate causal inferences may be profitably be balanced out with more broadly imagined studies that conceptualize the dependent variable in a greater variety of ways. If one is taking a granular approach, it makes sense to conceptualize many outcomes as a binary variable – wins or losses, successes or failures. But wins and losses can differ in their magnitude. An outcome is often a mixed bag that is hard to classify as either a win or a loss. The costs and benefits may be manifest on different dimensions and prove difficult to commensurate. Business often seeks to minimize the magnitude or impact of a "loss" or "failure" by having policy written in the least harmful way or having the harms partially offset. Additionally, outcomes do not exist on their own in a vacuum. They are linked dynamically over time, and they are linked to other outcomes that occur at different levels and in different branches of government. Without a sense of the magnitude and nature of the wins and losses – and how

they are connected with other wins and losses over time in the political system –
it can be fairly easy to misjudge and misinterpret business influence. The kind of
high-technique studies rightly encouraged by de Figueiredo and Richter (2014)
might be complemented by – and even embedded in – broader over-time studies
like Vogel (1989), Martin (1991), Hacker and Pierson (2010), Phillips-Fein
(2010), and Chapin (2017).

Looking over the literature on regulatory capture, Carpenter and Moss
(2014) urge scholars to distinguish between weak and strong capture, suggest
different types of capture, and outline various mechanisms of capture. Students
of business influence have taken analogous steps, especially in terms of mapping out the channels through which business has sought to influence public
opinion. Smith (2000) and Phillips-Fein (2010) highlight the role of business-
financed think tanks as a source of influence, and Walker (2014) examines the
activities of public affairs consultants. But further steps along these lines can
and should be taken.

A final point is that the evidence is still not clear that the business influence
distorts the quality of democratic representation, although suspicions continue to run justifiably high. Significant empirical and theoretical work is
required before definitive conclusions may be drawn. One thorny issue is
the question of how to measure business preferences. Smith (2000), Baumgartner et al. (2009), and Gilens and Page (2014) measure business preferences based on the (more or less) public positions that different business
groups takes on policy questions. But deciphering business preferences is
tricky business. Business is more than capable of strategically misstating what
it wants (Broockman, 2012, Chen, 2012), and fine-grained information about
the changing and heterogeneous economic interests of firms and industries can
sometimes be required to draw sound inferences (Swenson, 2018). Another
issue is how to think about representation when many of the policy issues that
business sets out to influence are matters of high complexity and low salience.
How should public opinion be measured on such issues? Vast sums of taxpayer money could be at risk, but Americans may not really know what they
think. How do we think about responsiveness when it comes to these types of
issues, and how do we measure it? A final issue has to do with the influence of
business on public opinion, which Smith (2000) and Walker (2014) regard as
a major source of business influence in the political system. How should we
think about representation in instances when business lobbies for the adoption of a particular policy and launches a public-relations campaign at the
same time? What if public opinion eventually becomes consistent with business preferences?

On these and other questions, more intellectual clarity is required before it
will be possible to understand whether the quality of democratic representation
is compromised by business influence.

During the Trump era, suspicions have only grown stronger that American democracy operates in the private interest.

Examples abound. One of the most highly salient involved the Environmental Protection Agency (EPA) under Scott Pruitt. Lindsey Dillon and her collaborators conclude that the prospect of "regulatory capture" at the EPA has deepened beyond a level not seen since Reagan's first term, when his EPA administrator resigned after only 2 years on the job (Dillon et al., 2018). Drawing loosely on an analytical framework proposed by Daniel Carpenter and David Moss (2014), Dillon and her collaborators (Dillon et al., 2018, p. S89) argue that the EPA under Pruitt departed in numerous ways from "its statutory mandate to protect human health and the environment." For instance, Pruitt's inaugural speech did not mention health or the environment and instead defined the EPA's goals as providing "certainty to the regulated" and enhancing "economic growth." Breaking with historical precedent, Pruitt permitted lobbyists to serve on the EPA's Scientific Advisory Board, and he met far more frequently with corporate and trade groups than other kinds of group (Dillon et al., 2018, p. S91).

Developments around Trump's primary legislative achievement, known as the Tax Cut and Jobs Act of 2017, would seem to offer grounds for similar misgivings. The legislation among other things provided for a cut in the corporate tax rate from 35 to 21 percent (Andrews and Parlapiano, 2017), and it was passed in a highly partisan, 3-month rush starting in the final week of September. Three business groups spent more than $56 million lobbying for it in the last quarter of 2017, presumably directing most of their attention to the Republicans in control of the process. These groups included the US Chamber of Commerce ($16.8 million), the National Association of Realtors ($22 million), and Business Roundtable ($17.35 million) (Brody, 2018).

Months after the bill was passed, many top legislative aides who worked on the bill decamped to "K Street" and other private-sector groups with use for their knowledge about the inner workings of the legislation and their close connections to lawmakers. The main tax attorney for the Senate Finance Committee on the Republican side, Mark Prater, was hired by Pricewaterhouse Coopers as managing director in its Tax Policy Services unit (Lorenzo, 2018). Brendan Dunn, one of Sen. Mitch McConnell's (R-KY) top legal advisors, joined Akin Gump Strauss Hauer & Feld, a legal and lobbying powerhouse that earned $38.7 million in income from lobbying last year – evidently the highest among its peers (Jagoda, 2018, Rozen, 2018). Shahira Knight, deputy director of the National Economic Council and the "top tax staffer" at the White House (Cook, 2017), joined The Clearing House Association (CHA) to head up its public affairs operation (White and Cook, 2018). The CHA is merging with the Financial Services Roundtable (Blackwell, 2018), and the new group will continue to lobby and advocate on behalf of large banks and other financial institutions (Lane, 2018). Much of the value that Prater, Dunn, Knight, and other tax specialists provide to their new employers is related to various forms of assistance they can offer during the implementation stage over the next few years (Levine and Meyer, 2018).

The signs of regulatory capture and the monetization of political connections that can be observed in the Trump era are surely not unique to the period, but it seems difficult to reject the claim that business influence is declining – or even standing still. If anything, example after example suggests that American business is more politically potent at the national level than it has been in years, forging and exploiting close ties with the party in power during a period of unified government. In the political arena no less than in the marketplace, American business may be subject to "fluctuating fortunes." But its fortunes appear to be fluctuating upward at the moment.

Unified government ended with the 2018 midterms, but there may be a deeper way in which the political fortunes of business will remain on the upswing in the United States for the foreseeable future.

In *Capital in the Twenty-First Century*, Thomas Piketty's celebrated treatise on economic inequality under capitalism, Piketty argues that a renovated form of patrimonial capitalism is taking hold in our globalized time (Piketty, 2014, p. 200). In contrast to the capitalism that prevailed in nineteenth-century Europe, when low rates of economic growth heightened the importance of inherited wealth and led to an economic system dominated by the rentier (who lived comfortably on the income or "rents" thrown off by their inherited ownership of certain assets such as land or government bonds), capitalism in the twentieth-first century, especially in the United States, is dominated by a combination of rentiers and supermanagers (usually but not exclusively top executives who earn extremely high incomes from their positions at large firms, both financial and nonfinancial) (Piketty, 2014, pp. 331, 377, 379, 380). Rentiers and supermanagers "cohabit" the upper centile of the income distribution, where labor income is the largest share of total income for individuals in the lowest fractiles of the upper centile, and capital income (including capital gains) is the largest share of total income when one reaches the top 0.1 percent (Piketty, 2014, p. 377). Piketty stresses that the distinction between the two groups can be overdrawn – for instance, rentiers and supermanagers can be the same individual, and the children of supermanagers can become rentiers (Piketty, 2014, p. 331). But the cohabitation of the two groups at the top of the income distribution is a defining characteristic of the new, global patrimonial capitalism.

Piketty finds that the number and income of "supermanagers" in the United States began to grow rapidly after the top marginal tax rate was reduced from 80–90 percent in the 1930–1980 period to 30–40 percent in the 1980–2010 period, hitting a low of 28 percent after the passage of the Tax Reform Act of 1986 (Piketty, 2014, pp. 420–422, 652–653). This is because executives were incentivized to push harder for larger and larger compensation packages, quickly realizing that they could keep much more of what they were paid. Since determining executive pay is inherently tricky due to the difficulty of identifying and valuing the individual contribution of a particular executive to the output of a firm, "top managers found it relatively easy to persuade boards and stockholders that they were worth the money, especially since compensation committees were chosen in a rather incestuous manner" (Piketty, 2014, p. 655).[13]

The specific mechanism underpinning the growth of economic inequality since 1980 is not without political implications. It suggests that the takeoff of inequality, driven in substantial measure by the multiplying number of corporate executives who command enormous pay packages, may have set off a feedback loop in which the high incomes of such executives help to amplify their political influence, which they wield to press for the continuation of policies that make their high incomes possible. "[T]he decrease in the top marginal income tax rate," Pikketty writes, "led to an explosion of very high incomes, which then increased the political influence of the beneficiaries of the change in the tax laws, who had an interest in keeping top tax rates low or even decreasing them further and who could use their windfall to finance political parties, pressure groups, and think tanks" (Pikketty, 2014, pp. 422–423). Mizruchi may be right that the cohesive, publicly minded corporate elite of yesteryear has fractured beyond recognition (Mizruchi, 2013), but to the extent that "supermanagers" share broadly similar views about taxes, labor, regulation, and other shared policy issues – which is a topic that certainly merits further research – it may not be necessary for a corporate elite to exist and operate in exactly the same way as it did in the postwar period. The form of patrimonial capitalism that has taken root in the United States today – one in which "supermanagers" are front and center alongside rentiers – may very well confer a kind of structural advantage in politics to business. As a result, despite its considerable heterogeneity, American business may continue to find the political winds at its back.

Still, strong conclusions remain fiendishly difficult to reach. How politically powerful is business? Does the political power of business distort the quality of democratic representation? Are our political institutions organized at a sufficient scale to serve as a counterweight to the new, globalized forms of faction that may be appearing today?

We have reams of scholarship on hand about these important questions, but there are few definitive answers to them, as pressing as they may be. Perhaps the anxieties we have about the matter are not so ill-founded after all.

---

[13] Piketty and his collaborators argue that executive compensation is not related to marginal productivity; they find that firm performance is correlated with sources of variance outside the firm that the executive does not control (such as the performance of other firms in the same industry) as opposed to sources of variance inside the firm that the executive does control. It seems that corporate executives are paid for luck more than they are paid for performance (Piketty, 2014, pp. 421–422).

REFERENCES

Akey, Pat. 2015. "Valuing Changes in Political Networks: Evidence from Campaign Contributions to Close Congressional Elections." *Review of Financial Studies* 28: 3188–3223.

Andrews, Wilson, and Alicia Parlapiano. 2017. "What's in the Final Republican Tax Bill." *New York Times*, December 18. Retrieved from www.nytimes.com/inter active/2017/12/15/us/politics/final-republican-tax-bill-cuts.html (last accessed January 2, 2019).

Ansolabehere, Stephen, John M. de Figueiredo, and James M. Snyder, Jr. 2003. "Why Is There So Little Money in U.S. Politics." *The Journal of Economic Perspectives* 17 (Winter): 103–130.

Baumgartner, Frank, Berry, Jeffrey M., Hojnacki, Marie, Kimball, David C., and Leech, Beth L. 2009. *Lobbying and Policy Change*. Chicago: University of Chicago Press.

Bertand, Marriane, Matilde Bombardini, and Francesco Trebbi. 2014. "Is It Whom You Know or What You Know? An Empirical Assessment." *American Economic Review* 104: 3885–3920.

Blackwell, Rob. 2018. "Top White House Official to Join Big-Bank Group." *American Banker*, June 4. Retrieved from www.americanbanker.com/news/top-white-house-official-to-join-big-bank-group (last accessed January 2, 2019).

Blanes I. Vidal, Jordi, Mirko Draca, and Christian Fons-Rosen. 2012. "Revolving Door Lobbyists." *American Economic Review* 102: 3731–3748.

Bauer, Raymond A., Ithiel de Sola Pool, and Lewis A. Dexter. 1963. *American Business and Public Policy*. New York: Atherton Press.

Bernstein, Marver H. 1955. *Regulating Business by Independent Commission*. Westport, CT: Greenwood Press.

Block, Fred. 1977. "The Ruling Class Does Not Rule: Notes on the Marxist Theory of the State." *Socialist Revolution* 33 (May–June): 6–28.

Brody, Ben. 2018. "Business Groups Spent Big on Lobbying during the Tax Overhaul." *Bloomberg*, January 23. Retrieved from www.bloomberg.com/news/articles/2018-01-23/tax-bill-prompts-business-to-pay-heavily-for-lobbying-campaigns (last January 2, 2019).

Broockman, David A. 2012. "The 'Problem of Preferences': Medicare and Business Support for the Welfare State." *Studies in American Political Development* 26 (October 12): 83–106.

Carpenter, Daniel. 2010. *Reputation and Power*. Princeton: Princeton University Press.

Carpenter, Daniel, and David A. Moss, eds. 2014. *Preventing Regulatory Capture: Special Interest Influence and How to Limit It*. New York: Cambridge University Press.

Chapin, Christy Ford. 2017. *Ensuring America's Health: The Public Creation of the Corporate Health Care System*. New York: Cambridge University Press.

Chen, Anthony S. 2012. "Virtue, Necessity, and Irony in the Politics of Civil Rights: Organized Business and Fair Employment Practices in Postwar Cleveland." *What's Good for Business*, ed. Kimberly Phillips-Fein and Julian Zelizer. New York: Oxford University Press.

Cook, Nancy. 2017. "White House Advisor Clashes with Mnunchin over Tax Plan." *Politico*, July 27. Retrieved from www.politico.com/story/2017/07/27/the-trump-administration-cant-agree-on-how-to-do-tax-reform-either-241000 (last accessed January 2, 2019).

Dahl, Robert A. 1961. *Who Governs? City.* New Haven: Yale University Press.

Dahl, Robert A., and Charles Lindblom 1976. *Politics, Economics, and Welfare.* New Brunswick, NJ: Transaction.

de Figueiredo, John M., and Emerson H. Tiller. 2001. "The Structure and Conduct of Corporate Lobbying: How Firms Lobby the Federal Communications Commission," *Journal of Economics and Management Strategy* 10 (2001): 91–112.

de Figueiredo, John M., and Brian Kelleher Richter. 2014. "Advancing the Empirical Research on Lobbying." *Annual Review of Political Science* 2014: 163–185.

Dillon, Lindsey, Christopher Sellers, Vivian Underhill, Nicholas Shapiro, Jennifer Liss Ohayon, Marianne Sullivan, Phil Brown, Jill Harrison, and Sara Wylie. 2018. "The Environmental Protection Agency in the Early Trump Administration: Prelude to Regulatory Capture." *American Journal of Public Health* 108: S89–S94.

Domhoff, G. William. 1967. *Who Rules America?* Englewood Cliffs, NJ: Prentice-Hall.

1978. *The Powers That Be.* New York: Random House.

Drutman, Lee. 2015. *The Business of America Is Lobbying.* New York: Oxford University Press.

Dye, Thomas R. 1978. "Oligarchic Tendencies in National Policy-Making: The Role of Private Policy-Planning Organizations." *Journal of Politics* 40 (May).

Ferguson, Thomas. 1983. "Party Realignment and American Industrial Structure: The Investment Theory of Political Parties in Historical Perspective." *Research in Political Economy* 6 (1983): 1–82.

1984. "From Normalcy to New Deal: Industrial Structure, Party Competition, and American Public Policy in the Great Depression," *International Organization* 38 (Winter): 41–94.

1995. *Golden Rule.* Chicago: University of Chicago Press.

Gilens, Martin, and Benjamin I. Page. 2014. "Testing Theories of American Politics: Elites, Interest Groups, and Average Citizens." *Perspective on Politics* 12 (September): 564–581.

Goldman, Eitan, Jorg Rochell, and Jongil So. 2009. "Do Politically Connected Boards Affect Firm Value?" *Review of Financial Studies* 22 (June): 2331–2360.

Groll, Thomas, and Christopher J. Ellis. 2014. "A Simple Model of the Commercial Lobbying Industry." *European Economic Review* 70: 299–316.

2016. "Repeated Lobbying by Commercial Lobbyists and Special Interests." CESinfo Working Paper #5809.

Grossman, Gene M., and Elhanan Helpman. 1994. "Protection for Sale." *American Economic Review* 84 (1994): 833–850.

Hacker, Jacob S., and Paul Pierson. 2010. *Winner-Take-All Politics.* New York: Simon and Schuster.

Hall, Richard L. 1996. *Participation in Congress.* New Haven, CT: Yale University Press.

Hall, Richard L., and Frank W. Wayman. 1990. "Buying Time: Moneyed Interests and the Mobilization of Bias in Congressional Committees." *American Political Science Review* 84 (September): 797–820, esp. 802.

Hall, Richard L., and Alan V. Deardorff. 2006. "Lobbying as Legislative Subsidy." *American Political Science Review* 100 (February): 69–84.

Hamilton, Alexander, James Madison, and John Jay. 2008. "The Federalist, 10 (Madison)." *In The Federalist Papers,* edited by Lawrence Goldman. New York: Oxford University Press.

Hart, David M. 2004. "'Business' Is Not an Interest Group: On the Study of Companies in American National Politics." *Annual Review of Political Science* 7: 47–69.

Hartz, Louis. 1955. *The Liberal Tradition in America.* New York: Harcourt, Brace.

Hertel-Fernandez, Alexander. 2014. "Who Passes Model Bills? Policy Capacity and Corporate Influence in U.S. State Politics." *Perspectives on Politics 12* (September): 582–602.

2016. "Explaining Durable Business Coalitions in U.S. Politics: Conservatives and Corporate Interests Across America's Statehouses." *Studies in American Political Development 30* (April): 1–18.

Hertel-Fernandez, Alexander, and Theda Skocpol. 2015. "Asymmetric Interest Group Mobilization and Party Coalitions in U.S. Tax Politics." *Studies in American Political Development 29* (October): 235–249.

Hofstadter, Richard. 1955. *The Age of Reform.* New York: Vintage Books.

Hojnacki, Marie, Kathleen M. Marchetti, Frank R. Baumgartner, Jeffrey M. Berry, David C. Kimball, and Beth L. Leech. 2015. "Assessing Business Advantage in Washington Lobbying." *Interest Groups and Advocacy 4* (September): 205–224.

Huntington, Samuel P. 1952. "The Marasmus of the ICC: The Commission, the Railroads, and the Public Interest." *Yale Law Journal 61* (April): 467–509.

Igan, Deniz, and Prachi Mishra. 2014. "Wall Street, Capitol Hill, and K Street: Political Influence and Financial Regulation." *Journal of Law and Economics 57* (November): 1063–1084.

Igan, Deniz, Prachi Mishra, and Thierry Tressel. 2012. "A Fistful of Dollars: Lobbying and the Financial Crisis." *NBER Macroeconomics Annual 26(1)*: 195–230.

Jagoda, Naomi. 2018. "Ex-MccConnell Policy Aide Joining Lobby Firm." *Politico,* May 21. Retrieved from https://thehill.com/business-a-lobbying/388607-ex-mccon nell-policy-aide-joining-lobby-firm (last accessed January 2, 2019).

Jayachandran, Seema. 2006. "The Jeffords Effect." *Journal of Law and Economics 49* (October): 397–425.

Key, Jr., V. O. 1948. *Parties, Politics, and Pressure Groups*, 2nd edition. New York: Crowell.

Kolko, Gabriel. 1963. *The Triumph of Conservatism.* New York: Free Press.

Kroszner, Randall S., and Thomas Stratmann. 1998. "Interest-Group Competition and the Organization of Congress: Theory and Evidence from Financial Services' Political Action Committees." *American Economic Review 88* (December): 1163–1187.

2000. "Congressional Committee as Reputation-Building Mechanisms." *Business and Politics 2*: 35–52.

2005. "Corporate Campaign Contributions, Repeat Giving, and the Rewards to Legislator Reputation." *Journal of Law and Economics 48* (April): 41–71.

Lane, Ben. 2018. "Big Bank Influence Grows: The Clearing House Association Merging with Financial Services Roundtable." *Housingwire*, March 13.

Levine, Marianne, and Theodoric Meyer. 2018. "It's a Great Time To Be a Tax Specialist." *Politico*, May 22.

Lindblom, Charles. 1977. *Politics and Markets.* New York: Basic Books.

Lorenzo, Aaron. 2018. "GOP Staffers Who Wrote the Tax Bill Cash in with Lobbying Gigs." *Politico*, June 4.

McCarty, Nolan, and Lawrence S. Rothenberg. 1996. "Commitment and the Campaign Contribution Contract." *American Journal of Political Science* 40 (August): 872–904.

McCarty, Nolan, Keith T. Poole, and Howard Rosenthal. 2013. *Political Bubbles: Financial Crises and the Failure of American Democracy*. Princeton: Princeton University Press.

McConnell, Grant. 1966. *Private Power and American Democracy*. New York: Knopf, 1966.

Martin, Cathie J. 1991. *Shifting the Burden*. Chicago: University of Chicago Press.

Mian, Atif, Amir Sufi, and Francesco Trebbi. 2010. "The Political Economy of the U.S. Mortgage Default Crisis." *American Economic Review* 100 (December): 1967–1998.

2013. "The Political Economy of the Subprime Mortgage Expansion." *Quarterly Journal of Political Science* 8: 373–408.

Mills, C. Wright. 1956. *The Power Elite*. New York: Oxford.

Milyo, Jeff, David Primo, and Timothy Groseclose. 2000. "Corporate PAC Campaign Contributions in Perspective." *Business and Politics* 2: 75–88, esp. 82.

Mintz, Beth, and Michael Schwartz. 1985. *The Power Structure of American Business*. Chicago: University of Chicago Press.

Mizruchi, Mark. 2013. *The Fracturing of the American Corporate Elite*. Cambridge, MA: Harvard University Press.

Novak, William. 2014. "A Revisionist History of Regulatory Capture." In *Preventing Regulatory Capture*, ed. Daniel Carpenter and David Moss. New York: Cambridge University Press.

Nunez, Stephen, and Howard Rosenthal. 2004. "Bankruptcy 'Reform' in Congress: Creditors, Committees, Ideology, and Floor Voting in the Legislative Process." *Journal of Law, Economics, and Organization* 20 (October): 527–557.

Peltzman, Samuel. 1984. "Constituent Interest and Congressional Voting." *Journal of Law and Economics* 27 (April): 181–210.

1985. "An Economic Interpretation of the History of Congressional Voting in the Twentieth Century." *American Economic Review* 75 (September): 656–675.

Phillips-Fein, Kim. 2010. *Invisible Hands*. New York: Norton.

Phillips-Fein, Kim, and Julian Zelizer. 2012. "Introduction." In *What's Good for Business: Business and American Politics since World War II*, ed. by Kim Phillips-Fein and Julian Zelizer. New York: Oxford University Press.

Piketty, Thomas. 2014. *Capital in the Twenty-First Century*. Cambridge, MA: Belknap Press of Harvard University Press.

Richter, Brian Kelleher, Krislert Samphantharak, and Jeffrey F. Timmons. 2009. "Lobbying and Taxes." *American Journal of Political Science* 53 (October): 893–909.

Rozen, Miriam. 2018. "Akin Gump Boosts Partner Profits as Deals, Lobbying Spur Gains." *The American Lawyer*, February 5. Retrieved from www.law.com/ameri canlawyer/2018/02/05/akin-gump-boosts-partner-profits-as-deals-lobbying-spur-gains/?slreturn=20181123192330 (last accessed January 2, 2019).

Schlesinger, Jr., Arthur M. 1957. *The Age of Roosevelt, Volume 1: The Crisis of the Old Order, 1919–1933*. Boston: Houghton Mifflin.

1958. *The Age of Roosevelt, Volume 2: The Coming of the New Deal*. Boston: Houghton Mifflin.

1960. *The Age of Roosevelt, Volume 3: The Politics of Upheaval, 1935–1936*. Boston: Houghton Mifflin.

Schlozman, Kay, and John Tierney. 1986. *Organized Interests in American Democracy* New York: Harper and Row.

Schlozman, Kay, Sidney Verba, and Henry E. Brady. 2012. *The Unheavenly Chorus*. Princeton: Princeton University Press.

Sklar, Martin. 1960. "Woodrow Wilson and the Political Economy of Modern United States Liberalism." *Studies on the Left 1* (Fall).

Sklar, Martin J. 1988. *The Corporate Reconstruction of American Capitalism, 1890–1916*. New York: Cambridge University Press.

Smith, Mark A. 2000. *American Business and Political Power*. Chicago: University of Chicago Press.

2010. "The Mobilization and Influence of Business Interests." In *The Oxford Handbook of American Political Parties and Interest Groups*, ed. by L. Sandy Maisel, Jeffrey M. Berry, and George C. Edwards, III. New York: Oxford University Press.

Snyder, Jr., James M. 1990. "Campaign Contributions as Investments: The U.S. House of Representatives, 1980–1986." *Journal of Political Economy* 98 (December): 1195–1227.

1992. "Long-Term Investing in Politicians: Or, Give Early, Often." *Journal of Law and Economics* 35: 15–43.

Stigler, George J. 1971. "The Theory of Economic Regulation," *Bell Journal of Economics and Management Science* 2(1): 3–21.

Stratmann, Thomas. 2002. "Can Special Interests Buy Congressional Votes? Evidence from Financial Services Legislation," *Journal of Law and Economics* 45 (October): 347.

2005. "Some Talk: Money in Politics. A (Partial) Review of the Literature." *Public Choice 124* (July): 135–156.

Swenson, Peter A. 2018. "Misrepresented Interests: Business, Medicare, and the Making of the American Health Care System." *Studies in American Political Development 32* (April): 1–23.

Tripathi, Micky, Ansolabehere, Stephen, and James J. Snyder, Jr. 2002. "Are PAC Contributions and Lobbing Linked? New Evidence from the 1995 Lobby Disclosure Act." *Business and Politics 4*: 131–155.

Truman, David B. 1955. *The Governmental Process*, New York: Knopf.

Useem, Michael. 1984. *The Inner Circle*. New York: Oxford University Press.

Van Houweling, Robert Parks. 2007. "An Evolving End Game: Partisan Collusion in Conference Committees, 1953–2003." In *Party, Process, and Change in Congress*, Volume 2, ed. by David W. Brady and Mathew McCubbins. Palo Alto: Stanford University Press.

Vogel, David. 1989. *Fluctuating Fortunes*. New York: Basic Books, 1989.

Walker, Edward T. 2014. *Grassroots for Hire*. New York: Cambridge University Press.

Waterhouse, Benjamin C. 2013. *Lobbying America: The Politics of Business from Nixon to NAFTA*. Princeton, NJ: Princeton University Press.

Weinstein, James. 1968. *The Corporate Ideal in the Liberal State*. Boston: Beacon.

White, Ben, and Nancy Cook. 2018. "Shahira Knight Leaving White House for Clearing House Banking Group." *Politico*, June 4. Retrieved from www.politico.com/story/2018/06/04/shahira-knight-white-house-622815 (last accessed January 2, 2019).

Yackee, Jason Webb, and Susan Webb Yackee. 2006. "A Bias Toward Business? Assessing Interest Group Influence on the U.S. Bureaucracy." *Journal of Politics 68* (February): 128–139.

3

The Interest Group Top Tier

Lobbying Hierarchy and Inequality in American Politics

Lee Drutman, Matt Grossmann, and Timothy LaPira

Critiques of American democracy often juxtapose the interests of the public and those of "special interests" – and Americans believe the "interests" are now in control: nearly 70 percent say the "government is pretty much run by a few big interests looking out for themselves" rather than for "the benefit of all the people."[1] Donald Trump drew on these concerns in his unexpectedly victorious 2016 campaign, repeatedly promising to "drain the swamp" in Washington to empower the American people. Likewise, Bernie Sanders waged a surprisingly strong Democratic primary challenge by promising to lead a "political revolution" against the billionairs and their lobbyists.

Recent political science research justifies voters' suspicion that political influence is not spread equally. Government follows the wishes of the top income earners rather than those of the broader public and listens to groups that represent business interests more than others (Gilens and Page, 2014). The rise in income inequality in the United States has stimulated a vast literature on political inequalities within the public, leading to a new consensus that only a small subset of Americans is likely to have their voice heard in policy debate (McCarty, Poole, and Rosenthal, 2008, Bartels, 2010, Gilens, 2012, Page, Bartels, and Seawright, 2013, Gilens and Page, 2014). Lobbying is seen as a key mechanism by which the rich and big business dominate politics.

But even swamp creatures come in very different sizes. Among the actively organized groups seeking to influence policy in Washington, resources are far from equally distributed. Within the interest group community, a limited number of organizations at the very top of the resource distribution have escalated their political investments in ways that increasingly distinguish them

---

[1] The American National Election Studies has regularly asked this question since 1964. The results are available at http://anesold.isr.umich.edu/nesguide/toptable/tab5a_2.htm.

from the rest of the pack. This population of groups at the top of the distribution is becoming increasingly stable over the last two decades. This group of top organizations – which we call the *top tier* – is positioning itself as a distinct class.

Our assessment comes from a comprehensive new analysis of the 37,706 interest groups reporting any lobbying activity between 1998 and 2012. We are the first to analyze lobbying trends across all of these groups, allowing us to revise common stylized claims about interest groups and to provide a macro-level description of their activities over a long period. This allows us to update the traditional story of lobbying growth: more competition has diluted the relative standing of most groups. Instead, we think this competition has enabled a select group of exceedingly well-resourced and committed organizations to pay a premium to rise above the noise.

These top tier organizations are analagous to the current generation of very wealthy families who now pay for every conceivable tutor so that their children can be advantaged in applying to elite prep schools and colleges, which are now more and more essential to getting ahead in our increasingly economically stratified society. In both circumstances, financial resources and social connections build up over time, reinforcing stratification. Money does not guarantee outcomes. But it helps reinforce inequalities by widening the gap between the very top and everyone else.

Although we cannot directly assess the policy influence of top tier groups here, we are able to show that their dominance is consistent with the evolution of the interest group system over time. Like prior scholars, we track these trends while acknowledging that the true explanations for policy influence are multifaceted, and that the evidence for them is often unobserved (Baumgartner and Leech, 1998, Lowery, 2007). Despite generations of attempts, there are still no agreed-upon measures among social scientists for measuring lobbying influence. We suspect this is in part because lobbying participation and expenditures are endogeneous and long term, and wins are not always clear or easily measurable. Success begets success; investment begets investment; and few fights in Washington are every truly settled (Drutman, 2015). We note that some of the most important findings in the interest group literature, such as "the advocacy explosion" and "the dominance of institutions," were largely descriptive (Salisbury, 1984, Berry, 1989). Trends in group mobilization and the distribution of representation have always garnered attention and prompted theoretical revision.

The divergence between the activities of the top tier and all other organized interests may provide a new explanation for a puzzle in the interest group literature: some scholars find policy influence by the highest-spending groups (Hacker and Pierson, 2010, Gilens, 2012, Gilens and Page, 2014), but others find that money does not consistently correlate with policy success (Baumgartner et al., 2009). We can often observe macro-patterns of imbalance – and find compelling examples of well-known groups securing policy gains (see

Grossmann, 2014) – without being able to demonstrate micro-patterns of direct influence. We provide a possible resolution: the disproportionate lobbying spending by top tier groups may buy them a privileged position in the interest group hierarchy in the long run, not just policy success in a given conflict in the short run.

THE EVOLUTION OF INTEREST GROUP REPRESENTATION

Scholars have long agreed on two general empirical trends: (1) the number of interest groups is growing; and (2) the most well-represented groups dispro-portionately represent business and other well-off sectors of society (Schattschneider, 1960, Schlozman and Tierney, 1986, Walker, 1991, Gray and Lowery, 1996, Baumgartner and Leech, 1998, Schlozman, Verba, and Brady, 2012). Over the last several decades, the outside demands on the political system have steadily increased, while the capacity of the government to process those demands has not increased commensurately – providing an opening for interest groups to fill the gap (Baumgartner and Jones, 2015).

But even as new groups proliferated, scholars struggled to find consistent evidence that group mobilization had led inexorably to the long prophesied interest group takeover of government (Olson, 1982). After observing the growth of interest groups in Washington from the 1960s to the 1980s, Robert Salisbury noted a "paradox:" more groups had actually led to less clout for established players because each group had a harder time standing out from the crowd, making the interest group community as a whole less influential (Salisbury, 1990). He pointed to several trends from the 1960s through the 1980s: (a) more organizations and more lobbyists; (b) a change in the compos-ition of interests away from member-based associations and toward institu-tions, think tanks, and advocacy groups, as well as an increased reliance on lobbying firms; and (c) a fragmentation of sectors into narrower policy domains focusing on minor issues.

These trends, Salisbury argued, brought volatility and uncertainty; they upset the traditional influence of entrenched interests and, as a result, reduced the overall role of groups in policymaking. More groups brought too many voices for any one voice to be meaningfully heard. Following Salisbury's observations, the number of interest groups has continued to expand (Walker, 1991, Baumgartner and Leech, 1998, Schlozman, Verba, and Brady, 2012), and the strategies available to groups have multiplied and been more widely utilized (Grossmann, 2012, Karpf, 2012, Schlozman, Verba, and Brady, 2012). Many scholars accepted Salisbury's verdict with little criticism, with concerns over "hyperpluralism" and specialized rent-seeking superseding traditional concerns about a few dominant elite groups (Rauch, 1995, Baumgartner and Leech, 1998, Teles, 2013).

But the earlier interest group explosion of the 1960s and 1970s also corres-ponded to what Frank Baumgartner and Bryan Jones call the "Great Issue

Expansion:" to tackle more issues generally, the number of committees and subcommittees, expert staff, and points of entry proliferated in Congress in an effort to process all the external pressures (Baumgartner and Jones, 2015). Although this period of congressional capacity expansion, subcommittee proliferation, and new agency creation ended in the late 1970s, the interest group community expansion has continued at a much greater pace. For example, between 1981 and 2006 the number of organizations listed in the *Washington Representatives* directory doubled (Schlozman, Verba, and Brady, 2012). But government capacity and productivity have all slowed since the 1980s. Put another way, more groups are now fighting over declining territory.

In contrast to Salisbury's speculation that "more groups" would mean "less clout" for the most established interests, we argue that a small number of exceptionally active organizations – the top tier – are counteracting these trends by increasingly standing out from the crowd. The small subset of organizations who dominate the interest group hierarchy are willing to do whatever it takes – spend more money, retain more lobbyists, and engage on more issues and from more angles – to do so. Certainly, all this spending does not guarantee that the groups in the top tier will always get their way. Sometimes, they may fight amongst themselves or face an unyielding government opposition. Yet we argue standing atop the pile of groups does make it more likely that top tier groups' concerns will be prioritized amidst the fire hose of information and demands. Outsized spending has allowed these top organizations to achieve a ubiquity that gives them a central role in the political process, and relegates the vast majority of groups to ancillary roles.

Prior Research on the Distribution and Stability of Interest Group Lobbying

In studies of how lobbying activity changes over time, the main concern has been how groups respond to government. The expansion of the size and scope of government has long been a primary explanation for how, why, and when group mobilization exploded (Walker, 1991). Studies typically measure the lobbying and government agendas at the policy topic level, showing that changes in the aggregate issue focus of Congress change the aggregate issue focus of interest groups. All else equal, congressional attention to certain topics is associated with lobbying on those topics (Leech et al., 2005). This relationship between governing and lobbying attention to particular issue areas transcends jurisdictional boundaries across separate branches and levels of government (Baumgartner, Lowery, and Gray, 2009, Baumgartner et al., 2011).

Yet despite short-term fluctuations of government activity and lobbying across issue domains, most lobbying is relatively stable. Most groups continue to lobby at the same amount in the same issue areas as the prior year (Leech et al., 2005, Baumgartner et al., 2011), and the overall structure of the interest group network varies little over time (LaPira, Thomas, and Baumgartner,

2014). The issue agenda of interest groups on the whole is remarkably unchanging and out of step with the priorities of the public (Kimball et al., 2012). Not all changes in interest group attention follow the same mobilization process: in some cases, well-established groups simply shift attention from one issue area to another; in others, new groups establish a Washington presence solely to take advantage of new government actions (LaPira, 2014). When in conflict, the new groups usually lose to established players (Grossmann, 2005). This suggests caution in extrapolating from the initial findings on lobbying dynamics: the total population of groups may grow on the fringes in response to the government agenda, but only the disproportionately resource-rich groups have the ability to successfully spread themselves across a broadening agenda with more resources and activities.

UNDERSTANDING THE TOP TIER'S DOMINANCE OF LOBBYING

Major lobbying operations are not mere reflections of a broader stability among top economic actors. Consider a corporation with a household name that is also a Washington institution: AT&T. In the 1980s, AT&T faced an antitrust settlement and forced breakup. Many more interest groups, including its (now-independent) former regional telephone companies and other new business competitors, began jockeying for attention: Just as AT&T lost its landline telephone monopoly, it also began to face increased lobbying competition. AT&T's more recent evolution has also been far from smooth. It again faced business turmoil in the 1990s, transforming itself from a landline telephone provider to a cable company to a mobile data firm. After buying up all of the cable television assets it could, it abruptly sold them off. It even had a near-death experience before the reabsorption of its mobile component (and the larger Cingular network) via its purchase by SBC, which took the AT&T name. AT&T's recent political environment has been equally unsettled: the issues and opponents it confronts have multiplied, the parties in control of the presidency and Congress have changed back and forth, and its former political strategy of contributing large amounts of soft money to both political parties has been outlawed. Throughout its turmoil, AT&T's Washington lobbying operation has remained stable, massive, and powerful.

Regardless of what is happening in its business or in its politics, AT&T spends considerable sums to stay among the interest group top tier. In 2012, it spent $17.4 million to pay 91 lobbyists to weigh in on 150 bills across 19 different issue areas. Among the bills AT&T reported lobbying on that year were the FAA Air Transportation Modernization and Safety Improvement Act, the Iran Threat Reduction and Syria Human Rights Act of 2012, the Pipeline Infrastructure and Community Protection Act of 2011, and the Federal Agriculture Reform and Risk Management Act of 2013. Very few people outside AT&T's lobbying team would recognize any obvious connections these bills have on the company's bottom line. But, with 91 lobbyists, AT&T has the relationships and capacity to make sure the company registers its opinion on anything that could possibly affect its business. Doing so allows AT&T to achieve participatory ubiquity – to be present at all conversations that might affect its business – to maintain the kind of long-term relationships necessary for political success. Facing an uncertain Trump administration, it even paid Trump's personal lawyer to offer unspecified insights. Almost certainly, AT&T's top-level investment in Washington has contributed to its ability to come out of a tumultuous period as one of the remaining telecom giants.

This example generalizes to other leading interest groups that have faced far less business disruption. A small number of organizations like AT&T commonly account for a very disproportionate share of lobbying activity. AT&T's consistency is typical of the top tier: A handful of powerful lobbying organizations increasingly consistent from year to year, regardless of political or economic change. Yet this comes at an increasing price: the cost to maintain a top tier lobbying operation in Washington is rising while the mobility in and out of the top tier is declining.

Why the Top Tier Arises

Elected and appointed officials carry out American policymaking with tremendous constraints on their time and limited abilities to gather information. As Herbert Simon (1956) argued, officials rely on their habitual practices and interactions to find acceptable solutions, rather than search for the optimal solution using all available information sources. The limited carrying capacity of government means officials constantly struggle to prioritize issues and problems (Jones, 2001, Jones and Baumgartner, 2005, Baumgartner and Jones, 2015). Like ordinary citizens, policymakers adopt cognitive shortcuts to ease the demands of decision making. Members of Congress use cues such as colleagues' positions (Matthews and Stimson, 1975, Kingdon, 1989), and identifiable constituencies and subconstituencies (Arnold, 1990, Evans, 2002, Miler, 2010) to simplify their policy choices in an information-overloaded environment (Whiteman, 1995). Interest groups and lobbyists are prime sources of information in this frenzied environment (Esterling, 2004, Kersh, 2007), but they must develop relationships to become go-to sources (Wright, 1996). They also must demonstrate that they will continue to be around, and that they can be counted on to credibly commit to cooperating with (or competing against) policymakers in the future.

The continuing rise of new groups increases competition to be a go-to source, making it more difficult to stand out from the noise (Salisbury, 1990). But not all ties are equal: a small number of repeat policy entrepreneurs and institutional leaders are the most important actors in Congress and the administration; these important policymakers seek out other influential players rather than each serving as a spokesperson for a different group's concern (Mayhew, 2000, Grossmann, 2014). Some interest groups are able to develop identities as informed sources and representatives, commanding the flow of information and creating lasting reputations (Heaney, 2004). Interest groups learn about the most influential players and reinforce their central roles via regular interaction in networks of communication, coalition formation, and issue debate (Heaney, 2014). The major players become the taken-for-granted participants in policy debates, standing in for broader stakeholders (Grossmann, 2012), and serving as de facto staff for their supporters in Congress, who often lack their own policy resources (Hall and Deardorff, 2006). And in an era in which Washington lobbying is dominated by the "revolving door," top tier organizations can more readily buy their way into every social network they might need to be influential, yet another advantage they have over less well-resourced organizations. And connections beget connections: top tier lobbying organizations are more likely to have their first pick at hiring and retaining top lobbyists because of their existing lobbyist relationships.

There are also organization-level reasons to expect increasing stability at the system level. The decision to establish a lobbying presence is self-reinforcing. Once companies establish government relations departments, personnel in those departments find ways to justify and expand their existence, often building on previous successes, and corporate managers come to see politics as important, finding more reasons to stay involved (Drutman, 2015). Although many of the policy changes they advocate are unlikely to succeed in any given session of Congress, sometimes all it takes is one minor but financially significant policy change – such as a special tax break or a small change in regulatory implementation – to more than justify a decade's worth of lobbying expenditures (Drutman, 2015). Years of lobbying, for example, likely paid off for some businesses in 2017's complicated corporate and individual tax reform. But this may be more than many smaller organizations can ever point to. Moreover, policy fights have a way of carrying on for many years. Once an organization gets pulled into a policy fight, sunk-cost and arms-race dynamics can demand continued attention and investment in the long run, and lobbyists for these organizations can keep these battles on the agenda.

Moreover, interest groups may continue to spend significant resources just to signal that any threats to a favorable status quo will be met aggressively (Baumgartner et al., 2009). Groups may spend additional resources, hire more lobbyists, and expand their policy agendas to maintain their reputation, even if it means subsidizing a lawmaker's policy objectives for lower priority issues (Hall and Deardorff, 2006). If so, then top tier groups' policy priorities and lobbying spending will not fluctuate with shifts in the government agenda, but should regularly increase over time to signal their important role in Washington. Even when they disagree with dominant groups' issue positions, lawmakers will see the top tier groups as well-known repeat players that are difficult to defeat. This all has a self-reinforcing logic. As organizations spend more, they increase their relative status. But once that status has been achieved, it has to be maintained.

Status Quo Bias and Top Tier Dominance

The unequal structure does not guarantee policy influence, but it may help explain seemingly contradictory findings on group influence. Across a random sample of nearly 100 policy battles between interest groups, Frank Baumgartner and colleagues find that no measure of resources is consistently associated with victory. But they also find that the best predictor of victory is being on the side of the status quo – it is far easier to play defense than offense in American politics. Yet high spending groups are the most likely to have already "won" a favorable status quo and be invested in keeping it. As they conclude, " . . . existing public policy is already the fruit of policy discussions . . . if the wealthy are better mobilized and more prone to get what they want in Washington, they should already have gotten what they wanted in previous rounds of the policy process" (Baumgartner et al., 2009, pp. 19–20). Put another way: winners stick around because policy outcomes distribute gains to them, gains worth defending.

A study of the policy influence of the most well-known and highest-spending interest groups by Martin Gilens and Benjamin Page (2014) shows more regular group influence, but agrees that status quo bias may play the largest role. Gilens collected the positions on policy proposals taken by interest groups with reputations for influence and industries that spent the most on lobbying; he finds that these interest groups are more likely to take positions in favor of the status quo and more likely to win if they do so. By our calculations with Gilens' (2012) data, the typical top interest group favored 54 policy changes and opposed 94.[2] In other words, the most powerful groups are much more likely to oppose a major policy change as they are to support a major policy change.

Although lobbying disclosure data do not directly observe the positions taken by all the lobbying groups in our population or their success in achieving their objectives, we believe that the inequalities and dynamics we document may be helpful in explaining the patterns of influence that are already found in the literature: although money does not guarantee influence in any particular battle, the most resourceful groups usually win over the long term, especially when they are defending the status quo. Their resources also give them the luxury to go on the offense; like good venture capitalists, they can continue to seed potential policy changes even with low rates of success.

GROWTH AND INEQUALITY IN THE LOBBYING COMMUNITY

Our empirical objective is to assess the distribution and evolution of influence activities in the interest group system. To do so, we compiled the population of all organizations that reported lobbying in Washington at any time between

---

[2] Our calculations are based on data that is publicly available at www.russellsage.org/economic-inequality-and-political-representation. Of course, it is important to note that Gilens' data is limited to issues on which there is public polling, which tend to be relatively high-salience issues.

1998 and 2012.[3] The full Lobbying Disclosure Act (LDA) data set is cleaned and managed by the Center for Responsive Politics (CRP), and consists of 37,706 unique organizations. Our population includes clients of lobbying firms, organizations lobbying on their own behalf, and those using both firms and their own staff. Lobbying reports include estimates of expenditures and the names of individual lobbyists. If an organization spends more than $5,000 per quarter (or, in years prior to 2008, $10,000 per semi-annual period) on direct-contact lobbying, it is required to report its activity with the Clerk of the House or the Secretary of the Senate. Likewise, lobbying firms contracted by organizations must also file reports on the organization's behalf. The CRP data aggregate all reported lobbying activity to the organization, even though in-house and contract reports are filed separately, to avoid double-counting of expenditures. Unique in-house and contract lobbyists are linked to the organization that reported lobbying.

Using these data, we generate annual sums at the organization level of analysis[4] for the amount of money spent on lobbying activities, the number of in-house staff lobbyists, and the number of external contract lobbyists for each organization. Since lobbying expenditures apply mostly to human resources, these three measures are correlated (at $r = 0.6$ for in-house lobbyists and total spending, $r = 0.5$ for contract lobbyists and spending, and $r = 0.5$ for in-house and contract lobbyists, all at the $p < 0.01$ level), but we use all three to show that the trends that we identify hold regardless of the measure.

As interest group scholars have long observed, the interest group population in Washington continues to grow. The total number of registered lobbying organizations more than doubled between 1998 and 2012,[5] growth that is consistent due to the initially documented advocacy explosion in the *Washington Representatives* commercial directory from the 1960s through the 1980s. In addition, we coded all organizations by the same organization types

---

[3] The Lobbying Disclosure Act of 1995 began requiring detailed expenditure and lobbying activity reports be filed in calendar year 1996. The Senate Office of Public Records began making these reports available electronically in calendar year 1998. Data prior to 1998 do not exist.

[4] The Center for Responsive Politics' (CRP's) method to address mergers, acquisitions, and organizational name changes is to treat all newly formed or named firms or organizations as new, distinct entities. For example, the Association of Trial Lawyers of America (ATLA) changed its name to the American Association for Justice (AAJ) in 2006. This change makes it appear as if ATLA dropped out of the top tier, and AAJ entered, when in fact the organization sustained its top tier status. We identify this example anecdotally, but CRP does not systematically indicate the timing of these changes, so we have no reliable way to link incumbent organizations with their antecedents (in and out of the top tier, across the entire time period). If anything, our methodological choice to treat these instances as new organizations works against our hypothesis that the top tier is increasingly persistent, so we are confident that our findings are robust against any systematic error it introduces.

[5] Although the raw trends appear to reverse course starting in 2009, LaPira (2015) shows that this decline is primarily an artifact of new lobbying disclosure rules, a congressional earmark ban, and other causes unrelated to the relative disparity in lobbying resource allocation between the top tier and the remainder of the interest group population.

Share of lobbying activity done by business

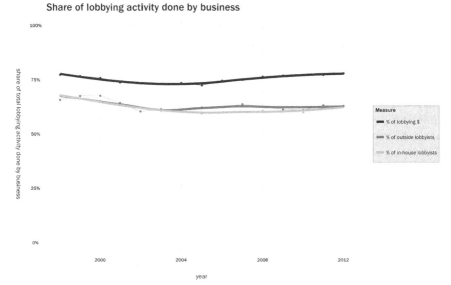

FIGURE 3.1 **Business Share of Lobbying Dollars and Lobbyists, 1998–2012.**
The figure reports the share of all disclosed lobbying dollars, in-house lobbyists, and outside lobbyists (at lobbying firms) accounted for by individual businesses, trade associations, and business associations and in each year, as complied by the Center for Responsive Politics (CRP) and categorized by the authors.

identified in prior studies. We confirmed that the distributions for the first year closely match those previously reported.[6] The proportion of individual businesses remains relatively stable, and clearly dominant. As a share of all lobbying organizations, businesses were 39.0 percent in 1998 and 38.4 percent in 2012. Of course, businesses do not only lobby directly, but also join business and trade associations to advocate their interests. To simplify, we collapse individual businesses, business associations, and trade associations into a single business category, with all others labeled "nonbusiness." As shown in Figure 3.1, groups in the collapsed business category consistently account for a majority of lobbying activity. They spend about three of every four dollars on lobbying, and employ or retain a majority of the lobbyists in Washington.

Across categories, lobbying resources are far from equally distributed. Figure 3.2 plots the densities for lobbying expenditures for the full populations

---

[6] Our distribution matches those of Baumgartner and Leech (2001) and remains relatively consistent from year to year. Trade associations, the next most common category, have declined from a high of 15.8 percent in 1998 to 11.1 percent in 2012. Institutions (a somewhat diverse category that includes hospitals and universities) increased from 8.3 percent of all organizations in 1998 to 10.2 percent in 2012. Citizen groups have hovered at between 3 percent and 4 percent of organizations; nonmember nonprofits have made up only between 2 percent and 3 percent; and labor unions have only represented about 1 percent.

(a)

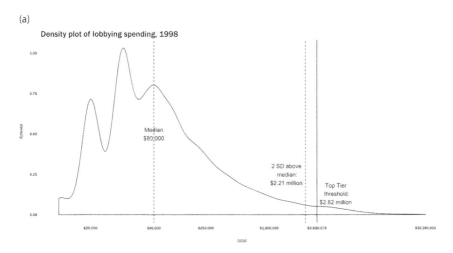

(b)

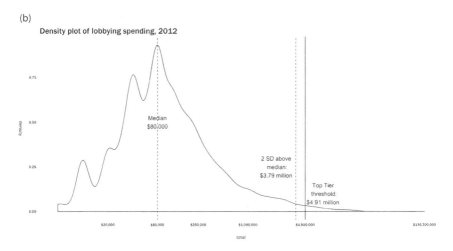

FIGURE 3.2 Distribution of Lobbying Spending on a Logged Scale, 1998 and 2012.
Panel A: 1998
Panel B: 2012
The figure reports the distribution of lobbying spending (on a logged scale) across all organizations in each year reporting nonzero lobbying expenditures on lobbying disclosure reports, as complied by the Center for Responsive Politics (CRP) and the authors. Lines mark the median organization, two standard deviations above the median, and the threshold for reaching the top 100 organizations in each year.

for 1998 and 2012, on a logged scale and in constant 2012 US dollars. As expected, the distributions in all 15 years are extremely skewed and leptokurtotic.[7] The high peaks and long tails of these distributions are visible, even with the x-axes plotted on a logarithmic scale. In 1998, interest organizations spending two standard deviations more than the median interest group spent 46.5 times as much as the group at the midpoint of the distribution. By 2012, an interest group at least two standard deviations from the median organization spent 50.2 times the group at the midpoint. Not only is the distribution of lobbying expenditures skewed, the disproportionate amount spent by those in the tail end increases over time. Spending by both the median group and those two standard deviations above the median went up from 1998 to 2012, but the latter increased at a greater rate. The percentage changes were 72.3 percent and 86.0 percent, respectively. That the distribution of lobbying spending is highly skewed and increasingly lopsided over time provides the first clues that the gap in spending between those organizations at the top and the rest of the population is increasing.

To better test our expectations, we operationalize top tier lobbying organizations as the 100 organizations that spent the most money lobbying in each year from 1998 through 2012.[8] This subset of interest organizations consistently spent greater than two standard deviations above the mean. We acknowledge that the annual top 100 is an arbitrary round number with no other special significance. Alternative thresholds do not substantially change the trends or associations that we document below. Regardless of the proper threshold, the top tier organizations in any given year are overwhelmingly more engaged than the typical interest group, as shown by the solid reference lines in Figure 3.2. The lowest ranking top tier organization spent more than 70 times what the median lobbying organization spent per year in both 1998 and 2012.

By definition, top tier groups outspend the rest of the population – but the differences are staggering. Figure 3.3 reveals that money also buys them a disproportionate share of the human resources that go into their lobbying efforts, especially in-house staff lobbyists. The top 100 groups consistently have at least one-third of the in-house lobbyists in Washington, and hire about one in five contract lobbyists from multiclient lobbying firms. Although Figure 3.3 shows some decline in the top tier share of resources between 1998 and 2009, readers should keep the growth in groups in mind while interpreting these

---

[7] The distributions in Figure 3.1 have skewness of 15.7 and kurtosis of 370 (Shapiro-Wilk $W = 0.15$, $z = 26.01$, $p < 0.001$) for 1998, and skewness of 49.6 and kurtosis of 3737 (Shapiro-Wilk $W = 0.09$, $z = 26.20$, $p < 0.001$) for 2012. We can also reject the null hypotheses that the distributions are normally distributed for years 1998–2012, though do not display them in Figure 3.1.

[8] Additional information available upon request includes rank orders of all top tier organizations, their mean spending, number of lobbyists, and number of issue area mentions on LDA reports, and the number of years during the 1998–2012 period in which they were among the annual Top 100.

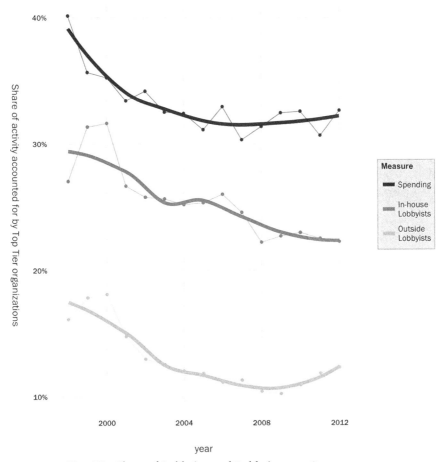

FIGURE 3.3 **Top Tier Share of Lobbying and Lobbyists, 1998–2012.**
The figure reports the share of all disclosed lobbying dollars, in-house lobbyists, and outside lobbyists (at lobbying firms) accounted for by the top 100 organizations in each year, as complied by the Center for Responsive Politics (CRP) and the authors.

trends: over a period in which the number of lobbying organizations more than doubled, the top 100's share of resources remained remarkably high and stable.

To account for any potential differences between business interest groups and other types of interests, we also analyze two separate top tiers: the business top tier and the nonbusiness top tier. Figure 3.4 reveals an increasing price of entry to reach the top tier among both business and nonbusiness organizations. Yet, business interests in the top tier are paying relatively more over time. The minimum lobbying expenditure for a top tier business organization more than doubled from 1998 to 2009, from $2.36 million to $4.93 million. Following 2009, the threshold to be in the top 100 has plateaued. Similarly, the threshold

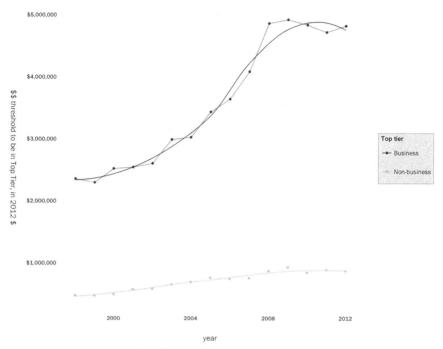

FIGURE 3.4 **Increasing Dollar Threshold for Top Tier, 1998–2012.**
The figure reports the amount of lobbying spending of the 100th highest business organization and nonbusiness organization in a ranking of lobbying spending in each year, as complied by the Center for Responsive Politics and analyzed by the authors.

for a nonbusiness organization in the top tier roughly doubled from 1998 to 2009, going from $480,000 to $940,000, with a similar plateau.

The organizations that make up this top tier are remarkably stable from year to year. Persistence in the top tier from one year to the next increases over time. Figure 3.5 shows that across our three measures of lobbying resources, the percentage of each year's top tier organizations that come from the prior year's top 100 is rising. This is true for both business and nonbusiness organizations. Put another way, turnover within the top tier is declining: the same organizations are increasingly entrenched in the top tier from one year to the next.

Among business organizations, the year-to-year persistence of the top tier as measured by spending has increased from 76 percent (1998–1999) to 91 percent (2011–2012). The trend is similar if we calculate the top tier by ranking organizations based on the number of lobbyists they retained. The year-to-year persistence of the nonbusiness top tier as measured by spending has increased from 69 percent to 88 percent (though there is no strong trend based on our measure of outside contract lobbyists). The top tier of the interest community is

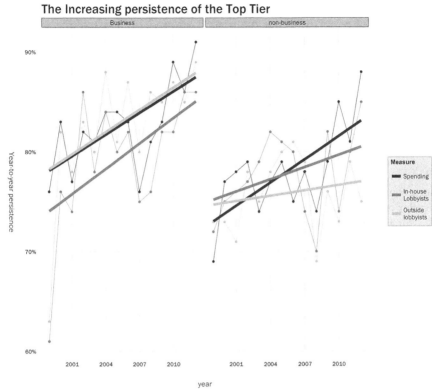

FIGURE 3.5 **Increasing Persistence of Top Tier Lobbying, 1998–2012.**
For each year, the figure reports the proportion of top 100 business and nonbusiness organizations in the prior year who are ranked in the top 100 in the current year in three different rankings of the top organizations by disclosed lobbying dollars, in-house lobbyists, and outside lobbyists (at lobbying firms), as complied by the Center for Responsive Politics (CRP) and analyzed by the authors.

becoming increasingly selective and stable each year, whether among business or among the lower-spending nonbusiness categories.

Not only are the same interest groups increasingly present in the top tier from year to year, but their ordinal position within the top tier is also increasingly consistent. To test this claim, we calculated the year-to-year Kendall's tau rank-order correlations for lobbying spending for both the top tier and the rest of the population. That is, we calculate the rank-order correlation between spending among the 100 top tier organizations at t_1 with their spending at t_2.[9]

---

[9] This procedure allows the correlation coefficient to account for the rank order associations of groups that may enter and exit the top 100 in t_2, so this measure is not redundant with our measure of persistence. Not doing so would simply case-wise delete groups that dropped out of

The rank-order correlations of top tier groups are always greater than that of the rest of the population, but the top tier groups' ordinal ranking increases over time relative to the rest of the population. The slope of the trend line for the top tier is $y = 0.13$, roughly four times greater than the slope of the trend for the rest of the population, $y = 0.03$. The increasing rank-order gap between the top tier and the rest reveals that the relative position of each top tier group is becoming more consistent over time.

A GROWING BUT DISTINCT AGENDA

The trends confirm that the interest group population has expanded while top tier groups have pulled away from the rest. Those at the top are increasingly regular and ubiquitous participants in the policy process, controlling valuable Washington real estate, both literal (physical office space) and metaphorical (agendas and attention). But to better assess the implications of this divergence, we assess whether the lobbying priorities of the top tier are different than the rest and how the top tier evolves. We assess the scope of the agenda in three ways: number of issue categories mentioned, number of agencies mentioned, and number of bill numbers mentioned. For each measure, we take the average among the top tier, and the average among all other groups. We find the same pattern across all three measures: a steady rise in the breadth of lobbying by the top tier, while the average among non top tier organizations remains flat. Compared to the average group, top tier organizations lobby in 5 times as many issue areas, target 5 times as many agencies, and address 50 times as many pieces of legislation. No matter how we cut it, we see top tier organizations doing more, while the average organization remains limited in its range.

Top tier organizations have not only expanded the scope of their combined agenda over time, but the content of that agenda is also very different from the rest of the population as well. For every predefined issue area on each organization's lobbying disclosure form, Figure 3.6 shows the ratio of top tier groups' issue area mentions to that of all other groups. The disproportionately important issue areas for the top tier include telecommunications, tort and copyright reform, and pharmaceutical regulation. These are hardly the issues at the top of the mind of the average citizen. They are not even topics of concern to most other interest groups. Top tier groups appear to be more concerned with economically significant regulatory issues, where they may face weaker competition and get their way more often (Hojnacki et al., 2015). The same dynamics may be apparent in policy debates surrounding the tax code, where top tier organizations disproportionately concentrate efforts to win and maintain their

the top 100 in t_2, which would artificially inflate the *tau* coefficient for that given year. In short, this is a conservative estimate of year-to-year rank-order correlation within the top tier. Results are available for replication from the authors.

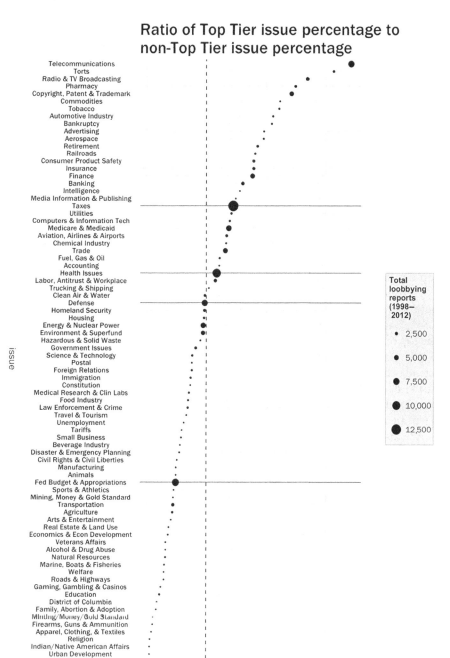

Ratio of Top Tier issue percentage to non-Top Tier issue percentage

issue

Telecommunications
Torts
Radio & TV Broadcasting
Pharmacy
Copyright, Patent & Trademark
Commodities
Tobacco
Automotive Industry
Bankruptcy
Advertising
Aerospace
Retirement
Railroads
Consumer Product Safety
Insurance
Finance
Banking
Intelligence
Media Information & Publishing
Taxes
Utilities
Computers & Information Tech
Medicare & Medicaid
Aviation, Airlines & Airports
Chemical Industry
Trade
Fuel, Gas & Oil
Accounting
Health Issues
Labor, Antitrust & Workplace
Trucking & Shipping
Clean Air & Water
Defense
Homeland Security
Housing
Energy & Nuclear Power
Environment & Superfund
Hazardous & Solid Waste
Government Issues
Science & Technology
Postal
Foreign Relations
Immigration
Constitution
Medical Research & Clin Labs
Food Industry
Law Enforcement & Crime
Travel & Tourism
Unemployment
Tariffs
Small Business
Beverage Industry
Disaster & Emergency Planning
Civil Rights & Civil Liberties
Manufacturing
Animals
Fed Budget & Appropriations
Sports & Athletics
Mining, Money & Gold Standard
Transportation
Agriculture
Arts & Entertainment
Real Estate & Land Use
Economics & Econ Development
Veterans Affairs
Alcohol & Drug Abuse
Natural Resources
Marine, Boats & Fisheries
Welfare
Roads & Highways
Gaming, Gambling & Casinos
Education
District of Columbia
Family, Abortion & Adoption
Mining/Money/Gold Standard
Firearms, Guns & Ammunition
Apparel, Clothing, & Textiles
Religion
Indian/Native American Affairs
Urban Development

0   1   2   3

ratio

Total
loobbying
reports
(1998–
2012)

·   2,500

•   5,000

●   7,500

⬤   10,000

⬤   12,500

FIGURE 3.6 Issue Lobbying Activity Ratio, Top Tier to The Rest.
The figure reports the ratio of the proportion of lobbying reports mentioning each issue area on lobbying disclosure forms submitted for the top 100 organizations (by total lobbying expenditures) to the proportion mentioning each issue area across all other organizations, as complied by the Center for Responsive Politics (CRP) and analyzed by the authors.

specific corporate tax benefits rather than competing in the appropriations process with all other groups for a small piece of the federal budget.

We also assess whether the overall changes in lobbying in the top tier were greater when the congressional agenda was more in flux, using data on the major topic areas of legislative hearings and congressional bills from the Policy Agendas Project (PAP). We found no association between the average percent changes in congressional attention across PAP topic areas and lobbying attention across lobbying disclosure categories among organizations in the top tier ($r = -0.1$, $p < 0.001$ level). The same is true of the year-to-year correlations in congressional topic areas compared to the year-to-year correlations of the topics of top tier lobbying ($r = 0.1$, $p < 0.001$ level). Groups in the top tier simply expand their policy agendas as government attention shifts to new issues rather than abandoning their highest priorities, they adapt to the constantly shifting landscape to find ways to make it work for them. Groups outside the top tier do not have the capacity for such a luxury.

Although the total number of groups lobbying on an issue area is associated with the level of government activity cross-sectionally by topic (Leech et al., 2005, Baumgartner et al., 2011), we show the same groups increasingly stay at the top of the lobbying hierarchy no matter what Congress is considering at any given moment. There were also no major changes in the top tier's lobbying agenda that correspond to changes in party control of Congress (in 2007 and 2011) or the White House (2001 and 2009). Partisan majorities may be insecure as elections come and go, but the lobbying top tier remains. It adapts to partisan agendas, without changing its own.

We also do not see evidence that the lobbying system changed dramatically following major punctuations in the issue agenda, such as after September 11, 2001. In other words, previously reported aggregate changes in lobbying by issue area does not covary with actual changes in the hierarchy of lobbying spending: the same major players continue to lobby disproportionately on their own priorities, even as they expand the scope of their agendas as new concerns draw attention from the government. Organizations that commit so many resources to politics have the capacity to weigh in on anything and everything, even if an issue is only tangentially related to their interests. This expanded scope of activity may not necessarily achieve immediate policy success, but instead sends a signal about the reach and capacity of these top organizations.

INTEREST GROUP HIERARCHY AND LOBBYING INFLUENCE

Our systematic description of lobbying trends reveals heretofore undocumented changes in how the select few top tier interest groups disproportionately engage with the policy process. First, the number of interest groups has continued to rise dramatically, and the business interest bias endures. Second, lobbying resources are distributed increasingly unevenly, with a top tier of organizations now spending at least 70 times what the median group spends. Third, top tier groups have steadily increased their lobbying activities. Reaching the top tier in 2012 requires roughly twice the money it did in 1998. Fourth, the top tier is becoming more stable, both in its overall population and in its internal rank ordering. Dominant organizations are more likely to stay dominant from one year to the next. Finally, the lobbying activities of the top tier are unrelated to changes in the governing issue agenda; top tier organizations simply add new issues to their existing priorities.

Although our analysis does not extend into the Trump administration, we see no reason to believe that either the trends or the consistent dominance we identify are changing. The swamp not only survives, but also thrives in an era of more open pay-to-play politics where industry-supportive players have moved into administrative agencies and big business can hold political events at Trump-branded properties. Like Obama before him, Trump has quickly exempted the administration from any new lobbying rules that stand in the way of his preffered apointments. Congress has likewise ignored populist concerns regarding dominant economic interests raised in both parties, continuing their high-dollar fundraisers and constant meetings with lobbyists. The ubiquity of the top tier may even help explain Washington's immunity from populist challenges. Whoever is elected is immediately met with a growing lobbying onslaught by the same big players.

Our findings may also help resolve seemingly contradictory findings in the literature on interest group influence. Although most scholars have been unable to consistently find that interest group lobbying dollars translate into policy success, others find considerable evidence that major interest groups gain clear benefits and enjoy high rates of success. More broadly, there is a mismatch between the economic literature on interest groups, which notes high returns to lobbying but does not specify how they are achieved, and the political science literature, which fails to detect statistical correlations between organizational political expenditures and policy outcomes. Perhaps only a few groups have the capacity for major policy influence, no matter what tools they and others use. This would be consistent with qualitative evidence from policy historians, who find that a small subset of major, repeat-player interest groups regularly help bring about policy change (Grossmann, 2014).

This analysis also suggests that scholars ought to treat political influence not only as a function of lobbying activities at a single point in time on a given issue, but also as a function of extended lobbying history, accumulated prior successes, and rank ordering in the lobbying hierarchy. Dozens of smaller organizations supporting a policy change may not amount to much influence even if their total spending eclipses that of a major player – whose size, reputation, and long-standing relationships may matter as much, if not more, than their allocation of resources toward that particular policy conflict. The success of the top-reputation groups and top-spending industries documented by Martin Gilens may not be as simple as the popular money-buys-influence folk theory. Rather, after decades in Washington, the top tier of interests has invested to establish and maintain their reputation and capacity as dominant actors, taking advantages of relationships and multiyear, multidomain strategies that take many years to execute. In the long run, that status, purchased with years of regular lobbying spending, likely pays off in policy responsiveness.

A REVISED VIEW OF INTEREST GROUP REPRESENTATION AND INEQUALITY

Opportunities for interest group influence are constrained by a simple arithmetic reality: if there are more groups in Washington but the time and attention of government officials is unchanged, a smaller share of interest groups will have their voices heard. This competition for limited attention has driven an increasing competition in which a decreasing proportion of organizations can be effective. Lobbying expenditures are distributed quite unevenly, with an increasingly immutable top tier that spends more money, retains more lobbyists, and lobbies on more issues. Rather than changing the balance of organization types or dislodging the major players of yesteryear, the crowding of the interest group community has coincided with a differentiated and increasingly stable top tier of groups.

These inequalities in lobbying among interest groups should play a broader role in discussions of the importance of growing economic inequality for policy outcomes. Just as a small subset of the richest members of the American public may account for public opinion's overall influence on policymaking, a similarly small subset of interest groups may be able to gain policymakers' attention. Public opinion scholars, who long expected influence to come from broadly shared opinions, have recently found that focusing on the disproportionate influence of the rich offers more compelling evidence that politicians listen to their constituents – they just focus on the select few rich enough to gain their ear. The resurgence of interest in political inequalities among citizens in the American public should be paired with increased attention to the coincident inequalities well-organized political class. The vast majority of individual citizens are not well equipped to influence policy when compared to lobbying outfits organized for that purpose alone. Even among these professional policy advocates, however, the capacity for influence is quite unequal. Just as a small proportion of individuals control access to wealth and political resources, a small subset of organizations dominates lobbying in the United States. Interest group inequality is likely to have just as much influence on how policy debates are resolved as the well-documented inequalities in civic and political participation among individual citizens.

These patterns have important implications for democratic representation and political equality. The pluralist ideal assumes that many different interests have the ability to effectively participate in the policy process, and that general interest legislation can emerge from bargaining among countervailing factions

(Galbraith, 1952, Dahl, 1956). Lobbyists often defend the current system by pointing out that everybody has a lobbyist in Washington. While it is true that lobbyists represent an impressive variety of causes (we found almost 38,000 different organizations showing up at least once in lobbying records over a 15-year period), there is a big difference between the $10,000 spent on lobbying in a single year by the National Campaign for a Peace Tax Fund (which advocates for conscientious objectors prefer not to have their taxes go to fund the military), and the roughly $15 million spent on average each year by Northrup Grumman, a defense contractor.

If having an effective voice in American national policymaking requires the ability to spend several million dollars per year on lobbying, effective participation will be limited to the unrepresentative sliver of groups with the capacity to do so – primarily large corporations and business associations. Spending $15 million per year buys the ability to hire dozens of well-connected lobbyists, who deeply understand the politics and policies around a set of issues and can make the most convincing case to all the important decision makers and their relevant staff, as often as needed. It also signals legitimacy and a credible commitment to engage the policy process in the long run, on a variety of issues, and to challenge any undesired outcome at every step of the way. Lobbying inequality raises serious anxieties about the representational capacities of American democracy. Americans are right to be concerned about the dominance of a few big interests, but not all lobbyists and interest groups should be considered equal.

The outsized lobbying role of the top tier provides a new way to think about the interest group community's expansion and institutionalization. It helps resolve a puzzle that emerged from seemingly contradictory findings: if more money does not consistently correlate to policy success, why do we see high-spending groups enjoying high success rates? Our analysis suggests that top groups enjoy a preeminent position; everyone else occupies a more marginal space. In the search for interest group influence, the top tier should be the first place to look. Any consideration of how well America can govern itself should also account for the disproportionate role that a small, unequal, and hierarchically distinct subset of interest groups play.

REFERENCES

Arnold, R. Douglas. 1990. *The Logic of Congressional Action.* New Haven: Yale University Press.
Bartels, Larry M. 2010. *Unequal Democracy: The Political Economy of the New Gilded Age.* Princeton: Princeton University Press.
Baumgartner, Frank R., Jeffrey M. Berry, Marie Hojnacki, David C. Kimball, and Beth L. Leech. 2009. *Lobbying and Policy Change: Who Wins, Who Loses, and Why.* Chicago: University of Chicago Press.
Baumgartner, Frank R., and Bryan Jones. 2015. *The Politics of Information.* Chicago: University of Chicago Press.

Baumgartner, Frank R., David Lowery, and Virginia Gray. 2009. "Federal Policy Activity and the Mobilization of State Lobbying Organizations." *Political Research Quarterly* 62(3): 552–567.

Baumgartner, Frank R., and Beth L. Leech. 1998. *Basic Interests: The Importance of Groups in Politics and Political Science.* Princeton: Princeton University Press.

2001. "Issue Niches and Policy Bandwagons: Patterns of Interest Group Involvement in National Politics." *Journal of Politics* 63(4): 1191–1213.

Baumgartner, Frank R., Larsen-Price, H.A., Leech, B.L., and Rutledge, P. 2011. "Congressional and Presidential Effects on the Demand for Lobbying." *Political Research Quarterly* 64(1): 3–16.

Berry, Jeffrey. 1989. *The Interest Group Society.* Glenview, IL: Scott, Foresman.

Dahl, Robert A. 1956. *A Preface to Democratic Theory.* Chicago: University of Chicago Press.

Drutman, Lee. 2015. *The Business of America Is Lobbying.* New York: Oxford University Press.

Esterling, Kevin. 2004. "Buying Expertise: Campaign Contributions and Attention to Policy Analysis in Congressional Committees," *American Political Science Review* 101(1): 93–109.

Evans, C. Lawrence. 2002. "How Senators Decide: An Exploration." In Bruce I. Oppenheimer (ed.), *U.S. Senate Exceptionalism.* Columbus: The Ohio State University Press.

Galbraith, John Kenneth. 1952. *American Capitalism: The Concept of Countervailing Power.* Boston: Houghton Mifflin.

Gilens, Martin. 2012. *Affluence & Influence: Economic Inequality and Political Power in America.* Princeton: Princeton University Press.

Gilens, Martin, and Benjamin I. Page. 2014. "Testing Theories of American Politics: Elites, Interest Groups, and Average Citizens." *Perspectives on Politics* 12(3): 564–581.

Gray, Virginia, and David Lowery. 1996. *The Population Ecology of Interest Representation: Lobbying Communities in the American States.* Ann Arbor, Michigan: University of Michigan Press.

Grossmann, Matt. 2012. *The Not-So-Special Interests: Interest Groups, Public Representation, and American Governance.* Stanford: Stanford University Press.

Artists of the Possible: Governing Networks in American Policy Change Since 1945. New York: Oxford University Press.

Grossmann, Matt. 2005. "The Dynamics of a Disturbance: New and Established Interests in Technology Policy Debates." *Knowledge, Technology, & Policy* 18(3): 95–113.

Hacker, Jacob S., and Paul Pierson. 2010. *Winner-Take-All Politics.* New York: Simon & Shuster.

Hall, Richard L., and Alan V. Deardorff. 2006. "Lobbying as Legislative Subsidy." *American Political Science Review* 100(1): 69–84.

Heaney, Michael T. 2004. "Outside the Issue Niche: The Multidimensionality of Interest Group Identity." *American Politics Research* 32(6): 611–651.

2014. "Multiplex Networks and Interest Group Influence Reputation: An Exponential Random Graph Model." *Social Networks* 36(1): 66–81.

Hojnacki, Marie, Kathleen M. Marchetti, Frank R. Baumgartner, Jeffry M. Berry, David C. Kimball, and Beth L. Leech. 2015. "Assessing Business Advantage in Washington Lobbying." *Interest Groups & Advocacy* 4(3).

Jones, Bryan D. 2001. *Politics and the Architecture of Choice: Bounded Rationality and Governance.* Chicago: University of Chicago Press.

Jones, Bryan D., and Frank R. Baumgartner. 2005. *The Politics of Attention: How Government Prioritizes Problems.* Chicago: University of Chicago Press.

Karpf, David. 2012. *The MoveOn Effect: The Unexpected Transformation of American Political Advocacy.* New York: Oxford University Press.

Kersh, Rogan. 2007. "The Well-Informed Lobbyist: Information and Interest Group Lobbying." In Allan J. Cigler and Burdett A. Loomis (eds.), *Interest Group Politics*, 7th ed. Washington: CQ Press.

Kimball, David C., Frank R. Baumgartner, Jeffrey M. Berry, Marie Hojnacki, Beth L. Leech, and Bryce Summary. 2012. "Who Cares about the Lobbying Agenda?" *Interest Groups & Advocacy* 1(1): 5–25.

Kingdon, John W. 1989. *Congressmen's Voting Decisions.* Boston: Little, Brown.

LaPira, Timothy M. 2014. "Lobbying After 9/11: Policy Regime Emergence and Interest Group Mobilization," *Policy Studies Journal* 42(2): 226–251.

2015. "Lobbying in the Shadows: How Private Interests Hide from Public Scrutiny, and Why That Matters," *Interest Group Politics*, 9th Ed., Eds. Allan J. Cigler, Burdett A. Loomis, and Anthony Nownes. Washington: CQ Press.

LaPira, Timothy M., Herschel F Thomas III, and Frank R. Baumgartner. 2014. "The Two Worlds of Lobbying: Washington Lobbyists in the Core and on the Periphery." *Interest Groups & Advocacy* 3(3): 219–245.

Leech, Beth L., Frank R. Baumgartner, Timothy M. LaPira, and Nicholas A. Semanko. 2005. "Drawing Lobbyists to Washington: Government Activity and the Demand for Advocacy." *Political Research Quarterly* 58(1): 19–30.

Lowery, David. 2007. "Why Do Organized Interests Lobby? A Multi-Goal, Multi-Context Theory of Lobbying," *Polity* 39: 29–54.

Matthews, Donald R., and James A. Stimson. 1975. *Yeas and Nays: Normal Decision-Making in the US House of Representatives.* New York: Wiley.

Mayhew, David R. 2000. *America's Congress: Actions in the Public Sphere, James Madison through Newt Gingrich.* New Haven: Yale University Press.

McCarty, Nolan, Keith T. Poole, and Howard Rosenthal. 2008. *Polarized America: The Dance of Ideology and Unequal Riches.* Cambridge: M.I.T. Press.

Miler, Kristina C. 2010. *Constituency Representation in Congress: The View from Capitol Hill.* New York: Cambridge University Press.

Olson, Mancur. 1982. *The Rise and Decline of Nations.* New Haven: Yale University Press.

Page, Benjamin I., Larry M. Bartels, and Jason Seawright. 2013. "Democracy and the Policy Preferences of Wealthy Americans." *Perspectives on Politics* 11(1). 51–73.

Rauch, Jonathan. 1995. *Demosclerosis: The Silent Killer of American Government.* New York: Three Rivers Press.

Salisbury, Robert. H. 1984. "Interest Representation: The Dominance of Institutions." *American Political Science Review* 78(1): 64–76.

1990. "The Paradox of Interest Groups in Washington—More Groups, Less Clout." In *The New American Political System*, 2nd ed., Anthony S. King (ed.). Washington, DC: American Enterprise Institute.

Schattschneider, Elmer E. 1960. *The Semisovereign People: A Realist's View of Democracy in America*. New York: Holt, Rinehart and Winston.

Schlozman, Kay Lehman, Sidney Verba, and Henry E. Brady. 2012. *The Unheavenly Chorus: Unequal Political Voice and the Broken Promise of American Democracy*. Princeton: Princeton University Press.

Schlozman, Kay Lehman, and John T. Tierney. 1986. *Organized Interests and American Democracy*. New York: Harper Collins.

Simon, Herbert A. 1956. "Rational Choice and the Structure of the Environment." *Psychological Review* 63(2): 129–138.

Teles, Steven M. 2013. "Kludgeocracy in America." *National Affairs* 1(17): 97–114.

Walker, Jack L. 1991. *Mobilizing Interest Groups in America: Patrons, Professions, and Social Movements*. Ann Arbor: University of Michigan Press.

Whiteman, David. 1995. *Communication in Congress: Members, Staff, and the Search for Information*. Lawrence, KS: University of Kansas Press.

Wright, John R. 1996. *Interest Groups and Congress: Lobbying, Contributions, and Influence*. Boston: Allyn & Bacon.

4

Developments in Congressional Responsiveness to Donor Opinion

Brandice Canes-Wrone and Nathan Gibson

Large majorities of Americans presume that campaign contributions influence legislative policymaking.[1] A recent Ipsos poll suggests that over 90 percent of the public believes policymakers listen more to campaign contributors than to voters (Hensel, 2016). Consistent with this result, the poll also finds that "money in politics" was the fifth largest issue for voters in the 2016 elections (Hensel, 2016). Other surveys indicate that 85 percent of Americans assume incumbents regularly choose policies to assist donors (Americans' Views on Money in Politics, 2015) and that over 75 percent believe money has "greater influence on politics today than before" (Desilver and Van Kessel, 2015).

In contrast to this widely held view, the political science literature provides little evidence that congressional roll call voting corresponds to campaign contributions. In fact, study after study suggests that contributions by political action committees (PACs) are not associated with roll call votes. Ansolabehere, de Figueiredo, and Snyder (2003, p. 114) summarize the available evidence, concluding that in 75 percent of the cases the contributions "had no statistically significant effects on legislation or had the 'wrong' sign – suggesting that more contributions lead to less support." This state of affairs has led some to conclude that campaign contributions may lack any impact on policymaking; as Milyo (2015, p. 1) surmises, "decades of research reveal very little evidence that campaign contributions or even lobbying has significant effects on the content of public policy."[2]

---

[1] The authors are grateful for helpful suggestions from Charles Stewart, participants in the SSRC Anxieties of Democracy Working Group, and seminar participants at NYU, Princeton, and Washington University in St. Louis.
[2] Other research emphasizes that PAC contributions may influence legislative activity outside the roll call process (e.g., Hall and Wayman, 1990, Powell, 2013) or by affecting the outcome of elections (e.g., Poole, Romer, and Rosenthal, 1987, Fox and Rothenberg, 2011).

This paper investigates a different avenue by which campaign donations may influence legislative voting. In particular, we focus on individual donors rather than PACs. Individuals are now the single-largest source of contributions for congressional candidates, outpacing both PACs and political parties by substantial amounts. In the 2012 elections, for instance, donations from individuals comprised 79 percent of the total raised by Senate candidates, 63 percent of that raised by House candidates, and 74 percent of that raised by presidential candidates (Barber, Canes-Wrone, and Thrower, 2017). These percentages contrast with elections as recent as the early 1990s, when the median federal candidate still received a plurality of campaign funds from PACs (Jacobson, 2012). The recency of this development is consistent with scholars' earlier focus on PACs and suggests that any influence of individual donors on roll call voting may be relatively new.

Notably, if such influence occurs, it probably comes at the expense of the members' within-district constituencies. As Gimpel, Lee, and Kaminski (2006) document, individual contributors are often not from a legislator's district or state. For instance, for the median reelection-seeking senator in 2012, 63 percent of his or her donors did not reside in-state (Barber, 2016). Moreover, contributors are not only geographically but also demographically dissimilar from the general electorate. In particular, the former have higher incomes, are wealthier, older, more educated, and more likely to be male and white (e.g., Francia et al., 2003). Thus, responsiveness to donor opinion – even to individual contributors – diverges from responsiveness to the general public.

To investigate whether congressional members are indeed responsive to individual contributors' preferences, we examine two datasets that enable the comparison of state-level opinion with the policy positions of the national pool of donors. The first dataset is from almost 30 years ago, when individual donors were less dominant in campaign finance. In particular, the 1988–1992 American National Election Study (ANES) Senate Study (Miller et al., 1999) was designed to measure state-level opinion and includes multiple policy questions that can be linked to roll calls. The second dataset, the Cooperative Congressional Election Study (CCES) (Ansolabehere and Pettigrow, 2014, Schaffner and Ansolabehere, 2015) also facilitates estimating state-level opinion on a set of issues associated with roll call votes but for the more recent period of 2006–2014.[3]

The analyses reveal a significant association between donor opinion and congressional roll call voting since 2006. As donors have become more supportive of a policy position, senators have become more likely to adopt it even after accounting for mass opinion in the state, partisan opinion, the preferences of the affluent, the senator's party, and other factors. By comparison,

---

[3] As we detail subsequently, the few other studies that compare legislators to donors differ in important ways. For instance, Bafumi and Herron (2010) and Barber (2016) calculate ideal points that are not based on the national pool of donors.

the average relationship between donor opinion and roll call voting was not significant in 1988–1992, suggesting that the overall effect has increased over time. In each time period, the impact is strongest when senators face an electoral environment favorable to their reelection. In the earlier years, however, the typical senator faced a more competitive electoral environment. Together, these results suggest that the public anxiety over money in politics is not entirely misplaced. Over the past 10 years senators have indeed been responsive to a national donor pool that is not representative of in-state constituents. At the same time, the conditional impact offers the possibility that the problem is not immutable and, correspondingly, could be reversed or at least diminished by policy reforms.

This chapter proceeds as follows. The "Related Literature" section provides an overview of the literature on individual contributors. The "Theoretical Foundation" section lays out alternative theoretical perspectives. The details of the analysis are described in the "Data, Specifications, and Methods" section, followed by the presentation of findings in the "Results" section. The "Discussion and Conclusion" section wraps up the chapter with a discussion of the broader implications of the findings as well as how they relate to the literatures on congressional representation, campaign finance, and accountability.

RELATED LITERATURE

A variety of research suggests that candidate ideology influences contributions from individuals. For instance, scholarship on house races shows that ideologically extreme candidates receive more out-of-state contributions from individuals (Gimpel, Lee, and Pearson-Merkowitz, 2008) and that extreme challengers receive more financial contributions in general (Stone and Simas, 2010). Johnson (2010) similarly demonstrates that ideologically extreme house candidates tend to rely on individual contributions, although he further finds that more moderate ones rely on PAC and party contributions. Barber, Canes-Wrone, and Thrower (2017) do not focus on ideological extremity per se but instead analyze how donors' policy preferences, as measured by an original survey, correspond to the roll call behavior of incumbent senators. This work also finds that donors, including out-of-state ones, are motivated by candidate ideology in choosing to contribute to campaigns.[4]

These findings are consistent with evidence from case studies and surveys that examine donors' motivations. For instance, several surveys have explicitly asked donors about their goals, and these analyses suggest the goals include a mix of ideology, professional interests, and social engagement (Brown, Hedges, and Powell, 1980, Francia et al., 2003). The case studies in Masket (2016) also

---

[4] Bonica (2013) develops candidate ideal points based on donor behavior and finds a higher fit in specifications that include ideological goals.

stress donors' ideological motivations. For instance, he documents how donors have become integrated into state parties' networks and therefore part of the party establishment.

Another strand of scholarship compares contributors' and voters' preferences in order to assess the extent to which donors are representative of the general public. As noted earlier, these studies find individual contributors tend to be wealthier, older, more educated, male, and white (e.g., Francia et al., 2003). The literature also suggests that donors are more ideologically extreme than the general electorate or even strong partisan voters (e.g., La Raja and Schaffner, 2015, Hill and Huber, 2017). Combined with the evidence that contributors select candidates strategically, this body of work suggests candidates have incentives to cater to donor preferences that are unrepresentative of the broader public.

Relatedly, a couple of pieces estimate the ideal points of donors, voters, and congressional members (Bafumi and Herron, 2010, Barber, 2016). However, the ideal point studies do not analyze the national pool of donors. Barber (2016) uses a survey of donors in the 2012 elections to estimate senator-specific donor ideal points from individuals who contributed to the given senator in that election along with donors in the senator's state. Likewise, Bafumi and Herron's (2010) ideal points are based on within-district donors.

In sum, the current literature does not assess whether congressional members are catering to out-of-district donors through roll call voting, and if so, whether this responsiveness varies across political context and has increased in recent years. Of course, it might seem straightforward that roll call voting will reflect the preferences of a national donor pool given that individual donors target contributions on the basis of candidate ideology. Yet congressional members face a variety of incentives that are not limited to fundraising, including responsiveness to voters' preferences (e.g., Erikson and Wright, 2000, Canes-Wrone, Brady, and Cogan, 2002). As such, even if one grants that there exist incentives to cater to donors' preferences, theoretical predictions regarding whether and when this should occur depend upon a variety of assumptions concerning voters, congressional members, and donors.

THEORETICAL FOUNDATION

Two theoretical strands present divergent perspectives regarding the conditions that encourage congressional members to cater to contributors' preferences. The first of these strands is formalized in Baron's (1994) model of informed and uninformed voters, which we refer to as the Informed and Uninformed Voters Theory. The second school of thought, which is more recent, considers campaign funds a means by which congressional members can increase their party influence (Cann, 2008, Powell, in press). We label this second perspective the Exchange Theory of Party Influence.

In the Informed and Uninformed Voters Theory, interest groups with preferences more extreme than the median voter have the ability to provide contributions that enable politicians to "buy" the votes of uninformed voters through advertising (Baron, 1994). In order to obtain the contributions, however, politicians must move toward the groups' positions.[5] Thus fundraising carries a direct electoral advantage but in order to obtain this advantage, politicians must be responsive to contributors' positions. In the theory, politicians are less responsive to the groups' preferences in the case where one candidate has an electoral advantage than in the case where no candidate has an ex-ante advantage. (Likewise, when one candidate has an inherent advantage, less money is raised from outside groups.) Accordingly, the theory is consistent with the prediction that an incumbent's responsiveness to donor opinion should be negatively associated with the favorability of the electoral environment she or he will face.

While the Informed and Uninformed Voters Theory focuses on advertising in campaigns, the Exchange Theory of Party Influence considers how internal congressional dynamics and fundraising interact (Cann, 2008, Powell, in press). The latter perspective has particular relevance to recent decades given that seniority has afforded congressional members less influence. With the Republican takeover in 1995, the party established term limits on committee chairmanships and enacted other rules that reduced the importance of seniority for committee and chairmanship assignments (e.g., Deering and Smith, 1997). The Democratic Party, upon regaining a majority in 2007, also became less reliant on seniority for committee posts (although so far has shied away from term limits) (e.g., Stewart, 2012). In seniority's wake, fundraising has become an important determinant of party leadership posts, including for committee chairs as well as for positions such as speaker, majority or minority leader, whip, or caucus chair (Cann, 2008, Powell, in press). Correspondingly, in both parties, members are given fundraising expectations based on their internal positions, with those in more powerful positions expected to raise higher amounts for the party and partisan colleagues (Powell, in press).

According to the Exchange Theory of Party Influence, a member's responsiveness to donor opinion need not produce a direct electoral advantage. Indeed, it could even be disadvantageous to the member's district popularity and vote margins. Accordingly, when donor and district opinion diverge, the perspective suggests that the congressional members most likely to cater to donor opinion will be those in relatively safe districts. These members can afford to become less popular in their districts and increase their influence within the party by raising funds that can be targeted to other races.

---

[5] In the model, candidates only move from the median voter in order to seek campaign funds if there are a sufficient number of uninformed voters and for particularistic policies.

The two theoretical perspectives thereby offer opposing predictions about the relationship between the electoral favorability of a member's district and their incentive to cater to donor opinion. According to the Exchange Theory of Party Influence, members in favorable districts will be more likely to cater to donor opinion; by contrast, according to the Informed and Uninformed Voters Theory, it is members in less favorable districts who will be more likely to do so. The empirical analysis, in addition to testing for an average effect of donor opinion, assesses these predictions by analyzing whether any such impact depends on the electoral favorability of a member's district.

DATA, SPECIFICATIONS, AND METHODS

To examine congressional responsiveness to individual donors, we analyze two datasets that include information about national donor opinion and state-level mass opinion. The first is the ANES Senate Study, which provides data on donor and state opinion from 1988 to 1992 (Miller et al., 1999). The second is the CCES, which corresponds to the 2006–2014 Senate elections (Ansolabehere and Pettigrew, 2014, Schaffner and Ansolabehere, 2015).

ANES Senate Study Data and Variables

The ANES Senate Study was unusual for its time in soliciting sufficient responses for state-level opinion estimates; in the pre-internet period the high expense of state-level samples tended to make them impractical. Numerous previous studies support the use of these surveys as estimates of state-level opinion (e.g., Erikson, 1990, Stewart and Reynolds, 1990, Norrander, 2001).[6] Several items concern preferences on policies relevant to roll calls, including ones on trade policy, abortion, and the death penalty. More specifically, after examining the full ANES Senate Study, we identified four questions that linked closely to roll call votes. These questions ask about trade imports, use of the death penalty, parental consent for teenage abortions, and government funding of abortions.[7]

For each policy item, the survey data contain information about multiple constituencies that could affect senators' roll call votes. In generating these opinion variables, we use the survey weights calculated by the ANES. *State Opinion* equals the percentage of all respondents in the senator's state who favored the liberal position on the issue (for its time): pro-protectionism, anti–death penalty, anti–parental consent, and pro–government funding of abortion.[8] Thus for the death penalty, the variable equals the percentage

---

[6] For full details on the ANES Senate Study, see Miller et al. (1999).
[7] Specifically, the questions are from variable numbers PS0571, PS0587, PS0579, and PS0583.
[8] Unfortunately, the ANES sample size does not permit estimating the percentages of Republicans and Democrats within a state who favor a policy; however, the CCES data will enable doing so.

of respondents in the state who were not in favor of the federal death penalty. *National Partisan Donor Opinion,* which is based on the population of respondents who self-identified as making a political donation in the current election cycle and as being a member of the senator's party, is coded similarly. In particular, the variable equals the percentage of such respondents who favored the liberal position on the issue. The variable is not limited to donors in the senator's state, given that such a high percentage of campaign donations are from out of state. Thus for Democratic senators, the variable is based on the national pool of Democratic donors, and for Republicans it is based on the national pool of Republican donors.

As a measure of senators' roll call behavior, we have created indices, akin to interest group ratings, of their votes on these topics. For each of the four survey items, we collected from *Congressional Quarterly* all available senate roll calls specifically on the issue. With the roll calls we then created an index of the percentage of each senator's votes that favored the liberal position: pro–protectionism, anti–death penalty, anti–parental consent, and pro–government funding of abortions. These roll call indices constitute the dependent variable *%Liberal Roll Calls$_{ijt}$* for each Senator i on issue j in Congress t. Across the congresses seven survey items were associated with a set of roll call votes, producing a dataset of 700 observations.

CCES Data and Variables

We conduct a similar analysis for the CCES data using available interest group ratings, CCES survey items, and the set of variables that match those available for the ANES analysis. Because the CCES does not include questions on the death penalty, we cannot analyze this issue. However, for both abortion and trade policy there are CCES survey items in multiple years. Indeed, for abortion there is a regular general item regarding the respondent's view on whether abortion should be impermissible, permitted under specified conditions, or generally allowed.[9] For trade policy, there is not a similarly general question but we can use items that ask about specific trade agreements to estimate pro–free trade opinion.[10]

The 2006–2014 CCES surveys contain at least 30,000 respondents in each year and over 50,000 respondents in the later years. *National Partisan Donor Opinion* and *State Opinion* are measured analogously as with the ANES data, and given the large sample sizes, for many states and years *Partisan State Opinion* can also be estimated. More specifically, Partisan State Opinion equals the percentage of respondents in the senator's state and party who favored the liberal position. For some years and states there are small sample sizes of

---

[9] The survey items for each year include v3019 for 2006, CC310 for 2008, CC324 for 2010 and 2012, and CC14*323*2 for 2014.

[10] A trade question is available in the 2006, 2008, and 2012 surveys.

in-state partisan respondents, and we require at least 100 respondents for this variable to be estimated; we accordingly present results with and without the control for partisan state opinion. Interest group ratings on abortion are available from the National Right to Life Committee and on trade policy from the Cato Institute. These ratings combined with the public opinion data on donor and state opinion produce 800 observations.

The CCES includes policy questions not just on abortion and trade but also on a range of salient roll calls taken during the previous (6-year) senate term. The number of roll calls per survey ranges from 5 to 9, generating a total of 31 unique roll calls across the five election cycles of 2006–2014. These roll calls encompass domestic and foreign policy issues such as immigration, taxes, NSA surveillance, health care, and gay marriage, among others.[11] This range of issues enables stronger within-senator identification. Each senator tends to have some issues on which national donor opinion is similar to state opinion and others on which they diverge. For instance, for Senator Max Baucus (D-MT), national donor and state opinion are fairly similar on the Korea Trade Agreement of 2011, with 55 percent and 58 percent supporting the agreement, respectively. By comparison, only 40 percent of Democratic donors supported the Keystone pipeline in 2012 while 85 percent of Montana residents supported it. For Senator Rob Portman (R-OH), there is more tension between donor and constituency opinion on trade but little on the Middle Class Tax Cut Act of 2012. In the case of the former, 64 percent of Republican donors favored the free trade agreement while only 44 percent of Ohio respondents did. In the case of the tax cut, 59 percent of both groups favored the bill.

We accordingly examine the CCES data with two different types of analyses. The first focuses on the issues available in the 1988–1992 ANES Senate Study. The second considers the broader set of CCES roll call votes. The latter enables assessing whether any observed effects for the issues in the ANES exist for a broader set of policies.

Specifications

The initial analyses of the ANES and CCES data estimate the following general specification for each Senator i on issue j in Congress t:

$$\%\text{Liberal roll calls}_{ijt} = f(\text{National partisan donor opinion}_{ijt},$$
$$\text{State opinion}_{ijt}, \text{Controls}_{ijt}), \qquad [4.1]$$

where the controls are defined below as well as in Appendix Table 4A, which provides a description of each variable, its measurement, and sources. For the broader set of CCES roll calls, the independent variables are similar but the

[11] Full details on the roll call votes and surveys are given in Ansolabehere and Pettigrew (2014) and Schaffner and Ansolabehere (2015).

dependent variable reflects the probability that senator j voted in a liberal direction. Specifically, *Liberal Vote* equals 1 if the senator voted with the position that the majority of senate Democrats favored and 0 otherwise.[12]

In addition to Equation [4.1], which estimates the average effect of donor opinion, we also examine whether this effect varies according to the electoral favorability of the state. Equation [4.2] describes this specification:

$$\%\text{Liberal roll calls}_{ijt} = f(\text{National partisan donor opinion}_{ijt},$$
$$\text{State opinion}_{ijt}, \text{National partisan donor opinion}_{ijt} \times$$
$$\text{Electoral favorability}_{ijt}, \text{State opinion}_{ijt} \times \text{Electoral}$$
$$\text{favorability}_{ijt}, \text{Electoral favorability}_{ijt}, \text{Controls}_{ijt}),$$

$$[4.2]$$

where Electoral Favorability, as with the controls, is defined subsequently. In Equation [4.2], a positive coefficient on the interaction term between electoral favorability and donor opinion would indicate that donor opinion has a larger association with senate roll call voting when the electoral context is more favorable; by comparison, a negative coefficient would suggest this occurs when congressional members face tougher districts. Thus a positive effect would support the Exchange Theory of Party Influence and a negative effect the Informed and Uninformed Voters Theory.

Control Variables and Political Context

The control variables account for each senator's partisan affiliation, the policy preferences of high-income respondents, and intertemporal change. Specifically, *Democratic Senator* equals 1 if the senator caucuses with the Democrats and 0 otherwise. We expect that independent of state and donor opinion, Democrats will be more likely than Republicans to vote in a liberal direction.

Gilens (2012) finds that the policy preferences of the top 10 percent of the income distribution in the national population have an outsized influence over national legislative activity. *Affluent Nondonor Opinion* accounts for this possibility. More specifically, in both the ANES and CCES, respondents self-report their income within ranges, and we match these categories to the census data on the national income distribution. While Gilens notes that campaign contributions are one reason the affluent may have greater influence on public policy, there are other potential reasons as well, such as greater activism (e.g., Verba, Schlozman, and Brady, 1995). Therefore, in order to disentangle the impact of affluence from donations, Affluent Nondonor Opinion is based on the percentage of the top 10 percent who do not report donating to a

---

[12] This coding follows Gailmard and Jenkins (2007).

candidate or campaign. As with the other public opinion variables, it equals the percentage who favor the liberal position.

Finally, the controls include a set of year indicators. These year effects capture variation in the ratings scales across congresses as well as any otherwise unaccounted for intertemporal differences in the propensity of senators to vote in a liberal direction.[13]

In addition to including all control variables, Equation [4.2] accounts for how a senator's responsiveness to donor opinion may vary according to the favorability of the electoral environment the senator will likely face. We measure this variation in two related but distinct ways. First, *Electoral Favorability* equals the statewide percentage of the two-party vote received by the presidential candidate of the senator's party in the most recent election. Second, *Normalized Electoral Favorability* equals the difference between this percentage and the national average received by the presidential candidate of the senator's party in the most recent election. The first of these measures captures not only state ideology but also national tides given that congressional races may be influenced by the presidential election (e.g., Jacobson, 2012). The second measure, by comparison, focuses on a state's relative liberalism/conservatism to other states in an effort to assess how district ideology alone may alter the impact of donor opinion. In regressions that include interactions involving these variables, all main effects are included.

Methods

In an effort to impose as few constraints on the data as possible, we begin with an ordinary least squares regression of Equation [4.1]. The standard errors are clustered by senator to account for senator-specific correlation in voting behavior. As an alternative way to capture the within-senator correlation, we have also analyzed a mixed effects specification that includes random intercepts by senator, as well as models with fixed effects for the senators, and these findings are substantively similar to those presented.[14]

A separate econometric issue involves the high collinearity between national partisan donor opinion and state partisan opinion in the CCES data. This issue is similar to the one faced by Gilens (2012) in his analysis of higher- versus lower-income citizens' influence on public policy outcomes; on many policies, the different income groups have similar preferences. Gilens (2012) significantly reduces the collinearity in the main analyses by examining only those policies on which the groups' preferences diverge by at least 10 percentage points. We adopt a similar approach. While the level of correlation between national partisan donor opinion and state partisan opinion is 0.9 for the full dataset, it is only 0.6

---

[13] Over the years of the ANES data, majority status in Congress does not change. For the CCES data, controlling for majority status does not alter the substantive findings.

[14] All alternative analyses are available upon request.

TABLE 4.1 *Senator Responsiveness to National Donor and State Opinion, 1988–1992.*

	[1]	[2]
National partisan donor opinion	−0.053	−0.055
	(0.196)	(0.122)
State opinion	0.593[b]	0.592[b]
	(0.117)	(0.121)
Affluent nondonor opinion	−0.004	—
	(0.234)	—
Democratic senator	0.408[b]	0.409[b]
	(0.036)	(0.037)
Constant	−0.058	−0.058
	(0.050)	(0.048)
Year effects	Included	Included
N	700	700

Dependent variable equals %Liberal Roll Calls. Clustered standard errors by senator in parentheses.
[a]$p < 0.05$, [b]$p < 0.01$, two-tailed.

for cases where these variables diverge by at least 15 percentage points and 0.8 if the variables diverge by at least 10 percentage points. We therefore focus on regressions that use the 15 percentage point divergence cutpoint. The results are robust to using either cutpoint or including all observations.

RESULTS

We begin by analyzing the average impact of national donor opinion according to the 1988–1992 ANES data. Table 4.1 presents these results.

Column [1] shows the main specification and column [2] shows the one that excludes the control for affluent respondents. As is immediately apparent, the average effect of donor opinion in this earlier period is not statistically significant. Indeed, the sign of the coefficient is even negative. This is the case regardless of whether affluent opinion is included as a control.

By comparison, several of the controls have significant effects. For instance, mass opinion is significantly associated with senator roll call behavior.[15] More specifically, if state opinion shifts 10 percentage points in a liberal (conservative) direction on an issue, the senator's percentage of liberal (conservative) votes on that issue shifts by approximately 6 percentage points. A senator's party also has a significant effect. In particular, the findings suggest that the roll call indices of Democratic senators are on average 40 percentage points more liberal than those of otherwise comparable senators from the Republican Party.

[15] As noted earlier, state partisan opinion is not included because the ANES sample sizes are not designed to be sufficient for measuring this variable.

TABLE 4.2 *Senator Responsiveness to National Donor and State Opinion,*
2006–2014.

	[1]	[2]	[3]	[4]
	%Liberal roll calls	%Liberal roll calls	Pr(Liberal vote=1)	Pr(Liberal vote=1)
National partisan donor opinion	0.563^b (0.061)	0.905^b (0.162)	2.761^b (0.245)	3.480^b (0.958)
State opinion	0.516^b (0.117)	0.737^b (0.258)	−0.419 (0.364)	−2.035 (1.322)
Affluent nondonor opinion	0.600^b (0.104)	−0.371 (0.262)	0.541 (0.396)	2.066 (1.163)
Democratic senator	0.488^b (0.031)	0.443^b (0.081)	0.777^b (0.092)	0.156 (0.295)
Partisan state opinion	—	−0.108 (0.233)	—	1.806 (1.677)
Constant	-0.660^b (0.082)	−0.277 (0.188)	-1.920^b (0.155)	-2.985^b (0.507)
Year effects	Included	Included	Included	Included
N	800	120	3048	505

Columns [1] and [2] report OLS coefficients and columns [3] and [4] report probit coefficients.
All columns report clustered standard errors by senator in parentheses. $^a p < 0.05$, $^b p < 0.01$,
two-tailed.

Also according to Table 4.1, the policy preferences of the affluent who are
not donors have no effect on senator roll call voting in 1988–1992. In supplemental analysis, we find that this lack of effect occurs even if donor opinion is
not included as a variable. While this finding – combined with the lack of
influence of donors – seemingly differs from that in Gilens (2012), the latter is
focused on overall policy enactments rather than senator roll calls and furthermore, includes a time span that extends back to Reagan and up to Bush 43. By
comparison, Table 4.1 is limited to a set of three policy issues in 1988–1992.
It is possible that in other years and/or on other issues, a significant effect of
affluent opinion emerges even for senator roll call voting.

Table 4.2 presents such analysis.

Column [1] analyzes the CCES data, which spans 2006–2014, with a
specification analogous to those for the 1988–1992 ANES data. Interestingly,
for this later period, a significant effect emerges not only for affluent nondonor
opinion but also for national donor opinion. As the national donor pool from a
senator's party becomes more liberal on an issue, the senator becomes significantly more liberal in their roll call behavior on that issue.

This effect holds for the additional specifications in Table 4.2 as well. Column [2] continues the specification analogous to the ANES analysis, but also controls for partisan state opinion for cases with at least 100 respondents and for which partisan state opinion diverges from national partisan donor opinion by at least 15 percentage points. (Between these two conditions, the divergence between partisan state opinion and donor opinion is the more constraining; this condition alone reduces the sample size to 166.) Columns [3] and [4] include all roll calls from the CCES data, not simply those on trade and abortion, with column [3] reporting the results from the full dataset and column [4] from the analysis that controls for partisan state opinion. In all of these analyses, the coefficients on national donor opinion are in the predicted direction and significant at conventional levels.

The size of this effect varies slightly across the specifications but in all cases is of substantive importance. In the analysis of the trade and abortion ratings in column [1], a 10 percentage point shift in donor opinion in a conservative (liberal) direction is associated with a 6 percentage shift in the percentage of a senator's conservative (liberal) votes on that issue. The analogous impact for the sample for which partisan state opinion is available is 9 percentage points, as shown in column [2]. In the probit analysis of the broader set of roll calls in column [3], a 10 percentage point increase in donor opinion is associated with a 10 percentage point increase in the probability that the senator votes in this direction (at the means of the independent variables, as is standard in probit analyses). Likewise, when partisan state opinion is accounted for in column [4], this estimated magnitude increases to 13 percentage points.

The effects of the controls are less consistent across the models than those for national donor opinion. In the specifications analogous to the ANES analysis, the coefficients on state opinion are significant. However, for the broader set of issues analyzed in columns [3] and [4], they are not, suggesting that perhaps the impact is higher for the issues of abortion and trade, which comprise the data in columns [1] and [2]. Affluent nondonor opinion also has a significant effect in column [1] and a marginally significant effect ($p<0.1$, two-tailed) in column [4]. These findings help to unpack the theoretical rationales in work that suggests an individual's affluence increases their policy influence (e.g., Gilens, 2012, Gilens and Page, 2014); in particular, Table 4.2 indicates that some, but not all, of this impact is due to campaign contributions.

The coefficients on senator party affiliation are always in the expected direction and in all but one case significant at conventional levels. However, partisan state opinion does not have a significant effect, either for the specification based on that for the ANES data in column [2] or for the full set of CCES roll call votes in column [4]. According to these data, senators are not responding to their home-state partisan constituencies except to the extent that their preferences overlap with those of the national partisan donor constituency or the general electorate.

These results support the argument that donor opinion influences senators' legislative voting behavior. At the same time, we recognize that the design of the study is such that causation claims must be tempered. Within this context we have made additional efforts to assess whether there is mere correlation between senators' and donors' preferences, particularly within the context of a Congress that has polarized over time. In particular, we have reanalyzed the data with senator fixed effects, and these results support those presented, both in terms of the sign and significance of the coefficients. Naturally, even the fixed effects model is not a pure experiment and we do not claim it as such; it does suggest, however, that even holding each senator's preferences constant across issues and congresses, change in donor opinion is associated with a corresponding change in roll call voting.

In sum, the analysis in Table 4.2 suggests a robust effect of national donor opinion in the years of 2006–2014. As a senator's national donor base becomes more supportive of a position, the senator becomes more likely to take that position. This is the case even controlling for factors such as the senator's party and state opinion. By comparison, state opinion has an effect in only some specifications, and there is never a significant impact of the senator's in-state partisan voters. Of course, these factors, like donor opinion, may be affected by the political context. We therefore analyze whether the favorability of the electoral environment affects the extent to which donor and state opinion influence a senator's roll call behavior.

Political Context

Table 4.3 presents the results on political context for both the ANES and CCES data, for each measure of electoral favorability.

In every analysis senators become more likely to cater to donor opinion as their electoral context becomes more favorable. In other words, as a state becomes more ideologically disposed to reelecting a senator, he or she becomes more responsive to contributors' policy preferences. Thus senators are not behaving as if money can buy elections; instead, they are more responsive to donor opinion when unlikely to face a tough race.

Figure 4.1 plots the marginal effect of donor opinion with respect to each measure of electoral favorability. The solid line represents the combined impact of the main effect of donor opinion and its interaction with electoral favorability, while the dashed lines reflect the 95 percent confidence interval. The dashes on the x-axes denote the realized values of electoral favorability.

The top panels show that for the 1988–1992 sample, donor opinion typically does not have an effect that is statistically distinguishable from zero for the realized values of presidential vote. By comparison, and as depicted in the bottom panels, the effect is generally statistically significant for 2006–2014.

Figure 4.1 illustrates how the average impact of donor opinion can differ so much between the time periods, even though Table 4.3 suggests the coefficient

TABLE 4.3 *Electoral Favorability and Responsiveness to National Donor Opinion.*

	[1]	[2]	[3]	[4]
	1988–1992	1988–1992	2006–2014	2006–2014
Electoral favorability × National partisan donor opinion	5.444[b] (1.495)	—	2.741[b] (0.700)	—
Normalized electoral favorability × National partisan donor opinion	—	4.234[a] (1.619)	—	2.227[b] (0.708)
National partisan donor opinion	-2.674[b] (0.788)	-0.029 (0.200)	-0.903[a] (0.380)	0.485[b] (0.066)
Electoral favorability × State opinion	-3.085[b] (1.175)	—	0.834 (1.068)	—
Normalized electoral favorability × State opinion	—	-3.064[a] (1.464)	—	0.575 (1.201)
State opinion	2.129[b] (0.605)	0.563[b] (0.112)	-0.237 (0.580)	0.282[a] (0.121)
Affluent nondonor opinion	-0.143 (0.231)	-0.026 (0.237)	0.653[b] (0.106)	0.663[b] (0.108)
Democratic senator	0.394[b] (0.040)	0.422[b] (0.038)	0.483[b] (0.033)	0.477[b] (0.034)
Electoral favorability	-1.160 (0.653)	—	-2.057[b] (0.532)	—
Normalized electoral favorability	—	-0.361 (0.771)	—	-1.751[b] (0.550)
Constant	0.528 (0.362)	-0.057 (0.059)	0.573 (0.303)	-0.506[b] (0.088)
Year effects	Included	Included	Included	Included
N	700	700	800	800

Dependent variable equals %Liberal Roll Calls. Clustered standard by senator in parentheses below.
[a] $p < 0.05$, [b] $p < 0.01$, two-tailed.

83

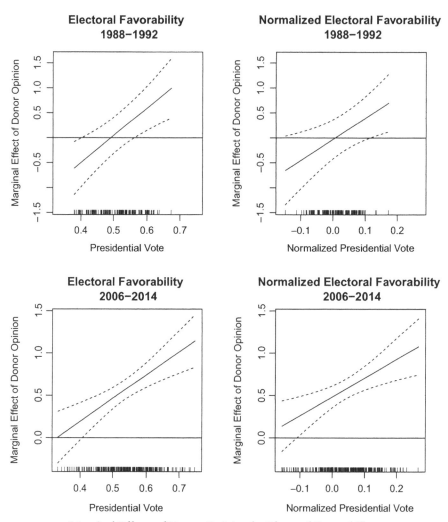

FIGURE 4.1 Marginal Effects of Donor Opinion by Electoral Favorability.

on the interaction term between donor opinion and electoral favorability is consistently significant across the years. Consider column [1] of Table 4.3. The combined results on the interaction and main effects imply that responsiveness to donor opinion becomes statistically significant once the percentage of the statewide vote for the candidate of the senator's party is at least 56 percent, as shown in Figure 4.1. This level of electoral favorability occurred for less than a quarter of the observations in 1988–1992. In column [2], which normalizes the presidential vote, even fewer observations are in the set for which donor opinion has a significant effect. Specifically, for only 3 percent of the cases is electoral favorability high enough such that donor opinion has a significant impact on senator roll call voting.

By comparison, for the 2006–2014 CCES data, Figure 4.1 shows that senators' responsiveness to donor opinion is significant for almost all of observed ranges of electoral favorability regardless of how it is measured. This wider coverage results not only due to differences in the estimates, but also the more favorable electoral context that the typical senator has enjoyed in recent years. As documented elsewhere (e.g., Fiorina, 2002), there are ever declining numbers of Blue Dog Democrats representing states that vote Republican in presidential elections and likewise, increasingly few Rockefeller Republicans representing states that tend to vote Democratic. Indeed, and as depicted by Figure 4.1, in the CCES years over half of the senators hailed from states in which more than 55 percent of the voters favored the presidential candidate from their own party.

As with all earlier results, the findings of Table 4.3 hold with fixed effects for the individual senators, suggesting that the estimates capture within-legislator variation. Moreover, the findings hold with both senator and issue fixed effects, indicating that the responsiveness occurs when donor opinion on an issue changes over time within a given senator's state and does not simply reflect variation across senators and issues. Still, as noted previously, we recognize that these data are observational rather than experimental. Moreover, there possibly is a positive feedback loop whereby the electoral favorability of the state and/or donor opinion are influenced by senators' roll call behavior; while these data do not enable testing this possibility, it is an interesting avenue for future research.

Overall, Table 4.3 and the robustness analysis with fixed effects are supportive of the Exchange Theory of Party Influence described earlier. According to that perspective, members who can afford to give up some district popularity will cater to donors at the expense of within-district voters. Conversely, the findings do not support the Informed and Uninformed Voters Theory, which suggests that members in competitive districts will raise funds in order to advertise to less-informed voters. Because the latter theory was developed with at least some orientation to PACs and interest groups, which dominated campaign finance at that time, it is perhaps not surprising that the Exchange Theory receives greater support.

Interestingly, the patterns observed for national donor opinion are transposed for state opinion in the earlier period. In columns [1] and [2], an increase in the favorability of the electoral context is associated with a decline in the impact of mass policy preferences. In the later years, however, the estimates on the interaction terms with state opinion are not at all significant. The other controls largely conform to expectations and prior results. Partisan affiliation has a consistently significant effect. Moreover, when the estimates on affluent opinion are significant, they are in the expected direction.

On the whole, the results of Table 4.3 suggest that the relationship between donor opinion and senator roll call behavior is conditional. On the one hand, such a result is reassuring because it suggests there are contexts under which no significant association exists. On the other hand, when a district is not ideologically balanced, responsiveness to donor opinion is substantial and congressional members have increasingly faced favorable electoral environments, making the conditional effect less comforting than it otherwise would be. Moreover, because there are issues on which donors from both major parties agree with each other but not with voters, this responsiveness to contributors has unsettling implications for representation.

DISCUSSION AND CONCLUSION

A commonplace concern about US government is that policymaking is shaped by the interests of campaign contributors rather than the public at large. For instance, the *Atlantic* has characterized the current system as reflecting "the new era of big money" and the government's "final capture by the powerful" (Bennet, 2012). Consistent with this view, a 2012 Democracy Corps survey found that when respondents were asked to name the two groups that most influence "how members of Congress vote" less than 15 percent cited voters while 45 percent cited campaign contributors (Democracy Corps, 2012). President Trump acquired office with a campaign that built upon these beliefs and declared the campaign finance system to be "broken" (e.g., Prokop, 2015). Yet study after study has investigated the effect of PAC contributions and found little or no effect.

We investigate this broad issue of money and politics differently, namely, by focusing on the largest source of campaign donations in today's political environment: individual donors. Three main findings emerge. First, we find a substantial effect of donor opinion as it relates to senate roll call behavior in 2006–2014; as the national donor pool from a senator's party becomes more supportive of a position, the senator becomes significantly more likely to take that position. Second, the electoral environment conditions this relationship. In less favorable environments, when a serious electoral challenge is likely, donor opinion does not have a significant association with roll call decisions. Once a state's ideology is sufficiently favorable to a senator's reelection chances, however, donor opinion has a substantial effect. Third, the impact is more substantial in recent years than in the late 1980s and early 1990s. While even in the earlier period the electoral environment conditioned the effect, the vast majority of senators did not have sufficiently high levels of electoral favorability for donor opinion to have a significant relationship with roll call behavior.

In combination, these findings have several implications. Most obviously, the work identifies a direct association between the campaign finance system and legislative voting. Individual donors are commonly seen as a less nefarious or more wholesome source of campaign contributions, perhaps because such financing is not thought to be related to access or lobbying. Yet this chapter highlights that individual donors may skew representation in important ways.

Moreover, given that these contributors' demographics and policy views do not reflect those of the general public (e.g., Hill and Huber, 2017), this influence should not be assumed to be wholesome or unproblematic. Even "small donors" are more affluent than nondonors (e.g., Magleby, Goodliffe, and Olsen, 2018). As such, donor responsiveness arguably paves the way for populists such as Trump to gain traction on claims that the system is broken.

An additional implication relates to the finding that the electoral context affects congressional responsiveness to donor opinion. Fiorina and Abrams (2009) provide evidence that elite-level polarization has not been the result of the partisan sorting of voters, or to the extent that it has occurred, geographic sorting. The results of this chapter do not counter that finding but do suggest that sorting could have policy implications beyond polarization. In particular, to the extent that sorting has contributed to more favorable electoral environments for incumbents, it may have encouraged greater congressional responsiveness to donor opinion. Finally, the intertemporal comparison indicates that the influence of individual contributors on legislative voting may have grown over time. Future work might use techniques such as multilevel regression and poststratification (MRP) to estimate state opinion over time on a range of issues, to see if the trend identified by these analyses holds up across a wider set of policies.

More generally, the findings in this paper speak to the broader literatures on representation and accountability. Several studies have suggested that Congress has been unrepresentative of the public. For instance, Fiorina and Abrams (2009) provide evidence that there is a "disconnect" between nationally elected representatives and mass opinion. Other research, such as Clinton (2006), shows that this disconnect is not merely due to the sorting of voters into more polarized and homogenous districts; on average, house members vote on roll calls in a more ideologically extreme manner than their general electorates would prefer. Consistent with these findings, Bonica and Cox (2018) find that since 1994, when majority status became competitive, the electoral penalty members have paid for being out of step with their districts has declined. Naturally, campaign finance is but one piece of the broader context of representation and accountability. The findings here are consistent with these works, however, in highlighting over time change that has incentivized members to cater to forces other than the general electorate.

There is currently a sense from Americans of both major parties that the federal government is no longer working well. As of 2015, only 25 percent of the public believed that the government has a positive effect on "the way things are going in the country" (Pew Research Center, 2015). Similarly, trust in government is low, with only 19 percent in 2015 and 18 percent since Trump's election believing that the government "does the right thing" most or all of the time (Pew Research Center, 2015, 2017). Obviously, campaign finance is only one of many issues affecting this dissatisfaction. At the same time, understanding how the campaign finance system affects representation is an important step in addressing public anxiety over how well our government is functioning.

REFERENCES

"Americans' Views on Money in Politics." 2015. *New York Times*. June 2. Retrieved from www.nytimes.com/interactive/2015/06/02/us/politics/money-in-politics-poll.html?_r=0 (last accessed September 19, 2016).

Ansolabehere, Stephen, John de Figueiredo, and James Snyder, Jr. 2003. "Why Is There So Little Money in U.S. Politics?" *Journal of Economic Perspectives* 17(1):105–130.

Ansolabehere, Stephen, and Stephen Pettigrew. 2014. "Cumulative CCES Common Content (2006–2012)." doi: 10.7910/DVN/26451, Harvard Dataverse, V5.

Bafumi, Joseph, and Michael Herron. 2010. "Leapfrog Representation and Extremism: A Study of American Voters and Their Members in Congress." *American Political Science Review* 104(3): 519–542.

Barber, Michael. 2016. "Representing the Preferences of Donors, Partisans, and Voters in the U.S. Senate." *Public Opinion Quarterly* 80(S1): 225–249.

Barber, Michael, Brandice Canes-Wrone, and Sharece Thrower. 2017. "Ideologically Sophisticated Donors: Which Candidates Do Individual Contributors Finance?" *American Journal of Political Science* 61(2): 271–288.

Baron, David P. 1994. "Electoral Competition with Informed and Uninformed Voters." *American Political Science Review* 88(1): 33–47.

Bennet, James. 2012. "The New Price of American Politics." Atlantic Monthly. October. Retrieved from www.theatlantic.com/magazine/archive/2012/10/the/309086/ (last accessed October 22, 2016).

Bonica, Adam. 2013. "Ideology and Interests In the Political Marketplace." *American Journal of Political Science* 57(2): 294–311.

Bonica, Adam, and Gary W. Cox. 2018. "Ideological Migration in the U.S. Congress: Out of Step but Still in Office." *Quarterly Journal of Political Science* 13(2): 207–236.

Brown, Clifford W. Jr., Roman P. Hedges, and Lynda W. Powell. 1980. "Modes of Elite Participation: Contributors to the 1972 Presidential Elections." *American Journal of Political Science* 24(2): 259–290.

Canes-Wrone, Brandice, David W. Brady, and John F. Cogan. 2002. "Out of Step, Out of Office: Electoral Accountability and House Members' Voting." *American Political Science Review* 96(1): 127–140.

Cann, Damon M. 2008. *Sharing the Wealth: Members Contributions and the Exchange Theory of Party Influence in the US House of Representatives*. Albany, NY: SUNY Press.

Clinton, Joshua D. 2006. "Representation In Congress: Constituents and Roll Calls in the 106th House." *Journal of Politics* 68(2): 397–409.

Deering, Christopher J., and Steven S. Smith. 1997. *Congress in Committees*, 3rd Edition. Washington, DC: *CQ Press*.

Democracy Corps. 2012. "Voters Push Back Against Big Money." Retrieved from www.democracycorps.com/attachments/article/930/dcor.pcaf.postelect.memo.111312.final.pdf (last accessed October 22, 2016).

Desilver, Drew, and Patrick Van Kessel. 2015. "As More Money Flows into Campaigns, Americans Worry about Its Influence." Pew Research Center Fact Tank. December 7. Retrieved from www.pewresearch.org/fact-tank/2015/12/07/as-more-money-flows-into-campaigns-americans-worry-about-its-influence/ (last accessed September 19, 2016).

Erikson, Robert S. 1990. "Roll Calls, Reputations, and Representation in the U.S. State." *Legislative Studies Quarterly* 15(4): 623–642.

Erikson, Robert S., and Gerald C. Wright. 2000. "Representation of Constituency Ideology in Congress." In *Change and Continuity in House Elections*, eds. David W. Brady, John F. Cogan, and John F. Ferejohn. Stanford, CA: Stanford University Press. Pp. 149–177.

Fiorina, Morris P. 2002. "Parties and Partisanship: A 40-Year Retrospective." *Political Behavior* 24(2): 93–115.

Fiorina, Morris P, with Samuel J. Abrams. 2009. *Disconnect: The Breakdown of Representation in American Politics*. Norman, OK: University Oklahoma Press.

Fox, Justin, and Lawrence Rothenberg. 2011. "Influence Without Bribes: A Noncontracting Model of Campaign Giving and Policymaking." *Political Analysis* 19(3): 325–341.

Francia, Peter L., Paul S. Herrnson, John C. Green, Lynda W. Powell, and Clyde Wilcox. 2003. *The Financiers of Congressional Elections: Investors, Ideologues, and Intimates*. New York: Columbia University Press.

Gailmard, Sean, and Jeffrey A. Jenkins. 2007. "Negative Agenda Control in the Senate and House: Fingerprints of Majority Party Power." *Journal of Politics* 69(3): 689–700.

Gilens, Martin. 2012. *Affluence and Influence: Economic Inequality and Political Power in America*. Princeton: Princeton University Press.

Gilens, Martin, and Benjamin I. Page. 2014. "Testing Theories of American Politics: Elites, Interest Groups, and Average Citizens." *Perspectives on Politics* 12(3): 564–581.

Gimpel, James G., Frances E. Lee, and Joshua Kaminski. 2006. "The Political Geography of Campaign Contributions." *Journal of Politics* 68 (August): 626–639.

Gimpel, James G., Frances E. Lee, and Shanna Pearson-Merkowitz. 2008. "The Check Is in the Mail: Interdistrict Funding Flows in Congressional Elections." *American Journal of Political Science* 52(2): 373–394.

Hall, Richard L., and Frank W. Wayman. 1990. "Buying Time: Moneyed Interests and the Mobilization of Bias in Congressional Committees." *American Political Science Review* 84(3): 797–820.

Hensel, Daniel. 2016. "New Poll Shows Money in Politics Is a Top Voting Concern." June 29th. Retrieved from www.issueone.org/new-poll-shows-money-in-politics-is-a-top-voting-concern/ (last accessed September 19, 2016).

Hill, Seth J., and Gregory A. Huber. 2017. "Representativeness and Motivations of the Contemporary Donorate: Results from Merged Survey and Administrative Records." *Political Behavior* 39(1): 3–29.

Jacobson, Gary. 2012. *The Politics of Congressional Elections, 8th edition*. Boston: Pearson.

Johnson, Bertram. 2010. "Individual Contributions: A Fundraising Advantage for the Ideologically Extreme?" *American Politics Research* 38(5): 890–908.

La Raja, Raymond J., and Brian F. Schaffner. 2015. *Campaign Finance and Political Polarization: When Purist Prevail*. Ann Arbor, Michigan: University of Michigan Press.

Magleby, David B., Jay Goodliffe, and Joseph A. Olsen. 2018. *Who Donates in Campaigns? The Importance of Message, Messenger, Medium, and Structure.* Cambridge, UK: Cambridge University Press.

Masket, Seth E. 2016. *The Inevitable Party: Why Attempts to Kill the Party System Fail and How They Weaken the Democracy.* New York, NY: Oxford University Press.

Miller, Warren E., Donald R. Kinder, Steven J. Rosenstone, and the National Election Studies. 1999. National Election Studies, 1988–1992. Merged Senate File [dataset]. Ann Arbor, MI: University of Michigan, Center for Political Studies [producer and distributor].

Milyo, Jeffrey. 2015. "Money in Politics." *Emerging Trends in the Social and Behavioral Science: An Interdisciplinary, Searchable, and Linkable Resource.* Edited by Robert Scott and Stephen Kosslyn. John Wiley & Sons. Pp. 1–9. Retrieved from http://dx.doi.org/10.1002/9781118900772.etrdso228 (last accessed April 27, 2017).

Norrander, Barbara. 2001. "Measuring State Public Opinion with the Senate National Election Study." *State Politics & Policy Quarterly* 1(1): 111–125.

Pew Research Center. 2015. "Beyond Distrust: How Americans View Their Government." Retrieved from www.people-press.org/2015/11/23/beyond-distrust-how-americans-view-their-government/ (last accessed April 27, 2017).

   2017. "Public Trust in Government: 1958–2017." Retrieved from www.people-press .org/2017/12/14/public-trust-in-government-1958-2017/ (last accessed May 23, 2018).

Poole, Keith T., Thomas Romer, and Howard Rosenthal. 1987. "The Revealed Preferences of Political Action Committees." *American Economic Review Papers and Proceedings* 77(2): 298–302.

Powell, Eleanor Neff. In press. *Where Money Matters in Congress: A Window into How Parties Evolve.* Cambridge, MA: Cambridge University Press.

Powell, Lynda W. 2013. "The Influence of Campaign Contributions on Legislative Policy." *The Forum: A Journal of Applied Research in Contemporary Politics* 11(3): 339–355.

Prokop, Andrew. 2015. "Donald Trump Made One Shockingly Insightful Comment During the First GOP Debate." *Vox*, August 6, 2015. Retrieved from www.vox .com/2015/8/6/9114565/donald-trump-debate-money (last accessed May 22, 2018).

Schaffner, Brian and Stephen Ansolabehere. 2015. "2010–2014 Cooperative Congressional Election Study Panel Survey." doi: 10.7910/DVN/TOE8I1, Harvard Dataverse, V6.

Stewart, Charles III. 2012. "The Value of Committee Assignments in Congress since 1994." MIT Political Science Working Paper No. 2012–7. Retrieved from file:///C:/ Users/bcwrone/Downloads/SSRN-id2035632.pdf (last accessed April 27, 2017).

Stewart, Charles III, and Mark Reynolds. 1990. "Television Markets and U.S. Senate Elections." *Legislative Studies Quarterly* 15(4): 495–523.

Stone, Walter J., and Elizabeth N. Simas. 2010. "Candidate Valence and Ideological Positions in U.S. House Elections." *American Journal of Political Science* 54(2): 371–388.

Verba, Sidney, Kay L. Schlozman, and Henry E. Brady. 1995. *Voice and Equality: Civic Voluntarism in American Politics.* Cambridge: Harvard University Press.

Appendix

TABLE 4A *Variables.*

Variable name	Coding	Sources
%Liberal roll calls	% roll call votes on which Senator j voted in liberal direction (pro-choice, pro-protectionist, anti–death penalty) on issue i in most recent Congress	1988–1992: % roll call votes on which Senator j voted in liberal direction (pro-choice, pro-protectionist, anti–death penalty) on issue i in most recent Congress. 2006–2014: interest group ratings provided by National Right to Life Committee (for abortion) and Cato Institute (for trade).
Liberal vote	1 if Senator j voted with a majority of Senate Democrats; 0 otherwise	Senate.gov roll call tables and CCES supplemental materials on Senate roll calls
National partisan donor opinion	Among respondents who are in Senator j's party and identify as a donor, the percentage who support the liberal position on the issue	ANES and CCES policy items, party id question, and item asking whether respondent made a political donation in the past year
State opinion	Among respondents who are in Senator j's state, the percentage who support the liberal position on the issue	ANES and CCES policy items and state identifiers
Partisan state opinion	Among respondents who are in Senator j's state and party, percentage who support the liberal position on the issue	CCES policy items, party ID question, and state identifier
Democratic senator	1 if Senator j caucuses with the Democrats; 0 otherwise	Senate.gov and CQ Press Congress Collection Member Profiles

(continued)

TABLE 4A *(continued)*

Variable name	Coding	Sources
Affluent nondonor opinion	Among respondents who are in Senator j's party, are not a donor, and are in the top 10 percent of income distribution, the percentage who support the liberal position on the issue	ANES and CCES policy items, party ID question, income question, item asking whether respondent made a political donation, and census data on income distributions.
Electoral favorability	Statewide percentage of the most recent two-party presidential vote supporting the candidate in Senator j's party	CQ Press Voting and Elections Collection
Normalized electoral favorability	The difference between Electoral Favorability and the national percentage of the two-party presidential vote supporting the presidential candidate of Senator j's party	CQ Press Voting and Elections Collection

5

Minority Protest and the Early Stages of Governmental Responsiveness in the Electoral Process

Daniel Gillion and Patricia Posey

On the evening of March 18, 2018, Stephon Clark, a 22-year-old unarmed Black man was shot at 20 times by two Sacramento police officers minutes after they arrived to respond to a vandalism complaint. Clark was struck seven times in his back according to a private autopsy report. He died on the scene in his grandmother's backyard (Del Real, 2018). His death sparked 2 weeks of protests in Sacramento among the city's Black residents who argued this was the latest example of a history of minority mistreatment by local authorities (Cava, 2018). Protests were held at city hall meetings, at the state capitol building, outside an National Basketball Association (NBA) game, on a highway, and near the site of the killing (Arnold et al., 2018, Kasler et al., 2018). The incident also sparked protests across the country from Portland, Oregon to Boston, Massachusetts, and Tampa, Florida and an investigation by the California Department of Justice. In response to this incident, California lawmakers submitted legislation (AB-931) to limit the use of police force (John, Elmahrek, and Winton, 2018). Stephon Clark. Terence Crutcher. Sandra Bland. Walter L. Scott. Tamir Rice. Michael Brown. Eric Garner (Almuktar et al., 2018). As the list of unarmed Black people killed as result of police use of lethal force grows, each death sparks minority protest and garners national attention.

Similarly, protests have defined Donald Trump's presidency. People stood in opposition to the inauguration, to march on behalf of women, to resist a travel ban targeting Muslims, to advocate for the importance of science, to express support for the rights of undocumented immigrants, to preserve and remove Confederate monuments, to demand gun control legislation, and to advocate for police reform (Chenoweth et al., 2017). Taking to the streets, for many, was the preferred way to express dissent. But while Trump's presidency energized protest activity, it inspired a backlash toward minority protests.

Donald Trump's election, like his campaign, brought renewed efforts to limit minority protest activity. Trump, along with other politicians, publicly condemned some demonstrations like the National Football League (NFL) kneeling protests against police brutality and other activities in support of Black Lives Matter (BLM). As these reactions themselves become news stories, politicians are criticized for when and how they respond to protests. Trump faced criticism from Democrat and Republican political leaders after refusing to condemn the role of white supremacists explicitly – protestors who chanted Nazi slogans and carried white supremacist symbols – in clashes with counterprotesters at a Charlottesville, Virginia "Unite the Right" rally. The rally ended with a man driving his car into a crowd of people protesting the rally, killing one person (Chenoweth and Pressman, 2017). Trump faced criticism from voters as people took to social media to lament that Trump was noticeably quiet as the violence erupted in Charlottesville. When he acknowledged the protests, he was further critiqued for the vagueness of his tweets and for not denouncing white supremacy unlike other Republican leaders (e.g., Republican House Speaker Paul Ryan) (Wang, 2017). Finally, when Trump held a press conference, he both defended his 48-hour delayed response to the events and emphasized that the white supremacists and the counterprotesters shared responsibility for the violence, which added to the bipartisan critique of how he responded to the protest (Thrush and Haberman, 2017). It is illustrative that this current political moment seemingly necessitates that political leaders address protest events.

In the 2 years leading up to the 2016 elections, the backdrop of an astonishing high number of unarmed Black people dying at the hands of police officers harkened the awakening of minority protest that reached new levels in both magnitude and intensity across the nation. From Baton Rouge to New York City, protesters marched throughout the streets, interrupted campaign events, and gathered by the thousands in Washington D.C., demanding government officials to direct their attention to outstanding issues of racial inequality. Even prominent groups but diffuse groups such as Black Lives Matter (BLM) created coherent political platforms to further direct their message to current politicians, with the hope that such officials in power would respond. If current politicians passively resisted action or actively refused to address these issues, then the hope was that the subsequent electoral reprisal would elect politicians more responsive to issues plaguing the Black community.

Similarly, during the height of the civil rights movement, the 1964 congressional election resulted in ushering a new wave of liberal Democrats into the stronghold of the South that were less conservative than their predecessors (Black, 1978, Bullock, 1981, Whitby, 1987, McAdam and Tarrow, 2013), establishing a "generational replacement" that some argue led to shifts in voting alignments (Fiorina, 1974). Even in the 1930s and 1940s, political activism associated with the Townsend movement led to the congressional election of candidates who were favorable to Social Security (Amenta et al., 1992).

Are these cases of citizen activism leading to dramatic electoral changes isolated incidents, or do they demonstrate the existence of a broader phenomenon that indicates the early stages of governmental responsiveness?

While voters have been described as having limited knowledge about politics (Delli-Carpini and Keeter, 1996), evidence suggests that they *are* more attuned to the current social and political conditions at any given time than the literature has assumed. Citizens' perceptions of conditions serve as shortcuts that inform them when voting. Bartels (1996) argues that when voters use these information shortcuts, the electorate produces results as if voters were fully informed of candidates' political platforms, suggesting that social realities can be informative to everyday voters in the aggregate. In this article, we explore whether minority protest is among the social conditions that the electorate uses to make voting decisions.

While a recent wave of scholarship has kindled a newfound interest in the political consequences of protest behavior (e.g., McAdam and Su, 2002, Amenta and Caren, 2004, Andrews, 2004, Soule and Olzak, 2004, Soule and King, 2006, Agnone, 2007, Giugni, 2007, King, Bentele, and Soule, 2007, Olzak and Soule, 2009, Luders, 2010), the majority of this research has focused on the ability of protest to influence policy, while only a few studies have assessed the impact of citizens' activism on voters themselves.[1] And none, to our knowledge, has examined the type of political candidates who manage and/or emerge from an environment of minority political protest. Among the few works that have examined the influence of protest on elections, the conclusions reached are far from conclusive. Some claim that protests can mobilize individuals behind a cause to elect political leaders who share a movement's goal (Amenta, Carruthers, and Zylan, 1992, Andrews, 2004, Amenta, 2006). Others contend that protest activists, in an effort to mobilize constituents around their cause, can engender a backlash from the broader public, thereby diminishing the impact that protest has on the electorate (McVeigh, Myers, and Sikkink, 2004, p. 678).

We see two problems arising from this debate that limit our general understanding of protest's influence on electoral outcomes. First, current literature provides little discussion of the competing ideological perspectives voiced in protest across various issues. Consequently, we know little about how minority protest activities, and the scope of these events, offer voters a collective understanding of protesters' grievances. Second, only a few scholars have examined the geographical location of protest events across multiple congressional districts, thus limiting the discussion of how local minority protests may uniquely impact constituents that reside within the district in which the protests

---

[1] In an analysis of 54 articles examining the outcomes or consequences of protest activity, Amenta et al. (2010, p. 293) report only one article that assessed protest's impact on elections. We are not the first to notice this (see McAdam and Tarrow [2010, 2013] who lament the lack of attention to the connections between social movements and electoral politics).

occurred. These two problems arise from a lack of data that captures the issues voiced in protest activities within a congressional district. Hence, the relative effectiveness of minority protest activity on electoral outcomes has not yet been established.

In this chapter, we provide the first analysis of the influence of minority protest on electoral returns across multiple congressional districts, and spanning various issues over time. Using protest data and election returns from 1960 to 1990, we demonstrate that citizens are attuned to the social conditions of their district and use protest behavior as an informative cue that shapes their voting behavior. More specifically, we place protests on an ideological scale and find that protests that express liberal issues lead to a greater percentage of the two-party vote share for Democratic candidates, while protests that espouse conservative issues garner a greater share of the two-party vote for Republican candidates. However, minority protests, which often express liberal issues, uniquely lead to a greater percentage of the two-party vote share for Democratic candidates. In addition, this study shows that minority protest produces a "vulnerability effect." That is, when legislators are not attentive to the issues raised by minority protest behavior, a fertile ground is fostered for challenger candidates to underscore the sitting politician's failure to address constituent concerns, leading to a greater number of quality challengers.

Thus, in this chapter, we demonstrate two electoral outcomes of minority protest. First, voting patterns of citizens respond to the ideological leaning of protest activity, and second, would-be, qualified candidates enter races to challenge sitting politicians, leading to changes in the makeup of government. By providing the first evidence that electoral returns are shaped by the ideological leanings of protest, our work suggests that minority protest is an informative cue that voters use to evaluate the state of social and economic conditions and potential politicians use to gauge their political fortunes. These are important findings because they suggest that minority protest is recognized by the American public. This recognition is reflected in their votes – which by determining who runs and gets elected – in turn shapes the makeup of government in the earliest stages.

THE RELATIONSHIP BETWEEN PROTEST AND THE ELECTORATE

Previous political events, and the attitudes associated with them, are often internalized by voters and shape their political behavior. Voters are informed by multiple social conditions that influence their vote. Fluctuating economic conditions (Kramer, 1971, Bloom and Price, 1975, Meltzer and Vellrath, 1975, Tufte, 1975, Fair, 1978, Kernell, 1978), political scandals, and government responses to natural disasters (Malhotra and Kuo, 2008), among other factors, have been shown to influence citizens' political engagement.

Scholars have theorized that protest behavior can be considered as one of these factors that influence citizens' political engagement. Both social movements and public opinion literature view grassroots movements as ways to shape citizens' political attitudes. Protest activities can influence voters' perceptions through what Lee (2002, p. 69) refers to as "mobilizing public opinion," where citizens are informed by their peers. This bottom-up approach to receiving information can be more influential to citizens than the views that come from political elites. Informative cues from like-minded groups can shape citizens' understanding of issues (Page and Shapiro, 1992). These groups can provide sufficient information for voters to make more informed decisions (McKelvey and Ordeshook, 1986). The reason for this, as it relates to protest, is because citizens' engagement in protest activity reflects some level of discontent that at least some part of the nation has against the status quo. When this discontent offers insight about current policies or politicians' records, protest activities can inform individuals' voting decisions (Lohmann, 1994, p. 518). Activists can influence voters directly by discussing issues with neighbors at home and with colleagues in the workplace, or indirectly by drawing citizens' attention to a salient issue (Claasen, 2007, p. 126).

For those involved in political activism, protest is only an extension of the many options citizens have in their political toolbox to influence government (Harris and Gillion, 2010). Thus, demonstrators do not abandon electoral politics, but rather engage in political activism while supporting their political party (Heaney and Rojas, 2011). Enlightened by the information provided by protest activity, citizens have often offered financial support toward the movement's cause while at the same time aiding institutionalized political parties.

Our theory of protest influence builds upon the work of several scholars who have argued that protest events are informative for citizens. In the next section, we attempt to broaden the influence of protest while restricting its geographical scope.

THEORETICAL LINK BETWEEN LOCAL MINORITY PROTEST EVENTS AND ELECTORAL OUTCOMES

Our theoretical claims begin by shifting the discussion of protest influence from protest at the national level to protest at the local level, because citizens are likely to be more attentive to minority protest behavior occurring within their own communities (Gillion, 2012, 2013). Minority protests that occur in citizens' communities build onto a larger understanding of their own social environment. Citizens' understanding of their environment can be informed by "casual observations" (Cho and Rudolph, 2008), simple observations conveyed by their neighbors' dress, home, or behavior. These observations contribute to what Baybeck and McClurg (2005) refer to as the "slow drip of everyday life." The social conditions in citizens' communities becomes the foundation of the social learning process that shapes their political preferences (McPhee, 1963, Sprague, 1982). In fact, many of the perspectives that citizens hold about politics stem from their local social environment (Eulau and Rothenberg, 1986, Huckfeldt and Sprague, 1987), which later influence their voting behavior (Kenny, 1992). Some have come to recognize the social environment as a vehicle to increase turnout by establishing norms of participation and providing social networks to mobilize potential voters (Rosenstone and Hansen, 1993, Verba, Schlozman, and Brady, 1995). Even being informed of another individual's actions within one's community can increase one's own voting activity (Großer and Schram, 2006).

We argue that minority protest, similarly, can become a part of the social learning process, and act as an avenue for social communication. In particular, it may serve as an informative cue that voters use to evaluate candidates as well as social conditions. Because protest places issues on the political agenda and makes certain issues salient, (Soule and King, 2006), protest has the potential to shift voters' evaluation of political candidates. Moreover, protest activities can educate the public on the particular details of an issue. Finally, protest can act as a mobilizing force that draws passion from constituents, heightening their interests in a relevant topic and increasing the likelihood that they turn out on Election Day. Rosenstone and Hansen (1993, p. 218) argue that had "social movements been as active in mobilizing voters in the 1980s as they were in the 1960s, even leaving the social structure and the condition of individual voters unchanged, reported voter participation would have fallen only 2.6 percent, rather than 11.3 percent." Thus, minority protests may be a resource for voters, who reflect upon such events when making electoral decisions.

However, not all potential voters are equally supportive of a given protest event. Information cues can resonate differently with different citizens (Bartels, 1996, pp. 204–205). Individuals who identify themselves as Democrats, for example, are supportive of the liberal views expressed in the civil rights movement (McAdam, 1982, Button, 1989, Luders, 2010), the women's movement (Costain and Costain, 1987, Young, 1996), and the environmental movement.[2] Republicans, on the other hand, have embraced conservative movements, such as those of the Christian right, anti–gay rights, gun rights, and antiabortion activists. Political parties have attempted to capitalize on these differences by claiming issue ownership on these topics, including activists' perspectives into their party platforms (Fetner, 2008).

We argue that the ideological leaning of any given protest is an important component for it to resonate with citizens. While protests on women's rights, for example, may address the specific grievances of gender inequality, these claims also fit within a larger appeal of equal rights and embody the larger grievance expressed by a liberal perspective. The specific topics of gun control or pro-life, likewise, can be captured under a general umbrella of conservatism.

---

[2] It is important to note that southern Democrats were an exception to this rule early in the 1960s. However, as the Black voter population increased in these districts so did the support for civil rights issues among southern Democrats (Black, 1978, pp. 448–449).

Because voters seek out and establish information networks that correspond to their own political preferences (Huckfeldt and Sprague, 1987), voters may use protest events as an informative cue that reinforces their political beliefs.[3] Based on the preceding argument, we introduce the following two hypotheses:

Voter Effect Hypothesis: Increases in protest activity that expresses a liberal (conservative) position will lead to a greater share of the two-party vote for the Democratic (Republican) candidate.

Voter Effect Minority Protest Hypothesis: Increases in minority protest activity will lead to a greater share of the two-party vote for Democratic candidates.

Protest and an Environment of Political Vulnerability

Potential challengers also consider political and social conditions in assessing whether they will run against an incumbent. At times, challengers can be deterred from running by an incumbent's fundraising efforts (Epstein and Zemsky, 1995). But quality challengers from the party in power are more likely to run for office when economic conditions are good, and quality challengers from the out-of-power party are more likely to run when the economic conditions are poor (Bianco, 1984, p. 361).

Incumbents attempt to inform voters of their previous activity through mailings and education material (Cover, 1977, Cover and Brumber, 1982), as well as through media outlets that are not available to challenger candidates (Mann and Wolfinger, 1980). The disproportionate flow of information from sitting politicians allows incumbents to shape perceptions of their performance record in the best light. Minority protest activity, however, can provide competing information that highlights grievances experienced during a politician's tenure.

When voters believe that incumbents have failed to deliver on promises or not implemented constituents' preferred policies, they can use that information to punish incumbents during reelection (Ferejohn, 1986, Austen-Smith and Banks, 1989). Here, protest activity can act as a double-edged sword, benefiting incumbents when protesters' concerns are ideologically aligned and hindering them when they are not.

Minority political protest, similarly, can alert politicians of a changing tide or of an issue that is rising in importance. Legislators are forward-looking, concerned about future issues that could potentially endanger their seats (Arnold, 1990). Thus, they consider "potential preferences" that citizens may value in the future (Sulkin, 2005). When legislators are not attentive to protest behavior, it provides fertile ground for challenger candidates to underscore the sitting politician's failure to address constituent concerns

---

[3] This view is similar to the initial steps of McPhee's (1963) vote simulator: first voters review information from the larger political environment and then form an opinion based upon their own predispositions.

(Sulkin, 2005).[4] Hence, politicians who ignore concerns voiced in district-level protest become vulnerable to political scrutiny. Minority protest can expose these weaknesses, making experienced challengers more likely to enter the race because they believe there is a higher chance of them winning the election (Banks and Kiewiet, 1989, Jacobson, 1990). The preceding argument leads us to put forth the following two hypotheses:

Vulnerability Hypothesis: Increases in district-level protest activity that express a liberal (conservative) position will increase the probability that a quality Democratic (Republican) primary challenger emerges.
Vulnerability Minority Protest Hypothesis: Increases in district-level minority protest activity will increase the probability that a quality Democratic challenger emerges.

DATA AND MEASURES

To evaluate our hypotheses, we use a combination of datasets that assess protest and election returns from congressional districts. The data cover house elections from 1960 to 1990. As is standard in the literature, we exclude all districts immediately following redistricting in order to avoid biased results that would arise from using different vote totals.

Measuring Election Returns and Candidate Quality

As the main dependent variable, we use election returns from the US House of Representatives from 1960 to 1990 (Cox and Katz, 1996). Based on our theoretical claims, we should expect protests to have divergent effects on the two major political parties, where liberal protests mobilize liberal voters thus are advantageous for Democrats but detrimental to Republicans; conservative protests mobilize conservative voters thus help Republicans but disadvantage Democrats. Thus, the nuances advanced in our theoretical claims require us to examine the impact that protests have on the Republican and Democratic parties separately. To this end, we split Cox and Katz's (1996) measure of election returns into the percent of the two-party vote received by the Democratic Party and the percent garnered by the Republican Party. As a second variable of electoral influence, we also use Jacobson's (1987) measure of candidate quality to capture the experience of a challenger from the opposing party, which is coded with a 1 if a challenger had previously held office and 0 otherwise. Similarly to vote share, we create separate measures of candidate quality for the two political parties.

---

[4] Sulkin (2005, p. 22) makes the point that "challengers may even be able to create the perception of weakness on issues simply by highlighting them in their campaigns."

District Level Measures of Minority Protest

We take a novel approach to measuring minority political protest. Previous studies of citizen activism have assessed minority protest at the national level, typically aggregating nationwide protest and analyzing its influence on national policies. For our purposes, it is important to capture the geographical location of protest activities over time. The geographical proximity to protest events could increase the probability that local citizens will be informed by other citizens' nearby activism (McVeigh, Myers, and Sikkink, 2004, p. 680). To this end, we draw on protest events reported in the *New York Times* from 1960 through 1990 that are contained in the Dynamics of Collective Action (DCA) database, arguably the most comprehensive source on national protest events. Newspaper accounts of protest are a "methodological staple" for studies of political protest (McAdam and Su, 2002, p. 74). With the help of the DCA database, the *Times* has emerged as the most widely used newspaper source for analyzing the link between protest behavior and governmental action in quantitative studies (see, for example, McAdam and Su, 2002, Earl, Soule, and McCarthy, 2003, King, Bentele, and Soule, 2007, Olzak and Soule, 2009, Soule and Davenport, 2009, Davenport, Soule, and Armstrong, 2011).

The DCA database has been described in detail in a number of published articles (e.g., McAdam and Su, 2002, Earl, Soule, and McCarthy, 2003, Van Dyke, Soule, and Taylor, 2004, Soule and Earl, 2005, Earl and Soule, 2006, Soule and King, 2006, King, Bentele, and Soule, 2007, Soule and King, 2008 Olzak and Soule, 2009, Soule and Davenport, 2009, Davenport, Soule, and Armstrong, 2011, Wang and Soule, 2012) and on the project's website.[5] However, there are a few notable features of the dataset that are worth mentioning in the context of our analysis. First, the data came from reading *all daily* editions of the *Times* over the specified time period, rather from using an index to locate candidate events (or simply coding the index to the *Times*). This is important because the biases associated with newspaper data are reduced (Earl et al., 2004). Second, newspaper articles were content coded by hand by trained coders such that information on many facets (e.g., size, duration, tactics used, police action) of each protest event was recorded. This is important for our purposes because, as we describe below, we wish to develop a measure of the *extent* of the informational cue sent by minority protests onto a district. Finally, protest events occurred all over the United States and not just in a particular geographic region. This is important for our work because we are interested in examining the effect of protest in congressional districts across the United States.

---

[5] www.stanford.edu/group/collectiveaction/cgi-bin/drupal/.

We add to, and transform, the DCA data in two fundamental ways. First, from the information provided in the DCA dataset, we sort all of more than 23,000 protest events into their respective congressional districts. To identify the location of minority protest, we referred to the place, local neighborhood, or city that is reported in the *New York Times*. When the *Times* only reported the city of where a protest occurred, we code the congressional districts that encompass that city.[6] Thus, one protest event can affect multiple congressional districts, as is often the case for marches, riots, or demonstrations that move across several locations. In identifying the location of political activism, we establish the first data source to link the geographical properties of protests to congressional districts over time.[7]

Second, rather than examining a simple count of protest events or just confirming whether or not a protest event occurred, we develop a measure designed to tap the scope or extent of the informational cue sent by protest events in a district in a given year.[8] Following Gillion (2013), we conceptualize the scope of information within protest in terms of levels of *salience*. Salient political protest is defined as including any of the following: (1) protest activity that involves more than 100 individuals, (2) protest activity that lasts more than a day, (3) protest activity that is supported by a political organization, (4) protest activity that results in property damage, (5) protest activity that draws a police presence, (6) protest activity that leads to an arrest, (7) protest activity that involves individuals carrying weapons, (8) protest activity that leads to injury, or (9) protest activity that involves death. We transfer the nine definitions given above into binary variables and then sum across the binary variables to calculate a saliency score for each instance of

---

[6] While the information provided in historical newspapers limits the precision of location for some protest events, our coding procedures provide a good proxy that allows us to test our theoretical claims. We argue that protests may affect voters in multiple congressional districts, residing in the local vicinity. We more forcefully posit that voters in the local vicinity of a protest event will be more likely to be informed and influenced by protest than are citizens who reside in a different part of the state, in another state, or a different region of the United States (the more traditional units of analysis in this literature). In other words, proximity to a protest event should matter, since proximity increases the probability of hearing about the protest event.

[7] Some may argue that coding protest across multiple districts might in some way bias our results. Our data show that 53 percent of the protests could be classified into a single district. In addition, 75 percent of the protests could be classified into four neighboring districts or fewer. To examine this potential bias, we create a controlled dummy variable, where districts that consisted of mobile protest (meaning these protest span across various districts) were coded with a 1 and districts with unique protest (meaning these protests only occurred in one district) were coded with a 0. The inclusion of this variable did not change the substantive results. As a further robustness check, we also explore the potential regional bias that is introduced by using *The New York Times*. We create a northeast dummy variable that comprises the nine states used by the Census: NY, VT, MA, ME, NH, CT, PA, RI, and NJ. Again, the substantive results remained unchanged.

[8] To create a general measure of protest, we assess a wide range of citizen behavior that includes the following: demonstrations, rallies, marches, vigils, pickets, civil disobedience, information distribution, riots, strikes, and boycotts.

protest. Computed in this fashion, a given protest event can have a saliency score that ranges from 0 to 9. To create an annual saliency score, we take the protest events that occurred in a congressional district for an election year and aggregate their level of salience.[9]

After creating an annual saliency score for each district, we then account for the ideological leaning, or *valence*, of the protest events in each district. To do this, we subtract the saliency scores of liberal protests from those of conservative protest in a district. In order to identify the grievance of protesters and categorize protest events by whether they expressed liberal or conservative concerns, we borrow from several established classifications of issue ownership drawn largely from Petrocik (1996), Petrocik, Benoit, and Hansen (2003), Damore (2004), and Sigelman and Buell (2004). As a second form of robustness, we drew upon several public opinion polls and calculated citizens' favorability toward an issue based on their political leanings. Generally, the following are classified as liberal issues: civil rights, feminism or women's rights, peace, international human and civil rights/democratization, environmental or green activism, pro-abortion, and animal rights. The following are classified as conservative issues: pro-life, Christian right, anti-crime, anti-immigrant/anti-foreigner/anti-asylum, and anti–"transnational union."[10]

The final protest measure, then, is one that encompasses multiple aspects of protest activity. First, our measure builds upon previous designs by including aspects of protest that affect its ability to resonate with voters; that is, this is a measure of protest salience, as we discuss above. Viewed in this manner, protest can be conceived as falling along a continuum, where higher scores indicate more informative events, and scores that approach zero indicate less informative behavior. Second, our measure of protest captures the ideological direction of the political signal being sent to the government; that is, this is also a measure of ideological valence. When the measure is positive, the political arena is dominated by protest activities that express liberal views; when it is negative, protests that advocate a conservative perspective have the louder voice. Finally, our measure captures how voters perceive protest. Few voters rely on a single source of information, but rather are informed by multiple sources and multiple perspectives, which together influence voters in a holistic fashion. Likewise, multiple protest events collectively offer voters a general understanding of their fellow citizens' concerns. In other words, our measure synthesizes multiple protests into a general message, which then influences electoral outcomes as people respond to this message at the polls.

---

[9] The saliency score is calculated as follows: *yearly salience* $= \overset{\cdot}{\Sigma}$ *level of salience*, where N represents the total number of protest events in a congressional district over the course of a year.

[10] See Appendix 5A for a complete table of protest issues and whether they are coded as liberal or conservative.

Liberal and Conservative Protests (1960s)   **Liberal and Conservative Protests (1970s)**

Liberal Leaning   Conservative Leaning   Liberal Leaning   Conservative Leaning
Protests   Protests   Protests   Protests

Liberal and Conservative Protests (1980s)   **Liberal and Conservative Protests (1990s)**

Liberal Leaning   Conservative Leaning   Liberal Leaning   Conservative Leaning
Protests   Protests   Protests   Protests

FIGURE 5.1 The Location of Liberal and Conservative Protest in the United States. *Notes:* The data used to produce the map for the 1990s cover protest events from 1990 to 1995. Our regression analysis, however, only goes through 1990 because of data constraints on election data.

Figure 5.1 graphically presents our measure. In this figure, we report the location of liberal and conservative protests by county.[11] The darker shades of liberal protest dominate the map and are initially concentrated in the south and northeast in the 1970s. Yet by the 1970s, liberal protests are widespread. In addition to the variation of protest activities across counties, there is also considerable variation over time. Protests in the 1960s and 1970s largely expressed liberal views. Driven by the civil rights movement and the anti-Vietnam movements, 90 percent of protests were liberal in both decades. The percentage of liberal protests, however, dropped to 86 percent in the 1980s,

---

[11] We use counties and not congressional districts for this illustration because we could not obtain accurate electronic maps of congressional districts for the 1960s and 1970s. Nevertheless, the illustration of counties provides a good understanding of the geographic distribution of protests.

and then to 78 percent in the 1990s, mirroring a similar trend of overall declining protest activity.[12]

While the overall level of protest has declined, the number of protests expressing conservative views has increased. Conservative protests began to emerge in a greater number of counties in the 1980s, with 14 percent of all protests expressing conservative values. By the 1990s, this percentage had increased to 21 percent. Protest events located in counties such as Teton, Wyoming and Butler, Pennsylvania shifted from expressing liberal issues in the 1980s to expressing conservative issues in the 1990s (see also Soule and Earl, 2005).

Our measure of protest fits nicely with historical accounts of citizen activism. What we add with our visualization, however, is the ability to locate when and where competing concerns expressed in public protest began to move in the direction of one or the other ideological position.

Alternative Explanations

While district-level minority protest activity may influence voters' perceptions, there are other important factors that will shape electoral outcomes. We begin by including standard measures used to assess the two-party vote share. Arguably, the most significant factor that predicts electoral outcomes is the incumbency status of political candidates. Incumbents enjoy a comfortable advantage over challenging candidates when heading to the polls (Gelman and King, 1990, Levitt and Wolfram, 1997).[13] The advantage that incumbents receive increases over a politician's tenure in office (Ansolabeher, Snyder, and Stewart, 2000), but this advantage has also become more significant for all incumbents over time.[14] We include a control for the incumbency advantage to account for the strong impact incumbents have on electoral outcomes.

Two other factors likely to explain electoral outcomes are the quality of a challenging candidate and the length of time a congressional member has served. In analyzing the quality of a challenging candidate as a dependent variable, several scholars have shown that experienced candidates, who have previously served in office, fare better than do inexperienced candidates (Leuthold, 1968, Huckshorn and Spencer, 1971). Thus, we incorporate the quality of a candidate as a control variable when testing the impact of protest on electoral returns. As for a representative's length of service, younger congressional leaders may be less likely to maintain a strong vote share because

---

[12] Since our protest data continues only through 1995, the 1990s figure represents protest data from 1990 to 1995. For the empirical analysis, however, we only make use of protest data from 1960–1990 in order to overlap with election return data that is restricted to this time period.

[13] Quality candidates are less likely to enter an electoral race when an incumbent is running for reelection (Leuthold, 1968, Huckshorn and Spencer, 1971, Banks and Kiewiet, 1989).

[14] The rise in television has also increased the incumbents' advantage (Prior, 2006).

they have not developed the name recognition, nor have they established a proven record, as many of their senior colleagues have done. Hence, we control for the number of years a representative has served in office.

We also control for other demographic factors that might impact the election. We control for congressional districts located in southern states and the population of the congressional district. While these variables will control for much of the variation across districts, there may remain an omitted district-level variable that could bias our results. Thus, for each model we include fixed effects for both district and year.

Finally, to understand the impact of minority protest activity on electoral returns, we implement an autoregressive distributed lagged (ADL) model for the main regression. The functional form of this estimation is as follows:

$$Y_{i,t}^{Vote\ Share} = \alpha + X_{i,t}\beta + \gamma_1 Y_{i,t-1} + \theta_1 (Protest)_{i,t} + \theta_2 (Protest)_{i,t-1} + \varepsilon_{i,t}$$

where i denotes the congressional district and t is the election year for the house. The vector X consists of district-level social and demographic characteristics. The vote share for the previous congressional race is included as a lagged independent variable. *Protest* captures the ideological leaning as well as the intensity of protest events that occurred in a district, as we describe above.[15]

RESULTS

In Table 5.1, we examine the impact of protest on congressional members' vote share. We distinguish the two-party vote share received from Democratic and Republican candidates to examine whether or not protest has a distinct impact upon the different ideological perspectives. Indeed, the social context of protest appears to motivate different segments of the electorate, and produce divergent effects on the candidates' vote share. When the coefficient on our protest measure is negative (indicating that the claims voiced in protest in a district are more conservative), the Republican vote share of the two-party vote increases. The impact of protest, however, is reversed for the Democratic vote share: When the coefficient on our protest measure is positive (indicating a more liberal position taken by activists), Democrats enjoy a larger portion of the two-party vote.

Importantly, the magnitude of these effects are quite substantial. For example, if the salience score of liberal protest in a district is 50 in an election year, the Republican vote share will decrease by 7 percent, and the Democratic vote share will increase by 2 percent, as was the case for Abner Mikva who

---

[15] Because our data are time-series cross-section (TSCS) data, the standard errors produced from ordinary least squares (OLS) regression are likely to suffer from heteroskedasticity and contemporaneous correlation (Beck and Katz, 2001). To overcome this problem, we use panel-correct standard errors (PCSEs), as recommended by Beck and Katz (1995).

TABLE 5.1 *Minority Protest Impact on the Democratic and Republican Vote Share.*

	Republican Model 1	Vote Share Model 2	Democrat Model 3	Vote Share Model 4
Vote Share$_{t-1}$	0.31^a	0.31^a	0.64^a	0.64^a
	(0.03)	(0.03)	(0.02)	(0.02)
Incumbent$_t$	7.86^a	7.91^a	5.43^a	5.46^a
	(0.58)	(0.58)	(0.63)	(0.63)
Incumbent$_{t-1}$	0.53	0.51	−3.32^a	−3.32^a
	(0.55)	(0.55)	(0.46)	(0.46)
Challenger Quality$_t$	−2.60^a	−2.54^a	−3.82^a	−3.80^a
	(0.41)	(0.41)	(0.42)	(0.42)
Challenger Quality$_{t-1}$	0.26	0.26	−0.23	−0.23
	(0.39)	(0.39)	(0.41)	(0.41)
Southern District	0.19	0.22	−0.10	−0.11
	(3.39)	(3.39)	(0.45)	(0.45)
Length of Service	0.04	0.04	0.05^a	0.04^a
	(0.03)	(0.03)	(0.02)	(0.02)
Population	−0.01	−0.01	−0.02	−0.01
	(0.02)	(0.03)	(0.03)	(0.03)
Protest$_t$	−0.14^a		0.04^a	
	(0.07)		(0.02)	
Protest$_{t-1}$	0.08		0.02	
	(0.07)		(0.02)	
Minority Protest$_t$		−0.08		0.03^a
		(0.06)		(0.01)
Minority Protest$_{t-1}$		0.01		0.03^a
		(0.06)		(0.02)
R^2	0.68	0.67	0.57	0.57
adj. R^2	0.59	0.59	0.56	0.56
N	1597	1597	1907	1907

Notes: Statistical significance is denoted as follows: significant at $^a p < 0.05$. The dependent variables are the Republican portion of the two-party vote as well as the Democratic portion of the two-party vote, respectively. The independent variable of interest, protest, is placed on a liberal-conservative scale, where negative values indicate that the majority of protests events in a district expressed a conservative perspective while positive values indicate a more liberal position. Controls for election years and congressional districts were also included in the model but are not reported in the table above. The full model can be found in the supplemental materials.

benefited from protest activity in 1968. During this year, 40 protest events which occurred in Illinois second congressional district expressed liberal concerns that ranged from civil rights to anti-war protests. The protest salience score from these events was 54, indicating a 2 percent increase in the Democratic vote share and a 7 percent decrease in the Republican's vote share. Representative Mikva, who ran on a platform that supported these liberal concerns, not only defeated the more moderate incumbent Democrat in the primary, Barratt O'Hara, but he went on to defeat the Republican challenger Thomas Ireland.

Republican candidates also benefit from protest activity, if that activity espouses conservative issues. If the salience score of conservative protest were 50, Republicans would increase their vote share by 7 percent, while Democrats would experience a decrease in their vote share by 2 percent.[16] During 1974, in Cleveland, Ohio, for example, a number of protest events confronted drug use in local neighborhoods and petitioned the police to take a stronger stance.[17] The salience score from these conservative protest events was 21, providing a 3 percent increase in the Republican vote share. These protest events advantaged Republican representative William Stanton (R-OH) in his victory over the Democratic challenger Michael Coffey in the 1974 election for the eleventh congressional district house seat.

Notice that there is not a one-to-one trade-off between the loss/gains of the Republican Party's vote share to the Democratic vote share. Republican voters are more responsive to the salience of protest activity. Protest activity is three times more likely to impact the Republican vote share in comparison to the Democratic vote share. This finding is surprising given that liberal protest activities substantially outnumbered conservative activities during the time period under study. Perhaps it is the case that because liberal protest activity was so much more common during this period than was conservative protest, conservative activism was more surprising, and thus was met with a greater response by voters.

These results hold up against other competing explanations. As expected, the incumbency advantage in both models is strong. The positive coefficient on length of service shows that candidates who have spent more time in office receive an additional boost in the two-party vote share. The quality of the candidates also serves to explain their vote share. As suggested by previous scholarship (e.g., Leuthold, 1968, Huckshorn and Spencer, 1971, Cox and Katz, 1996) more experienced candidates fare better in our analysis. Finally, like previous research (e.g., Gelman and King, 1990), we find that demographic features of the district are not significant predictors of the vote share – neither population size, nor being located in a southern state, influenced our dependent variable.

---

[16] Given the construction of our protest salience measure, there are a myriad of ways in which a salience score of 50 might be obtained. For example, a district could have 50 events, each with a salience score of 1 (if, for example, all of these events each had more than 100 participants). Or, it could have a score of 50 if there were 10 protest events, each with a score of 5.

[17] The war on drugs has been a Republican issue since Eisenhower's establishment of the US interdepartmental Committee on Narcotics in 1954, which was followed by Nixon's message that drug abuse is "public enemy number one" and Nancy Reagan's "just say no" campaign.

Ironically, minority protests do not work in the same way as more general ideological protest. While liberal protests are able to lead to a decrease in Republican vote share, minority protest has little to no effect on Republicans' electoral returns. The coefficient in Model 2 of Table 5.1 is not statistically significant. The coefficient in Model 2 of Table 5.1 is not statistically significant. Democrats' vote share, on the other hand, is greatly affected by minority protest. However, the relationship between minority protest and electoral returns is a positive one. Greater levels of minority protest leads to an increase in the Democratic vote share. Minority protests, like protests more broadly, do not produce a one-to-one trade-off between the loss/gains of the Republican Party's vote share to the Democratic vote share.

These results offer support for the Voter Effect Hypothesis as well as the Voter Effect Minority Protest Hypothesis. The results reveal that protest serves to reinforce citizens' political attitudes as opposed to alternating individuals' beliefs. Protest is well-received among voters who already share a similar ideological perspective. The positive increase that minority protest has on the Democratic vote share could be due to the fact that political activism further mobilizes like-minded individuals to come out and vote on Election Day. While this could be one possible explanation, another possible rationale for why minority protest leads to an increase in the Democratic vote share is because activism produces more qualified candidates. We explore this possibility further in the next section.

We incorporate Jacobson's (1987, 1990) measure of candidate quality, a measure also used by Cox and Katz (1996), which is coded as 1 if a challenger has previous held office and 0 otherwise. The independent variable of interest, protest, is placed on a liberal-conservative scale, where negative values indicate that the majority of protests events in a district expressed a conservative perspective while positive values indicate a more liberal position. Controls for election years and congressional districts were also included in the model but are not reported in the table above. The full model can be found in the supplemental materials. Regression coefficients come a probit model. Statistical significance is denoted as follows: significant at $*p < 0.05$.

Protest As a Signal of Vulnerability

Table 5.2 presents the relationship between protests in a district and the quality of a challenging candidate. There are several factors that hinder quality political challengers from running for office. One of the most significant factors that deter challengers is the presence of an incumbent politician running for reelection. This deterrent effect is observed in both Democrats and Republicans, with quality Democratic candidates being more vulnerable to an incumbent candidate than a Republican candidate. In addition to the incumbency status, the length of service of an incumbent also dampens the likelihood that we would see a quality Republican challenger emerge in an election race to run against a

TABLE 5.2 *Minority Protest Impact on the Quality of Candidates Running for Office.*

	Quality of Model 1	Republican Challenger Model 2	Quality of Model 3	Democratic Challenger Model 4
Challenger Quality$_{t-1}$	−0.326[a]	−0.328[a]	0.362[a]	−0.317[a]
	(0.102)	(0.102)	(0.081)	(0.105)
Previous Vote Share	−0.023[a]	−0.023[a]	−0.034[a]	−0.034[a]
	(0.008)	(0.008)	(0.005)	(0.007)
Incumbent$_{t-1}$	0.188	0.179	0.051	0.027
	(0.147)	(0.147)	(0.093)	(0.127)
Incumbent$_t$	−1.100[a]	−1.086[a]	−0.762[a]	−0.983[a]
	(0.156)	(0.155)	(0.122)	(0.166)
Southern District	−3.696	−6.404	−0.057	−.0634
	(5.922)	(6.641)	(0.098)	(.0523)
Length of Service	0.002	0.001	−0.020[a]	−0.022[a]
	(0.009)	(0.009)	(0.006)	(0.008)
Population	0.002[a]	0.002[a]	−0.001	0.001
	(0.001)	(0.001)	(0.001)	(0.002)
Protest$_t$	0.014[a]		0.001	
	(0.006)		(0.003)	
Protest$_{t-1}$	0.009		−0.002	
	(0.007)		(0.003)	
Minority Protest$_t$		0.027[a]		0.022[a]
		(0.016)		(0.009)
Minority Protest$_{t-1}$		0.005		−0.005
		(0.016)		(0.009)
AIC	1894.926	1896.172	1747.219	3438.597
BIC	9206.126	9185.868	2258.121	12323.856
log L	412.537	407.914	−781.609	−119.299
N	1597	1597	1907	1907

Notes: Statistical significance is denoted as follows: significant at [a]$p < 0.05$. The dependent variables are the quality of the challenging candidates running for office.

well-established politician. While the regression results highlight several factors that would discourage potential challengers, protest events stand out as an impetus for electoral competition.

To further illustrate the effect of political protest, we graph the predicted probabilities of a quality Democratic candidate running for office given different levels of protest activity that express liberal concerns. As one might expect, the average salience level of protest in a congressional district is relatively low,

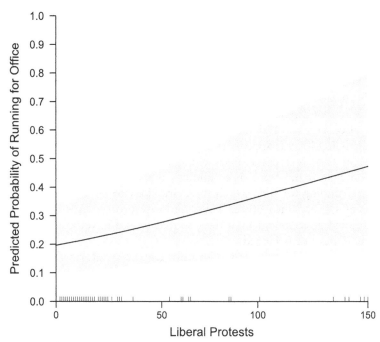

FIGURE 5.2 Predicted Probability of Quality Democrat Running for Office.
Notes: The graph depicts the predicted probability that a quality democratic runs for office given different levels of salient liberal protest. The tick marks on the x-axis represent actual saliency scores of protest activity found in the data.

with many of the raised ticks in Figure 5.2 clustering in the single digits. But as the context of protest changes, becoming larger, more contentious, or gleaning the support of liberal political organizations, quality Democratic challengers recognize an opportunity to benefit from the disgruntled sentiments expressed in a district. As Figure 5.2 shows, the predicted probability curve rises sharply with the increase of liberal leaning protest activity, moving from a low probability of a quality Democratic candidate emerging, at less than 20 percent, to a relatively higher probability, of almost 50 percent, holding all other variables constant at their means.

This was the case for New York's second congressional district in 1974. Liberal protest in favor of gay rights, feminist groups marching against sexual discrimination, and Black and Latino neighborhoods rallying for greater representation in government produced a very high protest salience score of 147 in the district. This significantly increased the probability of a quality Democratic challenger entering the 1974 election. Indeed, Thomas Downey (D-NY), who previously served as a New York Legislator for Suffolk County from 1972 to 1974, emerged to challenge the Republican incumbent, James Grover (R-NY). In this particular case, Downey's bid to run for office during a heightened level of liberal protest activity proved to be a shrewd decision. Downey defeated the 10-year incumbent, becoming one of the youngest members of Congress at age 25.

Minority protests also serve as a signal of vulnerability detected by potential political challengers against their incumbent opponents. Republican candidates are likely to face a more qualified Democratic challenger when minority protests occur in that district. Unlike general ideological protest, however, minority protests also serve as a signal for quality Republican candidates who have previously held office. It appears that potential political challengers believe that the issue of race is a contentious enough topic to sway voters. The ironic conclusion that stems from these findings is that if there are more qualified candidates running for office, then there are likely to be more qualified candidates being selected into office. Thus, minority protest ends up producing a more qualified government than the one that would have been produced had protest activities not occurred.

These results are illuminating. Not only are voters informed and mobilized by protest activities, but potential candidates also view protest activity as a signal that the timing is right to enter a race. That is, protest salience provides information to would-be challengers about citizens' concerns. In turn, as quality challengers enter races, the political opportunity structure for subsequent protest may be altered. To most scholars, the political opportunity structure (e.g., Tarrow 2011) is more or less open to claims made by challenging groups. And, some (Soule et al., 1999) note that protest activity can alter the political opportunity structure, such that subsequent protest will be more or less likely. Our findings suggest that perhaps one mechanism by which protest impacts the political opportunity structure is through encouraging quality challengers to enter electoral contests

DISCUSSION AND CONCLUSION

Minority protest has long been a form of civic engagement that marginalized citizens have relied upon to voice their grievances. Given that there is not an institutional procedure that recognizes the views of protesters, it is questionable whether the concerns voiced in minority protest activities are incorporated into the considerations of governmental institutions. Only recently have scholars of movement behavior and political participation begun to ask whether protest events can influence government, yet the lion's share of this work has focused on the effect of protest on governmental policy, and only a few studies have looked at its effects on electoral outcomes.

We argue that minority protest can have dramatic impacts on electoral outcomes and that these impacts are of two different types. First, we argue that minority protest can draw voters' attention to salient issues, educate voters on a topic, and lead them to vote for candidates whose platforms and ideological positions are consistent with the grievances expressed by protest. Second, we argue that information provided by protest events can also send a signal to potential challenger candidates that the timing is right to enter a race. Our empirical evidence is consistent with these arguments: protests that espouse liberal views lead Democrats to receive a greater share of the two-party vote in House elections, whereas protests that champion conservative views stimulate support for Republican candidates. Minority protest, in particular, leads to an increase in the vote share for Democratic politicians. Moreover, experienced, or quality candidates are more likely to run for office and challenge incumbents when there is a higher level of minority protest activity.

Our work suggests that citizens filter the information provided by protest through their own ideological prisms and that they use this information to inform their voting much in the same way that individuals' level of political engagement is shaped by their social context (Eulau and Rothenberg, 1986, Huckfeldt and Sprague, 1987, Cho and Rudolph, 2008). Our work is important because we introduce local protest activity into a discussion that has largely focused on social networks and organization membership to understand local-level political decisions. Minority protest events occurring in voters' communities are signals of political information that do not go unnoticed by the local electorate.

Recent data from the Crowd Counting Consortium shows the United States has seen four massive protests, each with well over 1 million participants since President Trump's inauguration.[18] These protests were objections to the Trump administration and its policies: the 2017 Women's March, the 2018 Women's March, the national student walkout on March 14 and the March for Our Lives on March 24 of 2018. The geographic breadth of each of these protest events is unprecedented as well as the range of issues (Arnold et al., 2018). The fervor of protest that ignited in the face of Trump's inauguration shows no sign of waning. If anything, the Trump political environment and presidency is inspiring more minority protests and more protests in general.

In response, elected officials are acknowledging and responding to the demands of protesters through their rhetoric and actions. After the police shooting of Stephon Clark, California legislators introduced legislation to limit police use of force (Koseff, 2018). West Virginia Governor Jim Justice agreed to the demands of the teachers by awarding a 5 percent salary raise. Florida state Governor and ally of the National Rifle Association Rick Scott signed into law a bill imposing a 21-year-old legal age requirement and 3-day waiting period on all gun purchases (Allen, 2018). These examples illustrate that elected officials are responding to protest activity. Consequently, voters can continue to use protest events for information and legislative response as metric for their voting behavior. It also means that possible political challengers have more information about their political environment.

---

[18] https://sites.google.com/view/crowdcountingconsortium/home?authuser=0

Our findings point to some suggestions for future research. First, in our analysis, there still remains the question of precisely *how* minority protest influences the vote share. Does protest mobilize new voters *or* does it increase turnout of a party's base? We suspect that it is a combination of both. However, untangling the different paths by which protest can influence individual voters is beyond the scope of this chapter. Instead, we seek to establish a strong foundation that protest does, indeed, feed into electoral outcomes, and we hope to stimulate others to investigate the precise mechanism by which this happens.

REFERENCES

Agnone, Jon. 2007. "Amplifying Public Opinion: The Policy Impact of the U.S. Environmental Movement." *Social Forces* 85: 1593–1620.

Almuhkhtar, Sarah, Mercy Bezaquen, Damien Cave, Sahil Chinoy, Kenan Davis, Josh Keller, K.K. Rebecca Lai, Jasmine C. Lee, Rochelle Oliver, Haeyoun Park and Destinée-Charisse Royal. 2018. "Black Lives Upended By Policing: The Raw Videos Sparking Outrage." *The New York Times.* Retrieved from www.nytimes.com/interactive/2017/08/19/us/police-videos-race.html (last accessed March 9, 2018).

Allen, Jonathan. 2018. "Florida Governor Signs Gun-Safety Bill into Law After School Shooting." *Reuters.* Retrieved from www.reuters.com/article/us-usa-guns-florida-law/florida-governor-signs-gun-safety-bill-into-law-after-school-shooting-idUSKCN1GL2RA (last accessed March 9, 2018).

Amenta, Edwin. 2006. *When Movements Matter: The Townsend Plan and the Rise of Social Security.* Princeton, NJ: Princeton University Press.

Amenta, Edwin, and Neal Caren. 2004. "The Legislative, Organizational, and Beneficiary Consequences of State-Oriented Challengers." In *The Blackwell Companion to Social Movements,* ed. David Snow, Sarah A. Soule, and Hanspeter Kriesi. London: Blackwell. Pp. 461–488.

Amenta, Edwin, Neal Caren, Elizabeth Chiarello, and Yang Su. 2010. "The Political Consequences of Social Movements." *Annual Review of Sociology* 36: 287–307.

Amenta, Edwin, Bruce G. Carruthers, and Yvonne Zylan. 1992. "A Hero for the Aged? The Townsend Movement, the Political Mediation Model, and U.S. Old-Age Policy, 1934–1950." *American Journal of Sociology* 98: 308–339.

Andrews, Kenneth. 2004. *Freedom Is a Constant Struggle: The Mississippi Civil Rights Movement and Its Legacy.* Chicago: University of Chicago Press.

Ansolabehere, Stephen, James M. Snyder Jr, and Charles Stewart III. 2000. "Old Voters, New Voters, and the Personal Vote: Using Redistricting to Measure the Incumbency Advantage." *American Journal of Political Science* 44: 17–34.

Arnold, R. Douglas. 1990. *The Logic of Congressional Action.* New Haven: Yale University Press.

Arnold, Jenna, Kanisha Bond, Erica Chenoweth, and Jeremy Pressman. 2018. "These Are the Four Largest Protests Since Trump Was Inaugurated." *The Washington Post,* Monkey Cage. Retrieved from www.washingtonpost.com/news/monkey-cage/wp/2018/05/31/these-are-the-four-largest-protests-since-trump-was-inaugurated/?noredirect=on&utm_term=.13d90a7ae1ea (last accessed May 31, 2018).

Austen-Smith, David, and Jeffrey Banks. 1989. "Electoral Accountability and Incumbency." In *Models of Strategic Choice in Politics*, ed. Peter Ordeshook. Ann Arbor: University of Michigan Press. Pp. 121–150.

Banks, Jeffrey S., and D. Roderick Kiewiet. 1989. "Explaining Patterns of Candidate Competition in Congressional Elections." *American Journal of Political Science* 33: 997–1015.

Bartels, Larry M. 1996. "Uninformed Votes: Information Effects in Presidential Elections." *American Journal of Political Science* 40: 194–230.

Baybeck, Brady, and Scott McClurg. 2005. "What Do They Know and How Do They Know It? An Examination of Citizen Awareness of Context." *American Politics Research* 33: 492–520.

Beck, Nathaniel, and Jonathan Katz. 1995. "What to Do (and Not to Do) With Time-Series Cross-Section Data." *American Political Science Review* 89: 634–647.

2001. "Throwing Out the Baby with the Bath Water: A Comment on Green, Kim and Yoon." *International Organizations* 55: 487–495.

Bianco, William T. 1984. "Strategic Decisions on Candidacy in U. S. Congressional Districts." *Legislative Studies Quarterly* 9: 351–364.

Black, Merle. 1978. "Racial Composition of Congressional Districts and Support for Federal Voting Rights in the American South." *Social Science Quarterly* 59: 435–350.

Bloom, Howard S., and H. Douglas Price. 1975. "Voter Response to Short-Run Economic Conditions: The Asymmetric Effect of Prosperity and Recession." *The American Political Science Review* 69: 1240–1254.

Bullock, Charles. 1981. "Congressional Voting and the Mobilization of a Black Electorate in the South." *Journal of Politics* 43: 662–682.

Button, James. 1989. *Blacks and Social Change: Impact of the Civil Rights Movement in Southern Communities*. Princeton, NJ: Princeton University Press.

Cava, Marco. 2018. "After Stephon Clark Shooting, Cries for Change — and Painful Echoes of Past Deaths." *USA Today*. Retrieved from www.usatoday .com/story/news/2018/03/29/sacramento-hopes-set-national-example-after-ste phon-clark-shooting/471713002/ (last accessed March 30, 2018).

Chenoweth, Erica, Jonathan Pinckney, Jeremy Pressman, and Stephen Zunes. 2017. "In Trump's America, Who's Protesting and Why? Here's Our February Report." *The Washington Post*, Monkey Cage. Retrieved from www.washingtonpost.com/ news/monkey-cage/wp/2017/04/05/in-trumps-america-whos-protesting-and-why-heres-our-february-report/?noredirect=on&utm_term=.022f0062ebc5 (last accessed April 5, 2017).

Chenoweth, Erica, and Jeremy Pressman. 2017. "Last month, 83% of U.S. protests Were Against Trump." *The Washington Post*, Monkey Cage. Retrieved from www.washingtonpost.com/news/monkey-cage/wp/2017/09/25/charlottesville-and-its-aftermath-brought-out-many-protesters-in-august-but-still-more-were-against-trump-and-his-policies/?utm_term=.38e79b8afb9b (last accessed September 28, 2017).

Cho, Wendy, and Thomas Rudolph. 2008. "Emanating Political Participation: Untangling the Spatial Structure Behind Participation." *British Journal of Political Science* 38(2): 273–289.

Claassen, Ryan L. 2007. "Floating Voters and Floating Activists: Political Change and Information." *Political Research Quarterly* 60: 124–134.

Costain, Anne, and Douglas Costain. 1987. "Strategy and Tactics of the Women's Movement in the United States: The Role of Political Parties." In *The Women's Movements of the United States and Western Europe*, ed. M. Katzenstein and C. Mueller. Philadelphia: Temple University Press. Pp. 196–214.

Cover, Albert D. 1977. "One Good Term Deserves Another: The Advantage of Incumbency in Congressional Elections." *American Journal of Political Science* 21: 523–541.

Cover, Albert D., and Bruce S. Brumberg. 1982. "Baby Books and Ballots: The Impact of Congressional Mail on Constituent Opinion." *The American Political Science Review* 76: 347–359.

Cox, Gary W., and Jonathan N. Katz. 1996. "Why Did the Incumbency Advantage in U.S. House Elections Grow?" *American Journal of Political Science* 40: 478–497.

Damore, David F. 2004. "The Dynamics of Issue Ownership in Presidential Campaigns." *Political Research Quarterly* 57: 391–397.

Davenport, Christian, Sarah Soule, and David Armstrong. 2011. "Protesting While Black? The Differential Policing of American Activism, 1960 to 1990." *American Sociological Review* 76: 152–176.

Delli-Carpini, Michael, and Scott Keeter. 1996. *What Americans Know about Politics and Why It Matters*. New Haven: Yale University Press.

Del Real, Jose. 2018. "Stephon Clark's Official Autopsy Conflicts with Earlier Findings." *The New York Times*. Retrieved from www.nytimes.com/2018/05/01/us/stephon-clark-official-autopsy.html (last accessed May 1, 2018).

Earl, Jennifer, Sarah Soule, and John McCarthy. 2003. "Protest under Fire? Explaining the Policing of Protest." *American Sociological Review* 68: 581–606.

Earl, Jennifer S., and Sarah A. Soule. 2006. "Seeing Blue: A Police-Centered Explanation of Protest Policing." *Mobilization: An International Journal* 11: 145–164.

Earl, Jennifer, Andrew Martin, John D. McCarthy, and Sarah A. Soule. 2004. "Newspapers and Protest Event Analysis." *Annual Review of Sociology* 30: 65–80.

Epstein, David, and Peter Zemsky. 1995. "Money Talks: Deterring Quality Challengers in Congressional Elections." *The American Political Science Review* 89: 295–308.

Eulau, Heinz, and Lawrence Rothenberg. 1986. "Life Space and Social Networks as Political Contexts." *Political Behavior* 8: 130–157.

Fair, Ray C. 1978. "The Effect of Economic Events on Votes for President." *The Review of Economics and Statistics* 60: 159–173.

Ferejohn, John. 1986. "Incumbent Performance and Electoral Control." *Public Choice* 50: 5–25.

Fetner, Tina. 2008. *How the Religious Right Shaped Lesbian and Gay Activism (Social Movements, Protest and Contention)*. Minneapolis, MN: University of Minnesota Press.

Fiorina, Morris P. 1974. *Representatives, Roll Calls, and Constituencies*. Minneapolis: Lexington Books.

Gelman, Andrew, and Gary King. 1990. "Estimating Incumbency Advantage without Bias." *American Journal of Political Science* 34: 1142–1164.

Gillion, Daniel Q. 2012. "The Influence of Protest Activity on Congressional Behavior: The Scope of Minority Protests in the District." *Journal of Politics* 74: 950–962.

2013. *The Political Power of Protest: Minority Activism and Shifts in Public Policy.* Cambridge, MA: Cambridge University Press.

Giugni, Marco. 2007. "Useless Protest? A Time-Series Analysis of the Policy Outcomes of Ecology, Antinuclear, and Peace Movements in the United States, 1977–1995." *Mobilization: An International Quarterly* 12: 53–77.

Großer, Jens, and Arthur Schram. 2006. "Neighborhood Information Exchange and Voter Participation: An Experimental Study." *The American Political Science Review* 100: 235–248.

Harris, Fredrick and Daniel Gillion. 2010. "Expanding the Possibilities: Reconceptualizing Political Participation as a Tool Box." In *The Oxford Handbook of American Elections and Political Behavior*, ed. Jan Leighley. Oxford University Press. Pp. 144–161.

Heaney, Michael T. and Fabio Rojas. 2011. "The Partisan Dynamics of Contention: Demobilization of the Antiwar Movement in the United States, 2007–2009." *Mobilization: An International Journal* 16: 41–54.

Huckfeldt, Robert, and John Sprague. 1987. "Networks in Context: The Social Flow of Political Information." *The American Political Science Review* 81: 1197–1216.

Huckshorn, Robert Jack, and Robert Clark Spencer. 1971. *The Politics of Defeat: Campaigning for Congress.* Amherst: University of Massachusetts Press.

Jacobson, Gary C. 1987. *The Politics of Congressional Elections.* Boston: Little, Brown. 1990. "The Effects of Campaign Spending in House Election: New Evidence for Old Arguments." *American Journal of Political Science* 34: 334–362.

John, Page, Adam Elmahrek, and Richard Winton. 2018. "Hundreds Rally in Sacramento After Stephon Clark Autopsy Raises New Questions in Police Shooting." *Los Angeles Times.* Retrieved from www.latimes.com/local/lanow/la-me-stephon-clark-protest-20180331-story.html (last accessed March 31, 2018).

Kasler, Dale, Tony Bizjak, Nashelly Chavez, and Hudson Sangree. 2018. "Protesters Block Golden 1 Center, Again, After Disrupting Council Meeting on Shooting of Stephon Clark." *The Sacramento Bee.* Retrieved from www.sacbee.com/latest-news/article207081079.html (last accessed March 28, 2018).

Kenny, Christopher B. 1992. "Political Participation and Effects from the Social Environment." *American Journal of Political Science* 36: 259–267.

Kernell, Samuel. 1978. "Explaining Presidential Popularity. How Ad Hoc Theorizing, Misplaced Emphasis, and Insufficient Care in Measuring One's Variables Refuted Common Sense and Led Conventional Wisdom Down the Path of Anomalies." *The American Political Science Review* 72: 506–522.

King, Brayden, Keith Bentele, and Sarah Soule. 2007. "Protest and Policymaking: Explaining Fluctuation in Congressional Attention to Rights Issues, 1960–1986." *Social Forces* 86: 137–163.

Koseff, Alexei. 2018. "Police Could Only Use Deadly Force When 'Necessary' under New California proposal." *The Sacramento Bee.* Retrieved from www.sacbee.com/latest-news/article207741689.html (last accessed April 10, 2018).

Kramer, Gerald H. 1971. "Short-Term Fluctuations in U.S. Voting Behavior, 1896–1964." *The American Political Science Review* 65: 131–143.

Lee, Taeku. 2002. *Mobilizing Public Opinion: Black Insurgency and Racial Attitudes in the Civil Rights.* Chicago: University of Chicago Press.

Leuthold, David A. 1968. *Electioneering in a Democracy: Campaigns for Congress*. New York: John Wiley & Sons.

Levitt, Steven D., and Catherine D. Wolfram. 1997. "Decomposing the Sources of Incumbency Advantage in the U. S. House." *Legislative Studies Quarterly 22*: 45–60.

Lohmann, Susanne. 1994. "Information Aggregation through Costly Political Action." *The American Economic Review 84*: 518–530.

Luders, Joseph E. 2010. *The Civil Rights Movement and the Logic of Social Change*. Cambridge: Cambridge University Press.

Malhotra, Neil, and Alexander G. Kuo. 2008. "Attributing Blame: The Public's Response to Hurricane Katrina." *The Journal of Politics 70*: 120–135.

Mann, Thomas E., and Raymond E. Wolfinger. 1980. "Candidates and Parties in Congressional Elections." *The American Political Science Review 74*: 617–632.

McAdam, Doug. 1982. *Political Process and the Development of Black Insurgency, 1930–1970*. Chicago: University of Chicago Press.

McAdam, Doug, and Sidney Tarrow. 2010. "Ballots and Barricades: On the Reciprocal Relationship between Elections and Social Movements." *Perspectives on Politics 8*: 529–542.

2013. "Social Movements and Elections: Toward a Broader Understanding of the Political Context of Contention." Pp. 325–346 in *The Future of Social Movement Research: Dynamics, Mechanisms, and Processes*. Edited by Jacquelien van Stekelenburg, Conny Roggeband, and Bert Klandermans. Minneapolis: University of Minnesota Press.

McAdam, Doug, and Yang Su. 2002. "The War at Home: Antiwar Protests and Congressional Voting, 1965 to 1973." *American Sociological Review 67*: 696–721.

McKelvey, Richard D., and Peter C. Ordeshook. 1986. "Information, Electoral Equilibria, and the Democratic Ideal." *The Journal of Politics 48*: 909–937.

McPhee, William. 1963. "Note on a Campaign Simulator." In *Formal Theories of Mass Behavior*, ed. William McPhee. New York: Free Press.

McVeigh, Rory, Daniel J. Myers, and David Sikkink. 2004. "Corn, Klansmen, and Coolidge: Structure and Framing in Social Movements." *Social Forces 83*: 653–690.

Meltzer, Allan H., and Marc Vellrath. 1975. "The Effects of Economic Policies on Votes for the Presidency: Some Evidence from Recent Elections: Reply." *Journal of Law and Economics 18*: 803–805.

Olzak, Susan, and Sarah Soule. 2009. "Cross-Cutting Influences of Environmental Protest and Legislation." *Social Forces 88*: 201–225.

Page, Benjamin I., and Robert Y. Shapiro. 1992. *The Rational Public: Fifty Years of Trends in Americans' Policy Preferences (American Politics and Political Economy Series)*. Chicago: University of Chicago Press.

Petrocik, John R, William L. Benoit, and Glenn J. Hansen. 2003. "Issue Ownership and Presidential Campaigning, 1952–2000." *Political Science Quarterly 118*: 599–626.

Petrocik, John R. 1996. "Issue Ownership in Presidential Elections, with a 1980 Case Study." *American Journal of Political Science 40*(3): 825–250.

Prior, Markus. 2006. "The Incumbent in the Living Room: The Rise of Television and the Incumbency Advantage in U.S. House Elections." *The Journal of Politics 68*: 657–673.

Rosenstone, Steven J., and John Mark Hansen. 1993. *Mobilization, Participation, and Democracy in America*. New York: Macmillan.

Sigelman, Lee, and Emmett H. Buell Jr. 2004. "Avoidance or Engagement? Issue Convergence in U.S. Presidential Campaigns, 1960–2000." *American Journal of Political Science* 48: 650–661.

Soule, Sarah, and Christian Davenport. 2009. "Velvet Glove, Iron Fist or Even Hand? Protest Policing in the United States, 1960–1990." *Mobilization: An International Quarterly* 14: 1–22.

Soule, Sarah, Doug McAdam, John McCarthy, and Yang Su. 1999. "Protest Events: Cause or Consequence of State Action? The U.S. Women's Movement and Federal Congressional Activities, 1956–1979." *Mobilization: An International Quarterly* 4: 239–256.

Soule, Sarah A., and Brayden King. 2006. "The Stages of the Policy Process and the Equal Rights Amendment, 1972–1982." *American Journal of Sociology* 111: 1871–1909.

Soule, Sarah A., and Susan Olzak. 2004. "When Do Movements Matter? The Politics of Contingency and the Equal Rights Amendment." *American Sociological Review* 69: 473–497.

Soule, Sarah A., and Brayden G King. 2008. "Competition and Resource Partitioning in Three Social Movement Industries." *American Journal of Sociology* 113: 1568–1610.

Soule, Sarah A., and Jennifer Earl. 2005. "A Movement Society Evaluated: Collective Protest in the United States, 1960–1986." *Mobilization* 10(3): 345–364.

Sprague, John. 1982. "Is There a Micro Theory Consistent with Contextual Analysis." In *Strategies of Political Inquiry*, ed. Elinor Ostrom. Beverly Hills, CA: Sage.

Sulkin, Tracy. 2005. *Issue Politics in Congress*. Cambridge: Cambridge University Press.

Thrush, Glenn, and Maggie Haberman. 2017. "Trump Is Criticized for Not Calling Out White Supremacists." *The New York Times*. Retrieved from www.nytimes.com/2017/08/12/us/trump-charlottesville-protest-nationalist-riot.html (last accessed August 12, 2017).

Tufte, Edward R. 1975. "Determinants of the Outcomes of Midterm Congressional Elections." *The American Political Science Review* 69: 812–826.

Van Dyke, Nella, Sarah A. Soule, and Verta A. Taylor. 2004. "The Targets of Social Movements: Beyond a Focus on the State." *Research in Social Movements, Conflict and Change* 25: 27–51.

Verba, Sidney, Kay Lehman Schlozman, and Henry Brady. 1995. *Voice and Equality: Civic Voluntarism in American Politics*. Cambridge: Harvard University Press.

Wang, Amy. 2017. "Trump Breaks Silence on Charlottesville: 'No Place for This Kind of Violence in America.'" *The Washington Post* Monkey Cage. Retrieved from www.washingtonpost.com/news/the-fix/wp/2017/08/12/trump-responds-to-charlottesville-protests/?utm_term=.0b39eaef6b97 (last accessed August 12, 2017).

Wang, Dan J., and Sarah A. Soule. 2012. "Social Movement Organizational Collaboration: Networks of Learning and the Diffusion of Protest Tactics, 1960–1995." *The American Journal of Sociology* 117(6): 1674–1722.

Whitby, Kenny J. 1987. "Measuring Congressional Responsiveness to the Policy Interests of Black Constituents." *Social Science Quarterly* 68: 367–377.

Young, Lisa. 1996. "Women's Movements and Political Parties." *Party Politics* 2: 229–250.

6

The Hollow Parties

Daniel Schlozman and Sam Rosenfeld

Party politics in twenty-first-century America presents a paradox. Our polarized age is unquestionably also an era of partisan revival. In the mass electorate, party identification predicts voting behavior better than any time since the dawn of polling. In government, interparty antagonism and intraparty discipline have reached unprecedented levels, placing severe strains on the very functioning of a Madisonian system of separated powers and triggering just the kind of chronic, rolling crisis in governance that motivates volumes such as this one. The national party organizations have become financial juggernauts even in a regulatory landscape that offers powerful incentives for political money to flow elsewhere. After languishing in the television-dominated campaign era of the late twentieth century, parties have ramped up their efforts in the field. During those same decades scholars deemed parties to be in permanent decline – but no longer. American parties are strong.[1]

And yet, even as the party divide defines the sides in America's political war, parties do not *feel* strong. They seem inadequate to the tasks before them – of aggregating and integrating preferences and actors into ordered conflict, of mobilizing participation and linking the governed with the government. This sense cannot merely be chalked up to popular misimpressions or to a mistakenly formalistic conception of the modern party. For years, warning bells had sounded. Parties' capacity to influence the political scene had grown brittle, they seemed to signal, and their legitimacy in the eyes of ordinary voters and engaged activists alike had abated. And then the warning bells became a honking siren. The developments of 2016 should upend any settled consensus that all is well in the party system. American parties are weak.

[1] We thank Tristan Klingelhöfer for excellent research assistance, and Devin Caughey, Joseph Cooper, Richard Katz, Eric Schickler, and participants in the Social Science Research Council (SSRC) Anxieties of Democracy Institutions Working Group Conference for helpful comments.

The solution to this paradox, we argue, lies in the reality that today's parties are hollow parties, neither organizationally robust beyond their roles raising money nor meaningfully felt as a real, tangible presence in the lives of voters or in the work of engaged activists. Partisanship is strong even as parties as institutions are weak, top-heavy in Washington, DC, and undermanned at the grassroots (Azari, 2016). The parties have become tarred with elements of polarization that the public most dislikes – from the screaming antagonism to the grubby money chase. More than any positive affinity or party spirit, fear and loathing of the other side – all too rational thanks to the ideological sorting of the party system – fuels parties and structures politics for most voters (Smidt, 2015, Abramowitz and Webster, 2016). Party identification drives American politics – but party loyalty, in the older sense of the term, has atrophied. Even the activists who do so much to shape modern politics typically labor outside of the parties, drawn to ideologically tinged "para-party" groups such as MoveOn.org on the left or the Koch-backed Americans for Prosperity on the right. The parties offer clear choices but get no credit.

The "Party Period" of the nineteenth century featured locally rooted and, in many instances, organizationally robust parties to which loyalties ran deep. Yet it aggregated participation into meaningful and distinct policy agendas only poorly. The party system often seemed little more than what a coalition of state parties could agree on. The situation has now reversed. Our new Party Period features a nationalized clash of ideology and interests but parties that are hollowed out and weakly legitimized. And much as nineteenth-century Americans were said to have lacked "a sense of the state," Americans in the contemporary era of party polarization can be said to lack a sense of party (Skowronek, 1982).

By legitimacy we mean foremost citizens' recognition that parties and partisan activity play a valid and important role in the polity, and additionally that, in party affairs, the actions and preferences of party elites merit due respect from loyal partisans. Americans need not celebrate everything about parties – ambivalence about political parties is as American as apple pie (Hofstadter, 1969, Ranney, 1975) – but they should recognize their distinct contributions not only as organizers of political conflict but as distinctive sites of small-d democratic and small-r republican citizenship.

While both parties are hollow, their hollowness manifests itself in divergent ways. The Democratic Party finds itself without a deep core. Organizationally, a party increasingly bourgeois in orientation fails to mobilize downscale irregular voters and nonvoters. Programmatically, its priorities appear little more than a list stapled together from particular constituencies. The Republican Party, by contrast, is less coreless than cleaved, starkly divided between a mass base and a well-heeled elite. Republicans have failed to embrace a positive vision that brings partisans together and that defines its boundaries against opponents and extremists alike.

We focus here on parties more than on partisans, but our assessment extends down to individuals. Even if "leaners" – independents who say they "feel closer to" one party – behave in the voting booth exactly like partisans, their increasing numbers should not be passed by so quickly. Instead, they suggest a reticence to march behind a party's banner (cf. Keith et al., 1992). At the same time, parties motivated by hatred for their opponents lose the capacity to enforce what Russell Muirhead and Nancy Rosenblum term "the discipline of regulated rivalry" (2016, p. 86, see also Rosenblum, 2008, Muirhead, 2014). They become vehicles for partisans' own venom and spleen, and their partial democratic visions descend into cabal and conspiracy.

The parties' long-term hollowing-out has cost the political system dearly. This essay seeks to delineate that cost, in the service of proposing a more robust and meaningful role for parties in American politics. We assuredly do not present such prescriptions as a "solution" to modern polarization. We affirm a politics defined by partisan combat over ideologically informed policy agendas. Indeed, our diagnosis emerges from an older view of responsible party government adapted for a new era. Ironic invocations of responsible party doctrine as laid out in the 1950 report by the American Political Science Association (APSA) Committee on Political Parties have become a staple of political science, usually pitched as a warning to "Be Careful What You Wish For" (Rae, 2007). We take a different view, reviving the prescription of an issue-oriented politics centered on the robust efforts of parties with real integrative tissue and policy capacity. If we paint a gloomier picture of the modern era, with its strong partisanship and hollow parties, than what many party scholars offer, that may be because we retain a more ambitious vision for responsible political parties as instruments of democracy.

PARTIES IN THEORY AND PRACTICE

Our polarized era has set the context for compelling and provocative new scholarly approaches to the study of parties. Group-centered theorists of parties have upended models predicting electorally induced partisan moderation, while a lively revival of skepticism toward procedural reform has occasioned new arguments for old-fashioned backroom politics. These two schools of thought share a self-conscious realism about the forces underpinning polarization along with a welcome leeriness of popular anti-party proposals that promise to restore moderation and comity to politics. But neither analysis accounts for the hollowness of contemporary parties or for the legitimacy problems that hollowness generates.

Advocates of a group-centered conception of political parties, chief among them a set of collaborators known as the "UCLA school," have done a great service by reinvigorating the scholarly discussion of parties for a new era of hyperpartisanship (Cohen et al., 2008, Bawn et al., 2012). Defining parties not as organized teams of politicians but rather as long coalitions of "intense policy demanders" – activists, interests, and ideologues all using politicians as agents rather than principals in the quest to achieve policy-related goals – the UCLA school helps account for the sustained absence of Downsian convergence in

American elections. Instead, its insights direct attention to the real stakes as parties vie to determine the distribution of society's goodies (Hacker and Pierson, 2014). Moreover, by collapsing the distinction between formal party organizations and the networks of nominally independent advocacy organizations and allied interest groups, the UCLA school's redefinition of parties provides a clearer picture of the actual combatants in contemporary political warfare.

Yet if parties appear only as the sum of the groups that comprise them, then parties have no intrinsic features *as parties*. Party politics in the UCLA school's account is a game of engaged elites who, once formally nominated and elected by duped and distracted voters, pursue relatively extreme agendas in office.[2] It is a testament to the cold-eyed, disillusioned bent of this work that the authors' normative conclusions have ranged from ambivalence to cautious endorsement of this very system and the structuring role that parties play in it (Cohen et al., 2008, pp. 360–363, Bawn et al., 2012, pp. 589–591, Cohen et al., 2016, pp. 707–708). Little in this analysis, however, engages the relative strength or weakness of parties as they seek to facilitate agreement among their groups, *or* the capacity of parties to mobilize participation and popular sentiment, *or* the consequences of shifts over time in the legitimacy of American parties.

The confounding events of 2016 have helped to lay bare the consequences. They highlight shortcomings in the theory of politics as a stable insiders' game among groups, and compel scholars to refocus their gaze on parties as parties. That the Republican Party failed so spectacularly to "decide" on its presidential nominee is hardly grounds to reject wholesale the theoretical insights for which the UCLA school's famous argument about party nominations served as an elaborate empirical test. But consider some of the causes of Donald Trump's victory: party actors so terrified of backlash from voters or media-advocacy institutions within their own coalition that they neglected to offer endorsements or take other decisive action; the fruitlessness of the elite signaling that did occur, stemming from a collapse in legitimacy; and a massive and exploitable chasm between the respective priorities and agendas of the parties' policy demanders and rank-and-file GOP voters. Rather than reflecting a victory of one faction over another (cf. Cohen et al., 2016), Trump beat all the established factions inside the party – and then, thanks to loyal support from Republican identifiers in the electorate, won the presidency.

A more openly prescriptive set of arguments from scholars and journalists loosely grouped under the moniker "new political realism" shares the UCLA school's hardheaded sense of democratic limits as well as their fateful blindness to parties' roles in bringing together disparate electorates and conferring legitimacy (La Raja, 2013, Cain, 2014, Pildes, 2014, La Raja and Schaffner, 2015, Persily, 2015, Rauch, 2015). Fittingly for an approach that celebrates the vote-maximizing transactional politics of a bygone era, the new realists adhere to an older conception of parties. They emphasize candidates' electoral needs and the

---

[2] Achen and Bartels (2016, pp. 297–328) analyze mass political behavior and tell a similar story.

imperatives of formal organization. Advancing a comprehensive critique of "romantic" democratic reforms in a number of different areas and institutions, the realists return consistently to a core prescription: empowering formal party actors and enriching formal party organizations relative to other players in the political system. Doing so, they argue, would channel power and resources away from more ideologically motivated and "purist" political actors to the sole institutions preoccupied chiefly with the practical task of winning elections, and thus incentivized toward moderation and bargaining. Stronger parties, the realists suggest, can save us from polarization.

Forceful arguments on behalf of parties as solutions to democratic failings are worth celebrating. But the new realists betray their own romanticism in presuming that a particular *kind* of long-faded party form, ideology-averse and ruthlessly transactional, could be revived in the twenty-first century. And their prescriptions to strengthen parties, which focus largely on helping them more freely and effectively vacuum up large financial donations, would only serve to magnify the parties' legitimacy crisis by doubling down on precisely the roles that the public finds most distasteful.

Nathaniel Persily, a leading new realist, has defined his view as a "'pro-party' 'bad-government' approach" (2015, p. 126). This essay, by contrast, reconstructs a good-government pro-party tradition, and applies it to contemporary dilemmas. Our outlook is "good government" in the sense that it retains the responsible-party commitment to the organization of political conflict around issues and public policy, and resists nostalgia for past political eras of blurred programmatic alternatives and rampant transactionalism. Nor do we find appealing the prospect of parties that wield vast influence entirely in service to their donors' bidding. Our differences with the new realists on this point recall disputes within the New York Democracy in the decades before the Civil War (Donovan, 1925, Earle, 2004). One faction, the "Hunkers," ignored slavery and hunkered after patronage. Their opponents, the "Barnburners," equally venerated political parties – and saw them as vehicles to rebuild society, foremost in opposing slavery. While in no way associating the new realists with the worst of the Hunkers, we place ourselves in the Barnburner tradition. Our vision is "pro-party," mean-while, in a more robust sense than the mere acceptance of the need for *somebody* to structure political choices – so why not parties? We emphasize instead the distinct and intrinsic qualities that, at their best, uniquely enable parties to mobilize popular participation, to integrate disparate groups, interests, and move-ments, and to foster meaningful choice and accountability in policymaking.

This outlook, we contend, emerges from a venerable intellectual lineage. The midcentury prescription for responsible parties went beyond a call for clearer lines of differentiation between the party programs. It was a vision to put the full force of American-style mass party organizations into the service of issue-based politics. E.E. Schattschneider and his allies celebrated the restless power-seeking energies of the two major American political parties even as they sought their reconstruction into forces for cohesive policy agendas. They shared the Progressive goal of issue-based politics but shunned the Progressive impulse toward anti-partyism.

As Schattschneider noted, middle-class Progressive anti-partyism was "formulated in language which seems to condemn all partisanship for all time but [was], in fact, directed at a special form of partisan alignment which frustrated a generation of Americans" trapped in the sectional System of 1896 (Schattschneider, 1956, p. 215). The New Deal had revolutionized national policymaking. A cross-party coalition of northern Republicans and southern Democrats had then stopped the Fair Deal in its tracks. For advocates of responsible parties, those conditions called for new approaches to parties and party reform. So, too, do we seek parties with real ideological meaning and mutual differentiation but also a tangible and felt presence in Americans' lives.

American parties are notoriously diffuse and infamously hard to define. They have no formal members. The entities that control parties' names and ballot access make up "the party" only in the most legalistic sense. We break no ground here; Schattschneider's own minimal definition that "a political party is an organized attempt to get control of the government" (1942, p. ix) still usefully separates parties from other entities that want influence and power. While recognizing the diverse actors inside American parties – elected officials, party functionaries, interest groups and social movements, lobbyists, grassroots activists, ordinary voters – we go against the modern party scholars who have treated parties chiefly as dependent variables, institutions created in response to needs and preferences derived elsewhere (cf. Aldrich, 2011). Treating parties as the end products of other actors' work – as vehicles for interests or office-winners for politicians – leaves parties' actual operations a black box.[3]

Instead, we treat parties principally as *collective* actors and as distinct institutions in their own right, focusing less on how they serve their constituent entities than on their capacities (or incapacities) in what Schattschneider called "the zone between the sovereign people and the government, which is the domain of the parties" (1942, p. 15). We ask not what other actors get out of parties, but how parties shape and reshape political combat.

A collective view of parties connects directly to the concept of responsible partisanship, with its recognition of party actors' linked fate. Without a collective party, a "there there" to link elites and masses and put forth a clear alternative, collective responsibility becomes impossible (Fiorina, 1980). And without some semblance of collective responsibility – in a far less formal sense than in Westminster systems, to be sure – a collective party will fail to make full use of its power.

Strong parties are not simply weak parties with strong bank accounts, but formal institutions that effectively and continually engage with voters, activists, and politicians to formulate and then implement party programs that clarify

---

[3] In seeking to fill these lacunae, political scientists would benefit from engagement with the sociological literature on parties. See Mudge and Chen (2014).

citizens' choices. In the sections that follow, we evaluate parties in the polarized era according to these criteria. We assess the strength and limitations of modern parties' organizational capabilities, their role in nominations, and their participation in agenda formulation, and then suggest some provisional approaches to reform in the direction of strong, responsible parties.

Any historically grounded account that indicts contemporary American parties runs the risk of golden-age-ism. If only the parties still dispensed turkeys at Thanksgiving, then somehow everything would be better again. But Americans have never had properly responsible parties in their history. Fully ideologically defined and sorted parties emerged only after the parties' coordinating capacities had collapsed, and to seek to revive those capacities is to pursue something new in American experience. Reconstruction of the parties begins, moreover, with the bedrock facts of a Madisonian political system, a sprawling state, and a distrustful public. The organizable alternatives in national politics flow from those harsh realities. Given the deep roots of contemporary polarization, our choices are circumscribed. Either Americans live with hollow parties or we reach for responsible parties.

ORGANIZATION

As parties in the electorate and parties in government have each revived, parties as organizations have tenaciously held on in the face of a broader American decline in federated membership groups (Putnam, 2000, Skocpol, 2003). The national party committees have modernized their operations and supercharged their fundraising since the 1970s (Cotter and Bibby, 1980, Conway, 1983, Reichley, 1985, Herrnson, 1988). Party organizations have not, however, built meaningful connections upward to elected officials or downward to voters.[4]

At the local and state levels, signs of revival in the era of polarization are hardest to identify – and hollowness most easily detected. Surveys of local party chairs in 1980 and in 2008 show remarkable continuity in parties' activities. In 1980, 60 percent of local Republican and 55 percent of local Democratic parties reported having a campaign headquarters at election time; in 2008, the figures were a near-identical 63 percent and 54 percent. And despite the avalanche of political money that pays canvassers for campaigns and "Super" political action committees (PACs) alike, local parties remain volunteer-led affairs. In 2008, as in 1980, only 6 percent of local Republican parties had any paid staff, while the figures for local Democratic parties rose only from 5 percent to 8 percent during the same period (Roscoe and Jenkins, 2014).

Meanwhile, state parties, central players in the American party system since Martin Van Buren, have become pawns in a mercenary, money-driven,

---

[4] For similar themes amid a less polarized polity, see Katz and Kolodny (1994) and Coleman (1994).

candidate-led, nationalized, and deinstitutionalized game. Party reform denied state parties the ability to control their delegations at national conventions. Yet even as parties in service, state parties have been supplanted; in off years, many "barely even have anyone around to answer the phone" (Greenblatt, 2015, see also Overby, 2015 and Ronanye, 2017). Legal legerdemain has pushed against statutory limits, without much benefiting state parties themselves (Allison, 2016, Confessore and Shorey, 2016, Vogel and Arnsdorf, 2016). A surviving piece of the Bipartisan Campaign Reform Act (BCRA) of 2002 bars the unlimited transfer of funds from national committees for party-building activities – the so-called soft-money loophole – and forces state parties to maintain separate state and federal accounts. Large donors in our nationalized polity, meanwhile, have failed to step up. Their dollars have gone directly to candidates or through new para-organizations.

The national party committees have held their own in the dollar chase, even as total spending by Independent Expenditure PACs ("Super PACs") now vastly surpasses the parties' own haul. The brief "soft money" boom that BCRA closed has left few footprints. Yet – and notwithstanding the new realists' hunches, based more on spending patterns than direct observation or analysis – we know little about national parties' actual operations, either inside their staff-led political shops or among their memberships, mostly elected by state committees. Members of each national committee elect its chair (or, when the party occupies the White House, rubber-stamp the president's pick for chair) – but how else do these well-networked individuals link candidates, causes, local notables, and national politics? The UCLA school has rightly shed light on informal interactions across partisan networks (e.g. Koger, Masket, and Noel, 2009). A perspective rooted in formal parties would apply their insights to far thicker interactions inside the nerve centers of parties themselves.

As the new realists correctly argue, the dance of congressional legislation and legal and agency interpretation has created a campaign finance system that uniquely constricts parties, with relatively generous limits on individual contributions, no limits on independent contributions or expenditures, and strict limits on donations to parties. But to view parties simply as financiers is to misdiagnose their contemporary predicament. The realists aim for strong parties but, despite some residual sympathy for turning back the clock on presidential nominations to the pre-reform era, principally aim to make it easier for party committees to raise and spend vast sums.

On the contribution side, the new realists risk blowback from the access afforded to donors and their preferences in the New Gilded Age. Giving parties a more prominent place in a financing system that most Americans regard as corrupt will hardly regain for parties their lost legitimacy or rebuild the frayed ties between insiders and ordinary partisans (Schmitt, 2015). Nor do the new realists reckon with the consequences of welcoming the super-rich into parties that, unlike narrowly focused pressure groups, putatively equalize political voice (Mann and Dionne, 2015). In the 2014 election cycle, 1 percent of

1 percent of Americans, a mere 31,976 donors, gave 29 percent of all dollars disclosed by federal election committees (Olsen-Phillips et al., 2015). Since their birth at the dawn of mass politics, parties at their best have been deeply egalitarian institutions. They should not become mere vehicles for plutocracy.

So, too, on the expenditure side. Nothing in a strategy to fund parties to the teeth will make them mobilize. Simply spending more money on television ads and, in swing states, on jerry-built campaign operations will not revitalize parties' fragile roots. Most dollars go into the interlocking network of political consultants and ad makers (Sheingate, 2016). Segregated independent expenditure units at the national and congressional committees target funds for media buys and explicitly cannot coordinate with the rest of the party. If a party in service to its candidates wants to maximize seats without an ongoing organization, then its television buyer – neither a professional politician nor a partisan in any older sense of the term – sits in the catbird's seat.

Assume away these principal-agent problems and even then the realists' model portrays a politics devoid of principled commitments. Politicians interested in winning as many seats as possible, or their minions, control resources – including to candidates who have no loyalty to a party's priorities. Ordinary partisans (or, for that matter, high-demanding groups) with strong preferences have no say in their choices. Accountability takes place only via exit, and not by voice. For the realists, the venerable "iron law of oligarchy" that Robert Michels (1915) developed to explain why socialist parties seemed the captives of career politicians morphs into a positive good.

As the spasms of discontent in 2016 signal, the long-term corrosive effects of popular disconnection from parties pose challenges for representative democracy far more severe than the mere ideological distance between the parties. It would be hard to invent a prescription more likely than the realists' to inflame the particular admixture of anti-partisan purity and anti-plutocracy zeal that powered Bernie Sanders. Nor would all the hedge-fund kings' horses and men in the realists' ideal system prove able to stop Donald Trump – or whoever the next Trump turns out to be. Simply opening the spigot would only worsen the parties' legitimacy problem and reduce their role in democratic life. Forgive any cynicism about the cynics that from such seeds will a hundred democratic flowers bloom.

MOBILIZATION

The torrent of partisan money has not only gone to television. Layered on top of these party structures lie the new purpose-built campaign operations, including both para-organizations such as the Kochs' Americans for Prosperity and jointly funded but candidate-led coordinated campaigns. Person-to-person canvassing, experiments have repeatedly found, motivates and persuades voters (Green and Gerber, 2015). And so, especially on the Democratic side, the field office has become a fixture of contemporary electoral politics (Masket, 2009, Nielsen, 2012, Darr and Levendusky, 2014). Yet despite breathless cheerleading heralding the return of old-fashioned shoe leather, candidates and parties still underinvest in mobilization even by their own metrics (Broockman and Kalla, 2014). If the parties spent directly on mobilizing voters, not only would more of them vote, but activists and ordinary citizens alike would have a greater sense of party.

The new field renaissance does not itself portend partisan renewal. Where parties' ward heelers once worked all the year round (Rakove, 1975), contacting now comes only when the electoral calendar demands. Although the hard work of canvassing remains in volunteers' hands, paid staff, parachuted in from afar and hoping for jobs in DC or perhaps the state capitol (before consulting or lobbying themselves), run the office (Schlozman, 2016). Early-twenty-somethings arrive to serve as organizers, reporting up to late-twenty-somethings on regional field desks. The campaign – in the most generous interpretation, the joint coordinated campaign – is the principal; party workers are its agent.[5] Obama for America emphasized building capacity among grassroots volunteers (McKenna and Han, 2015). It trained its captains and neighborhood team leaders extensively, but after election day in 2008 and again in 2012, let its organization wither on the vine.

The treatment must be compared with the control. Ryan Enos and Anthony Fowler (2018) estimate that the 2012 campaign raised turnout in swing states by about 7 or 8 percentage points. Yet intensive grassroots campaigning raises turnout so substantially above the baseline precisely because, absent extraordinary mobilization backed with formidable outside resources, ongoing political organization has fallen into such decay.[6]

Figures 6.1–6.4 encapsulate these trends.[7] Using data from the American National Election Studies (ANES), they show partisan contacting by Democrats and Republicans, in battleground states and non-battleground states, divided into income thirds for respondents aged 25–64. Specifically, the ANES asks: "Did anyone from one of the political parties call you up or come around to talk about the campaign?" We define battleground states as those in which the two-party vote in the average of the previous two presidential elections came within 5 percentage points in either direction of the national means – in other words, the states that both parties have a reasonable shot at potentially including in their winning coalitions.[8]

---

[5] This argument, never made explicitly, drives the analysis in Enos and Hersh (2015).

[6] Note the prevalence of highly competitive elections for Congress or governor even in states whose electoral votes are not much in doubt, underscoring the missed opportunity of disorganization and under-mobilization (Fraga and Hersh, 2016).

[7] These graphs merge the insights on stratification by income in Campbell (2007) and those across states in Beck and Heidemann (2014). Beck and Heidemann identify battleground states using a different measure, based on the long-run normal vote.

[8] This is the Partisan Voting Index developed in 1997 by election prognosticator Charlie Cook, with lower values indicating states closer to the national average. See Wasserman (2013). Results are similar using absolute margin of victory in past two presidential elections rather than deviation from national average.

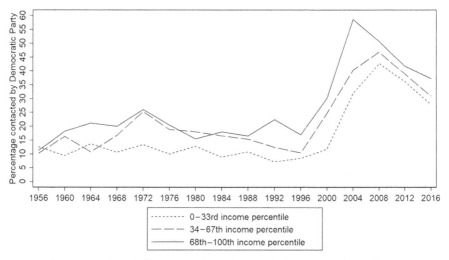

FIGURE 6.1 **Contacting by Democrats in Battleground States, 1956–2016.**
Source: American National Election Studies

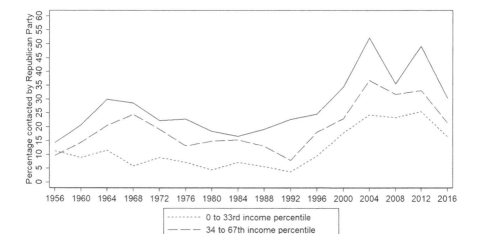

FIGURE 6.2 **Contacting by Republicans in Battleground States, 1956–2016.**
Source: American National Election Studies

As the figures show, the rise in contacting since 1996, as campaigns have grown closer and more expensive, has been principally limited to the band of closely contested states – and even there, fewer voters report being contacted in the most recent cycles. Patterns of class stratification appear consistent: across time, across levels of competitiveness, and for Democrats and Republicans,

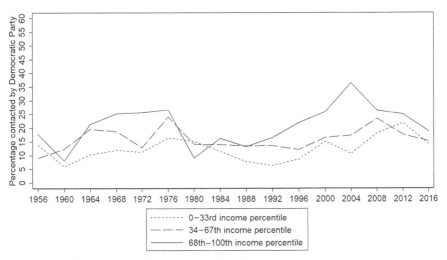

FIGURE 6.3 **Contacting by Democrats in Non-Battleground States, 1956–2016.**
Source: American National Election Studies

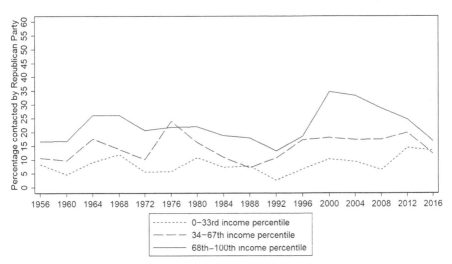

FIGURE 6.4 **Contacting by Republicans in Non-Battleground States, 1956–2016.**
Source: American National Election Studies

upper-income voters are more likely to report having been contacted by a political party. In 2016, 37 percent of upper-income battleground-state respondents reported being contacted by the Democratic Party and 30 percent by the Republican Party. Among low-income respondents in uncompetitive states, the figures are identical: 14 percent reported a contact from the Democrats, and 14 percent from the Republicans.

The parties have failed to mobilize their voters even in the much-vaunted new era of campaign analytics. Turnout among the voting-eligible population dropped from 61.6 percent in 2008 to 58.0 percent in 2012, and inched back up to just under 59 percent in 2016, with Donald Trump's popular vote total besting Mitt Romney's 4 years earlier while Hillary Clinton's share fell just short of Obama's. On-the-ground postmortems on the Clinton loss emphasized a field operation that amplified the pathologies of contemporary approaches to mobilization: overconfidence in analytics wizardry, disconnection from existing networks of activists and party workers rooted in their communities, and a consequent, yawning absence of local knowledge or capacity to adjust efforts in response to dynamics on the ground (Dovere, 2016, Parenti, 2016, Schlozman, 2016).

Whether one views parties as the creations of politicians or high-demanding groups, or as autonomous organizers of conflict, they exist to bring to the polls would-be voters who will elect a government that achieves backers' goals. As in the 1870s and 1880s, today's parties again stand evenly matched in national politics and fight each election aware that control over the entire government hangs in the balance (Lee, 2016). Yet neither party has organized to maximize its vote, and both suffer the consequences. Their failures to turn out potential voters are not just structural facts but *partisan* failures.

Critics from the left have long bemoaned the feckless Democrats (e.g., Piven and Cloward, 1988), but the devastating midterm losses of 2010 and 2014 followed by the shocking Electoral College upset in 2016 give the charge new salience – and new urgency. Gerrymanders, all the easier given patterns of residential dispersion, leave Democrats hobbled in state legislatures, and, absent the rare wave election, constrict their chances to win seats in Congress. The consequences have devastated groups at the very heart of the Democratic coalition. In Wisconsin, Michigan, and North Carolina, as well as in deep-red states, Republican legislatures have passed draconian restrictions on abortion rights and crippled unions in the public and private sectors alike.

For their part, Republicans have in the "voting wars" instituted voter ID requirements to protect against the miniscule problem of in-person voter fraud, and restricted voting procedures, such as early voting, disproportionately used by their political opponents (Hasen, 2012, Berman, 2015). Strategies of demobilization are nothing new in American politics. Jim Crow in all its electoral manifestations, from the literacy test to the white primary to the grandfather clause and, with a much weaker treatment, the northern pushback against the popular politics of the Party Period prove as much (McGerr, 1988). The modern voting wars raise larger questions about the racial odyssey of the Republican Party and the bounds of legitimate political competition. Yet the Republicans, too, suffer from failure to mobilize their would-be voters. In an influential analysis, Sean Trende (2013) attributed Mitt Romney's defeat in

2012 principally to 6 million "missing white voters," mostly downscale and outside the Greater South, who chose to stay home. A total outsider waged a hostile takeover of his party in 2016 by mobilizing many of those voters. Yet the nature of his victory more underscores the disconnect than solves it for the long term.

Perhaps, naysayers will reply, even with rising education levels the sky-high turnout of the late nineteenth century will never return. The video game and the app have replaced the torchlight parade while the Super Bowl provides the excitement once garnered by a booze-soaked election day waving the party ticket. The United States has not, however, put that hypothesis to a proper test. It is hard to imagine truly strong parties when such weak organization manifests in mediocre presidential and abysmal midterm turnout – and harder still to argue that the parties have really tried to mobilize their potential supporters (Crenson and Ginsberg, 2002).

NOMINATIONS

Parties still choose their nominees by the votes of delegates assembled at a national convention, as the Democrats have since 1832 and the Republicans have since 1856. The parties' formal authority still reaches its apex at "the pure partisan institution" of the convention (Shafer, 2010). Behind the debate over the ability of insiders – including elected officials, well-connected donors, and allied interest groups – to shape contemporary nominations lies a process that resists partisan appeals to authority. Like the new political realists (e.g., Persily, 2015, pp. 128–130), we think parties ought to control their nominations. But we would add a caution against Pyrrhic victories and poisoned chalices, in which procedures survive merely as much-criticized relics and party organizations endure quadrennial turns as punching bags.

From their Jacksonian institutional inheritance, the parties still retain influence. The states select delegates to a convention that is essentially a private meeting – and not a public utility subject to regulation. Proposals for a national primary have come and gone since the first presidential primaries without ever coming close to passage, not least because states like to set their own calendars in statute. In the Party Period, primitive practices mixed with a politics where parties mobilized mass electorates. Now only the forms linger, a product of a decidedly incomplete modernization. "If there is any arena where the rights of US states have survived the twentieth century, the New Deal, and all other expansions of the scope of the federal government," writes Walter Dean Burnham, "it is the conduct of elections" (2015, p. 32).

Yet even as the delegate hunt traces far back in American political history, the popular conversation increasingly accepts the plebiscitary logic of a national primary, wherein the candidate with the most votes automatically gets the nomination. Attacks against perceived violations of that norm come fast and furious. Parties and partisans offer only muted, and usually hypocritical, replies. One would be hard-put to find a full-throated defense of the party as the correct deciders of nomination – and still less, of the party as decider not simply because it will pick an electable nominee who will make a good president (Polsby, 1983) but because it will put forth an appropriate standard-bearer for the party's vision of democracy.

The most sustained attention to parties as arbiters of procedure comes from presidential contenders on their way to losing the nomination, and it is not pretty. The postreform era offers temptations unavailable to strategic politicians in earlier partisan constellations. Interminable campaigns and a thin sense of what party loyalty requires have rendered parties vulnerable to the predations of fair-weather friends. Especially once the debates have stopped, and there are few issues to pick over any longer, losing candidates turn their fire to a process that they claim to be rigged against them. Front-runners blithely ignore the complaints, keeping their eyes on November, and challengers attack the system. The ongoing Trump story, while broadly consonant with the idea that the contemporary parties prove weak defenders of their prerogatives, raises larger, still unsettled questions to which we return in the conclusion; the Democrats' lessons seem clearer.

No procedure has been more controversial than the unpledged Party Leader Elected Official delegates introduced by the Hunt Commission in time for the 1984 convention. The unpledged PLEOs, whom everyone terms "superdelegates," have always been a hard sell. They aimed to recreate the old process by which party leaders could judge their peers. In February 2016, Debbie Wasserman Schultz, the chair of the Democratic National Committee, offered the risibly incorrect view that superdelegates exist to allow grassroots activists a chance to attend the convention without having to run against elected officials to earn a slot (Borchers, 2016).[9] Even the chair of the national party could not defend with an appeal to public reason her party's hard-fought procedures.

Rather than seeking to take over the Democratic National Committee, Bernie Sanders's campaign sought to neuter it. In preconvention talks, Hillary Clinton's campaign acceded to a commission that will almost certainly strip DNC members of their unpledged first-ballot votes, and also to a left-leaning platform. Then, his demands met, Sanders became – poof! presto! – an apostle of party responsibility, waving a copy of the platform on late-night television (Wagner, 2016). None of the leading players in the Democrats' 2016 drama stuck up for party principle when it went against expedient interest.

PROGRAM

The paradox of parties dominating politics while seeming institutionally ancillary to that very domination – at once central and wraithlike – likewise

---

[9] In fact, the Democrats' pledged PLEO delegates, chosen by state party conventions or committees and allocated in proportion to candidates' vote share, precisely address Wasserman-Schultz's professed concern.

characterizes their programmatic functions. Parties structure policy choices and articulate conflict in twenty-first-century politics. Elites, activists, and the mass electorate alike have sorted into the "correct" party. The parties now take distinct positions on ever greater numbers of topics, along multiple issue dimensions (Layman et al., 2010). Just as members of Congress have polarized, as documented exhaustively using aggregate roll-call-based measures like NOMINATE, so too have positions in party platforms diverged over time (Paddock, 1992, Coffey, 2011, Gordon, Webb, and Wood, 2014).

This divergence is not only real but, perhaps just as importantly, *perceived*. At midcentury, the APSA Committee on Political Parties identified as a core problem of American politics the fact that "alternatives between the parties are defined so badly that it is often difficult to determine what the election has decided even in broadest terms" (1950, pp. 4–5). Even as a system of separated powers still stymies party responsibility, the twenty-first-century electorate at least recognizes that the parties offer genuine alternatives on election day. The proportion of Americans who saw "important differences in what the Republicans and Democrats stand for" rose from 46 percent in 1972 to 60 percent in 1992 to 81 percent in 2012 (American National Election Studies, 2018).[10] When contested, general elections now provide choices rather than echoes. The days of tweedle dum and tweedle dee are over.

Instead, our polarized era features a grand partisan battle over public purposes from which the parties themselves have receded. In place of programmatic formal parties are polarized networks of interest and advocacy groups, drawing on research and expertise from higher education and think tanks. A fluid midcentury landscape of "issue networks" working in ad hoc bipartisan coalitions has given way to a far more structured pattern of conflict between densely clustered partisan teams in civil society.

Yet platform-by-proxy imposes costs. Agenda formation carried out among less visible and formalized channels of elite actors faces real limits without the cross-fertilization of ordinary peoples' concerns, technical expertise, and political savvy that only parties can provide. So, too, the dominance of interest groups in generating policy with respect to their particular issues limits the potential for substantive coherence and responsibility in the party agendas. Finally, when issue activists perceive that parties are disconnected from the work of agenda generation, then any sense of party in the system further diminishes and the parties' legitimacy problems worsen further.

The weakness of American parties as vehicles for generating and articulating policy agendas is an old story. The *Sturm und Drang* of campaign rhetoric and the lofty bromides of party platforms notwithstanding, the major American parties have been held to be comparatively lacking in coherent policy agendas

---

[10] The relevant table is here: www.electionstudies.org/nesguide/text/tab2b_4.txt. Similarly, Americans are better able to identify the Republicans as the more conservative party; see www.electionstudies.org/nesguide/toptable/tab2b_5.htm.

or ideologies at least since the Party Period (cf. Gerring, 1998). Analysts have pointed variously to institutional fragmentation (Epstein, 1986, Samuels and Shugart, 2010), liberal anti-majoritarianism (Ranney and Kendall, 1956), and early mass suffrage (Katznelson, 1985, Shefter, 1994). Whatever the mix of causes, the result is a system in which formal parties lack the in-house research and policy operations typical among parties in parliamentary systems (Campbell and Pederson, 2014). Despite party organizations' sporadic twentieth-century experiments in formal policy work (Rosenfeld, 2018), American parties as a rule pursue agendas that are generated by satellite research and interest group networks engaging candidates and office holders directly.

The hollowness of the parties' programmatic efforts is evident along various fronts. The national party committees engage issues and policy largely through publicity efforts on behalf of the party "brand" rather than attempting to alter the brand itself through substantive research and deliberation. The modern platform-drafting process serves principally to gauge different factions' relative institutional clout within the party. Victorious nominees often use the platform as a consolation prize for vanquished candidates, while other times the documents are largely unmediated litanies of policy positions advocated by specific interest groups. As a logroll, the platform becomes the progeny of a thousand fathers; as meaningful expression of the party's agenda in government, it is an orphan.

The two major parties betray contrasting strengths and weaknesses in their approaches to program. The conservative movement transformed public policy expertise in the second half of the twentieth century by propounding a model of openly ideological think tanks exclusively engaged in a single party's extended network (Weaver, 1989, Ricci, 1993, Rich, 2005, Stahl, 2016). For all its pitfalls, that approach warrants appreciation from those interested in party responsibility. The turn away from a mythos of disinterested technocracy toward the mobilization of expertise in conscious conflict goes at least part of the way toward legitimizing parties as programmatic actors. Under conditions of twenty-first-century polarization, however, the right's policy infrastructure has bifurcated. At the programmatic core of the modern GOP's agenda, interest groups and donors have fought for upwardly redistributive economic policies notably lacking in mass support, even among Republican partisans (Hacker and Pierson, 2010). Outside of the narrow channels that generate such positions, however, lie populist campaigns of position-taking, symbolic conflict, and mobilized resentment that frequently merge seamlessly with the activities of the right's commercial media institutions (Ball, 2013). Both sides of the modern Republican approach to agenda generation – the narrow band of regressive policy commitments and the Fox-and-Breitbart world of permanent confrontation – only accentuate the gap between Republican elites and Republican voters on basic priorities and policy views.

The Democratic Party, for its part, enjoys comparatively robust policy capacity. Yet just as the formal parties' organizational hollowing out has augmented the upper-class bias of American politics, so does their absence from policy development, since parties bring in actors with experiences and priorities beyond the technocrats' ken. The class skew inherent to elite policy networks too often limits Democrats to expertise produced by white men with fancy degrees. As Daniel Patrick Moynihan once remarked tartly, "a party of the working class cannot be dominated by former editors of the *Harvard Crimson*" (Heilbrunn, 1997). Democratic policy elites have responded to rising inequality only fitfully, with solutions that retreat from larger questions of political economy (Weir, 1998). And as the politics of Obamacare well indicate, feedback from such opaque policymaking rarely shores up partisan loyalties (Oberlander and Weaver, 2015).

For leftist critics, elite technocratic control dovetails with the Democrats' reliance on large donors to produce elite agenda control. And because the party as a formal organization is not seen to actually participate in programmatic work, it gets none of the credit even when candidate nomination fights, movement mobilizations, or other intraparty dynamics actually help to produce significant and progressive changes in the party agenda. This dynamic played out like clockwork during the 2016 nomination contest, and helps explain why a substantive success story for insurgent energies seemed to produce so little in the way of new, positive attachments to the Democratic Party.

TOWARD MORE RESPONSIBLE MASS PARTIES

If hollowness provides the answer to the paradox of ineffectual parties in an age of hyperpartisanship, what achievable steps might imbue American politics with a stronger sense of party? In the search for a usable past, a good-government *pro-party* approach emphatically rejects a period that good-government *anti-party* advocates happily tout (cf. Rahman, 2016). In the Progressive Era, middle-class WASP reformers aimed to purify the political system by weakening parties. In their stead, they substituted a technocratic elite that would staff the burgeoning bureaucracy. In a fractured and pluralistic polity, we have no elite unified and confident enough, or invested with sufficient public support, to continue such a project today. The further recrudescence of the Progressive strategy to strengthen the presidency at the expense of party organizations and Congress hardly seems wise for a repeat run.

Nor do other rich democracies provide much in the way of helpful models. Indeed, the crisis of political parties extends far beyond American borders (Katz and Mair, 1995, Stokes, 1999, Blyth and Katz, 2005, Katz and Mair, 2009, Mair, 2013, Ignazi, 2014). Under proportional and majoritarian electoral systems alike, parties have grown hollow and lost legitimacy. The complaints here about too-powerful staff at the central office and frayed ties between party elites and the grassroots echo across the rich democracies. Populism, in many though by no means all instances fueled by racism and xenophobia, is on the march.

Yet the predicament of the center-left and the rise of the revanchist right, familiar transnational themes, manifest themselves unusually in the American context. Even as American parties remain, across a series of dimensions, comparatively weak, the United States retains as pure a duopoly as any democracy. While insurgent parties have reshaped party systems across Europe, challenges to the established order in the United States have at least so far come from within rather than without. The most notable third-party presidential candidates since Ross Perot, Ralph Nader in 2000 and Gary Johnson in 2016, won only 2.74 and 3.28 percent respectively. Precisely this fact of voice rather than exit makes renewal possible. Far easier to rehabilitate the parties, however fragile their gears, than somehow to reassemble them anew once they have split into shards.[11]

This configuration leads to a tempered conclusion. Given the strength of partisan loyalties in structuring political conflict, parties in the polity known for weak parties have the ingredients for renewal. At the same time, the fracture of so many once-strong organizations across the developed world tempers any enthusiasm that partisan renewal will be an easy or automatic process. The case for strong American parties rests less on successful contemporary models from abroad than on the bedrock reality of partisanship inside two parties. And indeed, though reversing America's century-spanning decline of federated membership organizations may not be in the cards, polarization arguably creates a setting distinctly suited *for parties in particular* to build more robust participatory organizations.

Parties must reinvigorate committees from the national all the way down to the precinct level. At the national and state levels, where staff working directly with top politicians typically run the show, their membership ought to reflect genuine commitment. When membership means more than adjudicating rules, it should appeal to activists, high-demanding groups' leaders, and politicians alike.

The nascent mobilizations of the twenty-first century – Dreamers, Occupy, Black Lives Matter, and also the Tea Party and the Alt Right – have generated energy aplenty. Some are more promising than others as partners to parties, and the parties have approached them in different ways (Parker and Barreto, 2013, Heaney and Rojas, 2015). As a general matter, however, while movements have reason to preserve their autonomy and parties to steer clear of doctrinaire elements that threaten electoral majorities, alliance between parties and movements not only generates votes on Election Day but institutionalizes movements' cadres and priorities once the initial ardor has faded (Schlozman, 2015). For all the inevitable frustrations, that promise remains. Parties will have to work to shape it to responsible ends.[12]

---

[11] We thank Henry Farrell for helping us to formulate this argument.
[12] For an incisive take from the left, see Shahid (2016).

American history provides examples of formal parties that combined robust organization with issue-oriented politics. Reformist Democratic state parties in the postwar era, such as the UAW-aligned Michigan Democratic State Central Committee and the Democratic Farmer-Labor Party that powered Hubert Humphrey's rise in Minnesota, serve as models for responsible parties (Buffa, 1984, Delton, 2002). Far from being mere ineffectual talking shops for white, upper-middle-class activists, in both states responsible parties pushed forward visions that, whatever their contradictions, offered powerful support for the black freedom struggle and linked racial and economic justice (Boyle, 1995, Lichtenstein, 1995, Thurber, 1999, Schickler, 2016). A half-century on from their heyday, the time has come for activists to step out of the shadows of party networks and walk forthrightly into the bright sunshine of open partisanship.

Those models of responsible partisanship were found at the state level, however, and they suggest one key point where midcentury theorists got the story wrong. As good New Deal liberals, the academic proponents of responsible national parties deplored sectionalism – above all in the Solid South – and sought coherent national parties oriented around national issue commitments. Yet they failed to anticipate how nationalized parties would hollow out the very organizations, reform as well as machine, that did the parties' work on the ground. Party-building in the twenty-first century requires sustained and continuous investment in state and local parties, and in our nationalized partisan era the onus falls on the national party organizations to carry that out. As long as shadow party organizations funded by big donors remain central to electoral politics, the staffers and elected officials who gatekeep and direct their giving ought likewise to steer rich donors to, and then reward them for, investment in state-level organizing and party-building. The fruits of sporadic twentieth-century efforts in this vein (Cotter and Bibby, 1980, Klinkner, 1994, Galvin, 2009, Conley, 2013), not to mention Howard Dean's short-lived but fruitful Fifty-State Strategy for the DNC early in the twenty-first (Kamarck, 2006, Jacobson, 2013, Kuttner, 2017), make the case for pursuing such activity as a core party task. The anti-Trump "Resistance" has begun to revive long-dormant local parties even in unlikely places (Galchin, 2018, Putnam and Skocpol, 2018).

Our vision for rejuvenated grassroots parties echoes Samuel Gompers's old line about what labor wanted: "We want more." We seek parties that organize consistently and effectively, and that see their purpose as persuading and mobilizing voters rather than simply "messaging" (Skocpol, 2017). The precise basket of activities they undertake will vary, but the basic model for local parties is no mystery. Nor, in the main, has the story much changed since the nineteenth century, except that local parties can no longer rely on the inducement of patronage. In an age of atomized polarization, as local parties puzzle how to rope in partisans with little sense of party, the humdrum work of party-building endures.

The model should be familiar to any veteran of local party politics, and so should the primary challenge local parties face: the institutional maintenance to keep a volunteer-led low-budget operation afloat leaves too little time for organizing. Local parties seek to engage and recruit volunteers as members and supporters with regular activities that offer solidary as well as purposive incentives (or, to cut the jargon, that mix in some fun). They support candidates up and down the ticket, encourage promising figures to run and offer assistance to those who do, monitor party affairs, and help make sure that state conventions, platforms, and the like reflect partisans' concerns. Revitalization would not replace such activities, but rather marshal people and resources so that they actually get performed. And that means shifting electoral resources further away from advertising and toward mobilization – continually and not just quadrennially.

A few points seem salient. First, local parties should both meet regularly and go beyond meetings to engage with voters all year round, rather than simply emerging Brigadoon-like at election season or for their formal tasks. The state of the art suggests that long-form "deep canvassing" would be particularly effective, given how person-to-person interaction with neighbors establishes rapport (Denizet-Lewis, 2016). Second, even if they hire an office worker or two, local parties are voluntary associations *par excellence*. In an age when formal meetings conducted under *Robert's Rules* hold ever less appeal, local parties must figure out how to hold volunteers' attention. At the most minimal level, that means giving volunteers meaningful tasks, the training to do them, and the opportunity for leadership. Third, analytics and "Big Data" should not restrict themselves to headquarters or to operatives churning among campaigns, consultancies, and Silicon Valley. A culture of experimentation works best when knowledge can be democratized and diffused. Local parties need not be backwaters, but creators of knowledge – and national and state parties ought to help them in that effort. Fourth, volunteer-led local parties serve as a bulwark against the predations of staff and of donors. Time is distributed more equally than money, and rare are the plutocrats who spend their evenings with the ward committee.

Strong parties support one another across levels of government. Local parties now find their work difficult because their counterparts above provide few activities between elections that serve as focal points to organize. The Democratic National Committee, for example, provides virtually no direct support for local parties or for field services.[13] By the standards of contemporary politics, local parties are cheap. A few bucks from above to rent a meeting hall and provide some food would seem money well worth spending – or, at the very least, a proposition about the efficacy of spending well worth testing.

Perhaps no partisan realm reveals such a gap between widespread norms and the institutional practices necessary for strong and vibrant partisanship as candidate selection. Even when party actors do succeed in "deciding" their

---

[13] We thank Kate Donaghue, a member of the DNC, for this insight.

nominations in the modern era, they do so in the shadows. 2016 revealed the brittleness of even their capacity for low-visibility signaling and deck-stacking. Small-d democratic norms serve as the default standard by which any potential reform to the system is judged, with perverse consequences for party responsibility. In this area, the central and most difficult task will come in changing those very norms among partisans themselves. Rolling back the Progressives' watershed introduction of primaries is unlikely. And the activists who powered the McGovern-Fraser reforms at the national level had their reasons, in spades (Plotke, 1996). But the first step in advancing the idea that permeable and issue-driven parties are entitled to a say in deciding who stands for office in their name is for party officers themselves to cease speaking out of the sides of their mouths in deference to their own legitimacy problems, and instead to begin forthrightly making the party's case. Democrats on the precipice of eliminating superdelegates to the national convention might first pause to take a long, sober look at the forty-fifth president of the United States. Republicans, of course, must take an even longer look.

Bringing parties back into the process of policy development may prove comparatively easy. The "diminishing oddness" of American parties has arguably rendered them *more* conducive to explicit programmatic work now than ever before (Rae, 2012, see also Pomper and Weiner, 2000). Pushing the parties in this direction would serve to instill a greater sense of party in American politics. For the UCLA school, parties are delegated with implementing policies chosen by the groups in the party coalition. But what if, alternatively, groups make their preferences clear and delegate to parties the task of forging policy? Given the integrative functions that parties alone possess at their best, such a process might be expected to produce agendas that better reflect the priorities of supporters and that bear the stamp of clearer, more responsible authorship. Twentieth-century experiments by both parties provide the precedents and potential forms that such programmatic work might take: formal policy councils housed in the party committees, party-sponsored publications covering substantive topics in public policy, and biennial issue conferences that once before and might once again serve as, in the words of James MacGregor Burns, "a transmission belt between movement politics and party politics" (Cronin, 1986, p. 536).

What might the two parties look like with more robust organizations and more significant roles in agenda development? The implications of responsible mass partisanship differ for the two major parties. Drawing on a growing body of scholarship documenting the especial contribution of the GOP to modern polarization, Matt Grossmann and David A. Hopkins (2016) argue for a more fundamental partisan asymmetry in American politics pitting a Democratic Party organized as a coalition of distinct social groups seeking benefits in the form of public policy against a Republican Party organized as a vessel for ideological conservatism.

For the Democrats, the very group-oriented log-rolling – at times reified in theories of pluralism and pragmatism – that can undercut the party's capacity to articulate a coherent agenda provides a rationale for party mechanisms that provide connective tissue and an *esprit de corps* to the party's coalition members. Since midcentury, when responsible partisanship left behind its Anglophiliac roots, liberals have proven its strongest adherents. As the Democratic Party now edges ever closer to the core dilemma of Western social democracy – how to sustain a working-class base while also attracting bourgeois votes (Przeworski and Sprague, 1986) – the promise of responsible, integrative parties remains as potent and relevant as ever before to long-term prospects on the center-left.

Our read on the disarray visible within the hollow parties inclines us toward skepticism about the significance of Republicans' alleged zeal, given that little in the way of ideological constraint appears to unite engaged Republican elites and the party's base voters behind a shared program. The gap between the two proved ripe for exploitation in 2016, with explosive results.

For our country's sake, responsible conservative partisanship remains a worthy goal, even in the age of Trump. The Republican Party would have to move beyond showmanship and position-taking on the one hand and a narrowly regressive policy agenda on the other hand (Douthat and Salam, 2008, Dionne, 2014). A rejuvenated Republicanism could no longer cede its messages to talk radio, Fox News, and Breitbart. Responsible partisanship, at its best, restrains partisans' worst impulses, muffling extreme voices and channeling energy toward the hard work of campaigning and governing. While political parties, even in democratic societies, can certainly be harnessed for malign purposes, a revitalized GOP would, we argue, be better placed to redirect the party's agenda beyond donor demands to the task of strengthening the frayed bonds of family and civil society, and to broaden its electoral appeal beyond a politics of white status anxiety and racial and ethnic nationalism. Perhaps the center-right mass party can no longer answer populist discontent. That these statements sounds so exhortatory precisely emphasizes the distance between hollow and responsible partisanship in contemporary Republicanism. Yet whatever the prospects for a responsible conservative party, the alternatives on the right seem far, far worse. When parties are susceptible to donors and demagogues, democracy becomes susceptible to takeover and breakdown.

The connection between party organizations and the lived experience of ordinary Americans has frayed over time. So, too, party responsibility for the policy conflicts that structure the party system has likewise attenuated. This essay has sought to diagnose the correct problem with American political parties in a polarized age. Our vision of responsible parties as the solution to hollow parties is unavoidably hooded and suggestive, as is our notion of how to get from here to there. Stronger parties will not solve the dilemma posed by the ill fit between disciplined ideological partisanship and Madisonian institutions – though we suspect they would mitigate the potential for crisis. But strong parties will help to clarify the nature of the conflict and mobilize Americans to participate as responsible citizens. A great partisan era calls for parties without apology.

REFERENCES

Abramowitz, Alan I., and Steven Webster. 2016. "The Rise of Negative Partisanship and the Nationalization of American Elections in the 21st Century." *Electoral Studies* 41: 12–22.

Achen, Christopher H., and Larry M. Bartels. 2016. *Democracy for Realists: Why Elections Do Not Produce Responsive Government*. Princeton: Princeton University Press.

Aldrich, John H. 2011. *Why Parties? A Second Look*. Chicago: University of Chicago Press.

Allison, Bill. 2016. "Millions from Maxed-Out Clinton Donors Flowed through Loophole." *Bloomberg*, August 26. Retrieved from www.bloomberg.com/politics/graphics/2016-dnc-contributions/ (last accessed December 8, 2018).

American National Election Studies. 2018. *The ANES Guide to Public Opinion and Electoral Behavior*. Ann Arbor: University of Michigan. Retrieved from www.electionstudies.org (last accessed December 8, 2018).

APSA Committee on Political Parties. 1950. *Toward a More Responsible Two-Party System: A Report of the Committee on Political Parties of the American Political Science Association*. New York: Rinehart.

Azari, Julia. 2016. "Weak Parties and Strong Partisanship are a Bad Combination," *Vox*, November 3. Retrieved from www.vox.com/mischiefs-of-faction/2016/11/3/13512362/weak-parties-strong-partisanship-bad-combination (last accessed December 8, 2018).

Ball, Molly. 2013. "The Fall of the Heritage Foundation and the Death of Republican Ideas." *The Atlantic*, September 25. Retrieved from www.theatlantic.com/politics/archive/2013/09/the-fall-of-the-heritage-foundation-and-the-death-of-republican-ideas/279955/ (last accessed January 2, 2019).

Bawn, Kathleen, Marty Cohen, David Karol, Seth Masket, Hans Noel, and John Zaller. 2012. "A Theory of Parties: Groups, Policy Demands, and Nominations in American Politics." *Perspectives on Politics* 10: 571–597.

Beck, Paul A., and Erik D. Heidemann. 2014. "Changing Strategies in Grassroots Canvassing: 1956–2012." *Party Politics* 20: 261–274.

Berman, Ari. 2015. *Give Us the Ballot: The Modern Struggle for Voting Rights in America*. New York: Farrar, Straus, and Giroux.

Blyth, Mark, and Richard S. Katz. 2005. "From Catch-all Politics to Cartelisation: The Political Economy of the Cartel Party." *West European Politics* 28: 33–60.

Borchers, Callum. 2016. "We Need More Questions Like This One from Jake Tapper to Debbie Wasserman Schultz." *Washington Post*, February 12. Retrieved from www.washingtonpost.com/news/the-fix/wp/2016/02/12/we-need-more-questions-like-this-one-from-jake-tapper-to-debbie-wasserman-schultz-video/ (last accessed December 8, 2018).

Boyle, Kevin. 1995. *The UAW and the Heyday of American Liberalism*. Ithaca: Cornell University Press.

Broockman, David, and Joshua Kalla. 2014. "Experiments Show This Is the Best Way to Win Campaigns. But Is Anyone Actually Doing It?" *Vox*, November 13. Retrieved from www.vox.com/2014/11/13/7214339/campaign-ground-game (last accessed December 8, 2018).

Buffa, Dudley W. 1984. *Union Power and American Democracy: The UAW and the Democratic Party, 1935–72*. Ann Arbor: University of Michigan Press.

Burnham, Walter Dean. 2015. "Voter Turnout and the Path to Plutocracy." In *Polarized Politics: The Impact of Divisiveness in the US Political System*," edited by William Crotty, pp. 27–70. Boulder: Lynne Rienner.

Cain, Bruce E. 2014. *Democracy, More or Less: America's Political Reform Quandary*. New York: Cambridge University Press.

Campbell, Andrea Louise. 2007. "Parties, Electoral Participation, and Shifting Voting Blocs." In *The Transformation of American Politics: Activist Government and the Rise of Conservatism*, edited by Paul Pierson and Theda Skocpol, 68–102. Princeton: Princeton University Press.

Campbell, John L., and Ove K. Pederson. 2014. *The National Origins of Policy Ideas: Knowledge Regimes in the United States, France, Germany and Denmark*. Princeton: Princeton University Press.

Coffey, Daniel. 2011. "More Than a Dime's Worth: Using State Party Platforms to Assess the Degree of American Party Polarization." *PS: Political Science & Politics* 44: 331–337.

Cohen, Marty, David Karol, Hans Noel, and John Zaller. 2008. *The Party Decides: Presidential Nominations Before and After Reform*. Chicago: University of Chicago Press.

2016. "Party versus Faction—In the Reformed Presidential Nominating System." *PS: Political Science & Politics* 49: 701–708.

Coleman, John J. 1994. "The Resurgence of Party Organization? A Dissent from the New Orthodoxy." In *The State of the Parties: The Changing Role of Contemporary American Parties*, edited by Daniel M. Shea and John C. Green, 311–327. Lanham: Rowman & Littlefield.

Confessore, Nicholas, and Rachel Shorey. 2016. "Democrats Are Raking in Money, Thanks to Suit by Republicans." *The New York Times*, October 1, p. A11.

Conley, Brian. 2013. "The Politics of Party Renewal: The 'Service Party' and the Origins of the Post-Goldwater Republican Right." *Studies in American Political Development* 27: 51–67.

Conway, M. Margaret. 1983. "Republican Political Party Nationalization, Campaign Activities, and Their Implications for the Party System." *Publius* 13: 1–17.

Cotter, Cornelius B., and John S. Bibby. 1980. "Institutional Development of Parties and the Thesis of Party Decline." *Political Science Quarterly* 95: 1–27.

Crenson, Matthew A., and Benjamin Ginsberg. 2002. *Downsizing Democracy: How America Sidelined Its Citizens and Privatized Its Public*. Baltimore: Johns Hopkins University Press.

Cronin, Thomas E. 1986. "On the American Presidency: A Conversation with James MacGregor Burns." *Political Science Quarterly* 16: 528–542.

Darr, Joshua P., and Matthew S. Levendusky. 2014. "Relying on the Ground Game: The Placement and Effect of Campaign Field Offices." *American Politics Research* 42: 529–548.

Delton, Jennifer A. 2002. *Making Minnesota Liberal: Civil Rights and the Transformation of the Democratic Party*. Minneapolis: University of Minnesota Press.

Denizet-Lewis, Benoit. 2016. "How Do You Change Voters' Minds? Have a Conversation." *The New York Times Magazine*, April 7, p. 48.

Dionne, E.J., Jr. 2014. "The Reformicons." *Democracy: A Journal of Ideas*, Summer.

Donovan, Herbert D.A. 1925. *The Barnburners: A Study of the Internal Movements in the Political History of New York State and of the Resulting Changes in Political Affiliation, 1830–1852*. New York: New York University Press.

Douthat, Ross, and Reihan Salam. 2008. *Grand New Party: How Republicans Can Win the Working Class and Save the American Dream*. New York: Doubleday.

Dovere, Edward-Isaac. 2016. "How Clinton Lost Michigan — and Blew the Election." *Politico*, December 14. Retrieved from www.politico.com/story/2016/12/michigan-hillary-clinton-trump-232547 (last accessed December 8, 2018).

Earle, Jonathan H. 2004. *Jacksonian Antislavery and the Politics of Free Soil*. Chapel Hill: University of North Carolina Press.

Enos, Ryan D. and Anthony Fowler. 2018. "Aggregate Effects of Large-Scale Campaigns on Voter Turnout." *Political Science Research and Methods* 6: 733–751.

Enos, Ryan D., and Eitan D. Hersh. 2015. "Party Activists as Campaign Advertisers: The Ground Campaign as a Principal-Agent Problem." *American Political Science Review* 109: 252–278.

Epstein, Leon. 1986. *Political Parties in the American Mold*. Madison: University of Wisconsin Press.

Fiorina, Morris P. 1980. "The Decline of Collective Responsibility in American Politics." *Daedalus*: 12–32.

Fraga, Bernard L., and Eitan D. Hersh. 2016. "Why is There So Much Competition in U.S. Elections?" Working paper. Retrieved from www.eitanhersh.com/uploads/7/9/7/5/7975685/fraga_hersh_compet_v3_1.pdf (last accessed December 8, 2018).

Galchin, Rivka. 2018. "The Teaching Moment." *The New Yorker*, June 4, pp. 38–43.

Galvin, Daniel J. 2009. *Presidential Party Building: Dwight D. Eisenhower to George W. Bush*. Princeton: Princeton University Press.

Gerring, John. 1998. *Party Ideologies in America, 1828–1996*. New York: Cambridge University Press.

Gordon, Soren, Clayton McLaughlin Webb, and B. Dan Wood. 2014. "The President, Polarization and the Party Platforms." *The Forum* 12: 169–189.

Green, Donald P., and Alan S. Gerber. 2015. *Get Out the Vote: How to Increase Voter Turnout*, 3rd ed. Washington: Brookings Institution Press.

Greenblatt, Alan. 2015. "The Waning Power of State Political Parties." *Governing*, December. Retrieved from www.governing.com/topics/politics/gov-waning-power-state-parties.html (last accessed December 8, 2018).

Grossmann, Matt, and David A. Hopkins. 2016. *Asymmetric Politics: Ideological Republicans and Group Interest Democrats*. New York: Oxford University Press.

Hacker, Jacob S., and Paul Pierson. 2010. *Winner Take All Politics: How Washington Made the Rich Richer—and Turned Its Back on the Middle Class*. New York: Simon & Schuster.

2014. "After the Master Theory: Downs, Schattschneider, and the Rebirth of Policy-Focused Analysis." *Perspectives on Politics* 12: 643–662.

Hasen, Richard L. 2012. *The Voting Wars: From Florida 2000 to the Next Election Meltdown*. New Haven: Yale University Press.

Heaney, Michael T., and Fabio Rojas. 2015. *Party in the Street: The Antiwar Movement and the Democratic Party After 9/11*. New York: Cambridge University Press.

Heilbrunn, Jacob. 1997. "The Moynihan Enigma." *The American Prospect*, July.

Herrnson, Paul S. 1988. *Party Campaigning in the 1980s*. Cambridge: Harvard University Press.

Hofstadter, Richard. 1969. *The Idea of a Party System: The Rise of Legitimate Opposition in the United States, 1780–1840*. Berkeley: University of California Press.

Ignazi, Piero. 2014. "Power and the (Il)legitimacy of Parties: An Unavoidable Paradox of Contemporary Democracy?" *Party Politics* 20: 160–169.

Jacobson, Louis. 2013. "Looking Back at Howard Dean's Fifty State Strategy." *Governing*, May 6.

Kamarck, Elaine. 2006. "Assessing Howard Dean's Fifty State Strategy and the 2006 Midterm Elections." *The Forum* 4. Retrieved from https://doi.org/10.2202/1540-8884.1141 (last accessed December 8, 2018).

Katz, Richard S., and Robin Kolodny. 1994. "Party Organization as an Empty Vessel: Parties in American Politics." In *How Parties Organize: Change and Adaptation in Party Organizations in Western Democracies*, edited by Richard S. Katz and Peter Mair, pp. 23–50. London: Sage.

Katz, Richard S., and Peter Mair. 1995. "Changing Models of Party Organization and Party Democracy: The Emergence of the Cartel Party." *Party Politics* 1: 5–28.

2009. "The Cartel Party Thesis: A Restatement." *Perspectives on Politics* 7: 753–766.

Katznelson, Ira. 1985. "Working Class Formation and the State: Nineteenth Century England in American Perspective." In *Bringing the State Back In*, edited by Peter B. Evans, Dietrich Reuschemeyer, and Theda Skocpol, 257–284. New York: Cambridge University Press.

Keith, Bruce E., David B. Magleby, Candice J. Nelson, Elizabeth A. Orr, Mark C. Westlye, and Raymond E. Wolfinger. 1992. *The Myth of the Independent Voter*. Berkeley: University of California Press.

Klinkner, Philip A. 1994. *The Losing Parties: Out-Party National Committees, 1956–1992* (New Haven: Yale University Press).

Koger, Gregory, Seth Masket, and Hans Noel. 2009. "Partisan Webs: Information Exchange and Party Networks." *British Journal of Political Science* 39: 633–653.

Kuttner, Robert. 2017. "Q&A: A New 50-State Strategy." *American Prospect*, January 17. Retrieved from http://prospect.org/article/qa-new-50-state-strategy (last accessed December 8, 2018).

La Raja, Raymond J. 2013. "Richer Parties, Better Politics? Party-Centered Campaign Finance Laws and American Democracy," *The Forum* 11: 313–338.

La Raja, Raymond J., and Brian Schaffner. 2015. *Campaign Finance and Political Polarization: When Purists Prevail*. Ann Arbor: University of Michigan Press.

Layman, Geoffrey C., Thomas M. Carsey, John C. Green, and Richard Herrara. 2010. "Activists and Conflict Extension in American Party Politics." *American Political Science Review* 104: 324–346.

Lee, Frances E. 2016. *Insecure Majorities: Congress and the Perpetual Campaign*. Chicago: University of Chicago Press.

Lichtenstein, Nelson. 1995. *The Most Dangerous Man in Detroit: Walter Reuther and the Fate of American Labor*. New York: Basic Books.

Mair, Peter. 2013. *Ruling the Void: The Hollowing of Western Democracy*. London: Verso.

Mann, Thomas E., and E.J. Dionne, Jr. 2015. "The Futility of Nostalgia and the Romanticism of the New Political Realists: Why Praising the 19th-Century Political Machine Won't Solve the 21st Century's Problems." Brookings Institution, June.

Masket, Seth E. 2009. "Did Obama's Ground Game Matter?: The Influence of Local Field Offices during the 2008 Presidential Election." *Public Opinion Quarterly* 73: 1023–1039.

McGerr, Michael E. 1988. *The Decline of Popular Politics: The American North, 1865–1928*. New York: Oxford University Press.

McKenna, Elizabeth, and Hahrie Han. 2015. *Groundbreakers: How Obama's 2.2 Million Volunteers Transformed Campaigning in America*. New York: Oxford University Press.

Michels, Robert. 1915. *Political Parties: A Sociological Study of the Oligarchical Tendencies of Modern Democracy*. Translated by Eden Paul and Cedar Paul. Republished Glencoe: Free Press, 1949.

Mudge, Stephanie L., and Anthony S. Chen. 2014. "Political Parties and the Sociological Imagination: Past, Present, and Future Directions." *Annual Review of Sociology 40*: 305–340.

Muirhead, Russell. 2014. *The Promise of Party in a Polarized Age*. Cambridge: Harvard University Press.

Muirhead, Russell, and Nancy L. Rosenblum. 2016. "Speaking Truth to Conspiracy: Partisanship and Trust." *Critical Review* 28: 63–88.

Nielsen, Rasmus Kleis. 2012. *Ground Wars: Personalized Communication in Political Campaigns*. Princeton: Princeton University Press.

Oberlander, Jonathan, and R. Kent Weaver. 2015. "Unraveling from Within? The Affordable Care Act and Self-Undermining Policy Feedbacks." *The Forum 13*: 37–62.

Olsen-Phillips, Peter, Russ Choma, Sarah Bryner, and Doug Weber. 2015. "The Political One Percent of the One Percent in 2014: Mega Donors Fuel Rising Cost of Elections." Center for Responsive Politics, April 30. Retrieved from www.open secrets.org/news/2015/04/the-political-one-percent-of-the-one-percent-in-2014-mega-donors-fuel-rising-cost-of-elections/ (last accessed December 8, 2018).

Overby, Peter. 2015. "Why State Parties Are Losing Out on Political Cash." *NPR*, February 9. Retrieved from www.npr.org/2015/02/09/384875874/state-political-parties-blames-congress-for-lack-of-funds (last accessed December 8, 2018).

Paddock, Joel. 1992. "Interparty Ideological Politics in 11 State Parties, 1956–1980." *Western Political Quarterly 45*: 751–760.

Parenti, Christian. 2016. "Garbage In, Garbage Out." *Jacobin*, November 18. Retrieved from www.jacobinmag.com/2016/11/clinton-campaign-gotv-unions-voters-rust-belt/ (last accessed December 8, 2018).

Parker, Christopher S., and Matt Barreto. 2013. *Change They Can't Believe in: The Tea Party and Reactionary Politics in America*. Princeton: Princeton University Press.

Persily, Nathaniel. 2015. "Stronger Parties as a Solution to Polarization." In *Solutions to Political Polarization in America*, edited by Nathaniel Persily, pp. 123–135. New York: Cambridge University Press.

Pildes, Richard H. 2014. "Romanticizing Democracy, Political Fragmentation, and the Decline of Government." *Yale Law Journal* 124: 804–852.

Piven, Frances Fox, and Richard A. Cloward. 1988. *Why Americans Don't Vote.* New York: Pantheon Books.

Plotke, David. 1996. "Party Reform as Failed Democratic Renewal in the United States, 1968–1972." *Studies in American Political Development* 10: 223–288.

Polsby, Nelson. 1983. *The Consequences of Party Reform.* New York: Oxford University Press.

Pomper, Gerald M. and Marc D. Weiner. 2000. "Toward a More Responsible Two-Party Voter: The Evolving Bases of Partisanship." In *Responsible Partisanship? The Evolution of American Political Parties Since 1950*, edited by John C. Green and Paul S. Herrnson, pp. 181–200. Lawrence: University Press of Kansas.

Przeworski, Adam, and John Sprague. 1986. *Paper Stones: A History of Electoral Socialism.* Chicago: University of Chicago Press.

Putnam, Lara, and Theda Skocpol. 2018. "Middle America Reboots Democracy." *Democracy Journal*, February 20. Retrieved from https://democracyjournal.org/arguments/middle-america-reboots-democracy/ (last accessed December 8, 2018).

Putnam, Robert D. 2000. *Bowling Alone: The Collapse and Revival of American Community.* New York: Simon & Schuster.

Rae, Nicol C. 2007. "Be Careful What You Wish For: The Rise of Responsible Parties in American National Politics." *Annual Review of Political Science* 10: 169–191.

   2012. "The Diminishing Oddness of American Political Parties." In *The Parties Respond: Changes in American Parties and Campaigns*, 5th ed., edited by Mark D. Brewer and L. Sandy Maisel, 25–46. Boulder: Westview Press.

Rahman, K. Sabeel. 2016. *Democracy against Domination.* New York: Oxford University Press.

Rakove, Milton L. 1975. *Don't Make No Waves … Don't Back No Losers: An Insider's Analysis of the Daley Machine.* Bloomington: Indiana University Press.

Ranney, Austin. 1975. *Curing the Mischiefs of Faction: Party Reform in America.* Berkeley: University of California Press.

Ranney, Austin, and Willmoore Kendall. 1956. *Democracy and the American Party System.* New York: Harcourt, Brace and Company.

Rauch, Jonathan. 2015. "Political Realism: How Hacks, Machines, Big Money, and Back-Room Deals can Strengthen American Democracy." Brookings Institution, May.

Reichley, A. James. 1985. "The Rise of National Parties." In *The New Direction in American Politics*, edited by John E. Chubb and Paul E. Peterson, 175–200. Washington: Brookings Institution Press.

Ricci, David M. 1993. *The Transformation of American Politics: The New Washington and the Rise of Think Tanks.* New Haven: Yale University Press.

Rich, Andrew. 2005. *Think Tanks, Public Policy, and the Politics of Expertise.* New York: Cambridge University Press.

Ronanye, Kathleen. 2017. "Out of Power, State Dems Frustrated with National Committee." Associated Press, January 3. Retrieved from http://bigstory.ap.org/article/4348e5c51f544fadb4f9229602c495d4 (last accessed December 8, 2018).

Roscoe, Douglas D. and Shannon Jenkins. 2014. "Changes in Local Party Structure and Activity, 1980–2008." In *The State of the Parties: The Changing Role of Contemporary American Parties*, 7th ed., edited by John C. Green, Daniel J. Coffey, and David B. Cohen, pp. 287–302. Lanham: Rowman & Littlefield.

Rosenblum, Nancy L. 2008. *On the Side of the Angels: An Appreciation of Parties and Partisanship*. Princeton: Princeton University Press.

Rosenfeld, Sam. 2018. *The Polarizers: Postwar Architects of Our Partisan Age*. Chicago: University of Chicago Press.

Samuels, David, and Matthew Shugart. 2010. *Presidents, Parties, and Prime Ministers: How the Separation of Powers Affects Party Organization and Behavior*. New York: Cambridge University Press.

Schattschneider, E.E. 1942. *Party Government*. New York: Holt, Rinehart and Winston.

    1956. "The Functional Approach to Party Government." In *Modern Political Parties: Approaches to Comparative Politics*, edited by Sigmund Neumann, pp. 194–215. Chicago: University of Chicago Press.

Schickler, Eric. 2016. *Racial Realignment: The Transformation of American Liberalism, 1933–1965*. Princeton: Princeton University Press.

Schlozman, Daniel. 2015. *When Movements Anchor Parties: Electoral Alignments in American History*. Princeton: Princeton University Press.

    2016. "The Lists Told Us Otherwise." *n+1*, December 24. Retrieved from https://nplusonemag.com/online-only/online-only/the-lists-told-us-otherwise/ (last accessed December 8, 2018).

Schmitt, Mark. 2015. "Democratic Romanticism and Its Critics." *Democracy: A Journal of Ideas*, Spring.

Shafer, Byron E. 2010. "The Pure Partisan Institution: National Party Conventions as Research Sites." In The Oxford Handbook of American Political Parties and Interest Groups, edited by L. Sandy Maisel and Jeffrey M. Berry, 264–284. New York: Oxford University Press.

Shahid, Waleed. 2016. "It's Time for a Tea Party of the Left." *The Nation*, May 10. Retrieved from www.thenation.com/article/its-time-for-a-tea-party-of-the-left/ (last accessed December 8, 2018).

Sheingate, Adam. 2016. *Building a Business of Politics: The Rise of Political Consulting and the Transformation of American Democracy*. New York: Oxford University Press.

Shefter, Martin. 1994. *Political Parties and the State: The American Historical Experience*. Princeton: Princeton University Press.

Skocpol, Theda. 2003. *Diminished Democracy: From Membership to Management in American Civic Life*. Norman: University of Oklahoma Press.

    2017. "A Guide to Rebuilding the Democratic Party, From the Ground Ip." *Vox*, January 5. Retrieved from www.vox.com/the-big-idea/2017/1/5/14176156/rebuild-democratic-party-dnc-strategy (last accessed December 8, 2018).

Skowronek, Stephen. 1982. *Building a New American State: The Expansion of National Administrative Capacities, 1880–1920*. New York: Cambridge University Press.

Smidt, Corwin D. 2015. "Polarization and the Decline of the American Floating Voter." *American Journal of Political Science*. doi:10.1111/ajps.12218.

Stahl, Jason. 2016. *Right Moves: The Conservative Think Tank in American Political Culture Since 1945*. Chapel Hill: University of North Carolina Press.

Stokes, Susan. 1999. "Political Parties and Democracy." *Annual Reviews in Political Science* 2: 243–267.

Thurber, Timothy N. 1999. *The Politics of Equality: Hubert H. Humphrey and the African-American Freedom Struggle*. New York: Columbia University Press.

Trende, Sean. 2013. "The Case of the Missing White Voters, Revisited." *Real Clear Politics*, June 21. Retrieved from www.realclearpolitics.com/articles/2013/06/21/ the_case_of_the_missing_white_voters_revisited_118893.html (last accessed December 8, 2018).

Vogel, Kenneth P., and Isaac Arnsdorf. 2016. "Clinton Fundraising Leaves Little for State Parties." *Politico*, May 2. Retrieved from www.politico.com/story/2016/04/ clinton-fundraising-leaves-little-for-state-parties-222670 (last accessed December 8, 2018).

Wagner, John. 2016. "Bernie Sanders, Elizabeth Warren Teaming Up Sunday to Pitch Clinton to Progressives." *Washington Post*, October 16. Retrieved from www.washingtonpost.com/news/post-politics/wp/2016/10/16/bernie-sanders-elizabeth-warren-teaming-up-sunday-to-pitch-clinton-to-progressives/ (last accessed December 8, 2018).

Wasserman, David. 2013. "Introducing the 2014 Cook Political Report Partisan Voter Index." *Cook Political Report*, April 4. Retrieved from http://cookpolitical.com/ house/pvi (last accessed December 8, 2018).

Weaver, R. Kent. 1989. "The Changing World of Think Tanks," *PS: Political Science and Politics* 22: 563–578.

Weir, Margaret. 1998. "Political Parties and Social Policymaking." In *The Social Divide: Political Parties and the Future of Activist Government*, edited by Margaret Weir, pp. 1–45. Washington: Brookings Institution Press.

Appendix 6A

DATA:

American National Election Studies, Time Series Cumulative Data File, 1948–2016.
Dave Leip's Atlas of US Presidential Elections, uselectionatlas.org.

PROCEDURE:

We include only respondents aged 25–64. Using the age variable (VCF0102), we drop all respondents younger than 25 (codes 0, 1) and older than 64 (codes 6, 7).

We recode the income variable (VCF0114) so that all respondents who are in the 0 to 33rd percentile of the income distribution displayed the same code (1, 2 to 1). We follow the same procedure for respondents in the 34th to 67th percentile (3 to 2) and in the 68th to 100th percentile (4, 5 to 3).

Battleground states are those with Partisan Voting Index (http://cookpoliti cal.com/house/pvi) whose absolute value is less than 5. Alaska and Hawaii in 1960 and 1964 and the District of Columbia in 1964 and 1968 are coded as non-battleground states.

For each year (VCF0004), for all three income groups, and for battleground and non-battlegrounds states, we plot the percentage of respondents who indicated that they were contacted by the Democratic Party (VCF9030b) and by the Republican Party (VCF9030c).

For 2012, we include the full sample (in-person and online). We employ sample weights (VCF0009z).

PART II

PROCEDURAL ANXIETIES

7

Does Regular Order Produce a More Deliberative Congress?

Evidence from the Annual Appropriations Process

Lee Drutman and Peter C. Hanson

> *"The House finds itself in a state of emergency. The institution does not function, does not deliberate, and seems incapable of acting on the will of the people. From the floor to the committee level, the integrity of the House has been compromised. The battle of ideas – the very lifeblood of the House – is virtually nonexistent."*
> Former Speaker John Boehner, September 30, 2010

It is common for scholars to observe that the quality of deliberation in Congress has deteriorated in recent years, and along with it, the institutional capacity of Congress to carry out its constitutional duties (Mann and Ornstein, 2006). In response, some scholars and practitioners have called for Congress to return to "regular order" (Mann and Ornstein, 2006, Green and Burns, 2010, Hanson, 2015). The call for regular order raises two questions. First, how do these calls fit with the scholarly understanding of how members pursue their legislative goals? Second, would debate on the floor under regular order constitute "deliberation" in the way its proponents have imagined? In the first section of this chapter, we define regular order and integrate it into existing scholarship on congressional organization. Second, we examine debate under open rules on House appropriations bills to assess deliberation under regular order.[1]

Our work is primarily descriptive. Most bills debated in the House in recent decades have been considered under closed rules that limit amending opportunities. Spending bills are the exception to this trend. They are commonly debated under open rules that permit amending by rank-and-file members of the minority and majority in accordance with the norm of regular order

---

[1] Chapter prepared for delivery at the 2017 Annual Meeting of the American Political Science Association, San Francisco, August 31–September 3. Earlier versions of this chapter were presented at the 2017 Annual Meeting of the Midwest Political Science Association and to the Anxieties of Democracy Working Group on Institutions, Princeton University.

(Hanson, 2016, Reynolds, 2016). This fact offers an opportunity to assess how debate unfolds on the floor in highly polarized conditions. We report the degree to which members of each party participate in debate, offer amendments, and succeed in winning passage of their amendments. We find ample evidence of bipartisan cooperation and consensus-building in appropriations. Members of the majority and minority routinely offer and win the adoption of amendments through one of two paths. Thirty-eight percent of amendments are decided with a voice vote. Most of those (83 percent) are adopted. Forty-two percent of amendments are regarded as more controversial and decided with a roll call vote. Most of these amendments (71 percent) are defeated, but of those that pass, 24 percent are supported by over half the members of both parties and another 35 percent are adopted primarily with the support of the minority party. Clearly, regular order gives minority party members the opportunity to present and win adoption of their policy proposals. On the negative side, our evidence shows that ideological extremists play an outsized role in debate. They offer more amendments than other members, and their amendments tend to win less support and face defeat more often than moderates. The paradox of regular order is that it simultaneously offers the opportunity for bipartisan deliberation over legislation while exposing the majority party to problems that may make its management of the floor more difficult.

   We begin by defining regular order and placing it in the context of theories of congressional organization. We present findings from two brief case studies to illustrate patterns in debate on appropriations bills. We then describe the quantitative data upon which this chapter is based, an original dataset of all amendments offered to appropriations bills in the House from 2005 to 2014. The chapter then reviews patterns in amending to appropriations bills. We examine the percentage of amendments offered by the majority and minority; whether or not amendments receive a vote; whether they are voted on by voice or roll call; whether they are adopted; patterns of support for amendments; and, the role of politically extreme members of the House in amending. We conclude by assessing calls for a return to regular order in the House.

THE CALL FOR REGULAR ORDER

A key duty of members of Congress is to manage the development and passage of legislation. Members have created various systems of rules, procedures, and institutions to meet this goal over time, updating them as needed to pursue their evolving interests (Binder, 1997, Schickler, 2001). Cox and McCubbins observe that power in the US House is centralized in some eras and decentralized in others (Cox and McCubbins, 2002). Speaker Thomas Reed famously built a coalition to adopt new rules to centralize power under the speaker at the turn of the twentieth century (Cox and McCubbins, 2005). In the mid-twentieth century, power was decentralized. Powerful committees dominated

Congress. Members shepherded bills along a carefully prescribed textbook path from committee consideration to the president's desk. In more recent decades, partisan polarization has created an incentive for members of the majority party to pursue partisan goals at the expense of broader collaboration with the minority party (Lee, 2009, Barber and McCarty, 2013, Lee, 2016). Members have collectively agreed to centralize power in majority party leadership, reduce the influence of once powerful committees, and more frequently adopt closed rules designed to prevent members of the minority from participating in lawmaking (Lee, 2015). Rather than following the textbook legislative path, members have been more likely to follow ad hoc procedures that vary so widely there can no longer be said to be a "normal" way of adopting legislation. In Sinclair's words, Congress now practices "unorthodox lawmaking" (Sinclair, 2012).

As it is used today, the term "regular order" appears to have developed in response to the shift toward unorthodox lawmaking. Regular order has a specific parliamentary meaning in certain contexts, but in practice the term is used to refer to a perceived set of norms about how legislation "should" be considered in Congress. It defines what is orthodox in a Congress characterized by unorthodox lawmaking. Mann and Ornstein describe regular order as the "process of going through multiple levels and channels of discussion, debate, negotiation, and compromise that make up a robust deliberative process" (p. 170). A former staff director of the House Rules Committee defined it as "those rules, precedents and customs of Congress that constitute an orderly and deliberative policymaking process" (Wolfensberger, 2013). Members emphasize the importance of deliberation in committee and open debate on the floor to regular order. A comment from Rep. Rick Nolan (MN-8), a Democrat in the minority, is typical: "The fact is we need to return to and restore regular order, where every bill brought to the floor of the House is required to be considered by committee, with open rules, where every amendment, every idea is debated, voted on, and fully considered."[2] Calls for regular order are frequently couched in language about the importance of respecting House traditions or the value of open debate and expertise. Steve King (R-IA), a conservative Republican often at odds with his party's leadership, is worth quoting in full because of the way he associates regular order with effective legislating:

There are 435 House districts and 100 Senators from the 50 States. The good ideas that come from our neighborhoods need to go into the eyes and ears of their Member of Congress, and we need to bring it here and bring those best ideas forward and compete. Put those ideas together in a competitive fashion so that as we sit down and first we draft a bill, that bill gets assigned to the committee of jurisdiction where the people have accumulated expertise on the topic are seated. There will be hearings for them to get better informed about the bill in question itself, and then in the subcommittee, a markup

---

[2] *Congressional Record*, September 9, 2014, H7305.

of the base bill that allows every member of the subcommittee to offer an amendment, any series of amendments, that are germane to the topic and the subject of the bill, which is assigned to the committee because of the jurisdiction of the committee, and then that subcommittee acts, in which case then the bill goes to the full committee for a similar process to the broader committee.

If it comes out of that committee improved in theory – and actually improved in practice most of the time – then that bill goes on the calendar here on the floor, where in which case it is subjected to the amendments that might come from all of the other Members, the Members that are on the committee of jurisdiction and the Members who are not on the committee of jurisdiction.

When this Congress is set up to function accurately, when we are defending, protecting, and respecting the jurisdiction of the various committees, we get the best product because we have the people on the committees that have – at least in theory – the most knowledge about the topic that comes before the committee. Some have years and years of expertise accumulated, some not quite as long, but they might bring that interest from their private life into the committee, as well.[3]

In this broad sense, "regular order" is an idealized vision of legislating based on the textbook Congress described by Sinclair. In practice, we interpret those who call for regular order to mean that they wish to see a return to a more routine, decentralized Congress: stronger, more independent committees developing and writing legislation, and a greater reliance on open rules during floor debates to allow all members the opportunity to offer amendments.

The scholarly case in favor of utilizing regular order more broadly is that it offers a superior way to deliberate over legislation than unorthodox methods of lawmaking. Regular order, by this line of argument, leads to better legislation because bills receive careful debate and scrutiny. This claim has not been tested systematically, but it has been made repeatedly by experienced observers of Congress. Green and Burns maintain that regular order "is necessary for the full and fair deliberation of issues" and that "ignoring regular order excludes many representatives from the legislative process, especially members of the minority, and risks enacting substandard legislation" (Green and Burns, 2010). Mann and Ornstein observe that the "suspension of regular order in Congress creates greater opportunities for parochial, special interest provisions to be added to legislation out of public view and for poorly constructed laws to get enacted without being properly vetted and corrected" (p. 217). Consistent with those claims, Hanson finds evidence that departing from regular order in the appropriations process reduces amending opportunities on the floor in the House and Senate (Hanson, 2015). Members have fewer opportunities to change legislation when regular order is not followed.

---

[3] *Congressional Record*, April 4, 2014, H2957.

REGULAR ORDER AND THE PURSUIT OF INDIVIDUAL INTEREST

Of course, the abstract desirability of any method of organizing Congress or managing legislation says little about whether Congress is likely to adopt it. The rational choice approach to the study of Congress assumes that members act strategically to advance interests such as the desire to win reelection. This approach treats observable features of Congress, including its organization, rules, and procedures, as the result of the combined efforts of 535 members independently pursuing their interests (Shepsle, 1992). The strategic decisions of members associating together in parties on questions such as how to manage legislation are similarly regarded as the result of members pursuing their individual interests. By this logic, the call for regular order is somewhat incongruous. Members likely utilize unorthodox methods of lawmaking because a sufficient number perceive it to be in their interest, and have concluded that following regular order is not.

Similarly, it is likely that calls from some members for regular order reflect a desire to redistribute power rather than a desire to improve deliberation. Arguments about procedure in Congress are arguments about power, and challenges to existing rules and procedures are commonplace as competing factions seek to maximize their influence. For example, disenfranchised liberals of the late 1960s and 1970s sought to wrest power away from southern committee chairs by attacking the seniority system (Rohde, 1991, Polsby, 2004). We interpret the current cry for "regular order" as the latest manifestation of this phenomenon – a demand to participate in lawmaking from members who are shut out of power so they can pursue their interests as they see fit.[4] Legislators making the demand are marginalized by the centralization of power in majority party leadership: idled committee chairs, majority party backbenchers, and members of the minority. They seek to shift power away from majority party leadership and create more opportunities for committees and rank-and-file members of both parties to influence legislative outcomes. For example, Republican members of the conservative Freedom Caucus, frustrated with their inability to advance their policy ideas, demanded that Speaker Paul Ryan agree to a more open legislative process prior to agreeing to give him their support as speaker (Reynolds, 2016).

As this discussion makes clear, calling for "regular order" is not simply a matter of reminding errant members to return to good legislative form and properly deliberate on legislation. We think it is unlikely that members place effective deliberation above other priorities that are more salient to them.

---

[4] See Debonis, Mike. 2015. "GOP Hard-Liners Seek More Power by Changing Rules. That Could Mean More Chaos." *Washington Post*, October 10. Retrieved from www.washingtonpost.com/politics/gop-hard-liners-seek-more-power-by-changing-rules-that-could-mean-more-chaos/2015/10/10/a54deaf2-6ec0-11e5-aa5b-f78a98956699_story.html?utm_term=.2d115bb6e5d7 (last accessed December 9, 2018).

Calling on leaders to adopt regular order is urging them to decentralize power in the chamber and shift legislative outcomes in ways that may be difficult to predict. A decision to allow more open rules, the focus of this chapter, would impact the core interests of members of the majority party, including their ability to shape policy and meet their electoral goals. Next, we review theories of congressional organization to assess in more detail how members of Congress make decisions about such issues.

The standard expectation of partisan theories of Congress is that members of the majority party have a powerful incentive to control the agenda when they are unified and ideologically distant from the minority, as they are today (Cox and McCubbins, 1993, Aldrich, 2011). They use their power over committees and floor debate to block consideration of legislation that might harm them and advance legislation that helps them meet policy or electoral goals. Special rules are a common tool to meet these goals. Under an open rule, members on the floor have the opportunity to amend a bill until it satisfies the median floor voter (Krehbiel, 1998). Bipartisan coalitions of support for amendments are more likely. Members of the majority party face the possibility that they will be unable to secure the adoption of their favored policies and increase the risk that they will be rolled by the minority party. Legislation adopted under closed rules is more likely to satisfy the typical member of the majority party in a highly polarized environment (Monroe and Robinson, 2008). Lee further demonstrates that close margins of control in the House in recent years have led members to prioritize opposing the other party and forcing votes that will cause their opponents political harm (Lee, 2016). Open debate in such conditions may expose legislation to delaying tactics, poison pill amendments, and political gamesmanship. Closed rules allow the majority party to suppress these tactics. Partisan theories of Congress offer little reason to believe that majority party members will have an incentive to follow regular order and adopt open rules as long as they are unified. Consistent with those expectations, power has been centralized in House leadership and most bills in the House are considered under closed rules that limit debate and amending opportunities (Drutman, 2015).

A second body of research finds members have a variety of interests, some of which are maximized through bipartisan cooperation. Members of Congress benefit from working together to solve major policy problems (Adler and Wilkerson, 2012). The chapter in this volume from Curry and Lee (Chapter 8) illustrates that the two parties continue to collaborate to pass major legislation despite high levels of polarization. Some policy domains may be conducive to bipartisan cooperation. According to the theory of distributive politics, members of both parties will cooperate to pass spending legislation in order to maximize the likelihood that they will receive benefits for their districts. Appropriations bills are generally debated in the House under an open rule (or no rule) on the floor (Reynolds, 2016). Previous research shows that there is a strong tradition of bipartisanship on appropriations because spending bills distribute funds to every district and benefit every member (Fenno, 1966,

White, 1989, Hanson, 2016). The benefits to members of the majority party from allowing open rules during times of high polarization are not well understood, in part because open rules are so rare. Research on appropriations bills shows that open rules create the possibility of productive debate and may ease the formation of a broad coalition of support (Hanson, 2016).

In short, past research suggests that the majority party's decision about how to manage legislation and the likelihood that open debate on the floor will be "deliberative" depends upon the particular bill in question and how all members perceive their interests relative to it. Should the majority opt for an open rule, it could face two possible outcomes. First, it could enable a vigorous debate over legislation, the consideration and passage of a variety of amendments from both parties, and increase the probability of bipartisan support for the final bill. Alternatively, it could expose itself to routine partisan squabbling that leads to delays and spurious, damaging amendments. Either outcome is likely to affect the reelection interests of members of the majority party. Open debate could shape policy outcomes in ways majority party members do not prefer or even find damaging. Alternatively, members may benefit by receiving credit for solving important policy problems even if the adopted policies represent a compromise. Open debate also carries the risk of exposing majority party members to minority party mischief and votes that could be used against them in a future campaign.

TWO VIGNETTES

We begin the empirical section of this chapter by describing the results of two brief case studies on the House appropriations process in 2005 and 2016 to provide a flavor for the kinds of debates we are analyzing and context for our quantitative findings. The debate over spending bills during these 2 years illustrates the costs and benefits of open rules for the majority party. They may help the majority party to build a winning coalition for a bill and provide opportunities for rank-and-file members to win passage of amendments important to them. They also expose the majority party to policy defeats by the minority and amendments designed to cause political harm rather than to advance a policy agenda.

2005

The 109th Congress (2005–2006) began as a moment of Republican ascendency in Washington. Republicans held control of both chambers of Congress and the presidency, and prepared a new push for conservative policies. "I earned capital in the campaign, political capital, and I intend to spend it," President George W. Bush stated after winning reelection.[5] It ended with the

---

[5] Stevenson, Richard. 2004. "Confident Bush Outlines Ambitious Plan for 2nd Term," *The New York Times*, November 5. Retrieved from www.nytimes.com/2004/11/05/politics/campaign/confident-bush-outlines-ambitious-plan-for-2nd-term.html (last accessed December 9, 2018).

party's reputation battered by a bungled response to Hurricane Katrina and the stage set for the Democrats to win control of the House and Senate in the 2006 midterm elections. The passage of appropriations bills in the House and Senate was notably smooth. The House of Representatives debated each of the dozen spending bills under an open rule that allowed the Democratic minority to freely propose amendments.[6] Democrats proposed 139 amendments to the bills, of which 54 (39 percent) were adopted. Republicans proposed 106 amendments to the bills, of which 43 (41 percent) were adopted. The spending bills were each adopted on an individual basis, avoiding the necessity of a catch-all omnibus spending bill. All won strong bipartisan support in the House with the exception of the routinely contentious Labor, Health and Human Services bill. Our review of *CQ Weekly*'s accounts of the debate on spending bills and the accompanying legislative record finds that it shows the costs and benefits of an open debate well.

We illustrate these findings using H.R. 3058, the Transportation, Treasury bill. Open debate contributed to the smooth passage of the bill, at least one significant policy defeat for the majority, and numerous opportunities for rank-and-file members of each party to advance their own agendas. The major area of controversy in the bill was the Bush administration's proposal to cut off public funding for the passenger rail service Amtrak, which was carried out in part by the House Appropriations Committee cutting Amtrak funding by 54 percent.[7] A Democratic attempt to restore funding in committee was defeated, but the issue came up again when the bill was brought to the House floor in late June. Taking advantage of the open rule, Republican Steven LaTourette (OH-14) and Democrat James Oberstar (MN-8) cosponsored an amendment (H. Amdt. 397) to restore Amtrak funding to $1.18 billion.[8] Opponents quickly concluded that the amendment would pass overwhelmingly, and sidestepped a strong showing by Amtrak supporters by allowing the amendment to pass by voice. A related amendment (H. Amdt. 401) offered by Democrat Corrine Brown (FL-3) struck additional legislative limitations on Amtrak from the bill, and was adopted with the support of 73 Republicans and 196 Democrats.[9] The action on Amtrak in the House was the first step in what later became a significant policy defeat for House leadership and the Bush administration on the bill. Following negotiations with

---

[6] The Legislative Branch bill was the exception. It is traditionally debated under a structured rule.

[7] Wolfe, Kathryn A. 2005. "House Panel Follows Authorizers' Lead on Transportation." *CQ Weekly* (June 27): 1751. Retrieved from http://library.cqpress.com/cqweekly/weeklyreport109–000001746773 (last accessed December 9, 2018)

[8] Wolfe, Kathryn A. 2005. "Amtrak Supporters Prevail in House." *CQ Weekly* (July 4): 1818–1819. Retrieved from http://library.cqpress.com/cqweekly/weeklyreport109–000001759933 (last accessed December 9, 2018).

[9] See House Roll Call Vote 336, June 29, 2005.

the Senate, the final version of the bill contained $1.3 billion for Amtrak. It was signed by the president.[10]

The remaining debate offered opportunities for legislative entrepreneurship by members on both sides of the aisle. A total of 12 amendments were adopted by roll call vote to the Transportation, Treasury bill, including nine Democratic amendments and three Republican amendments. Seven of the nine Democratic amendments were adopted with the support of less than half of the Republican conference. For example, Representative Chris Van Hollen (MD-8) won the adoption of an amendment (H. Amdt. 439) prohibiting the Bush administration from carrying out a rule allowing federal jobs to be contracted out to private companies with the support of 198 Democrats and 24 Republicans.[11] Republicans scored victories as well, winning passage of right-leaning amendments with the support of conservative Democrats. For example, Representative Mark Souder (IN-3) won adoption of an amendment (H. Amdt. 425) weakening the District of Columbia's gun control laws with the support of 209 Republicans and 50 Democrats.[12]

The successful passage of the Transportation, Treasury bill and hum of amending activity may help to explain why a House majority party would allow open rules at the cost of losing policy debates. Previous studies have shown that the norm of open rules in the House is maintained in part by the belief among members that open debate increases the support for appropriations bills by helping both parties to feel invested in the final product (Hanson, 2016). Our evidence does not prove that an open rule increased support for the Treasury, Transportation bill, but consistent with that account, it passed 405 to 18. The fate of the H.R. 3010, the Labor, Health and Human Services bill, later in the year demonstrates the danger to the majority party of attempting to pass a bill without seeking minority support. The bill initially passed the House after a debate under an open rule with a vote of 250 to 151. Fewer than 218 Republicans voted for the bill, and the winning margin came from 44 Democrats voting in favor.[13] Later that fall, the Democrats withheld their votes to protest spending cuts in the final version of the bill, and the majority party leaders could only summon 209 Republican votes in favor of it.[14] It was defeated, to their embarrassment, and passed a month later only after funding important to Republican defectors was restored.[15] The lesson is clear: when margins between

---

[10] Wolfe, Kathryn A. 2005. "Spending Bill Carries a Twist for Amtrak." *CQ Weekly* (November 21): 3135. Retrieved from http://library.cqpress.com/cqweekly/weeklyreport109–000001975293 (last accessed December 9, 2018).

[11] See House Roll Call Vote 357, June 30, 2005.

[12] See House Roll Call Vote 349, June 30, 2005.

[13] See House Roll Call Vote 321, June 24, 2005.

[14] See House Roll Call Vote 598, November 17, 2005.

[15] Swindell, Bill. 2005. "Labor-HHS Bill Survives Late Protest." *CQ Weekly* (December 26): 3391–3392. Retrieved from http://library.cqpress.com/cqweekly/weeklyreport109–000002018226 (last accessed December 9, 2018).

the parties are close, a few majority party defectors can doom a bill if the minority party is unified.

Evidence from the case study also indicates that open rules are valuable to rank-and-file members because they create the opportunity for members to be legislative entrepreneurs. Members receive the opportunity to offer amendments and build cross-party coalitions of support. No Republican amendment adopted by roll call vote to any of the 2005 appropriations bills in the House had sufficient support from the majority party alone to win adoption. The average majority party vote in favor of the 10 Republican amendments adopted by roll call vote was 181, with an average of 81 additional votes coming from the minority. Legislating on appropriations bills is a two-way street. Members of the minority may win some policy debates by attracting support from members of the majority, but majority party members also benefit from help from the minority.

2016

During the 114th Congress (2015–2016), power in government was split between Democratic president Barack Obama and a Republican Congress. House Republicans faced serious divisions in their ranks. Far-right members of the Freedom Caucus favored tactics such as government shutdowns to compel policy changes from President Obama that more moderate members believed would harm the party. Pressure from conservative lawmakers to force a shutdown ultimately persuaded Speaker John Boehner to resign the Speakership in the fall of 2015 and led to the election of Paul Ryan as his successor. Boehner's decision sidestepped the risk of an immediate shutdown, but did little to change the underlying dynamic. Ryan continued to face challenges governing the restive Republican caucus for the remainder of the 114th Congress.

An incident from the summer of 2016 illustrates the challenge facing the majority party when it adopts open rules for debate on appropriations bills. The skirmish began in reaction to an Executive Order signed by President Obama that prohibited discrimination on the basis of sexual orientation or gender identity by the federal government or its contractors.[16] Republicans adopted an amendment to the National Defense Authorization Act to provide a religious exemption to the order. In response, Democrat Patrick Maloney (NY-18) offered an amendment (H. Amdt. 1079) to the separate Military Construction and Veterans Affairs bill (H.R. 4974) requiring federal agencies to follow the order. The amendment initially appeared to pass, but was narrowly defeated 212 to 213 when Republican leaders held the vote open to persuade Republican members to change their vote.[17] The underlying bill

---

[16] "Exec. Order No. 13672." *Harvard Law Review*, February 10, 2015. Retrieved from http://harvardlawreview.org/2015/02/exec-order-no-13672/(last accessed December 9, 2018).

[17] See House Roll Call Vote 226, May 19, 2016.

passed later that day, but angry Democrats offered an identical amendment (H. Amdt. 1128) to the Energy and Water appropriations bill (H.R. 5055).[18] This time they scored a narrow win.[19] Support began to unravel for the Energy and Water bill, and to the surprise of leaders it was defeated 112 to 305.[20] Speaker Paul Ryan blamed Democrats for the chaos, stating, "The Democrats were not looking to advance an issue. They were looking to sabotage the appropriations process."[21]

The uncertainty of open rules ultimately proved to be too much for Ryan. Republicans overrode Democratic protests and adopted rules limiting amendments for the remaining four regular appropriations bills debated on the floor. The debate over the rule on first of those bills, Defense, revealed the central divide between the majority and minority. Republicans accused Democrats of abusing of open rules by seeking to score political points rather than legislating: "I know some of my colleagues are going to express concerns about procedure and the fact that this is a structured rule," observed Rules Committee member Bradley Byrne (AL-1). "Well, regular order means that the House works. Regular order doesn't mean chaos. Regular order doesn't mean that Members get to offer poison pill amendments just to kill a bill."[22] Democrats countered by accusing Republicans of unfairly shutting down debate in order to avoid painful votes. Democratic Whip Steny Hoyer (MD-5) responded: "As soon as it became clear … that House Republicans might have to take an up-or-down vote again on whether to ban discrimination against LGBT Americans, they shut the open process down."[23]

Discussion

A key lesson from the appropriations debates of 2005 and 2016 is that open rules create an unpredictable legislative environment for the majority party with costs and benefits that may be hard to anticipate in advance. The majority party has frequently followed the historic path of permitting open amendments based in part on a strategic assessment that giving all members the opportunity to amend the bills in combination with their distributive content would help

---

[18] Berman, Russell. 2016. "The Humbling of Paul Ryan: A Gay-Rights Amendment Takes Down a House Appropriations Bill, and With It Might Go the Speaker's Grand Plan to Revive the Congressional Spending Process." *The Atlantic*, May 26. Retrieved from www.theatlantic.com/politics/archive/2016/05/the-humbling-of-paul-ryan/484529/ (last accessed December 9, 2018).

[19] See House Roll Call Vote 258, May 25, 2016.

[20] See House Roll Call Vote 266, May 26, 2016.

[21] Fox, Lauren. 2016. "Ryan Pledges to Keep Regular Order After Floor Meltdown Over LGBT Provision," *Talking Points Memo*, May 26. Retrieved from http://talkingpointsmemo.com/livewire/ryan-just-saw-why-open-amendments-process-is-harder-than-it-looks (last accessed December 9, 2018).

[22] *Congressional Record*, June 15, 2016, H3837.

[23] *Congressional Record*, June 15, 2016, H3839.

to build a bipartisan coalition of support. That strategy was successful in 2005, when House members had a constructive debate on the Transportation, Treasury bill and passed it with a strong bipartisan vote. In 2016, open debate arguably destabilized the appropriations process. The LGBT amendment had both substantive and political value to Democrats. It advanced policy goals party members cared about, but it also threatened political harm to Republicans. Its passage undermined the coalition of support for the Energy and Water bill, ultimately leading to its defeat.

AMENDMENTS TO APPROPRIATIONS BILLS

We turn next to a longitudinal study of amending on appropriations bills. Responding to reformers calling for regular order requires scholars to consider a hypothetical: what likely outcomes would the majority party face today if it routinely followed regular order? In recent years, there has been little variation in the House that might help scholars answer that question. The House is in the midst of a period of high polarization and rarely brings legislation to the floor under open rules. We answer it by analyzing amending patterns on appropriations bills, which remain one of the few kinds of legislation routinely considered under open rules as the House has grown more polarized. We examine whether both parties succeed in offering and adopting amendments; voting patterns on amendments; and, amending activity ideological extremists in the chamber. Our findings are provocative, but they come with a caveat. We find evidence of productive debate and member mischief in our quantitative data, but we are unable to evaluate the extent to which they each characterize debate on appropriations bills. Nonetheless, they are broadly supportive of the fact that open debate on the floor creates both opportunity and risk for the majority party.

The data for this study come from an original dataset tracking all amending activity on regular appropriations bills between 2005 to 2014. We define a regular appropriations bill as those produced on an annual basis by the standing subcommittees of the House Committee on Appropriations, for example, the FY2005 Department of Agriculture Appropriations bill. There were 11 subcommittees in 2005 and 2006, and 12 thereafter. We do not include supplemental appropriations bills, omnibus appropriations bills, or continuing resolutions in our dataset. We reviewed the legislative history on Congress. gov of every bill that was reported from committee and received consideration on the House floor, and coded every amendment listed in that bill's legislative history to track whether it received a roll call or voice vote, whether it was adopted, and the level of support from each party if it received a roll call vote. Finally, we coded the type of rule under which the bill was considered. The dataset tracks legislative activity on a total of 2,512 amendments to 79 regular appropriations bills.

Our choice to focus only on regular appropriations bills offers some important advantages. The most important is consistency. The House aims to write and adopt the same set of appropriations bills every year. We take advantage of this fact to build a dataset in which comparisons over time can be made using a consistent set of bills. Relying on regular appropriations bills also imposes some limits on our analysis. First, while the House generally adheres to regular order in the initial stages of the appropriations process, there is some variation in whether each appropriations bill is debated on the floor every year under an open rule. Our analysis only describes amending activity on the set of bills that received individual floor debate under an open (or modified open) rule and not on those that only came to the floor in the context of an omnibus package or continuing resolution. A total of 79 regular appropriations bills were debated on the House floor between 2005 and 2014, while 39 were considered only as part of a package. Of the 79 bills that were debated, 58 were considered under open rules and 21 were considered under structured rules that required all amendments debated on the floor to be preapproved by the Rules Committee. Despite the apparently large proportion of bills considered under structured rules, we consider open rules to be the norm. All but two of the bills considered under a structured rule are accounted for by the 111th Congress (2009–2010), when the Democratic majority broke from the norm of adopting open rules for appropriations bills, and by the fact that the Legislative Branch appropriations bill is typically considered under a structured rule to avoid amendments on congressional pay. Table 7.1 shows the number of bills debated on the floor and the number of each type of rule adopted for each year in the dataset. Additionally, we only track appropriations bills through their initial passage on the House floor, and not through their negotiation with the Senate and final passage. Our data do not indicate whether the amendments adopted on the House floor were enacted in the final legislation.

TABLE 7.1 *Consideration of Annual Appropriations Bills, 2005–2014.*

Year	Open Rule	Structured Rule	Not Debated
2005	10	1	0
2006	9	1	1
2007	11	1	0
2008	1	0	11
2009	1	11	0
2010	0	2	10
2011	6	1	5
2012	8	1	3
2013	5	1	6
2014	7	2	3
Total	58	21	39

Our data are subject to at least three types of selection effects. First, there is a long-standing norm of nonpartisanship in appropriations that has endured even as the overall level of partisanship in the House has increased (Hanson, 2016). Second, within the population of appropriations bills, our dataset only includes those that were debated and presumably enjoyed more support in the chamber than those that were not. For example, the routinely controversial Labor, Health and Human Services Appropriations bill was not debated in 7 of the 10 years under study, while the less controversial Military Construction, Veterans Administration bill was debated every year. Finally, we analyze bills considered under open rules rather than those for which the Rules Committee selected amendments for debate. Our analysis accordingly captures amending activity in a legislative domain conducive to bipartisan cooperation, on a more popular set of bills within that domain, and on those debated under open rules. Despite these limits, the bills covered in the dataset meet our basic goal of providing a window into amending activity under open rules in a highly polarized House.

A DELIBERATIVE PROCESS?

Those who call for a return to regular order emphasize the need for all members to have the opportunity to participate in lawmaking through the opportunity to offer and debate amendments on the House floor. In this section, we evaluate how the majority and minority contribute to the *inputs* and *outputs* of the annual appropriations process through debate on the floor. By inputs, we mean members proposing ideas and seeking to shape policy on appropriations bills by offering amendments. By outputs, we mean members winning the adoption of their amendments and shaping the final version of the bill as passed on the floor. Our data do not allow us to characterize the nature of much of this legislative activity. We cannot state whether members are engaged in genuine policy debates or partisan gamesmanship. Instead, we describe the extent to which members of both parties are involved in the legislative process. We find that a substantial portion of members of both parties offer amendments to appropriations bills, that most these amendments are brought to a vote, and that amendments from both sides are adopted.

We turn first to the ability of both parties to offer amendments. The data show that substantial proportions of majority and minority party members offered amendments to appropriations bills during a Congress, consistent with the norm of open rules (Table 7.2). During the period under study, 41 percent of minority party members offered at least one amendment to an appropriations bill during a Congress, while 31 percent of majority party members offered at least one amendment. There is variation in the degree to which members of each side offer amendments over time, and in the total number of amendments offered during a Congress. In the 109th Congress (2005–2006) through the 111th Congress (2009–2010), a larger proportion of minority

TABLE 7.2 *Majority and Minority Members Offering Amendments.*

Congress	Proportion of Minority Offering Amendments	Proportion of Majority Offering Amendments	Total Minority Amendments	Total Majority Amendments	Minority Share of Amendments Offered	Party of Majority
109	0.49	0.36	295	260	0.53	R
110	0.52	0.24	375	106	0.78	D
111	0.09	0.03	24	7	0.77	D
112	0.45	0.46	243	389	0.38	R
113	0.43	0.46	265	301	0.47	R
Overall Average / Total	0.41	0.31	1202	1063	0.53	

TABLE 7.3 *Disposition of Amendments For Majority and Minority.*

Congress	Minority Roll Call	Minority Voice	Minority Not Voted	Majority Roll Call	Majority Voice	Majority Not Voted
109	113	92	90	91	108	61
	38.31	31.19	30.51	35.00	41.54	23.46
110	211	103	61	22	51	33
	56.27	27.47	16.27	20.75	48.11	31.13
111	22	1	1	7	0	0
	91.67	4.17	4.17	100.00	0.00	0.00
112	114	69	60	202	147	40
	46.91	28.40	24.69	51.93	37.79	10.28
113	76	135	54	102	161	38
	28.68	50.94	20.38	33.89	53.49	12.62
Total	536	400	266	424	467	172
Overall Average	44.59	33.28	22.13	39.89	43.93	16.18

party members offered amendments than of the majority party. That relationship reverses in the 112th Congress (2011–2012) and the 113th Congress (2013–2014), when a larger proportion of majority party members offered amendments. Similar patterns are visible in the total number of amendments offered during a Congress. Minority party members offered 53 percent of all amendments introduced during the time period.

Members must be able to bring their amendments to a vote to have a chance to influence policy on the House floor. Members voted on most amendments that were offered to appropriations bills during the period under study (Table 7.3). Forty-two percent (960) of amendments were brought to a roll call vote, 38 percent (867) to a voice vote, and 19 percent (438) were not voted upon. Figures for each party roughly match these proportions. Forty-five percent (536) of minority party sponsored amendments went on to a roll call vote, 33 percent (400) to a voice vote, and 22 percent (266) were not voted upon. Majority party amendments were disposed of with roll call votes in 40 percent (424) of cases, voice votes in 44 percent (467), and without a vote in 16 percent (172). There is substantial variation in the proportion of amendments falling into each category over the period of study. The proportion of minority amendments receiving a roll call vote ranges from 29 percent to 92 percent, voice votes from 4 percent to 51 percent, and without a vote from 4 percent to 31 percent. The comparable statistics for the majority are 21 percent to 100 percent, 0 percent to 53 percent, and 0 percent to 31 percent, respectively.

Both parties also have success winning approval of their amendments. Figure 7.1 illustrates the number of amendments sponsored by each party that were offered, voted on, and adopted in the five congresses under study. Across the full time period, 36 percent (428) of amendments offered by the minority

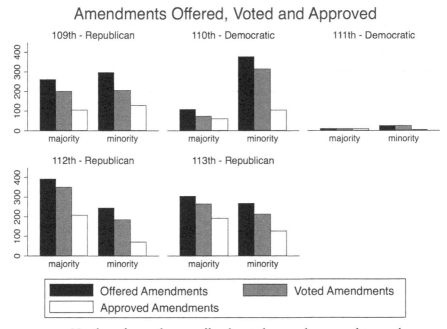

FIGURE 7.1 **Number of amendments offered, voted on, and approved to regular appropriations bills by minority and majority.**

were adopted and 53 percent (568) of amendments offered by the majority were adopted. While the minority party has a lower rate of approval for its amendments, its share of amendments that are passed is substantial. Minority party amendments constituted 43 percent (428) of adopted amendments, and majority party amendments constituted 57 percent (568).

These findings demonstrate that both parties contribute substantially to the inputs and outputs of the House appropriations process. The majority and minority both offer substantial numbers of amendments and most of those amendments receive a vote. The data also show that both parties win adoption of their amendments and that amendments from the minority constitute a significant proportion of those adopted by the full House. Next, we turn to an analysis of support patterns for amendments. Evaluating support for amendments is important for two reasons. First, it allows us to assess the degree to which all members can influence legislative outcomes. Second, it provides some leverage to characterize the nature of the amending activity by assessing the degree to which amendments provoke partisan debate or bipartisan agreement.

Voice Votes

We begin by analyzing amendments approved by voice votes in which no member's individual position is recorded. Voice votes are generally utilized

TABLE 7.4 *Amendments Considered and Adopted by Type of Vote.*

	Minority		Majority	
Congress	Roll Call (# Voted and prop. Adopted)	Voice (# Voted and prop. Adopted)	Roll Call (# Voted and prop. Adopted)	Voice (# Voted and prop. Adopted)
109	113	92	91	108
	0.40	0.89	0.25	0.76
110	211	103	22	51
	0.16	0.68	0.50	0.98
111	22	1	7	
	0.05	1.00	1.00	
112	114	69	202	147
	0.15	0.75	0.40	0.84
113	76	135	102	161
	0.17	0.84	0.41	0.92
Total	536	400	424	467
Average	0.21	0.80	0.39	0.87

for noncontroversial amendments with broad support in the chamber.[24] Thirty-eight percent (867) of amendments introduced between 2005 and 2014 were disposed of by voice vote, and 83 percent (722) of those amendments were approved. Minority and majority party amendments are both disposed of by voice vote, and both parties routinely win adoption of their amendments (Table 7.4). Members of the minority party offered 400 amendments that were considered by voice vote, and 80 percent (318) of those amendments were adopted. Majority party members offered 467 amendments that were considered by voice vote, and 87 percent (404) of these amendments were adopted. There is variation in the number of amendments considered and the rate of adoption over time. The minority party's rate of adoption ranged from a low of 67 percent in the 110th Congress to a high of 100 percent in the 111th. The majority party's rate of adoption ranged from a low of 76 percent in the 109th Congress to a high of 98 percent in the 110th.

---

[24] There are anecdotal cases of controversial amendments being accepted by voice vote because committee members do not wish to put the full House on record with a roll call vote. Committee members believe this tactic makes it easier to drop an amendment in later stages of the legislative process. Our data do not reveal the extent of this practice, but there is little evidence that characterizes most voice vote activity.

These findings strike us as important. Amendments adopted by voice vote constitute a significant portion of the amending activity on appropriations bills. Members of both parties cooperated to adopt 722 amendments to appropriations bills in the 10 years under study. These amendments may be regarded as minor on an individual basis, but taken as a whole they constitute a significant way for members on the floor to adjust the contents of legislation. They are also an example of routine bipartisan cooperation in a chamber characterized by extreme partisanship. We have a limited ability to characterize the amending activity in this study, but these amendments appear to fit easily into the category of routine and productive deliberation on legislation.

Roll Call Votes

Roll call votes are used to dispose of amendments that are regarded as controversial among members. Forty-two percent (960) of amendments offered to appropriations bills between 2005 and 2014 were decided with roll call votes. Adoption rates for amendments considered by roll call votes are much lower than for those considered by voice. Twenty-one percent (110) of minority party amendments and 39 percent (164) of majority party amendments considered by roll call vote were adopted. Table 7.4 shows that there is variation over time in the approval rates for the majority and minority. The minority party won approval for just 5 percent of its amendments in the 111th Congress, and reached of a high of a 40 percent approval rate in the 109th Congress. The majority party ranged from a low of 25 percent in the 109th Congress to 100 percent in the 111th.

Roll call votes offer a useful source of data about conflict and cooperation in the House because the position of every member is recorded. We placed each amendment into one of four categories (Figure 7.2) by plotting each amendment on a scatterplot according to the proportion of each party voting "yes" on the amendment. The categories are:

(1) Minority Dominant: over 50 percent of minority supports, under 50 percent of majority supports (upper left)
(2) Mutual Support: over 50 percent of each party supports (upper right)
(3) Mutual Opposition: over 50 percent of each party opposes (lower left)
(4) Majority Dominant: over 50 percent of majority supports, under 50 percent of minority supports (lower right)

These categories offer a convenient way to ascertain the degree of bipartisan cooperation or conflict in the chamber. Majorities in both parties might agree that an amendment is a bad idea (Mutual Opposition) or that it is a good idea (Mutual Support). The categories of Minority Dominant and Majority Dominant represent more typical partisan conflict in which an amendment leads most of one party to vote against most of another.

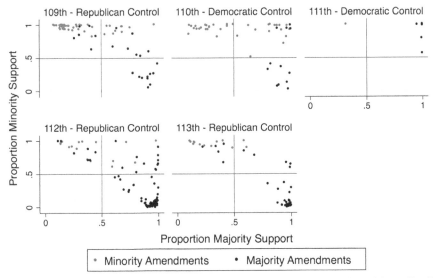

FIGURE 7.2 **Majority and minority party support for amendments adopted by roll call vote.**

The minority party accounts for a substantial portion of amendments that are adopted by the House through a roll call vote. Minority members sponsored 40 percent (110) of amendments adopted by roll call vote, while majority members sponsored 60 percent (165). Adopted amendments include those with support predominantly from one party and those with support from both parties. Figure 7.2 plots support from both parties for adopted amendments in each Congress under studied. It shows substantial evidence of members building cross-party coalitions. Of the 110 adopted amendments sponsored by the minority party, 71 percent (78) fell in the Minority Dominant category. Each of these cases represents an instance of the minority party rolling the majority by peeling off enough members of the majority party to win the vote. Twenty-nine percent (32) of minority party amendments were adopted with the support of over half the members of both parties. Of the 165 amendments sponsored by majority party members, 67 percent (111) fell in the Majority Dominant category and 21 percent (35) into Mutual Support. Interestingly, 11 percent (18) of majority amendments fell into the Minority Dominant category. These cases represent rolls of the majority party by a member of the majority party allying with members of the minority. It is noteworthy that cases falling into the Minority Dominant category are concentrated in the 109th and 110th Congresses, while cases falling into the Majority Dominant category are concentrated in the 112th and 113th Congresses. Minority party rolls have

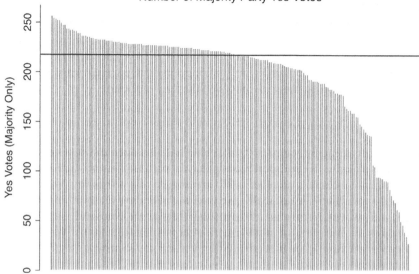

FIGURE 7.3 Number of "yes" votes from majority party for successful majority party amendments.

become less common over time, and majority party dominant votes have become more common.

The frequency of bipartisan coalitions supporting successful amendments may help to explain why regular order remains common on appropriations bills despite the potential for problems it causes for the majority party (Figure 7.3). Of the 165 majority party amendments adopted by roll call vote, only half had sufficient support from majority party members to be adopted without support from the minority. The success of majority party legislative efforts hinges not only on the opportunity to offer their amendments, but by winning the support of at least some members of the minority.

In summary, both parties have a significant role shaping the inputs and outputs of the annual appropriations process in the House of Representatives. Most of their legislative activity takes the form of offering and passing relatively noncontroversial amendments by voice vote – a finding we regard as a sign of healthy deliberation over the legislation. Both parties also offer amendments that win bipartisan support or that attract bipartisan opposition in roll call votes. The minority party's role is significant. It typically proposes hundreds of amendments during a Congress, most of the amendments it proposes are voted on, and many are passed. The importance of its role is evident from the composition of the pool of amendments that are adopted. The minority party sponsored 428, or 43 percent, of the 996 amendments adopted to appropriations bills by the House in the 10-year period under study. Seventy-four percent of the minority party's adopted amendments were passed by voice vote, 7 percent were adopted in a roll call vote with the support of both parties, and 18 percent were minority party rolls in which most members of the minority voted for an amendment and most members of the majority voted against it. The House appropriations process allows the minority party to participate in lawmaking and win the adoption of its amendments, sometimes over the opposition of most members of the majority party.

THE ROLE OF EXTREMISTS

Open rules may facilitate productive debate but also open the door to problems that make effective deliberation more difficult, such as dilatory tactics or efforts to politically embarrass members. We investigate this possibility by evaluating the extent to which ideologically extreme members are likely to offer amendments, and whether there is a relationship between ideological extremity and the degree of support an amendment receives on the floor. We find that ideologically extreme members of both parties are somewhat more likely to offer amendments, and that their amendments receive less support and are less likely to pass than those of ideological moderates. Absent further study, we cannot further characterize this amending activity, but it appears clear that the ideological extremists play an outsized role in open debate.

We turn first to the question of whether members who offer amendments are more ideologically extreme than those who do not. We measure the ideology of members of Congress using Poole and Rosenthal's DW-Nominate scale in which −1 is most liberal and 1 is most conservative. The data show that Democrats and Republicans who offer amendments on average are more ideologically extreme than those who do not. The mean DW-Nominate of a Democrat who offers an amendment is −0.38 compared to −0.35 of a Democrat who does not. Similarly, the mean DW-Nominate of a Republican who offers an amendment is 0.69 compared to 0.66 for Republicans who do not. That finding is generally consistent in each Congress under study with the exception of the 113th, when there is no difference between the Democrats.

We next turn to the question of whether extreme members offer more amendments than moderate members. The data in this case are highly skewed. Most members offer only 1 or 2 amendments, but a handful offer 10, 20, 30, or even 60 amendments during a Congress. We logged the total number of amendments offered by each member during each Congress under study and plotted the relationship of the resulting variable with the first dimension DW-Nominate score of each member (Figure 7.4). The pattern on the Republican side is not linear, but it demonstrates that far-right members are likely to offer large numbers of amendments. The pattern on the Democratic side is less distinct. The most extreme Democrats are likely to offer the most number of amendments in some Congresses but not in others. The Pearson's correlation

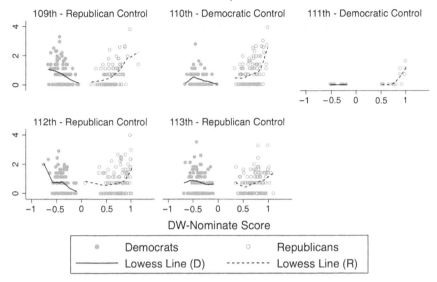

FIGURE 7.4 Relationship between ideological extremity measured by first dimension DW-Nominate score and number of amendments offered.

coefficient is stronger for Republicans than Democrats. The DW-Nominate score for Republican members is correlated with the number of amendments offered by a member at a magnitude of 0.32, compared to –0.22 for Democrats.

Do amendments offered by extreme members find support in the chamber? We estimated a series of regression models estimating whether or not the ideological extremity of an amendment sponsor reduced the proportion of votes the measure received in the chamber, the support it received from members of the sponsor's party, and its likelihood of passage. We do not report the full results from these models here. The results indicated that ideologically extreme Republicans were more likely, at statistically significant levels, to offer amendments that received little support in the chamber and, perhaps more importantly, among members of their own party. Amendments from extreme Republicans also were more likely to be defeated at statistically significant levels. The coefficients for Democrats were similar, but not always statistically significant. Pearson's correlation coefficients are consistent with the regression results. For example, a Republican sponsor's DW-Nominate score is negatively correlated with same party support at –0.29, compared to far weaker 0.12 for Democrats. We cannot more definitively characterize these findings absent additional analysis, but they are consistent with reports that amending activity from ideological extremists consumes substantial floor time without substantively contributing to the contents of appropriations bills.

CONCLUSION

Scholars who favor restoring regular order in Congress seek to improve deliberation by strengthening committees and bringing more legislation to the floor under open rules. This chapter offers evidence how such reform might play out in practice by analyzing the consideration of appropriations bills under open rules. We find that debate under regular order on appropriations bills is at times an island of productive lawmaking in which members of both parties have the opportunity to offer amendments, secure votes on them, and win passage. We see evidence of bipartisan cooperation to adjust legislation in the large number of amendments adopted by voice votes, and more substantial bipartisan policy changes in the passage of amendments through roll call votes with support from both parties. But, regular order is a doubled-edged sword. Regular order permits the minority party to offer amendments that may roll the majority party and potentially damage its reelection interests. It also permits more extreme members of the House to play an outsized role in debate. They offer more amendments than other members. These amendments generally win less support and are less likely to pass than those of more moderate members. The fundamental dilemma posed by regular order to party leaders is that it creates the potential for both more deliberative lawmaking and for mischief that could delay the passage of appropriations bills, cause members political harm, or undermine the interests of the majority.

While this finding is encouraging in many respects, appropriations bills have historically generated bipartisan support because most members see benefit in them and regard them as "must pass" legislation. Members may be more likely to see value in productive debate on appropriations bills than they are in other categories of legislation. Additionally, the case studies presented in this chapter show that open debate on appropriations bills occasionally contributes to the failure of a bill. This finding is important because it calls into question the central premise of reformers who seek to expand the use of regular order: that open debate will improve legislation by subjecting it to greater scrutiny and perfecting amendments. High levels of polarization combined with close margins of control may instead create a Tragedy of the Commons on the House floor in which members undermine legislation that will benefit the common good in their pursuit of individual interests. Consistent with that argument, Sinclair observes that unorthodox legislative practices arose in part due to the difficulty of conducting legislative business under regular order. Unorthodox legislative practices that allow leaders and committee experts to write legislation behind closed doors and push it through the floor with minimal change may fit scholars' expectations of a "deliberative" process better than allowing bills to become partisan piñatas on the floor. Future research should aim to test the hypothesis that open debate is consistent with ideals of effective deliberation and leads to "better" legislation than unorthodox methods.

Finally, we note that our data collection ended in 2014 prior to the beginning of Donald Trump's presidential administration. Not enough time has yet passed to assess whether the appropriations process has undergone any long-term changes that might alter the findings of this paper. It is noteworthy that the House of Representatives did not debate or adopt any of the regular appropriations bills in 2017 prior to adopting an omnibus appropriations bill in the fall of that year. The failure to debate the regular appropriations bills was unusual, but not unprecedented, in the House. Members debated that omnibus bill (H.R. 3354) under a structured rule under which amendments for both parties were allowed, but it was not taken up by the Senate. Instead, congressional leaders negotiated a 2-year bipartisan budget agreement that raised spending limits and paved the way for the adoption of a bipartisan $1.3 trillion omnibus spending bill in March of 2018. In theory, this budget agreement should stabilize appropriations while it is in effect. The coming years will be a good indication of whether past patterns in appropriations will endure or a new pattern will emerge.

REFERENCES

Adler, E. S., and J. D. Wilkerson. 2012. *Congress and the Politics of Problem Solving.* New York: Cambridge University Press.

Aldrich, J. 2011. *Why Parties? A Second Look.* Chicago: The University of Chicago Press.

Barber, M., and N. McCarty. 2013. Causes and Consequences of Polarization. In J. Mansbridge and C. J. Martin (eds.), *Negotiating Agreement in Politics*. Washington, DC: American Political Science Association.

Binder, S. 1997. *Minority Rights, Majority Rule.* New York: Cambridge University Press.

Cox, G., and M. McCubbins. 1993. *Legislative Leviathan: Party Government in the House.* Berkeley and Los Angeles: University of California Press.

Cox, G., and M. McCubbins. 2002. Agenda Power in the U.S. House of Representatives, 1877–1986. In D. Brady and M. McCubbins (eds.), *Party, Process, and Political Change in Congress: New Perspectives on the History of Congress.* Stanford: Stanford University Press.

2005. *Setting the Agenda: Responsible Party Government in the U.S. House of Representatives.* New York: Cambridge University Press.

Drutman, Lee. 2015. "The House Freedom Caucus Has Some Good Ideas on How the US House Should Operate." Retrieved from www.vox.com/polyarchy/2015/10/20/9570747/house-freedom-caucus-process-demands (last accessed October 17, 2016).

Fenno, R. 1966. *The Power of the Purse: Appropriations Politics in Congress.* Boston: Little Brown.

Green, M., and D. Burns. 2010. "What Might Bring Regular Order Back to the House?" *PS: Political Science and Politics* 43(2): 223–226.

Hanson, P. 2015. Restoring the Regular Order in Congressional Appropriations, *National Budgeting Roundtable.*

Hanson, P. C. 2016. The Endurance of Nonpartisanship in House Appropriations. In L. Dodd and B. Oppenheimer (eds.), *Congress Reconsidered*. Washington, DC: CQ Press.

Krehbiel, K. 1998. *Pivotal Politics: A Theory of U.S. Lawmaking*. Chicago: University of Chicago Press.

Lee, F. 2009. *Beyond Ideology: Politics, Principles, and Partisanship in the U.S. Senate*. Chicago: University of Chicago Press.

2015. "How Party Polarization Affects Governance." *Annual Review of Political Science 18*: 261–282.

2016. *Insecure Majorities: Congress and the Perpetual Campaign*. Chicago: The University of Chicago Press.

Mann, T., and N. Ornstein. 2006. *The Broken Branch: How Congress Is Failing America and How to Get It Back on Track*. New York: Oxford University Press.

Monroe, N. W. and G. Robinson. 2008. "Do Restrictive Rules Produce Nonmedian Outcomes? A Theory with Evidence from the 101st–108th Congress." *The Journal of Politics 70*(1).

Polsby, N. 2004. *How Congress Evolves: Social Bases of Institutional Change*. New York: Oxford University Press.

Reynolds, M. 2016. "Fights Loom Over Appropriations in the House and Senate." *New Republic,* January 3.

Rohde, D. W. 1991. *Parties and Leaders in the Postreform House*. Chicago: University of Chicago Press.

Schickler, E. 2001. *Disjointed Pluralism: Institutional Innovation and the Development of the U.S. Congress*. Princeton: Princeton University Press.

Shepsle, K. 1992. "Congress Is a "They," Not an "It": Legislative Intent as an Oxymoron." *International Review of Law and Economics 12*: 239–256.

Sinclair, B. 2012. *Unorthodox Lawmaking: New Legislative Processes in the U.S. Congress*. Washington, DC: CQ Press.

White, J. 1989. *The Functions and Power of the House Appropriations Committee*. Berkeley: University of California.

Wolfensberger, D. R. 2013. "Regular Order Is a Political Rorschach." *Roll Call.*

8

Congress at Work

Legislative Capacity and Entrepreneurship in the Contemporary Congress

James M. Curry and Frances E. Lee

> "Just as there are various ways to skin a cat, so there are various ways to make a law."
>
> Alan Rosenthal (2004, pp. 238–239)

Scholars and observers are increasingly concerned that Congress is losing its capacity to perform its functions in the American political system.[1] The contemporary Congress has been widely termed "broken" and "dysfunctional" (Mann and Ornstein, 2006, 2012, Hamilton, 2008, Smith, 2014), and public esteem for Congress has dramatically declined (Ramirez, 2009, Gerrity, 2014). Part of the blame for this state of affairs has been laid at the feet of the erosion of established legislative processes and norms (Thurber, 2011, Crespin and Madonna, 2016, Drutman, 2016, Lewallen, Theriault, and Jones, 2016). This view stems in part from widespread agreement that the decentralized, committee-driven legislative processes of the mid-twentieth century, often referred to as "regular order" processes, are superior to the more centralized, ad hoc, and "unorthodox" processes that characterize the contemporary Congress.

In this paper, we take stock of how changes to internal processes have affected Congress's institutional capacities. We make two interrelated arguments. First, we argue that Congress can take what Polsby (1975) calls "transformative" action whether the legislative process is centralized and leadership-led or whether it is decentralized and committee-led. Like Sinclair (2016), we argue that the centralization of processes is best viewed as an adaptation to the challenges of the contemporary partisan environment.

---

[1] We thank Doug Arnold, Jane Mansbridge, Eric Schickler, and the participants in the SSRC Anxieties of Democracy Institutions Working Group Conference for their helpful feedback and advice.

While Congress is frequently unable to avoid stalemate (Binder, 2003, 2014), unorthodox and leadership-led processes help Congress resolve conflicts and pass legislation on issues that could not navigate a more traditional process. Centralized processes provide lawmakers more flexibility to strike "grand bargains" and solve legislative logjams. The less-transparent nature of behind-the-scenes lawmaking makes cutting deals and crafting legislative packages more tenable in an era of intense partisanship. Importantly, while the congressional parties have polarized and opportunities for individual members to have input on major legislation have been curtailed, party leadership-led processes have not resulted in more partisan, programmatic lawmaking or the enactment of more laws by narrow majorities. Bills that become law in the contemporary Congress command a roughly equivalent level of bipartisan support as laws passed in earlier periods.

Second, we argue that Congress is better able than in previous eras to engage in conflict-clarifying representation[2] in order to express and educate the public on the positions of the parties and to give voice to the opinions of various groups in society. Today's Congress is a place where conflicts between the parties are dramatized more clearly than in the past, aiding public understanding of the issues at stake in elections. Centralized processes facilitate this kind of activity, allowing congressional parties to advance and vote on bills that communicate partisan messages. More broadly, today's members possess more opportunities for expressive and position-taking entrepreneurship than members of earlier eras. Given the vast revolution in communications technology, the contemporary Congress is a public arena where even backbench members can aspire to lead national constituencies.

We present an array of data on Congress's activities and processes and draw upon 24 in-depth interviews with long-serving lawmakers and high-level staffers to make these assessments.[3] Interview subjects were queried about contemporary internal processes, legislative negotiations, important recent legislative enactments, and how individual members can be effective as lawmakers in the current environment.

THE CASE FOR DECENTRALIZATION

Many congressional scholars, observers, and practitioners are dissatisfied with how congressional processes have changed. Once characterized by a decentralized policymaking process governed by institutional norms such as deference to seniority and committee autonomy, Congress today is much more centralized and frequently bypasses traditional deliberative processes when considering

---

[2] We thank Jane Mansbridge for suggesting this terminology.
[3] These interviews, which took place in 2014 and 2016–17, were largely open-ended. The anonymity of these subjects is protected, unless specifically waived. The Institutional Review Boards (IRB) at the University of Maryland, College Park and University of Utah approved this research.

legislation (Sinclair, 2016, Tiefer, 2016). A strong, independent, and effective Congress is thought to feature decentralized power, an internal division of labor organized around committees, and automatic and universalistic "regular order" decision making.

The work of Nelson Polsby (1968, 1975) underlies this perspective. Polsby (1975) broadly conceived of a continuum of legislatures, ranging from what he termed *arenas* on one end to *transformative* legislatures on the other. A transformative legislature actively generates and develops legislative proposals through internal processes. It is well-institutionalized (Polsby, 1968) with a complex division of labor among its members and its committees. Deliberative processes shape legislative proposals and mute external influences, such as parties, the executive branch, and interest groups. Internal institutional organization and processes primarily drive policymaking outcomes. Arena legislatures, in contrast, play a relatively small role in developing policy. Laws are drafted elsewhere, perhaps by party organs or by the executive, and are then presented to the legislature for ratification. Rather than deliberation, the primary purpose of an arena legislature is debate, expression, and representation, to allow for the "ventilation of opinion for the education of the country at large" and to "mobilize interest groups and proclaim loyalties" (Polsby, 1975, p. 281). Legislative procedures and institutions reveal little about policymaking outcomes in arena legislatures. The influence of external forces is foremost.

Most scholarship exhibits a preference for the decentralized and transformative Congress, as Polsby described it. This normative assessment stems from general agreement that deliberation is important, if not necessary, for representative democracy (see Mill, 1975, Gutmann and Thompson, 1996, Thompson, 2008). Accordingly, for Congress to legislate well, it needs to be a deliberative assembly with broad and decentralized participation wherein different voices and perspectives are heard and alternative policy proposals are analyzed and fairly considered through formal, open processes.

This view has manifested in scholarship on various aspects of "traditional" congressional organization and process. For instance, scholars have long emphasized the deliberative value committees bring to the legislative process through their abilities to develop expertise, uncover knowledge, and closely consider competing policy proposals (Maass, 1983, Bessette, 1994, Quirk, 2005, Bendix, 2016). Congressional division of labor is supposed to incentivize committee members to specialize, develop expertise, and produce well-crafted legislation (Gilligan and Krehbiel, 1990, Krehbiel, 1991). Beyond committees, Wawro (2000, p. 158) argues that decentralization generally encourages legislative entrepreneurship because it "provide[s] incentives for members to undertake legislative activity." Baumgartner and Jones (2015) argue that the congressional reforms of the 1970s devolving power to subcommittees made Congress more dynamic by spurring competition among members that resulted in effective policymaking. Shepsle (1988, p. 463) similarly argues that

Congress's system of specialization and division of labor is what makes it "capable of attracting and retaining talented and ambitious politicians."

Likewise, the traditional reauthorization process – by which Congress authorizes federal policies and programs for limited numbers of years – is viewed as "specifically designed to overcome dysfunction" (Lewallen, Theriault, and Jones, 2016, p. 181). Reauthorizations induce lawmakers to closely examine federal programs by holding hearings and engaging in deliberative markups (see Hall, 2004), thereby enabling Congress to recommend reforms in a timely and orderly fashion (Adler and Wilkerson, 2012). Drutman (2016) argues that decentralized processes foster legislative entrepreneurship and "political dynamism." Current and former members of Congress also frequently express a strong preference for traditional regular order processes (Crespin and Madonna, 2016).

In contrast, contemporary changes to Congress's institutional features and processes are viewed as a threat to Congress's capacity as a legislative institution.[4] Scholars typically portray centralized, party-led processes – those that make Congress appear as more of an arena – not only as anti-deliberative, but inadequate for Congress to serve its proper legislative role. Mann and Ornstein (2006, 2012) label Congress a "broken branch," and describe "a virtual collapse of genuine deliberations" (2006, p. 106). Omnibus legislating is often viewed as resulting in less deliberation and less scrutiny of legislative provisions (see, Krutz, 2005, pp. 5–7, 141), as are the centralized processes used in recent years to resolve standoffs over spending bills and avoid government shutdowns (Hanson, 2015). Centralized bill development and tight control over floor deliberations are understood to limit opportunities for debate and amendment by rank-and-file legislators (Smith, 2014), and mostly enable congressional majority parties to ram through partisan bills (e.g., Aldrich and Rohde, 2000, Cox and McCubbins, 2005).

The benefits of centralized processes are rarely discussed, but they may help Congress adapt to a difficult and partisan political environment and enable the passage of legislation (Wallner, 2013, Hanson, 2014, Sinclair, 2016). They may also help Congress highlight the strengths of arena legislatures relative to transformative legislatures, as Polsby (1975) described. Arena legislatures dramatize the contours of partisan conflict across different political issues and give expression to the preferences and opinions of different groups in the public. Earlier generations of scholars had criticized Congress's deficiencies as an arena. Notably, Schattschneider (1942, see also APSA Committee on Parties, 1950) advocated stronger, more disciplined parties in Congress, and more centralized authority for congressional party leaders, so the parties could offer voters meaningful, programmatic alternatives. There seems little doubt that today's

---

[4] Jenkins and Stewart's (2016) recent paper on the potential deinstitutionalization of Congress provides a nice overview of how in various respects Congress has found itself "backsliding" and becoming more of an arena.

Congress is more capable of giving voice to the major parties' competing visions for public policy, although this change rarely elicits positive comment.

MAKING LAWS VS. MAKING POINTS

> "We know how to work together to make things happen. We have done that in the past. . . . [T]he exercise we are going to have later today has nothing to do with making law and making a difference. It is about making a point."
>
> Senator Mitch McConnell (*Cong. Record*, Nov. 3, 2011, p. S7095).

Taking stock of the contemporary Congress's institutional capacity requires first distinguishing between its two primary functions: *lawmaking* and *representation*. Importantly, these two functions roughly align with the emphases of Polsby's (1975) transformative and arena archetypes.

Lawmaking is Congress acting in a transformative manner by developing, considering, and passing policy proposals. The American political system's bicameralism and separation of powers typically necessitate the construction of large, bipartisan majorities to clear the many veto points in the legislative process (Krehbiel, 1998, Mayhew, 2005). Consequently, when making laws Congress's primary concern is resolving conflicts and building sufficiently broad support to achieve enactment.

In contrast, *representation* does not entail resolving conflicts or building broad coalitions. A legislature-as-arena expresses, reflects, and gives voice to the divergent views of different political groups and constituencies. Most prominently, the major parties in a legislative arena communicate their policy stances, clarify lines of partisan cleavage, and thereby jostle for support in the broader public. We refer to this form of representation as *conflict-clarifying representation*, which we understand primarily as efforts by congressional parties to spearhead a party *message*. As acknowledged by Senator McConnell (above), the goal of messaging is not to make law but to "make points" – to allow the parties to make their case against one another in a public forum. The congressional processes utilized for messaging need not be deliberative, nor do they need to help minimize conflict. In fact, maximizing conflict may be preferred. Party messages are developed to give members of Congress issues to talk about on the campaign trail, and to clarify differences between the parties on a host of issues.

Messaging is not just a matter of giving speeches. Parties also communicate their differences via legislative initiatives designed to provoke partisan divisions – efforts typically referred to as "messaging votes." Members frequently contrast message votes with "substantive" or "serious" votes (Lee, 2016, pp. 143–148). The key distinction is that messaging bills and amendments are not expected to win sufficient support to be enacted as law.[5]

---

[5] Former Sen. Olympia Snowe (2013, p. 27) offers this definition: "Much of what occurs in Congress today is what is often called 'political messaging,' Rather than putting forward a

Messaging initiatives are designed to appeal to external constituencies, unite the proposing party, and elicit opposition from the other party. The rejection of an attractive-sounding idea allows the proposing party to criticize its party opposition, further clarifying the lines of conflict.

In the House, the majority party will often pass bills on party lines that members recognize have little or no chance of moving forward in the Senate or with the president. In many cases, such bills lay down a marker and communicate what parties would ideally like to do in policy terms. Given the supermajority thresholds frequently necessary to bring a measure to a vote in the Senate, a Senate majority party has less opportunity to pass messaging bills than the House majority. Instead, the Senate majority can publicize its message with repeated failed cloture votes. For their part, minority party lawmakers in both chambers will generally attempt to push their party's message via amendments designed to put the majority party on the spot.

Congress engages in messaging when policymaking is neither desired nor attainable. On many issues, bipartisan compromise simply cannot be found. In one example a staffer recounted, "Rep. Joe Barton (R-Tex.) said that he couldn't work with [Democrats on legislation to address climate change] because he couldn't work out a problem that he doesn't see as a problem."[6] When there is no prospect for sufficient bipartisan cooperation, lawmakers may opt for messaging bills to keep an issue salient. Yet, party leaders can also set out to message even in conditions where actual legislative achievement might have been possible. Parties often have incentives to engage in this kind of strategic disagreement as bipartisan compromise will blur party differences and take an issue off the table for the next election (Gilmour, 1995, Groseclose and McCarty, 2001, Lee, 2016). As former Rep. Barney Frank (D-Mass.) describes it: "You have to distinguish between situations of the normal rules of negotiation, where people want to sit down and do a deal, from situations where these normal rules do not apply."[7] At times members and leaders want to solve policy problems, but at other times members of one or both parties would prefer to message on the issue.

The key point is that messaging and lawmaking are different activities with different goals. *Lawmaking* is aimed at actually enacting a policy and requires resolving conflicts to build enough support to navigate the many veto points in the US policymaking process. Given bicameralism, the separation of powers, and frequent divided government, this almost always requires bipartisan negotiation. *Messaging* is not concerned with enactment, and members are not seeking to resolve conflicts and achieve the broad consensus necessary to enact

---

plausible, realistic solution to a problem, members on both sides offer legislation that is designed to make a political statement. Specifically, the bill or amendment is drafted to make the opposing side look bad on an issue and it is not intended to ever actually pass."

[6] Staffer, August 5, 2016   [7] From an interview with Frank, June 24, 2013.

legislation in most cases. Rather, conflict is often the goal, as members want to show where they disagree.

Lawmakers and staffers clearly distinguish between efforts at lawmaking and efforts at messaging. One veteran House staffer noted: "We did Obamacare repeal bills 50 times. Passed legislation to stop the EPA from doing its job. All these were just messaging bills – bills that would never get through the Senate or a president's signature."[8] In contrast:

When we decide we want to legislate, instead of doing a messaging bill, we talk to the Democrats very early in the process. ... When we work through regular order in committee and we are shooting to get a law enacted, those bills are either very bipartisan or even passed unanimously or by voice. When we message the votes are partisan in committee. So you can predict if we are headed to enactment or just sending a message earlier in the process than floor votes.[9]

Even lawmakers from the ideological wings of their party recognize the importance of bipartisan compromise when lawmaking. "The secret to crafting legislation," writes liberal Democrat Rep. Henry Waxman (D-Calif.), "is not ramming through a partisan bill, but rather designing one that is acceptable to all parties" (Waxman with Green, 2009, p. 62).

Sometimes efforts at messaging and lawmaking overlap. One longtime staffer described the lawmaking process as sometimes requiring staged conflict. In others words, after bipartisan negotiations, each side has to establish that the outcome was the result of hard bargaining in which no one had caved:

After we've established what the ultimate product was going to look like [via bipartisan negotiation behind the scenes], then we'll go out and everyone can fight with each other. There's the theatrical piece, the position piece, and the bottom line. You need all three. You have to do the theatrical. The fight is needed. If you don't have a fight, people will think you just caved. You have to stage it a little. It's like when Reagan was asked how he could be president with an acting background, and he said he didn't see how you could do the job if you weren't an actor.[10]

Another veteran Senate staffer stated that some messaging was aimed at raising the visibility of an issue so as to improve its legislative chances over the long run, but "there's also messaging where members aren't trying to legislate, not trying to work things out. ... [You're] not trying to make something happen. ... You're just out there jamming the bad guys."[11] Comments such as these indicate that partisan messaging efforts can sometimes be the public face of drawn-out partisan negotiations that will eventually result in compromise, but often these efforts are aimed principally at clarifying the lines of conflict between the parties.

---

[8] Member, July 28, 2016   [9] Staffer, October 17, 2016   [10] Staffer, July 15, 2016
[11] Staffer, October 30, 2014

PERSISTENT BIPARTISANSHIP IN LAWMAKING

There are, unfortunately, no systematic measures available to ascertain when Congress is engaged in messaging as opposed to efforts to enact legislation. We cannot measure legislators' internal motivations. However, it is possible to examine how members behave over time when Congress actually succeeds in making law. Figures 8.1 and 8.2 display for each Congress between the 93rd (1973–1974) and the 114th (2015–2016) levels of member support on roll call votes for bills that went on to become laws. For comparison, these figures also display levels of member support on roll call votes for bills that passed the chamber in question but did *not* go on to become law. The data compare only how each chamber voted the *first time* on these bills (initial passage), excluding later bicameral compromises that usually broaden support. The data exclude private bills, commemorative legislation, and simple resolutions.[12]

As shown, the contemporary Congress still legislates on the basis of large, bipartisan majorities. Even as the parties have polarized on roll call votes, generally, and even as congressional processes have centralized in the hands of party leaders, today's Congress rarely passes *laws* on the basis of narrow majorities or the support of a single party. Over the full time period, the average enacted law received the support of 89 percent of the House. There is, in fact, a slight upward trend over time – laws passed in more recent congresses have actually had broader support among the House membership ($p < 0.01$). This stands in contrast to bills passing the House that *did not* become law. These measures have seen a slight decline in overall chamber support over time ($p = 0.21$), and the gap between roll call votes on bills that did and did not become law has widened. A similar pattern is apparent in the Senate. Over the period, the average law received the support of 89 percent of the Senate on roll call passage votes. And as with the House, rates of support for laws has increased over time ($p < 0.01$), while support for bills that passed the Senate but that did not become law has declined ($p = 0.02$).

Figure 8.2 shows that these trends reflect continued high levels of support among minority party lawmakers on lawmaking votes. On average over the period, 81 percent of the members of the House minority party voted in favor of the bills that went on to become law. Overall, there is a slight upward trend since the 1970s ($p = 0.06$). While minority party support for new laws dropped between the 1970s and early 1990s, it has risen since 1995. In contrast, among bills not becoming law, minority party support has dropped significantly over time ($p = 0.02$). The patterns are similar in the Senate, with 81 percent of minority party senators supporting new laws over the full period. There is a slight downward trend in minority party support for new

---

[12] Votes on conference reports and simple resolutions (which only need to pass one chamber) are also excluded from this analysis. A replication including only bills considered under special rules on the House floor (1983–2016) finds the same patterns as those shown in Figure 8.1.

(a)

FIGURE 8.1 **Percent of Voting Members Supporting Bills on Initial Passage, 1973–2016.**
(a) House of Representatives
(b) Senate

laws, but it is statistically insignificant ($p = 0.35$). Among bills that did not go on to become law, minority party support is lower in almost every Congress, and there is a sharp decline in minority party support for these bills over time ($p = 0.02$).

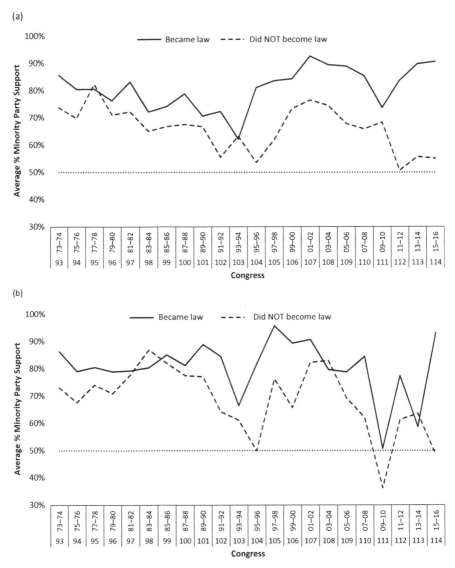

FIGURE 8.2 **Percent of Minority Party Supporting Bills on Initial Passage, 1973–2016.**
(a) House of Representatives
(b) Senate

The patterns in Figures 8.1 and 8.2 hold even among the most significant of enactments. Figure 8.3 assesses levels of support for final passage in the House and Senate for Mayhew's (2005) list of landmark laws, showing both the average percent of those voting in favor and the average percent of the minority

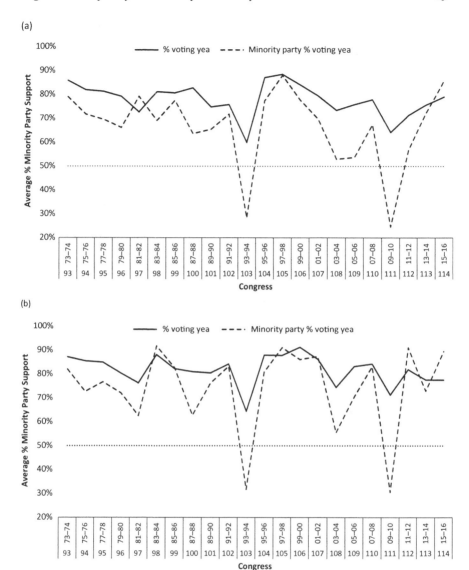

FIGURE 8.3 Support for Final Passage on Landmark Laws, 1973–2016.
(a) House of Representatives
(b) Senate

party voting in favor. From 1973–2016, support in the House and Senate has remained relatively stable (see also Arnold, 1990). The percent of those voting in support of passage has only had the slightest decline in the House and Senate, but neither trend is statistically significant (p = 0.13 for the House; p = 0.25 in the Senate). With few exceptions, minority party support for landmark laws has also remained high (slight downward trends are statistically insignificant: p = 0.28 for the House; p = 0.90 for the Senate). In fact, in several recent congresses, the percent of the Senate minority party supporting new landmark laws exceeded the overall rate of chamber support. Even in the contemporary partisan era, and under contemporary centralized processes, major laws routinely obtain the support of 75 percent of the House and 80 percent of the Senate.

Describing the post-2011 era, one member said simply: "the only bills that became law were bipartisan bills."[13] The starkly partisan votes that led to the enactment of the 2009 economic stimulus, the Affordable Care Act, and the Dodd-Frank Wall Street Reforms are highly atypical for lawmaking. As shown in the above figures, despite all the partisan and procedural change in Congress, lawmaking remains a bipartisan exercise. Just two congresses stand apart – the 103rd and 111th congresses – when Democrats held large majorities in both chambers and unified control of government. Under these conditions it appears Democrats were able to proceed with less buy-in from the minority. However, other periods of unified government (the 108th–109th for Republicans, and the 96th–97th for Democrats) do not exhibit the same pattern.

Figures 8.1 and 8.2 also reveal that in most congresses, bills that become law passed initially with wider margins of support than bills that passed without going on to become law. In both House and Senate, when Congress votes on passed bills that do not go on to become law, there is markedly less overall support and minority party assent, and minority support for these measures has been declining. In only a couple of congresses did unsuccessful passed bills win wider support in either chamber than bills that eventually became law. These instances occurred in some, but not all, congresses with unified party control.[14]

The patterns evident in Figures 8.1 and 8.2 are consistent with what one should expect considering Congress's dual activities of lawmaking and conflict-clarifying messaging. Messaging bills should attract lower levels of support because they are not intended or expected to successfully navigate all the veto points to result in a new law. This is by no means to claim that all the bills that pass one chamber without going on to become law were devised as messaging vehicles. But it is safe to conclude that some share of bills that pass without becoming law were taken up for messaging purposes, whereas bills that went on to enactment were drafted to successfully traverse the legislative process.

---

[13] Member, July 28, 2016.
[14] In the 103rd and 111th Houses, the bills that resulted in enacted laws garnered less support from the House minority party than the bills that only passed the chamber without becoming law. The same pattern was evident in the 108th and 109th Senates, when Republicans held unified party control of national government. However, the pattern does not hold in the 103rd and 111th Senates under unified Democratic party control, or in the 108th and 109th Houses under unified Republican party control.

TABLE 8.1 *Predicting Support for New Laws on Initial Passage, 1973–2016.*

	House		Senate	
	% voting yea	% minority party support	% voting yea	% minority party support
Bill-Level Variables				
Became law	0.071^b	0.148^b	0.083^b	0.132^b
	(0.004)	(0.009)	(0.008)	(0.014)
Sponsor distance from	0.077^a	0.179^b	−0.089	0.238
chamber median	(0.034)	(0.068)	(0.077)	(0.131)
Sponsor in majority party	-0.049^a	-0.094^a	−0.017	−0.007
	(0.022)	(0.044)	(0.036)	(0.061)
Sponsor distance from	-0.201^b	-0.491^b	0.050	−0.259
chamber median × Sponsor in majority party	(0.037)	(0.076)	(0.081)	(0.138)
constant	0.880^b	0.801^b	0.823^b	0.688^b
	(0.022)	(0.047)	(0.036)	(0.062)
Random Effects Parameters				
Congress	0.0013	0.0086	0.0011	0.0071
	(0.0004)	(0.0027)	(0.0005)	(0.0025)
N	5,912	5,912	1,712	1,712
AIC	−4717.5	3579.4	−1537.8	275.7

$^a p < 0.05;$ $^b p < 0.01$
Note: Analyses are multilevel mixed-effects linear regression analyses.

Multivariate analyses confirm the patterns found in Figures 8.1–8.3. Table 8.1 displays the results of multilevel mixed-effects linear regression analyses where the dependent variables are *% of yea votes on passage* and *% minority party support on passage.* These regressions control for the ideological position and party of the bill sponsor,[15] as well as an interaction between these two variables, and calculates random effects parameters for each Congress to account for changes in party polarization, inter-party homogeneity, and other important environmental factors shifting from congress to congress. Ordinary least squares (OLS) regression analyses also controlling for the degree of party polarization during each Congress,[16] the unity of the majority party during

[15] Ideological position is measured by the sponsor's first dimension DW-NOMINATE distance from the chamber median.
[16] Party polarization is measured as the difference between the first dimension DW-NOMINATE media of each party during each congress.

each Congress,[17] the majority share of chamber seats, and whether or not there existed divided government demonstrate the robustness of the findings in Table 8.1 and are found in the appendix.

The results indicate that, even after accounting for alternative sources of variation in overall member support for legislation, bills that eventually became law were approved with significantly more overall support and bipartisanship than passed bills that did not go on to become law. In the House, the models predict bills becoming law will have the support of a 9 percent larger share of the chamber, and a 23 percent larger share of minority party members than bills that do not go on to become law. In the Senate, bills becoming law are predicted to earn the support a 10 percent larger share of the chamber and a 19 percent larger share of minority party members. Overall, when Congress makes law, it has and continues to do so with levels of both overall and minority party support that significantly exceeds what is typical for bill passage.

Despite all the partisan conflict and position taking, even today's party-polarized and highly centralized Congress still makes law in the same long-standing way – with large, bipartisan majorities. There is at this point no clear trend toward lower levels of bipartisanship in lawmaking. Increases in partisan conflict unquestionably make it harder to legislate (Binder, 2003, 2014), and legislative efforts focused on messaging have clearly become more partisan, but most lawmaking efforts continue to result in broad support from both parties.

MAKING LAWS: A MORE CENTRALIZED, BUT STILL TRANSFORMATIVE LEGISLATURE

> "When I'm asked if Congress is broken, I'm uncertain how to reply. . . . Even now real legislation happens at crisis points." – Veteran House staffer[18]

The preceding analyses reveal no substantial changes over recent decades in the high levels of "bottom line" bipartisan support that enacted laws garner. At the same time, however, there is no question that legislative processes in Congress have changed markedly. Congress no longer follows the decentralized, committee-driven processes that characterized the transformative legislature described by Polsby (1975). That so much procedural change could occur while Congress still achieves such similar outcomes when enacting legislation suggests that these changes in process should be viewed as alternative paths to the same ultimate end. Along these lines, our interviews suggest that the decentralized processes of the mid-twentieth-century Congress are, in many cases, mala-dapted to today's difficult legislative challenges. Respondents express a prefer-ence for less centralized legislative processes, but such processes often cannot

---

[17] Majority party unity is measured as the inverse of the standard deviation of first dimension DW-NOMINATE scores among members of the majority party in each Congress.

[18] Staffer, August 5, 2016.

succeed in producing legislation under current conditions. In this section, we will consider how and why centralized legislative processes are employed so often, as well as what these changes mean for legislative entrepreneurship on the part of individual members.

A variety of indicators document the extent to which the legislative process in Congress has changed. Congressional committees today meet far more rarely than in the 1960s, 1970s, 1980s, and 1990s. According to *Vital Statistics on Congress* (Reynolds, 2018), committees hold about half as many meetings as committees did in the 1960s, and the frequency of Senate committee meetings has declined by one-third. Committee activity reached its peak in the 1970s, during the era of "subcommittee government" and has been declining ever since.

Committees are not only less active; they are less autonomous. "Today leadership is in control," said one veteran former member. "Chairs initiate very little without the consent of the Speaker." In contrast with the 1970s when he first came to Congress, "these days if a committee chair is holding a series of hearings with the aim of producing a piece of legislation, you can bet that he's already had a conversation with the leadership." "The process is less free-wheeling than it once was," he continued. "If you ask to do an exploratory hearing today, the leadership is likely to ask 'Who's testifying?' They might say, 'Don't you dare even *think* about bringing this up.'"[19]

Far more legislation comes to the floor without a formal committee report than in the past (see Bendix, 2016, Curry, 2016). Of course, reduced committee autonomy does not necessarily mean that committees and committee chairs are cut out of the legislative process. Chairs and committee staffs are often consulted in the informal processes that precede floor consideration, even when committees do not report bills. Drafting legislation is generally a collaborative effort between the leadership and committee chairs. As one staffer relayed it, "As a committee guy, I don't view increased leadership involvement as challenging committees, I see it as assisting us. Leadership is our ally helping clear the way for our committee initiatives."[20] Nevertheless, committee chairs today must still work within limits set by party leaders. On issues that are important to the party overall, committees must conform to "a broader idea about what we could do" set forth by leadership.[21]

Scholars often interpret the contemporary Congress's more centralized procedures as a means by which a majority party under polarized conditions can better steer policy toward its preferred position (Rohde, 1991, Aldrich and Rohde, 2000). However, the extent to which Congress continues to legislate on the basis of large, bipartisan majorities suggests, instead, that centralization in leadership has not facilitated more programmatic or partisan lawmaking.

[19] Member, July 27, 2016.   [20] Staffer, October 17, 2016.   [21] Staffer, July 15, 2016.

The leadership-driven bills of the contemporary Congress, like the committee-drafted bills of the twentieth-century Congress, still pass by wide assent.

In recent years, Congress has employed leadership-led and behind-the-scenes processes to successfully negotiate compromises and pass important policies, including some to address problems that had long proved intractable. Just since 2013, these efforts include: the 2013 Ryan-Murray budget deal, which ended more than 2 years of protracted budget standoffs; the 5-year reauthorization of federal surface transportation programs (the FAST Act, 2015) which, in addition to being the first full transportation reauthorization in 10 years, also ended a lengthy standoff over reauthorizing the Export-Import Bank; the 2015 reauthorization of the Elementary and Secondary Education Act (the Every Student Succeeds Act), which ended nearly a decade of debate over how to replace No Child Left Behind; the Medicare Access and CHIP Reauthorization Act of 2015, which found a permanent replacement for an ineffective Medicare cost-control measure that had been addressed on a temporary basis 17 times since 2002 (the so-called doc fix); and the USA Freedom Act, which reauthorized and reformed various provisions of the PATRIOT Act relating to intelligence surveillance, imposing new limits on the bulk collection of US citizens' telecommunication metadata by the National Security Agency (NSA) in a wake of the Edward Snowden controversy. These are among the actions Congress has taken in recent years on some of the more high-profile issues facing the nation. In each case, centralized, leadership-led, and behind-the-scenes processes were used. Each of these laws was also approved with wide, bipartisan support.

Asked to explain why Congress so frequently turns to leadership-driven, centralized processes, our interview subjects made a pragmatic case that more centralized procedures were often better adapted to the legislative challenges Congress faces today. In an era of polarized parties (Barber and McCarty, 2015), frequent divided government, and rampant obstructionism in the Senate (Wallner, 2013, Smith, 2014, Sinclair, 2016), decentralized processes often fail to yield legislation that can pass the opposing chamber and/or be signed by the president. Often, leaders are needed to manipulate legislative dynamics in order to build support for legislation (Arnold, 1990), and sometimes this requires the centralization of power and procedure in the hands of party leaders (Sinclair, 2016, Tiefer, 2016). In the interviews, two sets of factors stood out as pushing toward great centralization: (1) The *efficiency* of centralized processes and (2) the *secrecy* and *flexibility* provided by centralized processes, which can help congressional negotiators cut deals and craft legislative packages in a difficult political environment.

Efficiency, Crises, and Logjams

Congress often turns to centralized processes because decentralized, committee-led processes are prone to obstruction and deadlock in the contemporary political environment. Committee markups and open floor proceedings may allow lawmakers opportunities to substantively amend legislation, but they also create opportunities for obstructionists to throw a wrench in the proceedings – offer a large quantity of amendments for the purpose of delay and obstruction, push poison pill amendments to try to kill the legislation at hand, force lawmakers to take embarrassing votes, and more – rather than legislate toward an outcome. According to one staffer, many times, under these conditions, if "you try to work through an open mark-up or something, the bill gets weighed down in partisan attacks and nothing happens."[22] Faced with these prospects, leaders opt for tightly-managed processes: "When the other side isn't really trying to legislate through the process but is just putting up these partisan gotcha amendments, you have to move on. You have to close it down."[23]

The contemporary Congress does not always employ centralized processes, and today's legislative process is not uniformly leadership-driven. On many issues, committees of jurisdiction still proceed in much the same way as in the "textbook Congress" (Shepsle, 1989). For example, the annual National Defense Authorization Act (NDAA) is developed via a deliberative, committee-led process and approved via inclusive, open amending processes (Shogan, 2012). Centralization has not been needed to handle the NDAA, because Congress has not failed to pass the annual defense authorization in more than 50 years. The leadership will allow committees to take the lead, provided they can lead to a legislative result. Most rank-and-file lawmakers are happier if legislation can be worked up in that manner as well (Crespin and Madonna, 2016). But when decentralized processes are unable to produce an outcome, or appear headed for deadlock, leadership intervenes. As one committee staffer put it, "When we just couldn't resolve things with the Democrats we'd have to kick it to the leadership to work it out."[24]

The centralization of processes can happen in a number of ways and for various reasons, but "the number one reason it happens is timing."[25] When Congress is facing a tight deadline or some sort of crisis, leadership often steps in to expedite the process. As one staffer explained:

I see two processes. First, there is legislation done at the end when crisis looms. The House has passed something extreme. The Senate is log-jammed or passed something really different. In these processes, the leadership takes the lead. ... On lower profile bills, matters such as the FCC spectrum auction, the drug and device user fees that fund the FDA, and so on, the committee process still functions."[26]

Another explained it this way:

It's a crisis model. Leadership steps in when backs are against the wall and something has to be done. Expiring tax provisions, debt limit has to be raised. ... These days most of what's getting done is happening only in states of crisis. The leadership doesn't

---

[22] Staffer, December 4, 2017 (1).   [23] Staffer, October 11, 2017 (1).
[24] Staffer, December 5, 2017.   [25] Staffer, October 11, 2017 (1).   [26] Staffer, August 5, 2016.

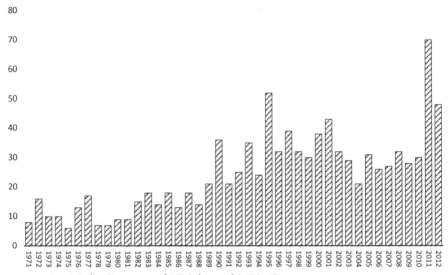

FIGURE 8.4 **Media Coverage of "Brinkmanship" in Congress**
Note: Values are the number of articles and editorials published by *The New York Times* mentioning both Congress and brinkmanship or standoff. Values were identified using *The New York Times'* historical database and searching for articles and editorials by year using the search terms: "Congress and (brinkmanship or standoff)."

want these crises. ... But the pressures just keep pushing issues up the food chain to the leadership.[27]

Sometimes, "There just isn't time to work through the traditional process."[28] This is not anyone's ideal: "It's a shame you can't do things differently... The time cycles we are working in speeds things up so you can't."[29]

The greater frequency with which the contemporary Congress copes with crises and legislative deadlines may be one reason centralized processes have been so prevalent in recent years. Figure 8.4 shows the number of *New York Times* articles and editorials each year from 1971 to 2012 that mention Congress and either "brinkmanship" or "standoff." The data indicate a steady increase in such news stories, with fewer than 10 or 20 articles identified each year in the 1970s, to three or four times that many mentioned in recent years. Notable spikes are apparent in 1995 and 2011, when high-profile showdowns over federal spending and the debt ceiling dominated congressional action. Overall, the data reveal an upward trend in crisis legislating in general. Party leaders play central roles in the management and resolution of these crises.

[27] Staffer, September 9, 2016.   [28] Staffer, October 11, 2017 (1).
[29] Staffer, December 4, 2017 (4).

Even absent a deadline or crisis, there are some issues that at the outset do not seem amenable to regular order, perhaps because obstructionists had derailed similar legislative efforts in the past, or because there is reason to believe they will this time. In such cases, the leadership may preempt committees or an open process. As one staffer described it, leadership will sometimes work around a committee, putting "together groups of senators to work on a bill. They essentially create ad hoc committees because they don't believe the regular committees can do it anymore. And they're right. They can't."[30]

In other cases, committee leaders themselves will "punt to the leadership to make key decisions," as they do not believe they can achieve success through a traditional process.[31] In these cases, leadership-led processes do not require initial committee failure. Leaders may convene a meeting early to help establish broad parameters for legislation that stands a chance of successfully passing both chambers and being signed by the president. Such a "blueprint"[32] will then guide bill development in committee. Or leadership may just lift a bill from committee consideration altogether.[33] Party leaders can assert control over negotiations at any point, particularly if time constraints are a concern. The 2009 Recovery Act, for example, went through no committee process and was negotiated quickly in leadership offices because the economic emergency demanded speed.[34]

Whether or not processes are centralized because there is a crisis, and whether processes are centralized at the behest of committee leaders or because the leadership intervenes, concerns about the capacity of decentralized processes to achieve a legislative result are often the critical consideration. Generally, centralization was portrayed as an adaptation to contemporary lawmaking challenges. The implication is that decentralized processes may have worked well in the past but do not fare well in today's challenging legislative environment.

Secrecy, Flexibility, and Constructing Legislative Deals

Centralized processes are also more secretive and flexible than decentralized processes, which helps aid dealmaking and the construction of legislative packages and the coalitions necessary to pass them. Traditional processes not only make it easier for opponents to obstruct and try to kill legislation, they can make it harder for a bill's proponents to engage in meaningful deliberations. As one staffer put it, "Transparency is a good thing in principle but it makes Congress more dysfunctional."[35] Doing things in a more secretive manner helps lawmakers find common ground, compromise, or hash out mutually beneficial deals in several ways.

[30] Staffer, December 4, 2017 (1).   [31] Staffer, October 17, 2016.   [32] Staffer, July 29, 2016.
[33] Staffer, August 2, 2016.   [34] Staffer, July 29, 2016.   [35] Staffer, September 9, 2016.

First, enhanced secrecy helps Congress mute lobbyist pressure. Traditional processes allow well-financed interest groups to monitor the proceedings and use their clout to influence reelection-minded legislators. As Arnold (1990, p. 275) put it, "Open meetings filled with lobbyists, and recorded votes, on scores of particularistic amendments, serve to increase the powers of special interests, not to diminish them." These efforts can bog down a legislative effort:

I know transparency is good, but it's very difficult with an issue like health care. There are so many interested parties on the outside. There is so much money involved; 15,000 lobbyists who want to be involved.[36]

Another reflected, "Once K Street knows you have a train leaving the station, they have umpteen things they want to get on it."[37] To cut a deal and get it through Congress, "you need the back-room discussions outside the view of the lobbyists, even if that's sacrilege to the open-government people."[38]

Second, the secrecy of centralized processes also enables Congress to mute pressures emerging from both parties' activist bases. A zealous party base can color the reactions of rank-and-file lawmakers to specific proposals, even those that comprise a small part of a larger deal, as there are "hyper-partisans on both sides that will turn everything into a wedge."[39] While at one time regular order processes allowed Congress to resolve conflicts, today, "Regular order is too messy and it's covered instantly in the media and it can create problems."[40] If information gets out about negotiations, "you run the risk of some members getting all riled up and the snowball starting rolling down the mountain and picking up steam. You just have to do it in a kind of secretive way."[41] Today, "the politics of each party's base has made [regular order] impossible."[42] Negotiating in the open in this environment makes reaching any deal difficult. Lawmakers cannot make offers that sound like capitulation, or even just engage in a give and take. If congressional leaders often appear overly secretive in their approach, it's because they feel they have to be:

There's so much divisiveness inside in the parties' caucuses that you render yourself pretty vulnerable if you're putting out your gives that publicly. I'll admit there is an increasing trend toward opaqueness and non-disclosure to the broader group, but part of it is this sense that the broader group will not handle the information responsibly.[43]

In contrast, the behind-the-scenes negotiations that are characteristic of centralized processes help negotiators come to agreements. Secrecy can allow negotiators to explore opportunities, float ideas, and manage sensitive issues with confidence that their counterparts will not leak the details. Negotiators,

---

[36] Staffer, August 2, 2016.   [37] Staffer, August 24, 2016.   [38] Staffer, October 10, 2017 (2).
[39] Staffer, October 11, 2017 (1).   [40] Staffer, December 6, 2017 (2).
[41] Staffer, December 5, 2017.   [42] Staffer, December 4, 2017 (3).
[43] Staffer, October 10, 2017 (1).

...need to have a theoretical discussion. But if a piece of the negotiation gets reported, it'll be seen in isolation from everything else we're trying to do, all the other moving parts. ... Social media will start churning information – all about one little piece. It spreads like wildfire. And all this even before you can have a discussion with the skeptics. By the time you can reach them, they've already made up their minds. They're not listening to you.[44]

Keeping things quiet is essential, "a leak can short-circuit the negotiations."[45] However, when negotiators all emerge unified around a single legislative package, it becomes hard to oppose. Instead, "everyone could say, 'Well, this or that part of it stinks, but at least it solves the overall problem.'"[46] Simply, in today's Congress, "it's in the backroom where the deal is made."[47]

Centralized processes also allow for more flexibility in constructing legislative packages and deals than is often possible through traditional, decentralized approaches. Committees, in particular, are often hemmed in by jurisdictional boundaries. When looking for trades or logrolls across issues to build legislative support, committees can only work within the policies and programs under their jurisdictions. "The committee process chops issues up, making larger negotiations impossible," one staffer explained.[48] For example, the Committee on Energy and Commerce cannot make cuts to programs under the jurisdiction of the Committee on Agriculture or provide more funding to programs under the jurisdiction of the Committee on Ways and Means in order to make a legislative package work or make it something that members will support.

Committee chairpersons and committee staff "are always a bit too in the weeds to some extent." Speaking of one committee chair in particular, this staffer noted, "[He] has proven he is the smartest guy in the room, but he gets lost in the bark of the tree and can't see the forest."[49] Discussing a health-care effort, one staffer reflected that committee members and staff, "were so focused on the little pieces. They had something like 17 meetings on just the nursing home provisions. They'd debate two lines, a comma, etc. It's just too much detail!"[50] Party leaders, by virtue of their position, are more focused on the big picture and are thus better suited to strike "grand bargains" as they can explore policy solutions across policies, programs, and jurisdictions, and put together legislative packages that can draw broad support for passage:

Leadership can open up the universe of policy to find the solution, taking into account the whole picture – the politics, the budget. These decisions get chased up to the leaders. ... There's no other decision maker who can get a deal to do things like keep the government open.[51]

In the contemporary Congress, "all the big deals tend to be leadership-driven."[52]

---

[44] Staffer, September 9, 2016.   [45] Ibid.   [46] Staffer, August 2, 2016.
[47] Staffer, October 9, 2017.   [48] Staffer, August 2, 2016.   [49] Staffer, October 10, 2017 (2).
[50] Staffer, August 2, 2016.   [51] Staffer, September 9, 2016.   [52] Staffer, August 24, 2016.

This flexibility is particularly helpful in trying to figure out how to pay for legislation in an era of tight budgets and large deficits. "Pay-fors" are often a sticking point. Identifying necessary offsets requires creativity and an ability to look across jurisdictional boundaries:

For anything you do, you have to find the money. Handling things at the leadership level allows you to go outside the relevant committee to find the money. Whatever problem you're trying to resolve – FAA, highway trust fund, whatever. The committee may not have jurisdiction over the policies that would allow you to get the pay-fors. So, the leadership needs to step in. The leadership is the place you go when you need to find offsets.[53]

Simply, "leadership has more flexibility to find the pay-fors," because it can work "outside the jurisdiction of any particular committee."[54] Finding offsets to pay for legislation entails political pain – cuts will have to be imposed or revenues raised: "When pain is involved, the leadership has to handle it."[55]

Leadership involvement does not necessarily mute committee influence. Some of those interviewed emphasized that the leadership can also make it easier for committees to move their bills through the rest of the legislative process:

Leadership gets involved for a lot of reasons. Sometimes it's to coordinate with the Senate. Sometimes it's to clear potential objections from other committees. . . . I know the leadership is a real ally to our committee in terms of waving off other committees, bad amendments, disgruntled members, and even clearing the way in the Senate and working with Senate leadership staff.[56]

Nor do centralized processes cut out the expertise of committee staff. Leaders can still draw on committee expertise for help. In their broad search for pay-fors the leadership will turn to committee staff for insight on what can be found within their jurisdiction. One staffer described how the "leadership tends to come to us for pay-fors in budget deals. We are often brought in for our expertise on Medicare, Medicaid savings, or other pay-fors like Spectrum sales or Strategic Petroleum Reserve sales."[57] The process today is often leadership-led, but committees are still involved in shaping legislative details.

Centralized processes also allow party leaders flexibility to decide who to, and to not, include in negotiations over legislative packages, and when they are brought into the fold. Managing this process enhances the odds of success. Leaders may need to work around traditionally important lawmakers, such as those sitting on a committee of jurisdiction. One leadership staffer, speaking about an attempt to cut a deal on health policy, noted:

If we involved the committee members, there would be too many demands to accommodate. [Ways and Means ranking member Sander] Levin would want the public option.

---

[53] Staffer, September 9, 2016.   [54] Staffer, August 24, 2016.   [55] Ibid.
[56] Staffer, October 17, 2016.   [57] Staffer, October 17, 2016.

[Ways and Means chairman Paul] Ryan would want to insist that the whole bill is paid for. Different groups would begin to impose their litmus tests on the package – we can't support it unless it has this or that feature.[58]

According to one longtime member: "As to whom you involve in the process, you can think in terms of concentric circles,"[59] where you start with yourself and your staff and build outward, bringing the most crucial members along the way. The process is one of identifying and winning the support of the "keys" and "umbrellas" who might ensure the passage of a piece of legislation (Huitt, 1961, p. 340). On anything dealing with entitlement programs like Medicare or Social Security, for example, Speaker John Boehner (R-Ohio) "knew that [Paul] Ryan was the one person he had to convince."[60] For such policies Ryan was both the "key," with other members taking cues from him, and the "umbrella," who provides political cover to those who stand behind him. Ryan's endorsement was expected to bring along enough fellow Republicans to allow the House to pass budget legislation.

Centralization and Legislative Entrepreneurship

Leadership-driven processes like these have significant implications for legislative entrepreneurship – *who* in Congress is able to have meaningful influence on important issues. Centralized processes widen inequities in influence. When negotiations occur behind closed doors in party leadership offices, the leadership is in the drivers' seat, determining who to bring into the negotiations and when. Party leaders are super-empowered in such processes, while most rank-and-file members are cut out. When relatively open processes like committee markups are sidestepped, the typical member of Congress has fewer formal and automatic opportunities for legislative entrepreneurship. Centralized processes are likely to present rank-and-file members with large, take-it-or-leave-it deals, with little time or resources to analyze the package in any detail (Curry, 2015).

Members' best bet for influence in the current environment is to make themselves a force to be reckoned with on a policy issue. In their search for "keys" and "umbrellas" (Huitt, 1961) for broadening support for a legislative initiative, leaders will reach out to lawmakers who are respected among their peers, either for their policy knowledge or for their ability to provide political cover to key constituencies. Given the extent to which actual lawmaking remains highly bipartisan, even minority party members who can influence their colleagues may be brought into the process.

Rank-and-file lawmakers can empower themselves by developing a reputation as an expert on a policy. Speaking of a particularly successful member, one staffer noted: "He was knowledgeable. He would just dig right in. . . . He had

---

[58] Staffer, August 2, 2016.   [59] Member, July 27, 2016.   [60] Staffer, August 2, 2016.

an impact because he knew what he was talking about."[61] Asked how a legislator can be effective today, one longtime member said simply, "You have to know policy. You have to be determined. You have to be patient."[62] In their study of legislative effectiveness, Volden and Wiseman (2014, pp. 197–210) rank developing "policy expertise" at the top of their list of "habits of highly effective lawmakers."

Lawmakers who can credibly claim to speak on behalf of organized groups of other lawmakers and promise to deliver or withhold their votes, such as leaders of the Congressional Black Caucus, the House Freedom Caucus, the Progressive Caucus, and other groups, can also be influential. For example, one staffer singled out Rep. Diana DeGette (D-Colo.) as a key player on a health-care bill: "She had no official role; she was not a committee head. But [the Democratic leadership] knew that we couldn't have her coming out against the bill with guns blazing."[63] DeGette had to be accommodated because, as cochair of the Pro-Choice Caucus, it was clear that she could create controversy regarding the legislation if she saw a threat to reproductive rights. Once she signed off on the deal, other pro-choice members could have confidence that their policy priorities were not endangered by the legislation, as well as political cover with pro-choice interest groups. Many members play similar roles in negotiating with leadership.

To be an effective legislative entrepreneur in the current environment means continually looking for opportunities. "Being effective is very situational. There is no set of steps. No roadmap. You just have to see opportunities to take advantage of."[64] Opportunities for entrepreneurship arise when leaders are actually attempting to legislate and want to broaden their support. "In legislating, you're making a quilt," said one former committee chair. "It's like Jesse Jackson's convention speech in 1988. My patch alone isn't big enough. You just have to keep adding patches."[65] When leaders are building coalitions to pass legislation, that is the time to ask for concessions. On the other hand, "it's hard to find a compromise if the other side doesn't care if it loses," said one longtime member.[66]

In other words, a would-be legislative entrepreneur cannot expect to make an imprint on policy when leaders are only pushing a messaging vehicle and are not seeking to enact a law. But when leaders "want to do something, you can always look for leverage points. Whatever the structure, the degree of centralization or decentralization, you can operate within it."[67] Individual members can advance their policy goals by being alert to circumstances when leaders are looking for additional support. At these times, members can trade their support in exchange for the incorporation of some of their policy priorities. Even in the minority, "I was able to make progress on key priorities [when the majority]

---

[61] Staffer, August 5, 2016.   [62] Member, July 28, 2016.   [63] Staffer, August 2, 2016.
[64] Staffer, August 5, 2016.   [65] Member, July 27, 2016.   [66] Member, July 28, 2016.
[67] Ibid.

had an agenda they wanted to pass."[68] As another longtime staffer described it, while members can make a lot of headway by being good team players and developing positive relationships with the leadership and with committee chairs, "being an asshole works sometimes, too, especially if leadership is in a fix and they need your vote."[69]

Leaders will turn to members who can be useful to them when they are seeking to achieve legislative success on issues. The "opportunities are less" for individual members to have input when highly centralized legislative processes are employed.[70] With fewer individual pieces of legislation passing and more highly centralized and omnibus legislating, today's legislative environment is undoubtedly more frustrating and restricted for would-be individual legislative entrepreneurs, and requires more creativity.

MAKING POINTS: CONFLICT-CLARIFYING REPRESENTATION

Congress is more than a lawmaking body. It is also a public sphere (Mayhew, 2000). Beyond Congress's lawmaking functions, the institution is also expected to give voice to the divergent perspectives of parties, groups, factions, and individual members. In some respects, today's Congress is more effective as a representative arena, as Polsby (1975) described it, than the Congress of earlier eras. This is particularly true in its ability to clarify the lines of party conflict.

Party Messaging

Parties in the contemporary Congress put their disagreements clearly on display. Party leaders continually use both roll call votes and communications efforts to convey party differences to external constituencies. Legislative parties of the twenty-first century are far better organized than those of the twentieth century to drive congressional debate so as to clearly define the stakes for external constituencies. Incentives to engage in party messaging are particularly strong in a context when party competition for control of Congress is tight and ongoing (Lee, 2016).

As shown above, very little actual legislation becomes law by narrow or partisan majorities, but the Congress nevertheless takes many roll call votes that pit one party against the other. Indeed, differences in Republican and Democratic voting behavior in Congress are wider than they have been at any point in 100 years (McCarty, Poole, and Rosenthal, 2006, Barber and McCarty, 2015). One simple indicator of the change is displayed in Figure 8.5, the percentage of votes in House and Senate that divide 90 percent or more members of one party against 90 percent or more members of the opposing party. By this measure, partisan conflict has been rising since 1981. In the 1970s, less than 2 percent of all roll call votes resulted in such stark party

---

[68] Ibid.   [69] Staffer, October 17, 2016.   [70] Staffer, August 5, 2016.

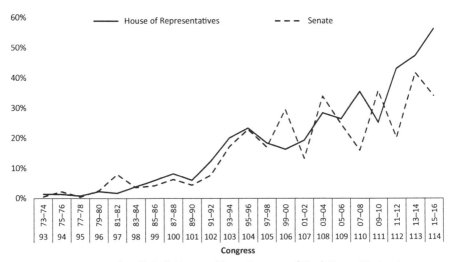

FIGURE 8.5 Percent of Roll Call Votes with 90 Percent of Each Party Voting in Opposition to the Other

divisions. Since 2011, better than 55 percent of House votes and 30 percent of Senate votes have pitted at least 90 percent of one party against at least 90 percent of the other party.

It is not possible to identify the precise share of roll call votes that are deliberately staged for party messaging purposes. The rise of party conflict in Congress has multiple causes (Theriault, 2008), including more polarization among party activists and high-information partisans outside the institution (Abramowitz, 2010, Layman et al, 2010) as well as the sorting out of constituencies along ideological lines (Fiorina and Abrams, 2009, Levendusky, 2009). Nevertheless, we know from media coverage as well as a growing body of scholarship that party leaders in both House and Senate intentionally and self-consciously use the floor agenda to drive party messages (Harris, 2005, Grimmer, 2013, Butler and Powell, 2014, Gelman, 2017). They do so by forcing votes and staging floor debate so as to exhibit sharp party cleavages. Majority parties regularly craft messaging bills – generally without much of a formal deliberative process – and bring them up to elicit party-line votes on the floor of both chambers. For their part, members of the minority party look for every opportunity to offer amendments, points of order, or otherwise force votes aimed at embarrassing the majority party (Egar, 2016). Regardless of the specific share of party-line votes that occur as a result of self-conscious political strategy, all this highly partisan voting in Congress has the effect of making the differences between the parties more visible to voters.

The contemporary Congress also invests substantial resources in a communications infrastructure designed to enable voters to better understand the issues at stake between the parties. In both House and Senate since the late 1970s,

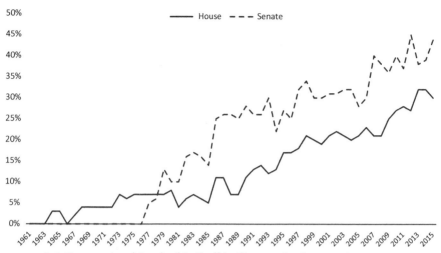

FIGURE 8.6 Congressional Leadership Staff in Communications, 1961–2015

Republicans and Democrats have developed and institutionalized extensive partisan public relations operations. As one indicator of this shift, Figure 8.6 displays the percentage of staff members working in House and Senate party leadership offices with job titles in communications.[71] On average throughout the 1960s and 1970s, less than 5 percent of leadership staffers were dedicated to communications functions. Beginning in the late 1970s, concomitant with increasing party conflict in roll-call voting, the congressional parties began to bring on board professional communicators to help the parties argue their case in public. These operatives work full-time on media strategies and outreach so as to drive a favorable narrative in public discourse. As one party communicator explained, "The goal [is] to provide a seamless integration of policy and messaging. We want to be communicating our values and priorities to the public and, of course, also effectively criticizing the bad ideas of the other side."[72] By the start of the 114th Congress (2015–2016), more than 40 percent of Senate leadership staffers worked in communications, with about 30 percent of House leadership staffers holding similar positions. Committees' communications capacities have grown as well, and this staff capacity serves to bolster the messaging done by the leadership. As one staffer explained, "We coordinate very closely with leadership communicators and we each augment each other's messaging. They help us, we help them."[73]

Congress has become a much more effective representational arena for purposes of articulating the major parties' competing visions for public policy. This steady stream of party messaging from Congress stands as one of the likely

[71] Data were compiled from *Congressional Staff Directories*.   [72] Staffer, September 12, 2014.
[73] Staffer, October 17, 2016.

explanations for the rising strength of partisan feelings in the electorate. Americans today are better able than they were in the 1960s and 1970s to see important differences between the parties, correctly place Democrats to the left of Republicans, and rate the parties as farther apart ideologically. Scholars date this shift as beginning in the 1980s (Bartels, 2000) and attribute it in great part to cue-taking from elites (Hetherington, 2001). The rise in party-line voting in Congress and the parties' increased investments in communications have probably contributed to better public understanding of partisan differences. A Congress in which party cleavages are clearly defined allows voters to ascertain where, why, and how the parties disagree with one another.

Individual Member Messaging

It is important also to take stock of how Congress-as-an-arena has evolved from the vantage point of individual members. Members not only seek to distinguish themselves as lawmakers, they also have strong electoral incentive to engage in position taking and credit claiming (Mayhew, 1974). Put in the terms used here, members of Congress today devote a lot of effort to messaging (Grimmer, 2013, Grimmer, Westwood, and Messing, 2015). Members' procedural opportunities to use the floor for their own messaging purposes has been restricted in key ways. However, changes in the broader communications environment have greatly expanded members' abilities to engage with external audiences.

Control of the floor in both House and Senate is more tightly managed in the contemporary Congress. Figure 8.7 shows the percentage of special rules issued by the House Rules Committee that were *restrictive* – meaning they limited opportunities to offer amendments – or *closed* – meaning they did not allow any amendments. The data show that while restrictions on amendments were once rare, they are now commonplace. Most bills now are considered under rules that limit amendments, with more than 40 percent of special rules shutting off amendments completely in recent congresses.

Figure 8.8 shows that floor amending has become less common in the Senate (Wallner, 2013), as well. The data indicate that at one time the Senate floor earned its reputation as a place of free-wheeling legislative business (Sinclair, 1989, Smith, 1989). In recent years, floor amending activity has declined precipitously. "Today's is a more controlled environment, more top-down," summarized a former member.[74] These constraints on floor amendments undoubtedly restrict members' opportunities to affect policy change. But considering the small share of floor amendments opposed by committee leaders that are actually incorporated into enacted legislation (Shepsle and Weingast,

---

[74] Member, July 27, 2016.

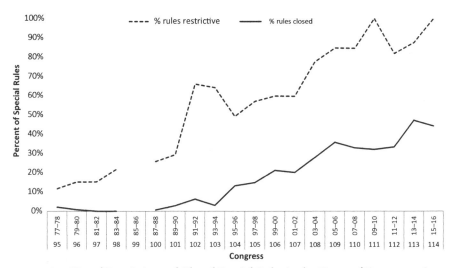

FIGURE 8.7 **Use of Restrictive and Closed Special Rules in the House of Representatives.**
Source: "Survey of Activities" reports published by the House Committee on Rules each congress

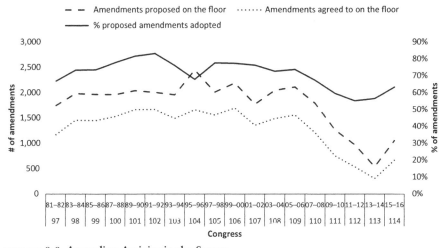

FIGURE 8.8 **Amending Activity in the Senate**
Source: Congress.gov

1987, Curry, 2016), the effect of a more constrained floor process has a larger effect on members' position-taking than on their policy influence.

On the other hand, changes in the media environment have greatly enhanced the ability of individual members to communicate with their constituents and even to cultivate a national following. The rise of electronic communications in all forms has transformed congressional communications capabilities. With the advent of email, the amount of mail traffic handled by congressional offices increased by an order of magnitude (Shogan, 2010). Official member websites, YouTube channels, and Facebook pages attract considerable traffic. Congress was fast to adapt to the changing technological landscape. As early as 2009, members of Congress collectively issued more than 1,100 tweets during a 2-week period (Glassman, Strauss, and Shogan, 2010). By 2013, every member of the Senate and more than 90 percent of House members had official Twitter accounts, which they use with great frequency (Straus et al, 2013). While cable news provides many outlets for lawmakers to reach external audiences, as does talk radio, social media enables members to curate their own public image directly (Golbeck, Grimes, and Rogers, 2010).

The proliferation of media platforms allows more members to engage in national messaging debates. No longer restricted to speaking on the floor or trying to draw the attention of a just a few national news outlets, today members can tweet and potentially become social media celebrities overnight. More members can turn to this kind of "outside" strategy. As one longtime member told us, "There are different types of entrepreneurs. There are people who work within the system. They can still do good work that way. But some go in a different direction and take more of an outsider's approach."[75] Another suggested that some members prefer to focus on messaging to the exclusion of legislative efforts: "A lot of the people who've been elected in recent years haven't really wanted to be legislators. They have been posturing, looking to make themselves famous. They are looking to become celebrities in the age of new media technologies."[76]

In the current environment, more members can seek to distinguish themselves as national opinion leaders and influence the substance of partisan messages. Changes in communication technology have lowered many barriers. "Electronic communications have virtually no direct marginal cost," writes Glassman (2014, p. 102):

Once a Member or constituent pays the startup and recurring costs of owning a computer, there is no further financial cost for each individual email communication between them. Almost all electronic communication media – be it email, social media, tele-townhalls, Web advertisements, and so forth – tend to have fixed capital or startup costs, but are then largely free on the margin.

The upshot is that even freshman members can directly communicate with national audiences, assuming only that they have the capacity to draw attention to themselves. These developments make for a highly entrepreneurial messaging arena. Party leaders seek to manage the overall image of their parties as much as possible, but they face continual competition both within their own ranks

[75] Ibid.   [76] Member, July 28, 2016.

and from the opposing party for the content of that message. These "new communication platforms ... help members create their own networks of support," remarked one staffer. "This makes managing party unity with some members difficult (i.e., Freedom Caucus). Members never had the opportunity to become celebrities unless they did something like drive into the Tidal Basin with a stripper. Now they all have Twitter to lead their followers into the pond!"[77]

From the vantage point of both parties and individual members, the contemporary Congress has evolved into a stronger, more vibrant representational arena. The sheer volume of communications going out to the public from Congress is higher than ever. Furthermore, these communications are instantaneous, allowing members to respond immediately to events and developments in an ongoing 24-hour news cycle. Parties have organized themselves to more fully exploit their institutional resources – both staff and roll call votes – to communicate their differences for external constituencies, making congressional party politics more meaningful and comprehensible for the broad public. At the same time, individual members also have more opportunities to cut a figure in national affairs. These changes have collapsed the distance between Congress and constituents in important ways. Assessments of Congress's performance as a democratic institution should take these developments into account.

DISCUSSION AND CONCLUSIONS

> "Nothing would be more disruptive to the Committee's work than bitter and extended partisan controversy."
>
> Richard F. Fenno (1962, p. 317)

In this paper, we assess how changes to Congress's internal processes have affected its institutional capacities. Following Polsby (1975), we consider how Congress performs both as a transformative lawmaking institution and as a representational arena. With lawmaking, we find that despite a tremendous increase in partisanship on roll call voting, when Congress actually enacts laws, it continues to do so as it always has – through the development of wide consensus and support from both parties. Since the 1970s, bipartisan support for the passage of laws has remained almost constant. That Congress is frequently unable to break through gridlock and address important policy issues is undeniably important. However, when Congress does act, in most cases it achieves roughly the same levels of broad bipartisan assent to laws as it did 40 years ago. Congress can rarely be indicted for ramming through bills with narrow or partisan majorities.

This basic fact about congressional enactments sets the wide-ranging changes in congressional procedure documented here in important context.

---

[77] Staffer, October 17, 2016.

The centralization of power in congressional leaders and the decline of "regular order" has not led to a rise in partisan *lawmaking*. Closed-door processes circumventing committee divisions of labor are not a means by which party leaders have systematically enabled the passage of partisan programs. Leaders may occasionally push through their policy priorities over the objections of their party opposition, but the constitutional system of bicameralism and separation of powers still almost always requires that congressional leaders assemble broad coalitions to succeed in legislating, no matter how intensely polarized the parties may be, and no matter what processes are used.

Rather than empowering majority parties, centralized processes are better understood as an adaptation to difficult contemporary conditions. Congress turns away from decentralized processes in great part because it needs to, in order to thread the needle to find legislation that can win a House majority, a Senate supermajority, and a presidential signature. When decentralized processes can succeed Congress still uses them, as with the annual NDAA. But the committee-led processes that worked so effectively in the mid-twentieth century are poorly suited for a contemporary era of sharp partisan conflict. Describing the low-conflict, consensual operations of the Appropriations Committee of the 1950s and 1960s, Fenno (1962, p. 317) recognized the threat that "bitter and extended partisan controversy" would pose to the committee's integration and its ability to perform its role in the institution. Subsequent developments have borne out Fenno's prescience.

The internal institutions and processes of the twentieth-century Congress have turned out not to be essential for Congress's functioning as a transformative legislature. Congress is transformative as long as it develops and enacts legislation that transforms public policy. The internal and procedural means by which it takes these actions are of limited consequence for its capacity as an institution. Generally, its transformative capacity stems from its powers and place within the constitutional system. The difficulties the contemporary Congress encounters in making law do not stem from process, but from pervasive two-party conflict. Indeed, Congress has many problems, but it does not appear processes are among the most pressing concerns. As former Congressional Budget Office Director Rudolph G. Penner famously said of deficits and the congressional budget process: "the problem is not the process; the problem is the problem."

While the centralization of processes has not damaged Congress's institutional capacity, it undoubtedly has had negative consequences for open deliberation and individual member input into legislation. Our interviewees almost universally preferred the decentralized processes of the textbook Congress (see also Crespin and Madonna, 2016). "The legislative process works so much better via committees," said one.[78] But when these processes do not work, leaders take advantage of the increased flexibility and reduced transparency

---

[78] Staffer, August 5, 2016.

that centralized processes allow. Under such circumstances, rank-and-file members have fewer formal opportunities to participate in lawmaking. We offered some perspectives on how individual members can engage in legislative entrepreneurship under these conditions. Principally, members can make themselves relevant as informal leaders by their capacity to influence other members, either as "keys" or as "umbrellas" (Huitt, 1961). When seeking to pass legislation, coalition leaders will turn to those members who can help them broaden their bases of support.

We also found that changes to the internal processes of Congress have strengthened its capacity as a representational arena, particularly by heightening its capacity for *conflict-clarifying representation* that allows for the "ventilation of opinion for the education of the country at large" and to "mobilize interest groups and proclaim loyalties" (Polsby, 1975, p. 281). Due in large part to the centralization of processes in the hands of leaders, congressional parties are much more effective at publicizing the nature and scope of their disagreement with one another, both by staging roll call votes that display party cleavages and by disseminating party messages in congressional debate and across news media. At the same time, individual members have greatly enhanced capacities to engage in entrepreneurial opinion leadership as well. Developments in electronic media technologies allow for many more and faster lines of communication between the Congress and the public. To the degree that rank-and-file legislators are cut out of the formal proceedings of the House and the Senate, they can turn to social media and cable news to try to influence the party's message and develop a national political following.

It is worth reflecting on these findings in the light of unified Republican government during the first 2 years of the Trump Presidency. Even with control of the House, Senate, and presidency, and the continued use of highly centralized processes, Republicans have largely been unable to enact partisan laws. High-profile attempts have failed, most prominently the 2017 effort to repeal and replace the Affordable Care Act. Omnibus budget and spending measures have been enacted using highly unorthodox processes but have been passed with strong bipartisan support or by cross-partisan majorities.[79] Only one partisan achievement stands out, the Tax Cuts and Jobs Act of 2017 (PL 115–97). At the same time, majority Republicans have continued to use their centralized procedural powers to take partisan messaging votes, including on an Americans with Disabilities Act reform bill,[80] a bill to ban abortions after 20 weeks of pregnancy,[81] and a bill to allow concealed carry permit holders from one state to legally carry their guns in any other state.[82] These bills are

---

[79] The 2018 budget agreement (H.R. 1892) passed the House 240–186 (D 73–119; R 167–67) and the Senate 71–28 (D 36–11; R 34–16). The FY 2018 omnibus appropriations (H.R. 1625) passed the House 256–167 (D 111–77; R 145–90) and the Senate 65–32 (D 39–8; R 25–23).
[80] H.R. 620 (D 12–173; R 213–19).   [81] H.R. 36 (D 3–187; R 234–2).
[82] H.R. 38 (D 6–184; R 225–14).

likely not headed to enactment, but will help the parties differentiate themselves in upcoming elections.

It is clear that taking stock of Congress's performance and capacity requires separate analysis of its functioning as both a representative arena and a transformative legislature. Differentiating between these two functions helps clarify some confusion about party leaders' role. Party leaders are vigorous partisans in the messaging arena. House leaders assemble partisan bills and jam them through. Senate leaders bring up bills they know will never pass in order to show the opposition party blocking their attractive ideas. Minority leaders continually try to embarrass the majority via harsh criticism and forcing painful votes. However, when lawmaking, party leaders often find themselves working closely with their counterparts across the aisle. No matter how tough they might be in prosecuting a party message, when lawmaking, party leaders must still work within the confines of a constitutional system that almost always requires broad support to function at all. Contemporary adaptations to process have provided congressional leaders with new tools to help achieve both goals.

REFERENCES

Abramowitz, Alan I. 2010. *The Disappearing Center: Engaged Citizens, Polarization, and American Democracy*. New Haven, CT: Yale University Press.

Adler, E. Scott, and John D. Wilkerson. 2012. *Congress and the Politics of Problem Solving*. New York: Cambridge University Press.

Aldrich, John H., and David W. Rohde. 2000. "The Consequences of Party Organization in the House: The Role of the Majority and the Minority Parties in Conditional Party Government." In Jon R. Bond and Richard Fleisher (eds.), *Polarized Politics: Congress and the President in a Partisan Era*. Washington, DC: CQ Press, pp. 31–72.

APSA Committee on Parties. 1950. "Towards a More Responsible Two-Party System." *Supplement, American Political Science Review* 44(3).

Arnold, R. Douglas. 1990. *The Logic of Congressional Action*. New Haven, CT: Yale University Press.

Baumgartner, Frank R., and Bryan D. Jones. 2015. *The Politics of Information: Problem Definition and the Course of Public Policy in America*. Chicago: University of Chicago Press.

Barber, Michael J., and Nolan McCarty. 2015. "Causes and Consequences of Polarization." In Nathaniel Persily (ed.), *Solutions to Political Polarization in America*. New York: Cambridge University Press, pp. 15–58.

Bartels, Larry M. 2000. "Partisanship and Voting Behavior, 1952–1996." *American Journal of Political Science* 44(1): 35–50.

Bendix, William. 2016. "Bypassing Congressional Committees: Parties, Panel Rosters, and Deliberative Processes." *Legislative Studies Quarterly* 41(3): 687–714.

Bessette, Joseph. 1994. *The Mild Voice of Reason: Deliberative Democracy and American National Government*. Chicago: University of Chicago Press.

Binder, Sarah A. 2003. *Stalemate: Causes and Consequences of Legislative Gridlock*. Washington: Brookings Institution Press.

2014. "Polarized We Govern?" Center for Effective Public Management, Brookings Institution. Retrieved from www.brookings.edu/wp-content/uploads/2016/06/Broo kingsCEPM_Polarized_figReplacedTextRevTableRev.pdf (last accessed December 11, 2018).

Butler, Daniel M., and Eleanor Neff Powell. 2014. "Understanding the Party Brand: Experimental Evidence on the Role of Valence." *Journal of Politics* 76: 492–505.

Cox, Gary W., and Mathew D. McCubbins. 2005. *Setting the Agenda: Responsible Party Government in the U.S. House of Representatives*. New York: Cambridge University Press.

Crespin, Michael H., and Anthony J. Madonna. 2016. "New Directions in Legislative Research: Lessons from Inside Congress." *PS: Political Science and Politics* 49(3): 473–477.

Curry, James M. 2015. *Legislating in the Dark: Information and Power in the House of Representatives*. Chicago: University of Chicago Press.

2016. "Knowledge, Expertise, and Committee Power in Congress." Presented at the Annual Meeting of the Midwest Political Science Association, April 6–10, 2016.

Drutman, Lee. 2016. "Political Dynamism: A New Approach to Making Government Work Again." Policy Paper, *New America*. Retrieved from www.newamerica .org/new-america/policy-papers/political-dynamism/ (last accessed December 17, 2018).

Egar, William T. 2016. "Tarnishing Opponents, Polarizing Congress: The House Minority Party and the Construction of the Roll-Call Record." *Legislative Studies Quarterly* 41(4): 935–964. DOI: 10.1111/lsq.12135.

Fenno, Richard F. 1962. "The House Appropriations Committee as a Political System: The Problem of Integration." *American Political Science Review* 56(2): 310–324.

Fiorina, Morris P., and Samuel J. Abrams. 2009. *Disconnect: The Breakdown of Representation in American Politics*. Norman: University of Oklahoma Press.

Gelman, Jeremy. 2017. "Rewarding Dysfunction: Interest Groups and Intended Legislative Failure." *Legislative Studies Quarterly* 42(4): 661–692.

Gerrity, Jessica C. 2014. "Understanding Congressional Approval: Public Opinion from 1974 to 2014." *The Evolving Congress*. Committee on Rules and Administration. United States Senate. Washington, DC: U.S Government Printing Office, pp. 189–216.

Gilligan, Thomas W., and Keith Krehbiel. 1990. "Organization of Informative Committees by a Rational Legislature." *American Journal of Political, Science* 34(2): 531–564.

Gilmour, John B. 1995. *Strategic Disagreement: Stalemate in American Politics*. Pittsburgh, PA: University of Pittsburgh Press.

Glassman, Matthew E., Jacob R. Straus, and Colleen J. Shogan. 2010. *Social Networking and Constituent Communication: Member Use of Twitter during a Two-Week Period in the 111th Congress*. Congressional Research Service Report for Congress, R40823, September 21, 2009.

Glassman, Matthew E. 2014. "Tweet Your Congressman: The Rise of Electronic Communications in Congress." *The Evolving Congress*. Committee on Rules and Administration. United States Senate. Washington, DC: U.S. Government Printing Office, pp. 95–106.

Golbeck, Jennifer, Justin M. Grimes, and Anthony Rogers. 2010. "Twitter Use by the U.S. Congress." *Journal of the American Society for Information Science and Technology* 61(8): 1612–1621.

Grimmer, Justin. 2013. *Representational Style in Congress: What Legislators Say and Why It Matters*. New York: Cambridge University Press.

Grimmer, Justin, Sean J. Westwood, and Solomon Messing. 2015. *The Impression of Influence: Legislator Communication, Representation, and Democratic Accountability*. Princeton: Princeton University Press.

Groseclose, Tim, and Nolan McCarty. 2001. "The Politics of Blame: Bargaining Before an Audience." *American Journal of Political Science* 45: 100–119.

Gutmann, Amy, and Dennis S. Thompson. 1996. *Democracy and Disagreement*. Cambridge, MA: Harvard University Press.

Hall, Thad E. 2004. *Authorizing Policy*. Columbus, OH: The Ohio State University Press.

Hamilton, Lee. 2008. "Congress Needs Proper Leadership." *Commentaries, Center on Congress*. Bloomington: Indiana University.

Hanson, Peter. 2014. *Too Weak to Govern: Majority Party Power and Appropriations in the U.S. Senate*. New York: Cambridge University Press.

  2015. "Restoring the Regular Order in Congressional Appropriations." New Ideas for Federal Budgeting: A Series of Working Papers for the National Budgeting Roundtable. Centers on the Public Service. School of Policy, Government and International Affairs. George Mason University.

Harris, Douglas B. 2005. "Orchestrating Party Talk: A Party-Based View of One-Minute Speeches in the House of Representatives." *Legislative Studies Quarterly* 30: 127–141.

Hetherington, Marc J. 2001. "Resurgent Mass Partisanship: The Role of Elite Polarization." *American Political Science Review* 95(3): 619–631.

Huitt, Ralph K. 1961. "Democratic Party Leadership in the Senate." *American Political Science Review* 55(2): 333–344.

Jenkins, Jeffrey A., and Charles Stewart III. 2016. "The Deinstitutionalization (?) of the House of Representatives: Reflections on Nelson Polsby's 'Institutionalization of the House of Representatives' at Fifty," Presented at the Congress & History Conference, Norman, Oklahoma, June 16–17, 2016.

Krehbiel, Keith. 1991. *Information and Legislative Organization*. Ann Arbor: University of Michigan Press.

  1998. *Pivotal Politics: A Theory of U.S. Lawmaking*. Chicago: University of Chicago Press.

Krutz, Glen S. 2005. *Hitching a Ride: Omnibus Legislating in the U.S. Congress*. Columbus, OH: The Ohio State University Press.

Layman, Geoffrey C., Thomas M. Carsey, John C. Green, Richard Herrera, and Rosalyn Cooperman. 2010. "Activists and Conflict Extension in American Party Politics." *American Political Science Review* 104(2): 324–346.

Lee, Frances E. 2016. *Insecure Majorities: Congress and the Perpetual Campaign*. Chicago: University of Chicago Press.

Levendusky, Matthew. 2009. *The Partisan Sort: How Liberals Became Democrats and Conservatives Became Republicans*. Chicago: University of Chicago Press.

Lewallen, Jonathan, Sean M. Theriault, and Bryan D. Jones. 2016. "Congressional Dysfunction: An Information Processing Perspective." *Regulation and Governance* 10(2): 179–190.

Maass, Arthur. 1983. *Congress and the Common Good*. New York: Basic Books.

Mann, Thomas E., and Norman Ornstein. 2006. *The Broken Branch: How Congress Is Failing America and How to Get It Back on Track*. New York: Oxford University Press.

2012. *It's Even Worse Than It Looks: How the American Constitutional System Collided with the New Politics of Extremism*. New York: Basic Books.

Mayhew, David R. 1974. *Congress: The Electoral Connection*. New Haven: Yale University Press.

2000. *America's Congress: Actions in the Public Sphere, James Madison through Newt Gingrich*. New Haven: Yale University Press.

2005. *Divided We Govern: Party Control, Lawmaking, and Investigations, 1946–2002*, 2nd ed. New Haven: Yale University Press.

McCarty, Nolan, Keith T. Poole, and Howard Rosenthal. 2006. *Polarized America: The Dance of Ideology and Unequal Riches*. Cambridge: The MIT Press.

Mill, John Stuart. 1975 [1861]. "Considerations on Representative Government." In *Three Essays*. Oxford: Oxford University Press.

Reynolds, Molly E. 2018. *Vital Statistics on Congress*. Washington, DC: Brookings Institution Press.

Polsby, Nelson W. 1968. "The Institutionalization of the U.S. House of Representatives." *American Political Science Review* 62(1): 144–168.

1975. "Legislatures." In Fred I. Greenstein and Nelson W. Polsby (eds.) *Handbook of Political Science*. New York: Addison-Wesley.

Quirk, Paul J. 2005. "Deliberation and Decision Making." In Sarah A. Binder and Paul J. Quirk (eds.), *The Legislative Branch*. New York: Oxford University Press, pp. 314–348.

Ramirez, Mark D. 2009. "The Dynamics of Partisan Conflict on Congressional Approval." *American Journal of Political Science*, 53: 681–694.

Rohde, David W. 1991. *Parties and Leaders in the Postreform House*. Chicago: University of Chicago Press.

Rosenthal, Alan. 2004. *Heavy Lifting: The Job of the American Legislature*. Washington: CQ Press.

Schattschneider, E. E. 1942. *Party Government*. New York: Farrar and Rinehart.

Shepsle, Kenneth A. 1988. "Representation and Governance: The Great Legislative Trade-Off." *Political Science Quarterly* 103(3): 461–484.

1989. "The Changing Textbook Congress." In John Chubb and Paul Peterson *(eds.)*, *Can the Government Govern?* Washington, DC: Brookings Institution, pp. 238–266.

Shepsle, Kenneth A., and Barry R. Weingast. 1987. "The Institutional Foundations of Committee Power." *American Political Science Review* 81(1): 85–104.

Shogan, Colleen J. 2010. "Blackberries, Tweets, and YouTube: Technology and the Future of Communicating with Congress: PS: *Political Science & Politics* 43(2): 231–233.

2012. "Defense Authorization: The Senate's Last Best Hope." In Jacob R. Straus (ed.), *Party and Procedure in the United States Congress*. Lanham, MD: Rowman and Littlefield, pp. 195–216.

Sinclair, Barbara. 1989. *The Transformation of the U. S. Senate*. Baltimore: Johns Hopkins University Press.

2016. *Unorthodox Lawmaking: New Legislative Processes in the U.S. Congress*, 5th edition. Washington: CQ Press.

Smith, Steven. 1989. *Call to Order: Floor Politics in the House and Senate.* Washington, DC: The Brookings Institution.

Smith, Steven S. 2014. *The Senate Syndrome: The Evolution of Procedural Warfare in the Modern U.S. Senate.* Norman, OK: University of Oklahoma Press.

Snowe, Olympia J. 2013. "The Effect of Modern Partisanship on Legislative Effectiveness in the 112th Congress." *Harvard Journal on Legislation* 50(1): 21–40.

Straus, Jacob R., Matthew Eric Glassman, Colleen J. Shogan, and Susan Navarro Smelcer. 2013. "Communicating in 140 Characters or Less: Congressional Adoption of Twitter in the 111th Congress." *PS: Political Science & Politics* 4(1): 60–66.

Theriault, Sean M. 2008. *Party Polarization in Congress.* New York: Cambridge University Press.

Thompson, Dennis S. 2008. "Deliberative Democratic Theory and Empirical Political Science." *Annual Review of Political Science* 11: 497–520.

Thurber, James A. 2011. "What Is Wrong with Congress and What Should Be Done about It." In Iwan Morgan and Philip John Davies (eds.), *Broken Government? Politics in the Obama Era.* London: University of London/Institute for the Study of the Americas Press.

Tiefer, Charles. 2016. *The Polarized Congress: The Post-Traditional Procedure of Its Current Struggles.* Lanham, MD: University Press of America.

Volden, Craig, and Alan E. Wiseman. 2014. *Legislative Effectiveness in the United States Congress.* New York: Cambridge University Press.

Wallner, James I. 2013. *The Death of Deliberation: Partisanship and Polarization in the United States Senate.* New York: Lexington Books.

Waxman, Henry with Joshua Green. 2009. *The Waxman Report: How Congress Really Works.* New York: Twelve.

Wawro, Gregory. 2000. *Legislative Entrepreneurship in the U.S. House of Representatives.* Ann Arbor: MI: University of Michigan Press.

Appendix 8A

TABLE 8.1A *Predicting Support for New Laws on Initial Passage, 1973–2016.*

	House		Senate	
	% voting yea	% minority party support	% voting yea	% minority party support
Became law	0.071[b]	0.148[b]	0.082[b]	0.131[b]
	(0.014)	(0.030)	(0.010)	(0.021)
Sponsor distance from chamber median	0.068[a]	0.147	−0.096	0.241
	(0.032)	(0.118)	(0.114)	(0.136)
Sponsor in majority party	−0.061[b]	−0.130[a]	−0.017	−0.004
	(0.015)	(0.051)	(0.044)	(0.065)
Sponsor distance from chamber median × Sponsor in majority party	−0.178[b]	−0.407[a]	0.037	−0.286
	(0.053)	(0.152)	(0.106)	(0.159)
Party polarization	−0.565[b]	−1.500[b]	−0.268	−0.748[a]
	(0.070)	(0.171)	(0.136)	(0.310)
Majority party seat share	−0.313[a]	−1.288[b]	−0.538[a]	−1.251[b]
	(0.139)	(0.365)	(0.224)	(0.416)
Majority party unity	2.289[b]	3.951[b]	−0.240	−0.652
	(0.452)	(1.184)	(0.214)	(0.393)
Divided government	−0.021	−0.044	0.007	0.024
	(0.011)	(0.028)	(0.014)	(0.025)
constant	−0.429	−0.640	1.506[b]	2.424[b]
	(0.381)	(1.043)	(0.275)	(0.487)
N	5,912	5,912	1,712	1,712
R-squared	0.163	0.329	0.154	0.263

Notes: [a]$p < 0.05$; [b]$p < 0.01$. OLS regression analyses with robust standard errors correcting for clustering by congress.

9

Dumbing Down?

Trends in the Complexity of Political Communication

Kenneth Benoit, Kevin Munger, and Arthur Spirling

DUMBING DOWN AS AN ANXIETY OF DEMOCRACY

Anxiety about the quality of public political discourse is nothing new. Beginning at least with Plato's call for "Philosopher Kings" to protect citizens from their own base impulses, this fear has its modern incarnation in commentators' concerns about the supposed dumbing down (Gatto, 2002) of politics, culture, and public life. Claims that elected officials and their output are less "intellectual" (e.g., Lim, 2008) than they used to be generally rely on the idea that contemporary politicians must appeal to a median voter who demands progressively simpler messages. This is despite, or perhaps because of, the increasing complexity of the modern world and the fact that information is no longer hard to acquire, but rather difficult to escape. According to this view, modern citizens are too busy or too distracted to absorb anything other than facile sound bites that the news media serves up on a 24-hour rolling basis. And the prognosis is that a bad situation will worsen. Thus, for example, the Guardian newspaper laments that the "state of our union is ... dumber,"[1] while other outlets describe Donald Trump's speeches on the campaign trail as having the standard of a fifth grader,[2] a fourth grader,[3] or even a third grader.[4]

In contrast to such pessimism, more sanguine commentators point to several interrelated trends suggesting we should not be worried. They argue that as the world has grown more complex, so has the public ability to absorb more – and more complex – information. In terms of formal education, the postwar period

---

[1] www.theguardian.com/world/interactive/2013/feb/12/state-of-the-union-reading-level

[2] www.washingtonpost.com/news/morning-mix/wp/2016/03/18/trumps-grammar-in-speeches-just-below-6t?utm_term=.175e0dddcfcf

[3] http://nypost.com/2016/03/17/donald-trump-speaks-at-a-fourth-grade-reading-level/

[4] www.politico.com/magazine/story/2015/08/donald-trump-talks-like-a-third-grader-121340

has seen a massive expansion in college enrollment, from around 45 percent of school leavers in 1959, to some 70 percent by 2009 by US Department of Labor figures. This pattern of increasing attendance, if not at identical rates, is not only true for historically privileged groups. It is also seen in women and African Americans, who joined the franchise in the United States much later than did white men. Thus, any claims that the extension of suffrage to relatively uneducated groups might be causing a decline in discourse quality (see Spirling [2016] for an application of this idea to the UK) are extremely dubious. Even if one does not accept that college adds much to students' core cognitive capacities, there is evidence at a more fundamental level that citizens can cope with more sophistication. The "Flynn Effect" describes the relentless year-on-year increase in IQ scores in multiple countries and societies, including the United States (Flynn, 1999). And in the specific domain of civics – presumably one of the more relevant subjects for political understanding – knowledge levels have been at worst flat in recent times (Galston, 2001).

In this chapter, we examine the evidence for these polar opposite positions in the debates on modern political discussion. In particular, we analyze long-term trends in the sophistication of language using similar metrics, comparing political and cultural texts across time and space. Our conclusions should be relatively anxiety-relieving. Put very simply, the State of the Union (SOTU) is probably an outlier as elite time series go, and the changes it has been through – which are by no means as stark as they first appear – are mostly a benign (and sometimes mechanical) consequence of other broader trends in language.

We proceed as follows. Because of its centrality to extant accounts of dumbing down, we reanalyze SOTU in some detail, and consider standard time series diagnostics and what they reveal. We also apply a sentence-level boot-strapping procedure to get a more accurate sense of how that corpus is – and is not – genuinely changing over time. We then provide a more general critique of the standard measure(s) of textual complexity and explain why they might be poorly suited for comparing speeches over such a long historical period. Our most important innovation below is to compare SOTU to other time series. In particular, we show that when we look at other branches of US government, comparatively to other countries (the UK), or to other cultural touchstones (such as Nobel prize literature announcements), there is little or none of the purported dumbing down we see for the SOTU texts. Finally, we look under the hood of the most widely used yardstick of "readability," the Flesch Reading Ease (FRE) measure, and decompose the patterns in our data into the component deriving from changes in sentence lengths versus the component that is a product of varying word lengths. We demonstrate that, while there is little systematic change in terms of word use, we live in an era of ever-shortening sentences. While this may well make for clearer, punchier rhetoric, we are unconvinced that it alone should provoke anxiety about the state of our democracy.

A NOTICEABLE TREND: THE SIMPLIFICATION OF
PRESIDENTIAL ADDRESSES

Since 1790, with only a few exceptions, the president has delivered an annual SOTU address to Congress. This makes it an unusually regular, if not especially frequent, source of data on the changing priorities of the executive. Importantly for our purposes, there is no requirement that it be a speech. Indeed, from Jefferson until around 1934, and even after on some occasions, the SOTU was generally submitted to Congress as a *written* document. Because the form of spoken English usually differs from that of written English, even for pre-written speeches, we might immediately expect that the change in formats is reflected in differences in the structure and complexity of the language, particularly in terms of the length of sentences. This induces an obvious problem of confounding: it is difficult to know whether changes over time are a product of some latent dynamic or simply the consequence of altering the means of the address. Nonetheless, studying the purported sophistication of this series has proved popular, both for academics (e.g., Lim, 2008) and journalists.

The most common measurement approach is to use (Flesch, 1948)'s "reading ease" (FRE) statistic. Based on a linear regression of reading comprehension on average sentence length and average number of syllables per word, the FRE has proved durable well beyond its mid-twentieth century origins. It consists of a linear combination of average word length (in syllables) and average sentence length, computed as

$$206.835 - 1.015 \left(\frac{\text{total number of words}}{\text{total number of sentences}} \right) - 84.6 \left(\frac{\text{total number of syllables}}{\text{total number of words}} \right)$$

In the initial application, FRE took values between 0 and 100, although technically the upper bound of a text's reading ease is 121.22, if a text consists exclusively of single-syllable, single-word sentences. Scores between 60–70 are considered "plain English," and easily read and understood by someone with an eighth- or ninth-grade education. (For comparison, the FRE of this chapter we calculated as 35.2.) In the 1970s, Kincaid et al (1975) introduced a linear rescaling of the formula designed to correspond more directly to the US grade school levels required to comprehend a text.

Whether or not FRE is suitable for a given application cannot be answered definitively from first principles. Still, some concerns are obvious. First, FRE is used in a context far from its original domain when applied to SOTU. It is doubtful whether judging the sophistication of SOTU addresses – designed for Congress and adult citizens who may be familiar with political terms in a way that minors are not – is best done with a measure invented for assigning books to school children. And if it is appropriate, the fact that the measure was last calibrated 70 years ago might give us pause. Here, one danger is that other than via syllable information, the FRE does not explicitly take into account the familiarity of the words used in a text. For a given word, this is something that surely varies over time: thus, citizens in 1940 would be have little trouble understanding *locomotive*, relative to voters in 1990, but by contrast may have struggled significantly with a term like *television*, which would be trivial for listeners later in the century. It is true that some other approaches do cater for familiarity explicitly (e.g., Dale and Chall, 1948), but in practice the scores for documents are highly correlated with those generated by FRE. This is also the case for the numerous other approaches that have proved less popular than FRE and its variants (e.g., Gunning, 1952, Spache, 1953, McLaughlin, 1969, Coleman and Liau, 1975).

More fundamental perhaps than the linguistic problems with FRE are the *statistical* problems that typically emerge with its use. For any given document, the FRE score provides what is essentially a *point estimate*, technically an out-of-sample prediction of the dependent variable ($\hat{y}$) from the original regression Flesch ran on school children. These predictions/estimates may then be plotted or analyzed. But for any systematic test of claimed changes over time, we also need to know our uncertainty around the point estimates. For this to happen, we require the sampling distribution of the FRE such that, for example, we can place 95 percent confidence intervals around the values. In this way, we can make statements about the whether the decline between two dates is statistically significant or merely due to sampling variation. In the measures presented below, we obtain bounds using the bootstrapping approach of Benoit, Laver, and Mikhaylov (2009), which resamples sentences with replacement within texts. This simulates variability while preserving dependencies among language within sentence units. For a given text with k sentences, we drew 100 samples (with replacement) of size k of those sentences. From the 100 samples, we computed the 95 percent confidence interval as the 2.5th and 97.5th quantiles of the replicates. Two factors in a text tend to influence the variability of readability statistics computed in this way. First, the more heterogenous the sentences of a text in terms of their sentence length and syllabic length, the more variable are the replicates. Second, shorter texts tend to produce larger intervals in the replicates, due to the higher resampling rates of sentences from texts with a smaller pool of sentences from which to draw.

In Figure 9.1, we plot the FRE point estimates and their associated 95 percent confidence intervals from this bootstrapping procedure. We also impose structural breaks (in the sense of Bai and Perron, 2003) on the time series. These are marked by solid vertical dark lines running to the height of the plot, while the shorter gray lines represent the confidence intervals.

The most evident pattern in Figure 9.1 is the upward trend in reading ease: from a typical level of 27 in the first period, to about 57 in the latest period. This corresponds to roughly a level requiring a college degree to understand the text, to requiring just having completed junior high school. From the break-point analysis, we observe three structural changes: in 1856, in 1934, and a third in 1981. After each break, the mean FRE increases. The first break, contemporaneous with the advent of the Third Party System, may reflect the

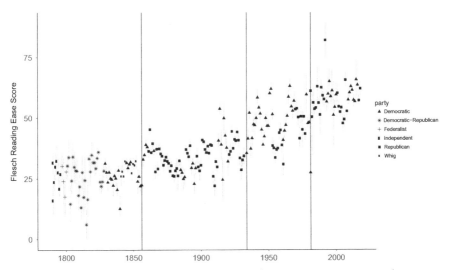

FIGURE 9.1 Flesch Reading Ease (FRE) Scores, with 95 Percent Bootstrapped Confidence Intervals, for the SOTU Address. The Solid Vertical Lines Are Estimated Structural Breaks.

greater role of broader-based party coalitions than had previously been the case. The second break corresponds to a shift in means of delivery: FDR delivered his addresses as speeches rather than written documents, and this was increasingly the norm thereafter. The final break occurs just after Carter's last address, which was by far the longest in history, and coincided with a period in which the president had returned (briefly) to delivering the SOTU report in writing.

Judging from the confidence intervals, however, we see that adding estimates of uncertainty about the reading ease statistics throws significant shade on claims about "dumbing down" in recent times. In particular, many of the confidence intervals from the last two periods in the data overlap. Taking this into account, it far from clear that speeches given around 2000 are any dumber, in a statistical sense, than speeches given in the 1940s and 1950s. Equally, it is not clear that the Republican speeches in the early years of the twenty-first century are statistically significantly different than those made 100 years earlier.

But even the point estimates may be misleading here. This is because, as noted above, they do not account for the practices of various presidents to deliver written, as opposed to spoken, addresses to Congress. Simply put, we might expect spoken texts to use simpler sentences, and therefore to score more highly on the reading ease index. To examine this claim, in the boxplots in Figure 9.2, we have distinguished the scores for our four time periods by whether the texts were spoken or written. As expected, spoken addresses tend score more highly on readability. Furthermore, the difference between spoken and written addresses is increasing over time: In the first period (1790–1856)

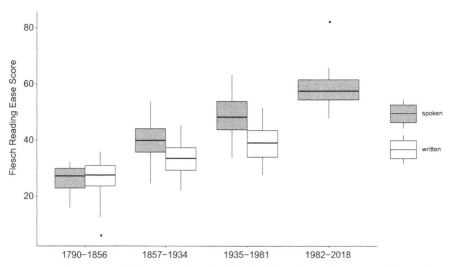

FIGURE 9.2 **Differences in Reading Ease by Method of Delivery, for State of the Union Addresses.**

there was no discernible difference in reading ease, regardless of whether the address was written or spoken, a sharp contrast to the era of 1935–1981 when there was about a 10-point difference between written and spoken addresses (a median 39 and 48, respectively).[5]

The difference appears to be that in the early years of the republic, even spoken addresses were designed for audiences with a nearly masochistic ability to endure long, convoluted speeches. While posterity remembers Abraham Lincoln's 2-minute speech on November 19, 1863, far fewer are aware that his immortal Gettysburg's address followed a 2-hour speech by former Secretary of State Edward Everett, a man widely acclaimed for his oratorical ability. In the early years of the Republic, longer texts, containing longer sentences, were far more common. The start of President John Adams's 1797 (spoken) address, for instance, contained the following sentence, inconceivable today:

Although I can not yet congratulate you on the reestablishment of peace in Europe and the restoration of security to the persons and properties of our citizens from injustice and violence at sea, we have, nevertheless, abundant cause of gratitude to the source of benevolence and influence for interior tranquillity and personal security, for propitious seasons, prosperous agriculture, productive fisheries, and general improvements, and, above all, for a rational spirit of civil and religious liberty and a calm but steady

---

[5] In the 1935–1981 period, 43 speeches were spoken and only 7 were written. This contrasts to the first and second periods, when the tallies were 56 to 12 and 67 to 10, respectively. In the era since 1982, all addresses have been spoken.

determination to support our sovereignty, as well as our moral and our religious principles, against all open and secret attacks. (John Adams, 1797)

While such passages are highly effective in reducing a text's reading ease score (it is −57.1 for that passage, and not even we can understand it!), few commentators would point to the death of such communication styles as a reason to be anxious about the quality of our democratic discourse or of political communication. Put more positively, fewer sentences of this nature are good for the clarity of political life.

COMPARING SOTU TRENDS TO OTHER TEXTS

We have thus far made the claim that the standard measures of complexity are not ideal, and that the point estimates they yield – at least as regards SOTU addresses – may be misleading. Still, there remains an undeniable long-term trend toward greater reading ease in the SOTU texts, which as a representative sample of elite discourse might provide a valid cause for concern. To assess whether the SOTU addresses is unusual, or part of a general troubling trend in increasing textual simplicity, we now compare the SOTU trends against several other benchmark corpora, observed over time. These texts include two other political series from the United States and two from a reasonably similar system, the United Kingdom.

The primary US corpora we examined are from Supreme Court (SCOTUS) opinions from 1790 to 2012 and executive orders from 1826 to 2017 (see Table 9.1).[6] The SCOTUS opinions not only represent legal language from the highest court in the United States, but also capture changing trends in both language and in subject matter. This is because changes in technology or political complexity may have affected the content of the documents in ways that might also have affected the SOTU corpus. The Executive Orders, some 4,451 in total, offer an alternative glimpse into presidential language, albeit in a different context. If the trends we observe in SOTU are absent from the judicial and alternative executive texts, we can perhaps dismiss claims about a general dumbing down of democratic discourse in the American context. We also have a short time series of machine readable text from the *Congressional Record*: in particular, representatives and senators speaking in floor debates (with the Speaker of either chamber removed) for the years 1995–2008. This allows us to compare executive texts with those from the legislature.

---

[6] For the SCOTUS corpus, we took a weighted sample of a total of 38,872 SCOTUS decisions. For all years in which there were fewer than 30 SCOTUS decisions recorded, we include all those from that year, but took a random sample of the decisions from years with more than 30. We also cleaned the text so that (e.g.) *Roe v. Wade* and other abbreviations such as *US* would not be counted as multiple sentences, and we eliminated any "sentence" appearing to contain fewer than four words.

TABLE 9.1 *Summary of the Texts Examined.*

Corpus	Date Range	Number of Texts	Max Words	Median Words
SOTU	1790–2018	232	31,920	5,716
SCOTUS	1790–2012	6,373	8,731	1,608
Congressional Record	1995–2008	819,978	3,677	36
Executive Orders	1826–2017	4,451	1,263	246
Nobel Prize Announcements	1901–2015	96	2,746	1,156
UK Party Manifestos	1918–2010	71	22,990	5,078
UK Party Election Broadcasts	1964–2001	84	2,202	1,362

As an additional benchmark against texts from a different, but in many ways similar political context, we also examined readability trends in two corpora from the United Kingdom: a set of 71 election manifestos from the Labour and Conservative parties, from 1918 to 2010, and a set of 84 party election broadcasts from 1964 to 2001. The latter are transcriptions of officially regulated radio and television broadcasts used by political parties to advertise their positions during election campaigns, in lieu of political advertising.[7] Both are aimed at the general citizenry and designed to broadcast party positions and to attract voters, although manifestos are written documents and party election broadcasts spoken.

Finally, we compare the SOTU addresses to the announcements of the winner for the Nobel Prize for Literature. These announcements typically explain why the committee is awarding the prize, and thus describe the merits and scope of the relevant author's work. We chose this time series because is relatively long and regular, and captures a broader, cultural spirit that is hopefully less explicitly political than the other data we have.

Comparing the SOTU trend to the other American political texts, we see in Figure 9.3 that unlike the SOTU texts, the Supreme Court opinions remained relatively constant in readability since 1790, at a Flesch score of around 40 for most of the period (with a dip around 1900). Even in the twenty-first century, this trend remained unchanged. Looking at the corpus of executive orders, we see that the reading ease of these presidential texts not only did not show an increase similar to the SOTU texts, but actually declined in the nineteenth century, remaining constant throughout the twentieth century, and then

---

[7] Party election broadcasts replace political advertisements in the United Kingdom, which are prohibited by law. Parties are allocated broadcast slots of around 5 minutes each, free of charge, using a formula set by Parliament. We obtained the broadcast transcripts from www.politicsre sources.net/area/uk/peb.htm.

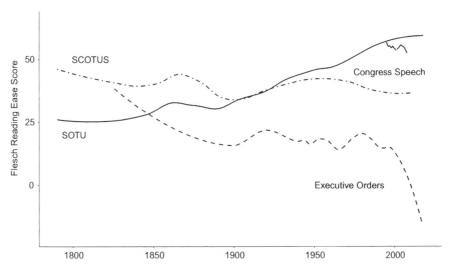

FIGURE 9.3 Comparing SOTU Reading Ease Trends to Other Governmental Texts: Supreme Court Decisions, Congressional Speeches, and Executive Orders.

declining sharply after 2000. So, while annual presidential addresses to Congress – and through live broadcast, to the public – became markedly more comprehensible, presidential text in the form of executive orders became markedly more dense. Thus, there seems to be a clear divergence in text that communicates goals and broad plans to a general audience (SOTU) and texts that deliver legally binding instructions from the president to the officers and agencies of the federal government (executive orders). As executive orders have increased in frequency and scope since the founding of the republic, they have clearly also grown in textual complexity. Executive political communication to the masses may have gotten markedly simpler, but executive orders are clearly exhibiting a tendency quite opposite to the "dumbing down" thesis.

To the extent we can draw firm conclusions from the congressional corpus, we see two things. First, the mean readability of these texts is high: certainly well above that of SCOTUS and the executive orders, and on a par with SOTU addresses around 1975. This perhaps makes sense given the texts here are spoken rather than written. But, perhaps more interestingly, any trend in simplicity from Congress is downward in the direction of *more complexity* not less. Recall that we have a great deal of data from Congress cross-sectionally (although not much over time). When we perform a t-test of means for the first and last year of the *Record* data, we easily reject the null of equal difficulty over time ($p < 0.01$).

Comparing the US speeches to the UK context and the international texts from Nobel prize announcements, we also see relative stability in these patterns compared to the trend to greater reading ease from SOTU. Figure 9.4 plots the

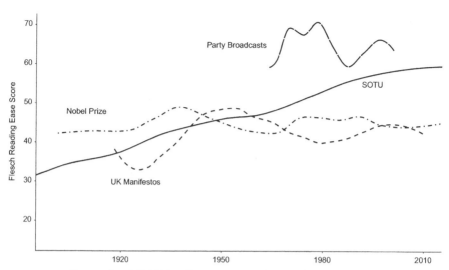

FIGURE 9.4 Comparing SOTU Reading Ease Trends to Other Text Series: UK Conservative and Labour Party Manifestos, UK Party Political Broadcasts, and Nobel Literature Prize Presentation Speeches.

time trends for UK manifestos, the party election broadcasts, and the Nobel Prize announcements. While Nobel Prize announcements gained in reading ease slightly from about 1930 to 1950, their scores remained relatively constant across that period, at around 50, similar to the relatively stable UK election manifestos. The stability in the reading ease of the UK manifestos is in many ways a remarkable contrast to the SOTU trend, because of significant changes in the character of the electorate and of political campaigning during this period. Finally, party broadcasts, while at a much higher reading ease level than the other texts generally, also showed relative stability within the 60–75 point range, the level at which texts are considered easily comprehended with only 8 or 9 years of formal education.

Overall, the conclusions from our benchmarking are clear: Compared to trends in judicial texts, congressional speeches, and other executive texts, the trend to greater simplicity of the SOTU texts appears to be a somewhat isolated phenomenon. Compared to political texts aimed at mass publics, such as the UK manifestos and party election broadcasts, the singular nature of the SOTU trend is upheld. Even the texts honoring some of the brightest users of language in the world, as indicated through the Nobel Prize texts, showed no real changes in complexity. Something unique is happening in the SOTU texts. To investigate what this might be, in the next section we decompose the drivers of the reading ease score. This allows us to assess whether the observed pattern appears to be coming from a change in sentence length or rather, because presidential addresses are using syllabically simpler words. If the latter, we might consider this be a form of "dumbing down," but if the former, then it probably reflects primarily stylistic differences in an evolving preference for shorter sentences.

DIGGING DEEPER INTO THE COMPONENTS OF READING EASE

As explained, the index of reading ease, which we have used to measure the sophistication of political communication, the FRE, consists of a linear combination of sentence length and word lengths. For each additional increase in the mean word length of a text's average sentence, the index decreases by 1.015, and it decreases by 84.6 for each one unit increase in a text's average word's number of syllables. And as noted, while these weights are specific to the Flesch index, the components, or some form of them, are common to nearly every index of readability.

Figure 9.5 plots the long-term trends in the three American text series, for the mean sentence length in words. Here we see a steady change in the measure for SOTU that mirrors the trend in the Flesch index that contains the mean sentence length as a component: from a typical sentence of 40 words around 1,800, to a typical sentence of around 20 words or fewer by 2,000. As measured by the Flesch index, a 20-word length change corresponds to an increase in the Flesch score of 20.3, which would explain two-thirds of the increase observed between the median texts in the first and last periods (Figure 9.1). If we compare the SOTU address with the longest sentences, James Madison in 1815 with an average sentence length of nearly 53.5 words, to an

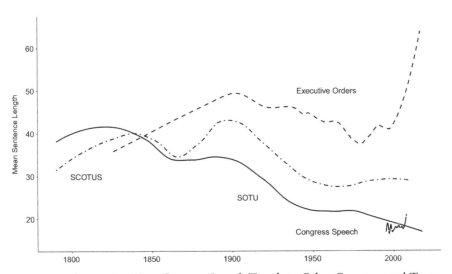

FIGURE 9.5 Comparing Mean Sentence Length Trends to Other Governmental Texts: Supreme Court Decisions and Executive Orders.

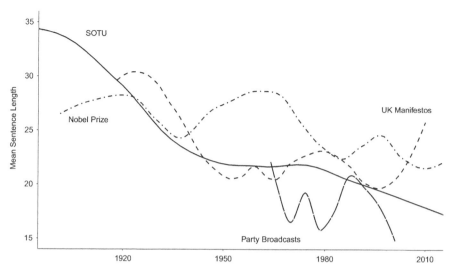

FIGURE 9.6 Comparing Mean Sentence Length Trends to Other Text Series: UK Conservative and Labour Party Manifestos, UK Party Political Broadcasts, and Nobel Literature Prize Presentation Speeches.

address with some of the shortest sentences, Donald Trump's speech in 2017 at around 17.5 words per sentence, this alone accounts for a difference in the Flesch score of over 36.5.

Examining the other corpora measured in Figure 9.5, we see generally similar trends to their Flesch scores. A key difference is a noticeable decline in mean sentence length for the SCOTUS texts between 1900 and 1950, of about 15 words on average. The sentence length of the executive orders increases steadily between 1825 and 1900, then holds relatively steady until increasing sharply following 2000. The latter shift in particular explains the sharp drop in the Flesch scores of the executive order texts from about 2000. As with the SOTU addresses, most of the changes appear to be driven by changes in sentence length. For the congressional speeches, although we were able to observe only a very short time series, the trend nonetheless looks approximately constant, with a very small recent increase in sentence length.

To compare trends in sentence length to our non–US benchmark corpora, Figure 9.6 compares the SOTU texts to the sentence length trends for the UK political texts and the Nobel Prize announcements. While they fluctuate over time, only the Nobel texts from 1920 to 1950 exhibit a strong downward trend, explaining the matching rise in reading ease during this period for the Nobel texts from Figure 9.4.

Turning to the other component of the reading ease measure, we examine trends in word lengths in Figures 9.7 and 9.8. The first shows the trends for our American political texts, and the second for the comparative benchmark

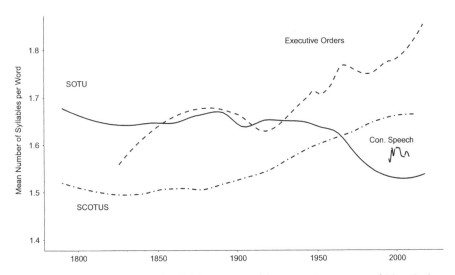

FIGURE 9.7 **Mean Number of Syllables Per Word for Four Governmental Text Series:** Supreme Court Decisions, Congressional Record, Executive Orders and for the State of the Union Addresses.

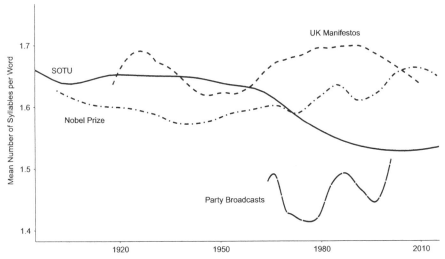

FIGURE 9.8 **Mean Number of Syllables Per Word for Four Text Series:** Nobel Literature Prize Presentation Speeches, UK Conservative and Labour Party Manifestos, Transcripts of UK Party Political Broadcasts, and for the State of the Union Address.

corpora. Here the trend for SOTU is relatively flat, until about 1960 when the trend drops to a new plateau around 2000. By contrast, the other three series show steady increases or stasis in mean sentence length. The executive orders have generally longer words from about 1920, and SCOTUS uses more syllables (on average) from about 1900. Congressional speeches don't move a great deal in this space: they begin and end in approximately the same place, syllablewise. Overall, this is a striking contrast: if anything, word lengths are getting longer in US political text, except for the SOTU addresses, which have shown a tendency toward shorter words, especially since 1960. Benchmarked against the comparative texts, we see the decline in SOTU word lengths (albeit for a shorter time series) in Figure 9.8, while the typical word lengths of the other texts has remained relatively constant.

While SOTU texts have declined in both word and sentence lengths, the contribution of gradually shortening sentences is far stronger than the move to progressively shorter words. To assess this, we can compare the coefficients in the Flesch formula that provide weights for each component, against the typical variation in each component among the SOTU speeches. By measuring a "standard deviation" in mean sentence length and mean word length across the texts, we can compare what a change in this standardized unit of variation would yield in scoring terms. For sentence length, the standard deviation is 8.9; for word length, this figure is a much smaller 0.7. This means that this typical change for sentence length results in just over 9 (8.9 × 1.015) in the Flesch index, while a typical change in word length changes the Flesch index by just under 6 (0.07 × 84.6). Sentence length changes are weighted 1.5 times more than word length changes for these texts, in terms of the coefficients of the Flesch formula. Given the steady and marked changes in sentence length over the evolution of the US presidential addresses, these changes explain most of the widely noted trend to greater reading ease in this corpus.

DISCUSSION

For some contemporary commentators, "anti-intellectualism" is ever present, as if culturally baked into the historical heritage of public life in the United States (Hofstadter, 1963). For others, today's "cult of ignorance" represents something new and more terrifying (Asimov, 1980). Thus, while 1968 presidential hopeful George Wallace railed against "pointy-head college professors who can't even park a bicycle straight," (current) Secretary of Education Betsy DeVos pushed this rhetoric further by encouraging college students to "fight against the education establishment" whose elites " ... tell you what to think."[8] It would seem that systematic evidence for evaluating such baleful trends would be easy to come by. And, to the extent that the SOTU addresses appear to show increasing reading ease, scholars and journalists who draw anxious conclusions

---

[8] "U.S. Secretary of Education Betsy DeVos Prepared Remarks at the 2017 Conservative Political Action Conference." Retrieved from www.ed.gov/news/speeches/us-secretary-education-betsy-devos %E2%80% 99-prepared-remarks-2017-conservative-political-action-conference (last accessed December 9, 2018).

from that corpus might well have a point. Having assessed the SOTU data in some detail, however, we are skeptical of the need for panic.

Our reexamination of the upward trend in the SOTU readability patterns has revealed several significant qualifications to the dumbing down thesis. First, if one is serious about uncertainty around the measures, the "standard" picture changes: while means tell one fairly clear story, appropriately accounting for sampling variation tells a more confusing tale.

Second, and importantly, the SOTU trend toward much greater reading ease is not general in political communication. Indeed, it appears to be unique even among presidential texts, for those we examined: presidential executive orders, after remaining fairly constant at a college-plus reading ease level, became considerably more complex around 2000 due to the shift toward longer sentences. The language complexity of the Supreme Court has remained almost unchanged since 1800. Other texts, such as the party platforms of the main UK parties, and the Nobel Prize acceptance speeches, are also unchanged in terms of their average simplicity. It is true that UK party broadcasts are less complex that SOTU addresses, but this is not a new phenomenon, and some modern ones are approximately on a par with those from the 1960s.

Third, examining the components of the reading ease index, sentence length and word length, we find that most of the changes are being driven by sentence length, although from about 1960 we acknowledge that there is also a trend toward shorter words in the SOTU addresses. In the first decade of SOTU addresses, the typical sentence was twice as long as the typical sentence from those in the 2000s. Part of this trend comes from the shift from written to spoken addresses but was evident even in those that were written. We suspect that shorter sentences – as noted above, common to most other series – are likely to reflect changing communication styles rather than being *per se* evidence of "dumbing down" of content. Related to style, the purpose of SOTU addresses is also changing. In earlier times, the documents were closer to dutiful if plodding reports on the health of the nation – and especially its finances. In today's more polarized climate, they represent a relatively rare opportunity for presidents to appear as magnanimous statesmen, while directly pushing pet policies and claiming credit. On this score, watching recent SOTU speeches is instructive: applause is expected (encouraged?) after virtually every sentence uttered; as recently as Carter, live response was much more muted. In the sense that these are mostly cosmetic changes, our efforts here should ameliorate anxiety about the quality of deep democratic discourse, at least from this particular source.

Statistical measures notwithstanding, there are also substantive reasons to doubt that simpler presidential addresses are a cause for concern for the health of democratic deliberation. In social science, when scholars have applied readability measures to link linguistic sophistication to outcomes, greater clarity is generally associated with beneficial outcomes. Put crudely, if one can understand a speech or document, one may find it easier to adjust behavior and hold the author to account. We have at least preliminary evidence of this when institutions such as central banks (Jansen, 2011) or courts (Owens and Wedeking, 2011) are clearer in their communication. Sometimes, a complex idea is best communicated using simple, short sentences – and this likely extends to political science itself (Diamond, 2002, Cann, Goelzhauser, and Johnson, 2014). Ultimately then, rather than fearing the changes we have documented, we might better embrace them as a positive development for our democracy.

REFERENCES

Asimov, Isaac. 1980. "A Cult of Ignorance." *Time*, January (21), p. 19.

Bai, Jushan, and Pierre Perron. 2003. "Computation and Analysis of Multiple Structural Change Models." *Journal of Applied Econometrics 18*: 1–22.

Benoit, Kenneth, Michael Laver, and Slava Mikhaylov. 2009. "Treating Words as Data with Error: Uncertainty in Text Statements of Policy Positions." *American Journal of Political Science 53*(2): 495–513.

Cann, Damon, Greg Goelzhauser, and Kaylee Johnson. 2014. "Analyzing Text Complexity in Political Science Research." *PS: Political Science & Politics 47*(3): 663–666.

Coleman, M., and T Liau. 1975. "A Computer Readability Formula Designed for Machine Scoring." *Journal of Applied Psychology 60*(2): 283–284.

Dale, Edgar, and Jeanne Chall. 1948. "A Formula for Predicting Readability." *Educational Research Bulletin 27*(1): 11–20.

Diamond, Larry. 2002. "What Political Science Owes the World." *PS: Political Science & Politics Online Forum*: 113–127.

Flesch, Rudolph. 1948. "A New Readability Yardstick." *Journal of Applied Psychology 32*(3): 221–233.

Flynn, James R. 1999. "Searching for Justice: The Discovery of Iq Gains Over Time." *American Psychologist 54*(1): 5–20.

Galston, William. 2001. "Political Knowledge, Political Engagement, and Civic Education." *Annual Review of Political Science 4*: 217–234.

Gatto, John Taylor. 2002. *Dumbing Us Down: The Hidden Curriculum of Compulsory Schooling*. Vancouver: New Society Publishers.

Gunning, Robert. 1952. *The Technique of Clear Writing*. New York: McGraw-Hill.

Hofstadter, Richard. 1963. *Anti-Intellectualism in American Life*. New York: Knopf Books.

Jansen, David-Jan. 2011. "Does the Clarity of Central Bank Communication Affect Volatility in Financial Markets? Evidence from Humphrey-Hawkins Testimonies." *Contemporary Economic Policy 29*(4).

Kincaid, J. Peter, Robert Fishburne, Richard Rogers, and Brad Chissom. 1975. *Derivation of New Readability Formulas (Automated Readability Index, Fog Count, and Flesch Reading Ease Formula) for Navy Enlisted Personnel*. Vols. Research Branch Report, pp. 8–75. Naval Air Station Memphis: Chief of Naval Technical Training.

Lim, Elvin. 2008. *The Anti-Intellectual Presidency*. New York: Oxford University Press.

McLaughlin, Harry. 1969. "SMOG Grading: A New Readability Formula." *Journal of Reading 12*(8): 639–646.

Owens, Ryan, and Justin Wedeking. 2011. "Justices and Legal Clarity: Analyzing the Complexity of Supreme Court Opinions." *Law & Society Review* 45(4): 1027–1061.

Spache, George. 1953. "A New Readability Formula for Primary-Grade Reading Materials." *The Elementary School Journal* 53(7): 410–413.

Spirling, Arthur. 2016. "Democratization of Linguistic Complexity: The Effect of Franchise Extension on Parliamentary Discourse, 1832–1915." *Journal of Politics* 78(1): 120–136.

PART III

ANXIETIES OF GOVERNANCE

10

Public Policy and Political Dysfunction
The Policyscape, Policy Maintenance, and Oversight

Suzanne Mettler and Claire Leavitt

In the 8 years following the enactment of the Affordable Care Act (ACA), the Republican Party in Congress called frequently and vociferously for its outright repeal. When it had passed in 2010, not a single Republican had voted in favor of it, despite its inclusion of several features that their party had promoted for years. Subsequently, in the polarized climate in Washington, Republicans found the ACA a perfect foil to distinguish themselves from Democrats. As implementation challenges mounted and health-care premiums rose, the GOP could chastise "Obamacare" and promise to repeal it as a means to rally their base, and the strategy helped the party to retake majorities in the House in 2010 and the Senate in 2014, and to win the White House in 2016. But no sooner had Republicans achieved unified government than it became evident that even in the House of Representatives, the party would have significant trouble corralling enough support to pass a repeal-and-replace bill (named, in acronymous likeness, the American Health Care Act). After the first failed attempt at passage in March 2017, Speaker Paul Ryan successfully forced the bill through the House 2 months later, only to have the Senate reject its passage in a dramatic late-night session in July. What explains the Republicans' failure to legislatively follow through on one of their key electoral promises?

The answer, in brief, is that over the 7 years of its existence, the new policy had taken on a life of its own and transformed politics in the process, and now it was impossible to simply eviscerate it. Though seemingly beleaguered, the ACA had restructured institutional and organizational arrangements for health-care delivery. Insurance companies and hospitals responded by altering their standard operating procedures, and they wanted neither to be forced to change them back again nor to face new uncertainties about health-care provision. Governors and state legislators who had welcomed the ACA's Medicaid expansion and the accompanying federal funds, including some Republicans, did not want to face disgruntled constituents or lose the resources on which their states relied. (As of June 2018, 33 states plus the District of Columbia have accepted federal funds to expand this program.) Among ordinary citizens, momentum shifted from proponents of repeal to those who either favored the law or disliked aspects of it but wanted to see it improved, a group that included many Republicans (Jacobs and Mettler, 2017). On the eve of the first scheduled House vote, reports came out that as few as 17 percent of Americans supported it (Firozi, 2017). With support for the bill fracturing his own caucus, Ryan withdrew it, announcing that "Obamacare is the law of the land" and that it would remain so "for the foreseeable future" (Conway, 2017). Despite Ryan's later success in passing a revised bill, lack of enthusiastic support across the party ultimately presaged its Senate death, and even a subsequent vote in that chamber on the "skinny bill" failed to garner enough support when three GOP members crossed party lines to defeat it. "It's time to move on," said a weary Speaker Mitch McConnell. Since then, despite the Trump administration's efforts to construct roadblocks to ACA implementation, the law prevails, with enrollments fairly steady and marketplaces intact.

The case of the ACA illustrates a fundamental truth about contemporary American politics: public policy itself now functions as a formidable part of the political landscape, shaping politics at both the mass and elite level and influencing future policy changes. We dwell today in what could be called a "policyscape," a political environment that is densely laden with policies such as these that were created in the past, particularly in the robust policymaking period of the 1930s through the 1970s that now structure the political order. On net, federal spending accounts for 1 in 5 dollars in the nation's economy, with an increase from 3.6 percent of GDP in 1930 to 20.5 in 2015 (Federal Reserve Bank of St. Louis, 2016). Besides allocating dollars, policies structure public and private life through a vast array of regulations. They connect the federal government with states and localities in a web of intergovernmental relations, through a variety of mechanisms that range from promotional to coercive. Policies include not only direct, visible forms delivered directly by government, but also numerous others channeled through the tax code or nonprofit and private organizations.

In order to understand contemporary American politics, public policies cannot be regarded simply as outcomes of the political process; rather, they have taken on the role of institutions, fixtures of the political landscape that are themselves highly consequential. "New policies," as E.E. Schattschneider observed long ago, "create a new politics" (1935, p. 288). Policies organize the terms of political conflict, both by creating standing commitments of the political parties and by energizing political activists, and these dynamics in turn have fostered polarization. Policies convey messages about the appropriate scope of government action and imbue citizens with a sense of their *status*, with implications for their civic engagement. Policies also influence interest groups' goals and, in some instances, even spur their creation.

By their very existence, public policies transform the character of politics and the realities of political opportunities and constraints. In contemporary American political development, the number and scope of policies have grown to a point that has intensified these tendencies. In addition, accumulated policies today exist in a polity of transformed political and institutional conditions, such as the rise of partisan polarization, and they may both affect and be affected by those circumstances. In this chapter, we will begin with an overview of the policyscape, and then we will probe four aspects of its impact. First, existing policies affect the possibilities for the creation of new public policies or policy reform and the shape that such developments take, foreclosing some and channeling others. Second, the thickening and multiplication of policies appears to interact with other contemporary institutional and political developments in ways that exacerbate gridlock and dysfunction. Third, policies require routine maintenance if they are to continue to function as lawmakers planned, rather than to deteriorate, become derailed, or grow outdated as circumstances change. Congress can engage in such action through reauthorization or other policy adjustments, but the accumulation of such responsibilities in tandem with other political developments appears to hinder these routines from occurring as regularly as in the past. Fourth, long-established policies also require regular monitoring through the oversight process, but Congress's capacity to fulfill such responsibilities varies over time as the institutional and political context changes, and it has been subject to deterioration over the past quarter-century. In sum, the investigation of how policies themselves influence and are affected by contemporary politics opens a vast and important area of inquiry that scholars have only begun to explore.

POLICIES AS INSTITUTIONS THAT SHAPE POLITICS: AN OVERVIEW

Although existing public policies have emerged as formidable institutions in their own right for at least half a century, not just in the United States but also in other affluent nations, scholars are still in the early stages of the investigation of the difference this development makes for contemporary politics. Political scientists have traditionally regarded public policies as a "dependent variable," an outcome of the political process, and focused on explaining the political circumstances under which lawmakers have succeeded or failed in creating them (Pierson, 1993). A growing number of scholars, however, have been directing attention to the accumulation of policies and how their collective density is reshaping the nature of politics itself (Fukuyama, 2014, Hacker and Pierson, 2014, Orren and Skowronek, 2014, Pierson, 2014, Jenkins and Milkis, 2015).

Certainly the presence of policies that were created in the past is nothing new, and newly elected public officials have never encountered a *tabula rasa*;

nonetheless, the proliferation of policies since the mid-twentieth century – their sheer number and complexity – has led to qualitatively different political dynamics than those of earlier times. Stephen Skowronek uses the term "the policy state" to describe the contemporary political order, one in which "problems of American political development present themselves as problems of public policy and policy choice" (2009, pp. 334–335). Richard Rose and Philip L. Davies wrote that policymakers are "heirs before they are choosers," as they "spend far more time living with the consequences of inherited commitments than with making choices that reflect their own initiatives" (Rose and Davies, 1994, pp. 1, 4–5). In Paul Pierson's book examining why both the Reagan and Thatcher administrations failed in many respects to achieve welfare state retrenchment, he observed that "policies inherited from the past" condition politics by facilitating the development of constituencies that defend those policies and by affecting the political strategies available to reformers and their opponents (Pierson, 1994, p. 9). More recently, Pierson and Jacob Hacker have referred to "policy as terrain," demonstrating that control over policy has become the "prize" over which political actors struggle in the electoral arena (Hacker and Pierson, 2014, p. 645). Stephen Teles refers to the modern American state as a "kludgeocracy," less distinctive for its size than for the complexity of public policy, which has developed in an incoherent manner that makes the system prone to failure (2013).

Precisely how policies shape politics is a matter that increasingly interests scholars but that is still early in its theoretical development and empirical examination. Theda Skocpol was one of the first scholars to coin the term "policy feedback," meaning that "policy, once enacted, restructures subsequent political processes" (Skocpol, 1992, p. 58). Pierson built on these ideas, suggesting that resources and interpretive mechanisms might be at play, influencing the demands and participation of interest groups and mass publics alike (Pierson, 1993, also see Schneider and Ingram, 1997). Several scholars have examined these dynamics empirically, particularly in the case of individuals (e.g., Campbell, 2003, Lerman and Weaver, 2014, Mettler, 2018).

Some suggest that policies, once established and plentiful, foster inertia in the political system, making the status quo or steady expansion of policies inevitable. Frances Fukuyama (2014) sees the contemporary welfare state as complicated and difficult to reform. Paul Pierson's early work (1994) indicated that policy feedback tends toward "lock-in" – positive, self-reinforcing dynamics. Other studies also reveal dynamics emanating from policies in which stability and entrenchment dominate (e.g., Rose and Davies, 1994, Ejdemyr, Nall, and O'Keefe, 2015, Nall, 2015,).

Yet policies do not necessarily exhibit durability. Kathleen Thelen and Wolfgang Streeck (2005) have argued that political institutions generally may confront "incremental process of change" that in time transform their character and effects, and public policies are no exception. Sometimes policies vary in their sustainability owing to the different political and institutional circumstances in which they were enacted or in which implementation began (Berry, Burden, and Howell, 2012, Maltzman and Shipan, 2012). In addition, as Eric Patashnik argues, longer-term sustainability may be affected by whether or not policies engender supportive administrative and legal structures (2008). Hacker (2004) has shown that, over time, policies are subject to "drift," which occurs when Congress fails to "update" current laws in accordance with evolving political, social, and economic conditions, leading to a fundamental incongruity between socioeconomic problems and policy solutions (Hacker and Pierson, 2001, McCarty, Poole, and Rosenthal, 2006). In short, policies may cease functioning as they once did because *external* circumstances change, and lawmakers fail to make necessary adjustments so that policies can keep pace. The failure to raise the gas tax for the highway trust fund as environmental circumstances change is a case in point, and it makes both maintenance of the infrastructure and new innovations much more difficult to accomplish.

In addition, policies can deviate from their intended purposes over time due to *internal* changes. *Policy design effects* may become manifest later on, for example, as particular features evolve to foster deterioration. Policies that lack automatic cost-of-living adjustments and that fail to rise automatically with inflation, such as the minimum wage and Pell grants, necessarily wither in value unless lawmakers take action to elevate rates, whereas those with such features, such as Social Security and tax expenditures, are protected. *Unintended consequences* occur when policies inadvertently provide incentives to individuals or organizations to act differently than they otherwise would, leading vested interests to emerge and engage in rent-seeking, thus derailing policy from its intended purposes. For example, the availability of federal student aid promoted the development of a for-profit sector of colleges and training institutes, which depended almost entirely on government funds, enriching shareholders but leaving students indebted and poorly trained, at taxpayer expense. *Lateral effects* occur when the development of an unrelated policy shapes a policy's own development, for example by squeezing resources or limiting the eligibility pool. Growing demands on state budgets for mandatory spending on Medicaid, K–12 education, and incarceration has led to reduced commitments to public higher education, the largest discretionary item in most state budgets (Mettler, 2014). Aaron Wildavsky long ago anticipated such dynamics, observing that over time "policy becomes more and more its own cause," as policies develop in ways that affect one another's growth (1979, p. 81).

We will argue that in the contemporary polity, the policyscape generates a vast and complex array of developmental dynamics, encompassing both those that perpetuate the status quo and "lock-in" as well as those that lead to deterioration of existing policies. The policyscape's emergence means that the task of public officials is different today than in the past; if government is to function well, they need to be knowledgeable about and committed to policy maintenance and oversight. As we will see, however, other forms of institutional decay undermine such capacities and the political incentives to pursue them.

HOW POLICIES INFLUENCE NEW POLICY DEVELOPMENT

Policies created in the past shape the prospects for new policy development, as well as the form such policies take, through multiple dynamics. Consider the centrality of concerns about taxing and spending in US politics today, as Americans appear to want government to address myriad social and economic problems but oppose tax increases to pay for new policies. This conundrum is often cast as solely a feud between liberals and conservatives and between the nation's major political parties, but closer examination reveals plenty of support for spending priorities on both sides of the aisle (Page and Jacobs, 2009). Already, existing policies themselves play a major role in locking-in both spending commitments and reduced tax obligations, and these in combination constrain lawmakers' capacity for policy innovation.

While the federal budget is vast, amounting to $4 trillion in spending in 2017, in fact it contains remarkably little leeway to permit resource allocations for new policies. In part this is because in the most recent calendar year, spending has surpassed revenues, as it has each year since 2001 (CBO, 2017a). Deficit spending is nothing new; the federal government has operated with deficits for most years in the post–World War II era, with the surpluses in several consecutive years during the late 1990s as the exception (CBO, 2015b). Two-thirds of federal spending, however ($2.5 trillion in 2017), is allocated to mandatory spending programs for which eligibility is determined by law and is nonnegotiable; the lion's share goes to Social Security, Medicare, and Medicaid, and a small portion to other income support programs. In addition, $263 billion went to pay interest on the debt. This leaves $1.2 trillion for discretionary spending, half of which is allocated to defense. Just 15.25 percent of the budget remains for discretionary domestic programs (CBO, 2017a, 2017b), and most of it is dedicated to well-established commitments in a wide array of areas including health-care and health research, transportation and economic development, education for K–12 and college students, vocational training, food and nutrition, housing assistance, science, energy and environmental programs, law enforcement, and diplomacy. Among the programs included in these categories are venerable entities such as Pell grants and WIC (Special Supplemental Nutrition Program for Women, Infants and Children), the Centers for Disease Control and Prevention (CDC), the national park system, and numerous others (CBO, 2015a, Center on Budget and Policy Priorities, 2016). It is also the case that congressional advocates of deficit reduction triumphed in recent years, forcing "sequestration" rules that limited spending across issue areas and further stymied maintenance of the policyscape. As a result of such constraints, new policies cannot be considered without engaging in difficult trade-offs, with cuts made to existing programs to permit new innovations.

Theoretically, the nation could opt to increase revenues by altering the tax code in ways that raise rates and rein in exemptions and loopholes. Despite vast fiscal challenges and rising economic inequality, this alternative has not gained favor. The problem is not only the absence of political will, but also the status of tax policy itself. Republican lawmakers since the Reagan era have repeatedly pursued aggressive tax cuts, further reducing revenues. With spending commitments largely locked in and tax revenues reduced, policymakers have been engaged in a war of attrition, with little capacity to pursue new ideas that cost money.

In 2001 and 2003, President George W. Bush and Congress agreed on large tax cuts, with benefits that would be bestowed particularly on the affluent, and would take effect gradually over the next decade (Hacker and Pierson, 2005a). As it happened, their largest impact in reducing federal revenues coincided with the years following the 2008 financial downturn, when the state of the economy already ensured a smaller inflow of resources. The long-run consequences of the Bush tax cuts therefore foreclosed opportunities for a larger economic stimulus during the Obama administration, one that might have promoted a stronger recovery, reached more Americans who are currently frustrated by long-term stagnation in incomes, and permitted other new spending commitments. Democratic lawmakers in 2010 did agree to raise revenues from the wealthiest taxpayers as a means to pay for provisions of the Affordable Care Act.[1]

In 2017, Republican majorities in Congress achieved their major goal in enacting the Tax Cuts and Jobs Act, which was signed into law by President Donald Trump. The primary aim of the legislation involved tax cuts, rather than reform: it reduced household tax rates, with those of the affluent trimmed by the greatest percentage, and it slashed the corporate income tax rate from 35 percent to 21 percent. Unlike the revenue-neutral approach adopted in the bipartisan effort to enact tax reform in 1986, the TCJA is projected to increase the deficit by amounts ranging from $1.6 trillion to $1.8 trillion, according to analyses from the Joint Committee on Taxation, Penn Wharton School, and Tax Foundation (Patel and Parlapiano, 2017). The TCJA tops even the Bush tax cuts of 2001 and 2003 in upwardly redistributional effects: Hacker and Pierson estimate that the new tax law provides approximately 60 percent of its benefits over 10 years to the top 1 percent (2005b).

The one major avenue that lawmakers have found for bypassing the taxing and spending conundrum, at least at the moment of policy enactment, is by spending through the tax code itself: offering new or expanded benefits in the form of tax expenditures – otherwise known as tax breaks – rather than direct spending in the form of income support for households or payment of services.

---

[1] In 2012, President Barack Obama reached a compromise with Congress to permit a small portion of the Bush tax cuts to expire, effectively raising taxes on high-income households (for married couples earning $450,000 or above). The deal also increased the tax on capital gains and dividends from 15 to 23.8 percent, though kept it well below the rate of 28 percent, which prevailed in the late 1980s and early 1990s (Burman and Slemrod, 2013,CBO, 2014, p. 8). Other major features of the Bush tax cuts, including other across-the-board rate cuts and estate tax exemptions, remained in place.

In doing so, they are building on a long, well-established component of US policy – what Christopher Howard has termed the "hidden welfare state," which includes part of what Jacob Hacker has called "the divided welfare state," and what one of us has termed "the submerged state." The largest tax expenditures are a triumvirate of policies, including the home mortgage interest deduction, established in 1913; the nontaxable status of employer-provided retirement benefits, in 1926; and the nontaxable status of employer-provided health benefits, in 1954 (Howard, 1997, p. 176). Given rising demands for government responsiveness to multiple issues but escalating antipathy to new taxes, lawmakers increasingly turned to tax credits and tax deductions, and their number grew from 81 in 1980 to 151 in 2010 (Mettler, 2011, p. 20). Tax expenditures became, as one lawmaker put it, "the only game in town": the sole approach that could garner bipartisan support for new policies across a range of purposes, from social welfare to college savings, job creation to energy conservation, and numerous others (Howard, 2002, p. 428). The 2017 tax cuts did scale back the scope of a few tax expenditures, such as the state and local tax deduction and mortgage interest deduction, but left most intact.

But while the "submerged state" strategy offers short-term gains in appealing to voters, in numerous ways such policies compound the difficulties lawmakers confront in creating constructive policy solutions to perceived problems. Tax expenditures worsen the nation's long-run problem of insufficient revenues by reducing the amount government collects. They easily become entrenched, furthermore, because once part of the tax code, they remain in place, not being subject to the annual appropriations process as are most direct spending programs. Many of them cultivate defenders in industries that benefit from their existence, such as realtors, homebuilders, and insurance companies, and the interest groups that defend them assiduously from reductions. Notwithstanding a few exceptions such as the Earned Income Tax Credit, tax expenditures overall benefit primarily the wealthiest Americans: the Congressional Budget Office (CBO) estimated that in 2013, 51 percent of the benefits in the 10 largest such policies accrued to households in the top fifth of the income distribution, with the top 1 percent alone netting 17 percent (CBO, 2014). As a result, these policies fail to mitigate inequality and reduce the source of revenues that could be applied to policies that do more to aid low- and middle-income people (Mettler, 2011). Ordinary citizens who utilize such policies, in contrast to those who use policies delivered directly by government, fail to gain an enhanced awareness that government has helped them or provided them with opportunities to improve their standard of living (Mettler, 2018). This in turn makes it all the more difficult to muster the political will necessary for grand bargains and tough compromises necessary for governing.

As a result of such dynamics, these policy designs immensely complicate opportunities for reform, and influence the form that they take. Take health care, for example. The United States long remained an outlier compared with other affluent nations because of its failure to extend health coverage to working age adults. Presidents from the time of Harry Truman aspired to achieve this goal, and faced charges of introducing socialism (Blumenthal and Morone, 2009). After President Dwight Eisenhower signed into law the provision noted above, excluding from taxation the amounts employers put aside for their employees' health coverage, more and more Americans benefited from these tax subsidies, but from all appearances, it was the private sector that actually provided the benefits. Insurance and pharmaceutical companies evolved into third-party beneficiaries of these arrangements. President Lyndon Johnson worked around this existing system by promoting and signing into law Medicare and Medicaid, for seniors and low-income people. As Hacker has noted (2002), this combination of arrangements increasingly made Americans think of health coverage for workers as the domain of the private sector, free of public interference, hindering the prospects for reform. When President Bill Clinton tried to promote health reform, insurance companies ran ads aimed to frighten Americans about a government takeover, and opposition quickly mounted among the public and in Congress. Clinton's reform plan was never even formally considered in Congress.

By the time President Barack Obama took office, he could glean lessons from 60 years of developments and failures. The ACA built on top of already existing programs and approaches. The new law extended health coverage to many people, for example, through an expanded version of Medicaid. Also, to the chagrin of Obama's supporters who had expected him to circumvent interest groups, he cut deals with groups that were already advantaged through existing policies so that they would support reform. As Lawrence Jacobs and Theda Skocpol have observed, the ACA came to fruition because public officials were willing to negotiate with major stakeholders such as insurance companies and drug companies (2010). Opponents depicted the ACA as a "government takeover," and yet the law's health insurance marketplaces (or "exchanges") are expected to bring 29 million customers to insurance companies by 2019, with a mandatory obligation and government subsidies to encourage sign-ups. By building on the existing system and negotiating with key players, Obama succeeded where Clinton and others had failed. Proponents of a single-payer system, vocal during the 2016 Democratic presidential primary, fail to acknowledge the inherent challenges in such a transformation in the United States, as it would require smashing an existing system that is deeply entrenched. Now, the political and organizational dynamics spurred by the ACA have enabled it to survive despite the calls for its repeal; future health reformers will need to work within its structure to improve health-care coverage, delivery, and costs.

In sum, when public officials seek to address issues today, they do not start on a policy frontier. Rather, they confront a dense policyscape, and must typically build atop or circumvent existing policies that already generate all sorts of effects that complicate reform and channel the path that it takes.

THE POLICYSCAPE AND OTHER POLITICAL INSTITUTIONS

Since the mid-1990s, American political institutions appear to be lapsing into greater dysfunctionality, none more than the US Congress. As numerous scholars have observed, gridlock appears to be on the rise. Gridlock refers to the inability of Congress to pass the legislation necessary for either updating and maintaining current laws or passing new ones to regulate modern life. However we measure it, whether as the number of important bills passed in a given Congress (Mayhew, 2005), the proportion of all salient items on the legislative agenda that a given Congress manages to pass (Binder, 2000, 2003) or the number of enacted bills that change, revise or restructure extant policy (Saeki, 2009), stalemate in the legislature presents unique and in many cases unprecedented challenges to the American polity in its third century. Gridlock has led to a decrease in public esteem for and trust in Congress as an institution (Binder, 2000, 2003) and to long-standing vacancies in executive agencies and federal courts, compromising those institutions' ability to perform their own constitutional roles (Binder and Maltzman, 2002, Teter, 2013, Mann and Ornstein, 2016).

The challenges presented by the policyscape may themselves be affected by deteriorating capacity of political institutions to perform routine tasks, and in turn it may be exacerbating those developments. Certainly Congress, the nation's primary policymaking body, has risen to confront far greater challenges in American history than policy accumulation, from war to the Great Depression. And as recently as the administration of President George H.W. Bush, Congress managed to enact numerous new laws and update existing laws effectively. Yet today the paired emergence of partisan polarization and the policyscape, both in the context of the traditional Madisonian system, seems to present growing challenges to governance.

The American political system is characterized by institutional arrangements that deter hasty or capricious decision making and action. The US Constitution deliberately poses numerous obstacles to policymaking, requiring a high degree of compromise and negotiation for it to succeed (Robertson, 2005, Chapter 8). Separation of powers means that the executive and legislative branches lack the degree of coordination inherent in parliamentary systems. Congress itself, consisting of two distinct chambers, each selected through different electoral procedures by different constituencies, heightens the challenges of enacting laws. Compounding the difficulties further, the Senate is structured in a manner that gives extra weight to low-population states, and it operates according to rules that empower the minority and individual members, presenting numerous roadblocks to collective action. In short, US institutions contain numerous "veto points," making change difficult (Fukuyama, 2014, p. 503).

While these institutional arrangements have prevailed throughout the nation's history, the rise of the policyscape may cause them to operate with even greater difficulty than is the norm. In a political system designed to make decision making multistaged, cumbersome, and impossible without widespread agreement and coordination, the accumulation of policy density and complexity may slow or deter action. The thickening of public policies may also stymie Congress's ability to maintain and oversee them effectively, as we will discuss in subsequent sections of this chapter.

The governing challenges of the policyscape have also emerged in tandem with the declining capacity of the political parties to function effectively. Early on in US history, lawmakers created political parties precisely in order to overcome the difficulties of institutional design. These organizations aim to coordinate public officials, enabling them to work together across chambers, branches, and time in order to achieve policy goals. At their best, the parties "grease the wheels" of the complicated machinery of US government, but in recent decades, they have more often clogged it, leading to gridlock, particularly in Congress. Some interpret this as the effect of rising ideological polarization, owing to the disappearance of political moderates and the rise of greater homogeneity withinin the two major parties in addition to a growing gulf between them (McCarty, Rosenthal, and Poole, 2006). Frances Lee attributes the rise of partisanship in Congress to the sharply increased competition between the parties, since 1980, in their struggle to control both chambers. The parties' chief political strategy – aimed at gaining an electoral advantage – has been to distinguish themselves from one another, and to adopt a strident "teamsmanship" even on nonideological votes as a means of conveying these distinctions to voters. This "perpetual campaign" approach to governing deprives lawmakers of the time needed to focus on policy matters and it imperils the requisite capacity to compromise and negotiate (Lee, 2016, pp. 48–60).

These transformations in Congress undercut policymakers' engagement in lawmaking and policy maintenance, just at the point in time when the emergence of the policyscape most requires it. The institution's capacity for information gathering, which is necessary to deal with complex issues, vacillates over time (Baumgartner and Jones, 2015). It has diminished recently, in part because of a reduction in the time allotted to hearings, which are held less often, are shorter, are more often one-sided, and are less oriented around problem-solving than in the past (Mann and Orenstein, 2006, p. 215, Lewallen, Theriault, and Jones, 2015, pp. 22–23). The rising cost of competitive campaigns puts pressure on officials to devote more time to fundraising, at the expense of intensive policy work. Lee also points out that party leaders have moved resources away from committee staff and toward public relations personnel in their own offices, in order to communicate the party brand to voters (2016, Chapter 5, also Drutman and Teles, 2015). Numerous long-serving members as well as staffers who were renowned for their policy expertise have retired or, in the case of some members, lost their seats. For all of these reasons, rising partisanship appears to deprive Congress of the capacity necessary to manage effectively the large array of complex policies that exist today.

It is also possible, furthermore, that the emergence of the policyscape itself has in part contributed to the rise of more ardent partisanship. Party leaders draw on differences in stances on policy issues to distinguish their party from the opposition, and activists also accentuate these distinctions. The growth of social welfare spending as a percentage of personal income may have reached a tipping point that heightens the liberal and conservative divide. The impact of policy accumulation on partisanship is a topic yet to be examined directly by scholars. What can be said, however, is that polarization or teamsmanship, together with the emergence of the dense, complex array of existing policies in the United States, combine to make navigating the nation's multiple institutional veto points increasingly difficult. Now we will examine how this mix influences policy maintenance and oversight.

POLICY MAINTENANCE

The large number of existing policies means that the "old business" section of the congressional agenda brims over with updating and maintenance tasks, according to E. Scott Adler and John Wilkerson (2012). Thad Hall explains that the 1946 Legislative Reorganization Act required some laws to be reauthorized, and by the 1960s, Congress attached sunset provisions to nearly all complex new domestic policies, as a means to reassert congressional authority over the executive branch (2004, pp. 17–19, 25). Adler and Wilkerson, using data from 1980 to 1998, find that Congress continued to reauthorize legislation even after other forms of dysfunctionality began to emerge, but Hall and James Cox detect that such policy maintenance itself began to wane by late in the 1990s (Cox, 2004, pp. 57–58, Hall, 2004, pp. 104–105).

As a cursory means to examine policy maintenance up to the present, we consulted the 20 policy areas identified by Americans in 2015 as top issue priorities, and then created an inventory of 34 policies that pertain to those priorities. Some of these policies require reauthorization, while others do not, but Congress has typically engaged in regular reform even of the latter types. The next step was to investigate how recently the law had been reauthorized or updated, and whether it was either formally overdue for such maintenance or informally so (in the case of laws that lack sunset measures but were updated more often in the past). This approach contains limitations, of course, as some might suggest additional policies that apply to each category, or point out that some categories do not refer to obvious federal legislation (e.g., "moral breakdown"), and so forth.

Overall, this assessment indicated that more than half of the policies were either overdue for reauthorization, or "out of date" in the case of those lacking sunset provisions but for which reforms had not occurred for a period longer than the number of years in between past reforms. Policies overdue for reauthorization include Head Start, the Higher Education Act, the Individuals with Disabilities Education Act, the Juvenile Justice and Delinquency

Prevention Act, Temporary Assistance to Needy Families, and Unemployment Insurance, each of which falls into an issue category that more than half of Americans consider a priority. Although 51 percent of Americans name the environment as a top priority, several key policies have languished now for 25 to 30 years, including the Clean Air Act Amendments, the Clean Water Act, and the Superfund. Policies that appear to be outdated include immigration, which previously permitted bipartisan grand bargains but is increasingly subject to partisan divides, particularly exhibited by the parties' failure to reach a legislative agreement on the Deferred Action for Childhood Arrivals (DACA) program that began as an Obama executive order and was overturned by President Trump; the Voting Rights Act, of which Section IV was invalidated by the Supreme Court in the 2013 decision *Shelby County v. Holder*; and policies governing lobbying and money in politics, among others (Mettler, 2016, pp. 380–382).

Inattention to policy has real consequences, illustrated, for example, by the deteriorating record of the nation's aid policies for college students. In the mid-twentieth century, the United States led the world in college graduation rates among young adults, but since then 10 other countries have surpassed it, and improvements among those who grow up in households below the median income have barely increased (Mettler, 2014, pp. 21–26). The United States also played a pioneering role in developing environmental policies up until the 1990s, but since then, as David Vogel has shown, it has lagged behind while European countries have leapfrogged beyond it (2012). Gridlock combined with policy complexity hinders not only the development of new policies but also the updating of existing ones.

Of course, policy neglect may be preferable to making changes if those alterations are hostile to a policy's intended aims or for other reasons leave it weakened or eviscerated. In 2017, for example, the Republican-led House of Representatives passed a reauthorization of the Higher Education Act that, if signed into law, would eviscerate regulations on for-profit colleges. The status quo, problems aside, may at least keep in place a modicum of policy functionality for public services that Americans rely on. As the Trump Administration is learning, policies, particularly those enacted as laws, offer a form of stability to American government and, unlike executive orders, once in place they are not easily dismantled.

OVERSIGHT

Policy maintenance depends almost as critically on Congress's second major, implicit constitutional responsibility: *oversight* of the presidency and of the administrative state. "Oversight" is a catch-all term that refers to Congress's dual ability to conduct retroactive investigations of executive branch activities as well as to consistently review administrative agency activities and implementation of programs (Pearson, 1975, see also Kaiser, 1988). Scholars have distinguished between the "more routine, accommodative" proactive surveillance of administrative agencies and the "adversarial, often confrontational, and sometimes high-profile nature of congressional investigations," but the vast number of activities that could conceivably huddle under the "executive oversight" umbrella makes the responsibility difficult to parsimoniously define and measure. Congressional oversight of the executive may include regular "nonlegislative"[2] hearings convened by budget, appropriations, and authorizing committees; informal meetings between legislative staff and executive officials; investigations of complaints from constituents and interest groups by individual members or committees; brokering communication and negotiations between constituents and government agencies (constituent casework); agency audits and reviews by the Government Accountability Office (GAO)[3] upon request by a member of Congress; statutory controls over administrative procedures; and constitutional responsibilities such as the ability to "advise and consent" on presidential nominees (in the Senate), to impeach and try the president for "high crimes and misdemeanors," and to reorganize executive agencies, among other institutional duties. Perhaps most importantly, Congress may continually request and gather information from the executive on how previous laws have been implemented in order to seriously consider whether a proposed piece of legislation will fit into the policy environment that already exists, as well as what kind of future choices the legislation might constrain. Woodrow Wilson, in his seminal 1885 study *Congressional Government*, argues: "Quite as important as legislation is vigilant oversight of administration, and even more important than legislation is the instruction and guidance in political affairs which the people might receive from a body which kept all national concerns suffused in the broad daylight of discussion." In its idealized form, then, we might even consider oversight to be a continuous public *conversation* between Congress and the executive over what has worked, what does work and what will work for achieving not only efficient and effective public administration but also broad legislative goals.

Congress's ability to monitor the executive branch is established, albeit indirectly, by the Constitution, both in the document's separated-institutions-sharing powers framework (to use Neustadt's famous term) as well as in the enumerated powers granted to Congress. Congress could not possibly exercise its Article I powers – such as appropriating funds from the US Treasury, declaring war, and organizing executive departments – without constant vigilance over executive branch activities, and the "necessary and proper" clause in

---

[2] "Nonlegislative" hearings refers to hearings where no specific piece of pending legislation is considered (see Baumgartner and Jones, 2015).

[3] The GAO (formerly the General Accounting Office) is an independent and nonpartisan government agency that provides auditing, evaluation and investigation of the executive branch for Congress; the GAO is frequently referred to as "Congress's watchdog" and is perhaps best described as the auditor of the American state.

Article I, Section 8 legitimizes secondary activities, such as oversight, that will help Congress achieve its primary legislative goals (Kaiser, 1988, Sunstein, 1993, Talbert, Jones, and Baumgartner, 1995). The oversight powers implicit in the Constitution were affirmed by the Washington Administration during the Second Congress (1791–1793), after the House of Representatives fiercely debated and ultimately passed a resolution to establish a committee to investigate War Department unpreparedness after the defeat of American troops at the hands of Native American tribes. President Washington determined that the House indeed had the right to investigate the executive branch, despite the Constitution's lack of *direct* guidance on this question, and agreed to provide any information the House committee requested that did not jeopardize national security (thus also setting the precedent for "executive privilege," which Washington did not need to invoke in this instance since none of the requested materials violated his national-security standard). Washington's decision "firmly established Congress's power to investigate the conduct of executive branch actors, and served as an important precedent for numerous congressional investigations throughout the nineteenth century" (Kriner and Schickler, 2014, p. 19).

In the twentieth century, the Supreme Court cemented Congress's right to compel information from the executive as well as to regularly review administrative activities, with some restrictions. In *McGrain v. Daugherty* (1927), the Supreme Court upheld Congress's right to investigate the Attorney General and the Justice Department for failing to prosecute administration officials who accepted bribes from oil companies in exchange for leases to extract petroleum on federal lands (the so-called Teapot Dome scandal). The Supreme Court again decided in favor of congressional oversight 2 years later in *Sinclair v. United States* (1929), mandating that Congress could legally hold in contempt any citizen who refused to provide information critical to an investigation. In *Watkins v. United States* (1957), while the Court established clear limits on the type of information Congress could legally compel private citizens to disclose, Chief Justice Earl Warren emphatically upheld Congress's investigative rights more broadly. Warren maintained in his majority opinion that "the power of the Congress to conduct investigations is inherent in the legislative process. That power is broad. It encompasses inquiries concerning the administration of existing laws as well as proposed or possibly needed statutes." Warren noted, however – in a comment that would provide considerable dramatic irony for future scholars studying the electoral benefits of position taking during hearings – that "investigations conducted solely for the personal aggrandizement of the investigators or to 'punish' those investigated are indefensible" (354 U.S. 178, 187). Later, in *US v. Nixon* (1974), the Court reaffirmed the right of Congress and special prosecutors to compel information essential to an ongoing investigation from the executive branch, significantly qualifying the president's "executive privilege" and empowering Congress.

Congress has also strengthened its executive authority through statute: the Administrative Procedures Act of 1946 was the first piece of legislation that established uniform standards for agency decision making; its progeny, the Freedom of Information Act of 1966, imposed strict disclosure requirements for executive agencies. The Legislative Reorganization Acts of 1946 and 1970 vastly expanded Congress's capacity to conduct investigations of the executive and, crucially, the 1970 Act expanded the GAO's right to conduct regular evaluations of executive programs in addition to financial audits of government agencies. More recently, as a result of the Clinton administration's "Reinventing Government" initiative, Congress enacted two critical statutes[4] that enhanced the accountability of government agencies by requiring all agencies to submit strategic and performance goals, and later all proposed rules and regulations, to Congress and the GAO before approval (Oleszek, 2010).

Congress has steadily increased its own capacity for oversight in order to establish the accountability of a rapidly growing administrative state both to the American people (through their elected representatives) and to Congress itself: persistent and consistent "watchfulness" over government agencies upholds the integrity of the principal-agent relationship between Congress, which authorizes policies and programs, and the agencies tasked with implementing them. Congruity between lawmakers' intent and actual policy outcomes (post-implementation) is especially difficult in light of the fact that agencies have to answer to multiple principals – various authorizing and appropriations committees, the full House and Senate chambers, the Office of Management and Budget (OMB), the GAO, and special interests both within and outside the federal government (see Moe, 1987). Thus, rigorous, sustained oversight is one of Congress's most important weapons for ensuring that agencies conform as closely as possible to lawmakers' preferences.[5]

That Congress *should* conduct rigorous oversight is uncontroversial among American political actors and in the academic literature; whether Congress regularly and effectively fulfills this responsibility is another matter. It's tempting to point to an apparent "golden age" of oversight from the late 1960s to late 1980s that reached high-water marks with congressional investigations of Vietnam war policy under Johnson and Nixon, the Watergate hearings, and the investigations of the Reagan administration's covert weapons sales to Iran in order to aid anti-Communist rebels in Nicaragua. Aberbach (1991) shows that, beginning in the early 1970s and continuing through the

---

[4] The Government Performance and Results Act of 1993 (GPRA) and the Congressional Review Act of 1996 (CRA).
[5] However, it's worth noting that oversight from multiple committees can sometimes make the process less effective; a fragmentation of information, activities, and preferences among several committees may lead to little or no information-sharing and an inability of the agency in question to respond effectively to its principals (see Lewis, 2008).

1980s, Congress significantly increased its oversight activities in response to the continued growth of the administrative state and to public dissatisfaction with government in general – but that, crucially, this period of enhanced oversight occurred "in an advocacy context ... in an environment of support for the basic goals of [the relevant] programs and agencies" (Aberbach, 2002, p. 61). In other words, Congress presented itself as less of an enemy and more of an ally to the administrative state. Whittington (2001) argues that, during the Nixon administration, Congress effectively constructed a new standard for oversight, pushing back against the perception – in both the White House and, increasingly, among the public – that the president should have ultimate discretion over foreign policy, a norm that remains intact today despite significant increases in executive power after the 9/11 terrorist attacks and the subsequent "War on Terror." Furthermore, congressional investigations of Nixon's abuses raised the level of discourse and diligence within Congress itself; Congress felt obliged to meet the same standards of conduct it imposed upon the executive (Whittington, 2001).

McCubbins and Schwartz (1984), focusing on the same political era, argue that what appears to be lax Congressional oversight is in fact a reflection of Congress's preference for a particular *type* of oversight: rather than expend resources on *ex ante* surveillance of agency activities (so-called police patrol oversight), Congress opts instead for "fire alarm oversight," a process through which Congress statutorily establishes a system of rules and procedures that permit constituents, interest groups, and other whistleblowers to sound "fire alarms" about administrative malfeasance. Congress will then respond to the charges through investigations. Far from neglecting its oversight duties, the authors argue, Congress has instead made a rational decision to delegate its administrative surveillance responsibilities to outside groups, who are better positioned to provide specific information about agency misdeeds, thus saving members time and resources that are all too precious in the federal legislature.

However, other assessments have not been nearly as optimistic. Writing *during* the supposed golden age of oversight, some scholars bemoaned Congress's inability to rigorously and vigilantly monitor the executive, calling the legislature's efforts "weak and ineffective" (Pearson, 1975, p. 281, see also Scher, 1963, Fiorina, 1981, Ogul, 2009). And more recent studies have affirmed past charges of Congress's being asleep at the wheel. Mann and Ornstein (2006) underscore Congress's abdication of its oversight responsibilities particularly since the beginning of the new century:

During the 1980s and into the 1990s ... Serious oversight was done by the Appropriations Committees in both houses and by a number of authorizing committees. When the Republicans took control of Congress, there was substantial aggressive oversight – for the period when Bill Clinton was president, that is – although the oversight of policy was accompanied by a near-obsession with investigation of scandal and allegations of scandal. But when George Bush became president, oversight largely disappeared. From homeland security to the conduct of the war in Iraq, from the torture issue uncovered by the Abu Ghraib revelations to the performance of the IRS, Congress has mostly ignored its responsibilities. (p. 151)

What happened? The oversight literature offers several prisms through which to view variations in oversight activity since the mid-twentieth century. If, as Fenno (1977) has suggested, members of Congress win reelection in their districts by running against Congress as an institution, then we might reasonably assume that those members have no incentive to prioritize oversight, which is in large part an institutional responsibility, over other activities. Members of Congress might also tend to view the bureaucracy as an "impenetrable maze" (Scher, 1963, p. 532) and, thus, oversight of unwieldy government agencies as a decidedly unpalatable and Herculean task. Scher (1963), Aberbach (1991), and Shipan (2005) attribute periods of lax oversight to Congress's increasing workload since the mid-twentieth century; as a result, they argue, Congress has become increasingly cognizant of the increased opportunity costs of oversight. Other scholars attribute variations in oversight to Congress's punctuated efforts to assert its own institutional power relative to the executive branch (Kaiser, 1988, Kriner and Schickler, 2014): bursts of oversight activity as well as statutes to enhance the oversight process have increased after consolidations (and, arguably, abuses) of executive power during the Franklin Roosevelt adminis-tration, the Nixon administration, and the George W. Bush administration.

Mayhew (2005) notes the precipitous drop-off in Congressional investiga-tive activities after 1980, but attributes this decrease in large part to exogenous factors such as the rise of investigative journalism after the Watergate scandal in the 1970s, special investigative commissions and independent counsels/ special prosecutors (see also Kaiser, 1988). As Mayhew points out, "by the time the House Judiciary Committee inherited the Clinton imbroglio in mid-1998, there was virtually nothing left to reveal or expose. An independent counsel's office plus the media had already performed the labor" (Mayhew, 2005, p. 76). Indeed, Congress has institutionally extended the investigative capacities of independent agencies (located within the executive branch and thus technically still under the president's purview) over the past several decades: 1978's Ethics in Government Act, a congressional response to the Nixon administration's abuses including the firing of Watergate Special Pros-ecutor Archibald Cox in 1973, established the protocols for appointing and removing independent prosecutors; that same year, Congress created Offices of Inspectors General (OIGs) in all federal departments and major agencies. In 1990, Congress placed agencies under even more scrutiny by passing the Chief Financial Officers Act, which created politically independent CFO positions to oversee the financial management of 23 separate federal agencies. While it is not immediately clear why Congress chooses to create independent oversight capacity rather than enhance its own institutional powers (and vice versa) at certain points in time, we suggest that political uncertainty motivated by increased partisan competition (see Lee, 2016) might explain why members wish to partially insulate executive oversight from attempts at partisan point-scoring in Congress.

Indeed, the subset of the oversight literature that we find most convincing focuses on oversight as an instrument for partisan teamsmanship. Partisan polarization has been increasing since the mid-1960s (see Green, Palmquist, and Schickler, 2002, McCarty, Poole, and Rosenthal 2006, Theriault, 2008, and Levendusky, 2009), but for the first time in American history, in the 111th Congress (2009–2011), the most conservative Democrat in either chamber was ideologically to the left of the most liberal Republican (Mann and Ornstein, 2016). Thus, under conditions of high polarization, "divided government"[6] reflects not simply interparty conflict but also ideological contention, and is also a significant predictor of legislative gridlock. Measured, broadly speaking and as previously discussed, as the proportion of important items on the policy agenda that become law in a given Congressional session, legislative productivity decreases under divided government (Kelly, 1993, Edwards, Barrett, and Peake, 1997, Coleman, 1999, Howell et al, 2000, Binder, 2003, and Rogers, 2005; importantly, however, see Mayhew, 2005). But does increased polarization also affect Congress's ability to perform its *other* major institutional responsibility? If so, how – and what motivates members to engage in oversight activity in the first place? We argue that these questions are extremely promising avenues for future research, and a number of scholars have already taken up the mantle, empirically assessing whether polarization under divided government adversely affects Congress's ability to monitor the administrative state and investigate the president. In the 1991 edition of *Divided We Govern*, David Mayhew found no significant difference between the number of "high-profile" executive branch investigations – that is, investigations that garnered substantial media attention – performed under united versus divided government. However, in the book's second edition (2005), Mayhew reported different results: The number of high-profile investigations over the last decade was greater under divided than under united government. Kriner and Schwartz (2008), using an updated version of Mayhew's data, confirm these more recent results, while Parker and Dull (2009) find that, under divided government, Congress conducts more investigations of the executive branch and those investigations are significantly longer than they are under united government. (The authors also show that the effect of divided government on Congressional investigations became more pronounced after the 1970s.)

Thus, it appears that under divided government and conditions of high partisan polarization, we might expect Congress to pass *fewer* pieces of

---

[6] Divided government refers to a condition wherein the presidency and Congress are controlled by opposing political parties.

legislation (i.e., for gridlock to increase) but to perform *more* oversight. Examining the use of oversight as a partisan weapon is one way to make sense of this apparent puzzle. Ginsburg and Shefter (1990) argue that investigations and legal proceedings have consistently been important tools in the partisan wars, while Shipan (2005) argues that divided government provides an additional incentive to prioritize oversight (see also MacDonald and McGrath, 2016):

> In part, [this incentive exists] for policy reasons; policy divergence is most likely to occur under divided government, so the majority party in Congress will want to constrain the agencies under the president's control. In addition, members of the majority party may believe that they can benefit from using active oversight to emphasize policy differences between their party and the president's party, and if in the course of such hearings and investigations they embarrass a president and his agency, this is a not insignificant side benefit. (Shipan, 2005, p. 437)

Kriner and Schickler (2014) and Kriner (2009) show that Congressional investigations of presidential decisions can diminish public support for the president's policy goals as well as his overall job approval, confirming the real-world political ramifications of executive investigations under divided government. Kriner (2010) also shows that criticism of the president by members of his own party during investigative hearings significantly diminishes public approval of the president; thus, under united government, members may have an incentive to either avoid targeted investigations altogether or to attempt to mute the rhetoric and publicity surrounding certain oversight activities. As former Republican representative (and future Obama administration Transportation Secretary) Ray LaHood put it in 2004: "Our party controls the levers of government. We're not about to go out and look beneath a bunch of rocks to try and cause heartburn" (quoted in Oleszek and Oleszek, 2012, p. 52).

Lee (2013) attributes the politicization of oversight to partisan polarization coupled with increased partisan loyalty and cooperation: "It is not only that the congressional parties today are better sorted out in ideological terms, they are also better coordinated in pursuing their political interests" (p. 788). Using an original data set, Lee shows that congressional charges of administrative malfeasance are significantly greater under divided than under united government.[7] These results match with the patterns we might intuitively expect under divided government: Investigations with a particularly political or partisan bent – oversight, in other words, that offers the opportunity for political point-scoring – occur more frequently under divided government. In Lee's (2015) words: "Despite a frenzy of investigatory activity under divided government, congressional oversight [on the whole] may be less effectual in the polarized

---

[7] Lee measures salient congressional charges against the executive branch according to the extent of front-page coverage of those charges in *The New York Times*; she shows that there are a significantly greater number of front-page stories of administration malfeasance under divided than under united government.

era, because of its obvious politicization and the dearth of critical voices from within the president's own party" (p. 272).

Party leaders do seem to be aware of the ability of oversight hearings to damage not just the incumbent president but other major political actors in the executive branch as well, some of whom might have aspirations for the top job. However, and importantly, members' knowledge of the political benefits of oversight does not necessarily indicate that oversight is *motivated* primarily by partisan considerations. For example, in mid-2015, well into the "invisible primary"[8] for the 2016 presidential race, House majority leader Kevin McCarthy of California praised the Republican caucus for the establishment of the House Select Committee on Benghazi to investigate the 2012 attacks on the US consulate in Benghazi, Libya. Of Secretary of State Hillary Clinton's repeated appearances before the committee, McCarthy said in a Fox News interview: "Everybody thought Hillary Clinton was unbeatable, right? But we put together a Benghazi special committee, a select committee. What are her numbers today? Her numbers are dropping. Why? Because she's untrustable. *But no one would have known any of that had happened had we not fought*" (emphasis ours).[9] McCarthy's remarks suggest two things: First, that oversight is an effective instrument for achieving partisan electoral goals, whether in presidential races or in what has become an almost biennial battle between the two major parties for control of Congress (Lee, 2016) – and politicians know it. Second, members take oversight seriously: McCarthy frames the Benghazi hearings as a prime example of Congress's effectively checking abuses within the executive branch, and any subsequent political damage to the administration as entirely justified and part and parcel of democratic accountability.

Similarly, in the months prior to the 2006 midterm elections, in which Democrats regained control of both chambers from Republicans, then-Minority Leader Nancy Pelosi and Democratic Congressional Campaign Committee Chairman Rahm Emanuel made the need for investigations into the Bush administration's handling of the Iraq war a central piece of their political platform (Parker and Dull, 2013, see also Goldberg, 2006, Toner, 2006). As Pelosi pithily put it: "We win in '06, we get subpoena power."[10] After their decisive victory, the Democrats made good on their campaign promise to make investigative activity a focal point of their agenda: In just their first 2 months in office, Democratic committee chairs held a combined 81 hearings on the Iraq

---

[8] The "invisible primary" refers to the period of approximately 2 years before each party's actual nominating contest, during which fund-raising, early opinion polls, public endorsements, and activist support produce a "front-runner" before the actual primary season begins (see Cohen et al, 2008).

[9] See Schleifer, Theodore. 2015. "Kevin McCarthy Backtracks Benghazi Comments," CNN.com, October 2. Retrieved from www.cnn.com/2015/10/01/politics/mccarthy-walk-back-benghazi-emails/ (last accessed December 9, 2018).

[10] See Goldberg, Jeffrey. 2006. "Central Casting," *The New Yorker*, May 29. Retrieved from www.newyorker.com/magazine/2006/05/29/central-casting (last accessed December 9, 2018).

war alone (Kriner, 2008). But for Democratic leaders, the political damage their investigations may have inflicted upon the Bush administration was simply a natural side effect of accountability. Oversight, maintained Carl Levin, who became the chair of the Senate Armed Services Committee in 2007, "becomes a significant moral issue";[11] as for the prolificacy of the hearings, in May 2007, House Energy and Commerce Committee Chair John Dingell pointed out that, after years of united Republican government, "we have a huge backlog, and we'll try to use what we can to get to everything."[12]

If oversight activities do significantly increase under divided government, as much of the empirical evidence suggests, can we attribute that increase to partisan teamsmanship and the politicization of a once-august institutional responsibility, or does the increase reflect a Congress finally in the position to demand real accountability from presidents and agency leaders that may have become a bit too comfortable under united government? While House and Senate majorities have clear political incentives to pare back or avoid major investigations when their party controls the White House, does more routine monitoring of the administrative state suffer under united government as well? Performing "police patrol" oversight may exact a powerful opportunity cost if committee resources must be diverted from political investigations that might pay valuable electoral dividends. What's more, the opportunities apparent in high-profile, politicized investigations may assume priority over lawmaking itself, if members believe that position taking in investigatory hearings confers more benefits than legislating, the latter of which often requires forging compromises and sacrificing ideological purity.

Thus, two major research questions emerge from our discussion of oversight. First is a question not only of degree but also of kind: Under which conditions (divided or united government) does Congress provide *more* oversight, and under which conditions does it provide "good" oversight? We suggest that, while oversight activities on the whole may increase under divided government, we can nevertheless expect to see significantly more measured, nonpartisan oversight under united government. How to define and operationalize "good" oversight, reliably distinguishing between partisan and nonpartisan activities, will be a challenge for congressional scholars, but it may also help researchers move beyond the police-patrol versus fire-alarm dichotomy and expand the conceptualization of meaningful oversight to include, as previously discussed, delegation to nonpartisan agencies such as the GAO, the Congressional Research Service, and inspectors-general. The Republican congressional

---

[11] See Babington, Charles. 2006. "Incoming Chairmen Ready to Investigate," *Washington Post,* December 16. Retrieved from www.washingtonpost.com/wp-dyn/content/article/2006/12/15/AR2006121501680.html (last accessed December 9, 2018).

[12] See Hearn, Josephine, and Jim VandeHei. 2007. "The Oversight Congress: Trouble for Bush," *Politico,* May 22. Retrieved from www.politico.com/story/2007/05/the-oversight-congress-trouble-for-bush-004137 (last accessed December 9, 2018).

majorities' track record in holding the Trump administration accountable for alleged abuses will also provide much qualitative fodder for political scientists over the next few years. In a *Washington Monthly* piece published right before Trump's inauguration, Daniel Stid (2017) argued that there was reason for optimism about the Republican Congress's willingness and ability to strengthen its oversight capacity and effectively monitor President Trump. How well Republicans have fared at checking Trump's executive management will become clearer as time passes and more data becomes available. However, the House Intelligence Committee's decision, in March 2018, to end its investigation of alleged Russian efforts to aid Trump's presidential campaign (and of alleged collusion between the Trump campaign and Russian agents) despite the ongoing probe by Justice Department-appointed Special Counsel Robert Mueller suggests that Congress might decide to take a backseat to nonlegislative actors precisely to avoid a direct political line from Republican leaders in Congress to their party's leader in the White House.

The Mueller investigation itself, aside from any concomitant congressional probes, illuminates the dearth of statutory checks on executive authority, an important component of oversight. There exists no immediately obvious recourse should Trump decide to fire Mueller, who was appointed by Deputy Attorney General Rod Rosenstein when Attorney General Jeff Sessions recused himself from the process.[13] The aforementioned Ethics in Government Act, which Congress passed in 1978 and reauthorized in 1987 and 1994, expired in 1999 and has not been reauthorized since, rendering the appointment and removal of special counsels solely unto Justice Department regulations. Trump, who considered firing Mueller twice and was talked out of it by White House officials (see Haberman and Schmidt, 2018), has made no secret of his distaste toward Muller's investigation – he has called it, among other hyperboles, the "greatest witch hunt in history" – and a bipartisan group of legislators has pushed for new legislation that would protect Mueller against Trump's making good on his repeated threats to dismiss the special counsel. The Special Counsel Independence and Integrity Act was introduced by two Republican and two Democratic senators, and in late April 2018 was approved 14–7 by the Judiciary Committee, earning the support of Judiciary Chair Chuck Grassley (R-IA) and three other Republicans on the committee. Senate Majority Leader Mitch McConnell has said publicly that he will not bring the bill to the floor, and it is highly unlikely that the bill or its House counterpart would make it to the House floor under Republican control. However, this particular legislative

---

[13] Sessions recused himself in order to comply with Title 28, Chapter I, Section 45.2 of the Code of Federal Regulations, which stipulates that agency officials shouldn't participate in any "criminal investigation or prosecution if [the agency official] has a personal or political relationship with … an elected official, a candidate (whether or not successful) for elective, public office, a political party, or a campaign organization." Sessions was an early Trump supporter and served as a senior advisor on his campaign.

battle underscores not only important lacunas in Congress's capacity to check presidential authority but also the constitutional ambiguity over what, precisely, prosecutorial discretion enables the president to do – and how far Congress can go to rein him in. The reauthorized Ethics in Government Act was challenged in the Supreme Court in 1988, and while the law was upheld 7–1 in *Morrison v. Olson*, Justice Antonin Scalia's dissent maintained that the establishment of an independent Office of the Independent Counsel violated the separation of powers by infringing on the executive's "exclusive control" over the exercise of prosecutorial power. These constitutional questions – which have been side-stepped by current protocols that place the special counsel's office firmly under Justice Department control – have already resurfaced as Congress attempts to establish control over Mueller's investigation while keeping its own probes alive.

The second major research question that emerges from our discussion of oversight is: do members of Congress prioritize oversight (particularly but not necessarily limited to politically motivated investigations) at the expense of lawmaking under divided government? As discussed, McCubbins and Schwartz (1984) have shown that members of Congress favor retroactive "fire alarm" oversight over preemptive "police patrol" oversight due to the resource and opportunity costs of the latter, and other work suggests that members may perceive an overall opportunity cost to ensuring bureaucratic compliance with congressional directives (see Scher, 1963, McCubbins, Noll, and Weingast, 1987). Because there is little direct link in the extant literature between oversight and members' goals – primarily reelection (Mayhew, 2004); plus advancement within the institution and making good public policy (Fenno, 1995); plus prestige and ambition for higher office (Cox and McCubbins, 1993) – we might simply assume that members will favor the imminent and tangible rewards of legislating over the more ambiguous benefits of oversight. But as partisan polarization and legislative gridlock have increased over the past few decades, there is reason to suspect that the instruments by which members use to achieve their goals may have shifted. In what is arguably the most highly polarized era in congressional history, during which partisan competition has become a consistent feature of legislative politics, might members derive more benefits from oversight, and the political damage it inflicts, than from policymaking itself? Thorough empirical research into this question will help clarify the nature of gridlock: If members of Congress aren't passing as many bills as they used to, what *are* they doing, and why? Is the decision to forego legislating for oversight a conscious decision made with an eye to electoral outcomes, or is it simply a natural consequence of the inability to get broad-based legislation approved by highly polarized chambers?

CONSIDERING IMPLICATIONS

Governing is complicated. Citizens expect both effectiveness – the provision of policies that function smoothly and efficiently to solve problems – and democracy, or responsiveness to widely shared priorities and full and fair inclusion of a diversity of views. The inherent challenges of collective action operate perennially to raise the voices of the well-heeled and well-organized over those of ordinary citizens. American political institutions, by design, present a series of obstacles to swift action and require officials to build broad coalitions of support if they are to overcome multiple hurdles required to enact laws – and to oversee those laws over the long term after they have been enacted. In recent decades, growing partisanship, rather than smoothing the process of building consensus, has in many respects made it more difficult to attain. In the midst of these circumstances and interacting with them, the policyscape presents yet another formidable challenge to effective governance.

Existing policies also affect the lawmaking process. They set much of the policy agenda, channeling reform efforts and influencing whether new policy alternatives are apt to be feasible or not. They hinder the creation of bold new policies, but they may ease the path of incrementalism. The existence of a wide array of policies means, on the one hand, that lawmakers in the past have acted to address myriad needs and those laws remain on the books and presumably make Americans better off than they would be in their absence. Yet, on the other, policies do not continue to function on autopilot to work as effectively as they once did, and they need to be maintained and subject to oversight. Growing partisanship makes the likelihood that policies will be cared for effectively less likely.

Ordinary citizens likely have little awareness of how much Congress is actually accomplishing in one period of time compared to another, particularly in terms of policy maintenance and oversight, but they are quite aware of the escalation of dramatic government failures (Light, 2014, Kamarck, 2016). They may also acquire a sense of less dramatic but real forms of deterioration, such as the decay of roads and bridges, the failure of schools to improve, insufficient public services, and so forth. If so, such perceptions may help to fuel the anti-government attitudes of our time. These questions, like many others we have raised, await further inquiry.

What is apparent to us is that modern political development in the United States has brought us to a perplexing time, when citizens' expectations of government in many ways outstrip the capacity of the political system to deliver. The institutional obstacle course set forth in the US Constitution combined with the complexity of our vast array of existing policies render the task of governance one that requires public officials who are knowledgeable about public policy, have the commitment to tending to it, and who are willing to compromise and negotiate for such purposes. Yet the deeply divided party system of our times operates in a manner that it antithetical to such goals.

One consequence of these developments is that presidents are left with far greater capacity than Congress to manage the executive branch and to drive the direction of policy implementation. The administrative state is enabled to flourish, virtually unchecked by Congress. Instead, the legislative branch increasingly focuses its oversight activities on a few matters that can be exploited for partisan purposes, rather than general monitoring of how well policies are functioning. This leads to arrangements quite different from the traditional understanding of separation of powers. Congress risks turning into a calcified institution that is incapable of performing its constitutionally ordained roles. By choosing to devote itself primarily to partisan battles, the institution is participating in making itself increasingly irrelevant. Meanwhile, existing policies are left to function unsupervised and to fall into disrepair or go off the rails. These trends undermine Congress's ability to govern responsively, the nation's laws' capacity to function well, and perhaps most worrisome of all, Americans' confidence in government.

How can the United States, in the twenty-first century, revitalize its capacity to govern effectively and in a manner that maintains and better realizes its democratic ideals? That is the challenge of our time.

REFERENCES

Aberbach, Joel D. 1991. *Keeping a Watchful Eye: The Politics of Congressional Oversight*. Washington, DC: Brookings Institution Press.
  2002. "Improving Oversight: The Endless Task of Congress." *Society* 40(1): 60–63.
Adler, E. Scott, and John D. Wilkerson. 2012. *Congress and the Politics of Problem Solving*. New York: Cambridge University Press.
Baumgartner, Frank R., and Bryan D. Jones. 2015. *The Politics of Information: Problem Definition and the Course of Public Policy in America*. Chicago: University of Chicago Press.
Berry, Christopher R., Barry C. Burden, and William G. Howell. 2012. "The Lives and Deaths of Federal Programs, 1971–2003." In Jeffery A. Jenkins and Eric M. Patashnik (eds.), *Living Legislation: Durability, Change, and the Politics of American Lawmaking*. Chicago: University of Chicago Press, pp. 86–110.
Binder, Sarah A. 2000. "Going Nowhere: A Gridlocked Congress?" *Brookings Review* 18(1): 16–19.
  2003. *Stalemate: Causes and Consequences of Legislative Gridlock*. Washington, DC: Brookings Institution Press.
Binder, Sarah A., and Forrest Maltzman. 2002. "Senatorial Delay in Confirming Federal Judges, 1947–1998." *American Journal of Political Science* 46(1): 190–199.
Blumenthal, David, and James A. Morone. 2009. *The Heart of Power: Health and Politics in the Oval Office*. Berkeley: University of California Press.
Burman, Leonard E., and Joel Slemrod. 2013. *Taxes in America: What Everyone Needs to Know*. Oxford University Press.
Campbell, Andrea. 2003. *How Policies Make Citizens: Senior Political Activism and the American Welfare State*. Princeton, NJ: Princeton University Press.
Congressional Budget Office (hereafter, CBO). 2014. "Updated Budget Projections: 2014–2024." Retrieved from www.cbo.gov/sites/default/files/113th-congress-2013-2014/reports/45229-UpdatedBudgetProjections_2.pdf (last accessed December 11, 2018).

CBO. 2015a. "The Federal Budget in 2015." Retrieved from www.cbo.gov/sites/default/ files/114th-congress-2015-2016/graphic/51110-budget1overall.pdf (last accessed December 11, 2018).

2015b. "Updated Budget Projections: 2015–2015." Retrieved from www.cbo.gov/sites/ default/files/114th-congress-2015-2016/reports/49973-UpdatedBudgetProjections_0 .pdf (last accessed December 11, 2018).

2017a. "The Federal Budget in 2017: An Infographic." Retrieved from www.cbo.gov/ publication/53624 (last accessed December 11, 2018).

2017b. "Discretionary Spending in 2017: An Infographic." Retrieved from www.cbo .gov/publication/53626 (last accessed December 11, 2018).

Center on Budget and Policy Priorities. 2016. "Policy Basics: Non-Defense Discretionary Programs." Retrieved from www.cbpp.org/research/policy-basics-non-defense-dis cretionary-programs (last accessed December 11, 2018).

Cohen, Marty, David Karol, Hans Noel, and John Zaller. 2008. *The Party Decides: Nominating Contests before and after Reform*. Chicago: University of Chicago Press.

Coleman, John J. 1999. "Unified Government, Divided Government, and Party Responsiveness." *American Political Science Review* 93(4): 821–835.

Conway, Madeline. 2017. "Ryan: Obamacare Is the Law of the Land for the Foreseeable Future." *Politico*. March 24. Retrieved from www.politico.com/story/2017/03/ obamacare-repeal-failed-paul-ryan-reaction-236478 (last accessed December 11, 2018).

Cox, James H. 2004. *Reviewing Delegation: An Analysis of the Congressional Reauthorization Process*. Westport, CT: Praeger.

Cox, Gary W., and Matthew D. McCubbins. 1993. *Legislative Leviathan: Party Government in the House*. Oakland: University of California Press.

Drutman, Lee, and Steven Teles. 2015. "A New Agenda for Political Reform." *Washington Monthly*. March/April/May. Retrieved from https://washingtonmonthly .com/magazine/maraprmay-2015/a-new-agenda-for-political-reform/ (last accessed January 2, 2019).

Edwards, George C. III, Andrew Barrett, and Jeffrey Peake. 1997. "The Legislative Impact of Divided Government." *American Journal of Political Science* 41(2): 545–563.

Ejdemyr, Simon, Clayton Nall, and Zachary O'Keefe. 2015. "Building Inequality: The Permanence of Infrastructure and the Limits of Democratic Representation." Retrieved from http://web.stanford.edu/~nall/docs/di.pdf (last accessed December 11, 2018).

Fenno, Richard F., Jr. 1995 (1973). *Congressmen in Committees*. Berkeley: Institute of Governmental Studies Press.

Fenno, Richard. 1977. "U.S. House Members in Their Constituencies: An Exploration." *American Political Science Review* 71(3): 883–917.

Federal Reserve Bank of St. Louis. 2016. "Federal Net Outlays as Percent of Gross Domestic Product," Economic Research. Retrieved from https://fred.stlouisfed.org/ series/FYONGDA188S (last accessed December 11, 2018).

Fiorina, Morris P. 1981. "Congressional Control of the Bureaucracy: A Mismatch of Incentives and Capabilities." In Lawrence C. Dodd and Bruce J. Oppenheimer (eds.), *Congress Reconsidered*, 2nd edition. Washington, DC: CQ Press.

Firozi, Paulina. 2017. "Poll: Just 17 Percent of Voters Back ObamaCare Repeal Plan." *The Hill*. March 23. Retrieved from http://thehill.com/policy/healthcare/325448-poll-majority-of-voters-disapprove-of-gop-obamacare-repeal-plan (last accessed December 11, 2018).

Fukuyama, Francis. 2014. *Political Order and Political Decay: From the Industrial Revolution to the Globalization of Democracy*. New York: Farrar, Straus, and Giroux.

Ginsberg, Benjamin and Martin Shefter. 1990. *Politics by Other Means: The Declining Importance of Elections in America*. New York: Basic Books.

Goldberg, Jeffrey. 2006. "Central Casting: The Democrats Think about Who Can Win in the Midterms—and in 2008." *The New Yorker*. 29 May. Retrieved from www.newyorker.com/magazine/2006/05/29/central-casting (last accessed January 17, 2019).

Green, Donald, Bradley Palmquist, and Eric Schickler. 2002. *Partisan Hearts and Minds: Political Parties and the Social Identities of Voters*. New York: Oxford University Press.

Haberman, Maggie and Michael S. Schmidt. 2018. "Trump Sought to Fire Mueller in December." *The New York Times*, April 10. Retrieved from www.nytimes.com/2018/04/10/us/politics/trump-sought-to-fire-mueller-in-december.html (last accessed December 11, 2018).

Hacker, Jacob S., and Paul Pierson. 2001. "Winner-Take-All Politics: Public Policy, Political Organization, and the Precipitous Rise of Top Incomes in the United States." *Politics & Society* 38(2): 152–204.

Hacker, Jacob, and Paul Pierson. 2005a. *Off Center: The Republican Revolution and the Erosion of American Democracy*. New Haven, CT: Yale University Press.

2014. "After the 'Master Theory': Downs, Schattschneider, and the Rebirth of Policy-Focused Analysis." *Perspectives on Politics* 12(3): 64362.

Hacker, Jacob S. 2002. *The Divided Welfare State: The Battle over Public and Private Social Benefits in the United States*. New York: Cambridge University Press.

2004. "Privatizing Risk without Privatizing the Welfare State: The Hidden Politics of Social Policy Retrenchment in the United States." *American Political Science Review* 98(2): 243–260.

Hacker, Jacob S., and Paul Pierson. 2005b. "Abandoning the Middle: The Revealing Case of the Bush Tax Cuts." *Perspectives on Politics* 3(1): 33–53. DOI: 10.1017/S1537592705050048

Hall, Thad. 2004. *Authorizing Policy*. Columbus, OH: Ohio State University Press.

Howard, Christopher. 2002. "Tax Expenditures." In Lester M. Salamon (ed.), *The Tools of Government: A Guide to the New Governance*. New York: Oxford University Press.

1997. *The Hidden Welfare State: Tax Expenditures and Social Policy in the United States*. Princeton, NJ: Princeton University Press.

Howell, William G., Scott Adler, Charles Cameron, and Charles Riemann. 2000. "Divided Government and the Legislative Productivity of Congress, 1945–94." *Legislative Studies Quarterly* 25(2): 285–312.

Jacobs, Lawrence R., and Theda Skocpol, 2010. *Health Care Reform and American Politics: What Everyone Needs to Know*. New York: Oxford University Press.

Jacobs, Lawrence R., and Suzanne Mettler. 2017. "Outside of Washington, There Is a New Vital Center in Health Care Reform." *Health Affairs*. July 31. Retrieved from www.healthaffairs.org/do/10.1377/hblog20170731.061320/full/ (last accessed January 2, 2019).

Jenkins, Jeffery A., and Sidney M. Milkis. 2014. "Introduction: The Rise of a Policy State?" In Jenkins and Milkis (eds.), *The Politics of Major Postwar Policy Reforms in Postwar America.* New York: Cambridge University Press.

Kaiser, Frederick M. 1988. "Congressional Oversight of the Presidency." *The Annals of the American Academy of Political and Social Science* 499: 75–89.

Kamarck, Elaine C. 2016. *Why Presidents Fail.* Washington, DC: Brookings Institution.

Kelly, Sean Q. 1993. "Divided We Govern? A Reassessment." *Polity* 25(3): 475–484.

Kriner, Douglas. 2010. *After the Rubicon: Congress, Presidents, and the Politics of Waging War.* Chicago: University of Chicago Press.

Kriner, Douglas L. 2009. "Can Enhanced Oversight Repair the 'Broken Branch?'" *Boston University Law Review* 89: 765–793.

Kriner, Douglas L., and Eric Schickler. 2014. "Investigating the President: Committee Probes and Presidential Approval, 1953–2006." *Journal of Politics* 76(2): 521–534.

Kriner, Douglas L., and Liam Schwartz. 2008. "Divided Government and Congressional Investigations." *Legislative Studies Quarterly* 33(2): 295–321.

Lee, Frances E. 2013. "Presidents and Party Teams: The Politics of Debt Limits and Executive Oversight, 2001–2013." *Presidential Studies Quarterly* 43(4): 775–791.

2015. "How Party Polarization Affects Governance." *Annual Review of Political Science* 18: 261–282.

2016. *Insecure Majorities: Congress and the Perpetual Campaign.* Chicago, IL: University of Chicago Press.

Levendusky, Matthew. 2009. *The Partisan Sort: How Liberals Became Democrats and Conservatives Became Republicans.* Chicago, IL: University of Chicago Press.

Lewis, David E. 2008. *The Politics of Presidential Appointments: Political Control and Bureaucratic Performance.* Princeton, NJ: Princeton University Press.

Lerman, Amy A., and Vesla M. Weaver. 2014. *Arresting Citizenship: The Democratic Consequences of American Crime Control.* Chicago, IL: University of Chicago Press.

Lewallen, Jonathan, Sean M. Theriault, and Bryan D. Jones. 2015. "Congressional Dysfunction and the Decline of Problem Solving." Paper prepared for presentation at the 2015 Midwest Political Science Association Meeting.

Light, Paul C. 2014. "A Cascade of Failures: Why Government Fails, and How to Stop It." Center for Effective Public Management, The Brookings Institution.

MacDonald, Jason A., and Robert J. McGrath. 2016. "Retrospective Congressional Oversight and the Dynamics of Legislative Influence Over the Bureaucracy." *Legislative Studies Quarterly* 41(4): 899–934. Retrieved from https://onlinelibrary.wiley.com/doi/pdf/10.1111/lsq.12138 (last accessed December 11, 2018).

Maltzman, Forrest, and Charles R. Shipan. 2012. "Beyond Legislative Productivity: Enactment Conditions, Subsequent Conditions, and the Shape and Life of the Law," In Jeffery A. Jenkins and Eric M. Patashnik (eds.), *Living Legislation: Durability, Change, and the Politics of American Lawmaking.* Chicago, IL: University of Chicago Press, pp. 111–134.

Mann, Thomas E., and Norman J. Ornstein. 2016 (2012). *It's Even Worse than It Looks: How the American Constitutional System Collided with the New Politics of Extremism.* New York: Basic Books.

2006. *The Broken Branch: How Congress Is Failing America and How to Get It Back on Track*. New York: Oxford University Press.

Mayhew, David R. 2004. (1974). *Congress: The Electoral Connection*, 2nd edition. New Haven: Yale University Press.

  2005. "Actions in the Public Sphere." In Paul J. Quirk and Sarah A. Binder *(eds.), The Legislative Branch*. New York: Oxford University Press, pp. 63–106.

  2005. (1991). *Divided We Govern: Party Control, Lawmaking, and Investigations, 1946–1990*, 2nd edition. New Haven: Yale University Press.

McCarty, Nolan, Keith T. Poole, and Howard Rosenthal. 2006. *Polarized America: The Dance of Ideology and Unequal Riches*. Cambridge: MIT Press.

McCubbins, Matthew D., and Thomas Schwartz. 1984. "Congressional Oversight Overlooked: Police Patrol versus Fire Alarms." *American Journal of Political Science* 28(1): 165–179.

McCubbins, Matthew D., Roger G. Noll, and Barry R. Weingast. 1987. "Administrative Procedures as Instruments of Political Control." *Journal of Law, Economics, & Organization* 3(2): 243–277.

Mettler, Suzanne. 2011. *The Submerged State: How Invisible Government Policies Undermine American Democracy*. Chicago, IL: University of Chicago Press.

  2014. *Degrees of Inequality: How the Politics of Higher Education Policy Sabotaged the American Dream*. New York: Basic Books.

  2016. "The Policyscape and the Challenges of Contemporary Politics to Policy Maintenance." *Perspectives on Politics* 14(2): 369–390.

  2018. *The Government-Citizen Disconnect*. New York: Russell Sage Foundation.

Moe, Terry M. 1987. "An Assessment of the Positive Theory of 'Congressional Dominance.'" *Legislative Studies Quarterly* 12(4): 475–520.

Nall, Clayton. 2015. "The Political Consequences of Spatial Policies: How Interstate Highways Facilitated Geographic Polarization." *Journal of Politics* 77(2): 394–406.

Ogul, Morris S. 2009. (1976). *Congress Oversees the Bureaucracy: Studies in Legislative Supervision*. Pittsburgh: University of Pittsburgh Press.

Oleszek, Mark J., and Walter J. Oleszek. 2012. "Institutional Challenges Confronting Congress after 9/11: Partisan Polarization and Effective Oversight." in David P. Auerswald and Colton C. Campbell (eds.), *Congress and the Politics of National Security*. New York: Cambridge University Press.

Oleszek, Walter J. 2010. "Congressional Oversight: An Overview." Congressional Research Service report No. R41079. Washington, DC: Congressional Research Service.

Orren, Karen, and Stephen Skowronek. 2014. "Pathways to the Present: Political Development in America." In Richard Valelly, Suzanne Mettler, and Robert Lieberman (eds.), *Oxford Handbook on American Political Development*. Oxford: Oxford University Press.

Page, Benjamin I., and Lawrence R. Jacobs. 2009. *Class War? What Americans Really Think about Economic Inequality*. Chicago, IL: University of Chicago Press.

Parker, David C.W., and Matthew Dull. 2009. "Divided We Quarrel: The Politics of Congressional Investigations, 1947–2004." *Legislative Studies Quarterly* 34(3): 319–345.

  2013. "The Weaponization of Congressional Oversight: The Politics of the Watchful Eye, 1947–2010." In Scott A. Frisch and Sean Q Kelly (eds.), *Politics to the*

Extreme: American Political Institutions in the Twenty-First Century. New York: Palgrave MacMillan, pp. 47–69.

Patashnik, Eric M. 2008. *Reforms at Risk: What Happens after Major Policy Changes Are Enacted*. Princeton, NJ: Princeton University Press.

Patel, Jugal K., and Alicia Parlapiano. 2017. "The Senate's Official Scorekeeper Says the Republican Tax Plan Would Add $1 Trillion to the Deficit." *The New York Times*, December 1. Retrieved from www.nytimes.com/interactive/2017/11/28/us/politics/tax-bill-deficits.html (last accessed January 2, 2019).

Pearson, James B. 1975. "Oversight: A Vital Yet Neglected Congressional Function." *Kansas Law Review* 23: 277–288.

Pierson, Paul. 1993. "When Effect Becomes Cause: Policy Feedback and Political Change." *World Politics* 5(4): 595–628.

1994. *Dismantling the Welfare State? Reagan, Thatcher, and the Politics of Retrenchment*. New York: Cambridge University Press.

2014. "Conclusion: Madison Upside Down." in Jeffery A. Jenkins and Sidney M. Milkis (eds.), *The Politics of Major Policy Reform in Postwar America*. New York: Cambridge University Press, pp. 282–302.

Robertson, David Brian. 2005. *The Constitution and America's Destiny*. New York: Cambridge University Press.

Rogers, James R. 2005. "The Impact of Divided Government on Legislative Production." *Public Choice* 123(1/2): 217–233.

Rose, Richard, and Phillip L. Davies. 1994. *Inheritance in Public Policy: Change without Choice in Britain*. New Haven, CT: Yale University Press.

Saeki, Manabu. 2009. "Gridlock in the Government of the United States: Influence of Divided Government and Veto Players." *British Journal of Political Science* 39(3): 587–607.

Schattschneider, E.E. 1935. *Politics, Pressure, and the Tariff*. New York: Prentice Hall.

Scher, Seymour. 1963. "Conditions for Legislative Control." *Journal of Politics* 25 (3): 526–551.

Schneider, Anne Larason, and Helen Ingram. 1997. *Policy Design for Democracy*. Lawrence: University Press of Kansas.

Shipan, Charles R. 2005. "Congress and the Bureaucracy." In Paul J. Quirk and Sarah A. Binder (eds.), *The Legislative Branch*. New York: Oxford University Press, pp. 432–458.

Skocpol, Theda. 1992. *Protecting Soldiers and Mothers: The Political Origins of Social Policy in the United States*. Cambridge: Belknap Press of Harvard University Press.

Skowronek, Stephen. 2009. "Taking Stock." In Lawrence Jacobs and Desmond King (eds.), *The Unsustainable American State*. New York: Oxford University Press.

Stid, Daniel. 2017. "Why the GOP Congress Will Stop Trump from Going Too Far." *Washington Monthly*, January/February. Retrieved from https://washingtonmonthly.com/magazine/januaryfebruary-2017/why-the-gop-congress-will-stop-trump-from-going-too-far/ (last accessed January 2, 2019).

Sunstein, Cass R. 1993. "The Myth of the Unitary Executive." *The Administrative Law Journal* 7(1): 297–308.

Talbert, Jeffery C., Bryan D. Jones, and Frank R. Baumgartner. 1995. "Nonlegislative Hearings and Policy Change in Congress." *American Journal of Political Science* 39(2): 383–405.

Teles, Stephen. 2013. "Kludgeocracy In America." *National Affairs*, 17(Fall). Retrieved from www.nationalaffairs.com/publications/detail/kludgeocracy-in-america (last accessed December 11, 2018).

Teter, Michael J. 2013. "Gridlock, Legislative Supremacy, and the Problem of Arbitrary Inaction." *Notre Dame Law Review* 88(5): 2217–2232.

Thelen, Kathleen, and Wolfgang Streeck, eds. 2005. *Beyond Continuity: Institutional Change in Advanced Political Economies*. New York: Oxford University Press.

Theriault, Sean M. 2008. *Party Polarization in Congress*. New York: Cambridge University Press.

Toner, Robin. 2006. "How the Democrats Would Rule the Hill." *The New York Times*, October 8. Retrieved from www.nytimes.com/2006/10/08/weekinreview/08toner.html?pagewanted=all (last accessed December 11, 2018).

Vogel, David. 2012. *The Politics of Precaution: Regulating Health, Safety and Environmental Risks in Europe and the United States*. Princeton, NJ: Princeton University Press.

Whittington, Keith E. 2001. *Constitutional Construction: Divided Powers and Constitutional Meaning*. Cambridge: Harvard University Press.

Wildavsky, Aaron. 1979. *Speaking Truth to Power: The Art and Craft of Policy Analysis*. Boston, MA: Little, Brown, and Co.

11

The Effects of Partisan Polarization on the Bureaucracy

David B. Spence

What does the new reality of partisan polarization imply for the modern American administrative state? We might assume, quite a lot. Agencies derive their mandate and funding from an increasingly polarized Congress. They sit within an executive branch headed by a partisan politician. They receive input from (what many scholars see as) an increasingly polarized electorate. And agencies are the central characters in one of the major disputes that is driving the parties apart: namely, question of the proper role of government in private and economic life. Recent debates over the Affordable Care Act, financial regulation, antitrust regulation, greenhouse gas regulation, and net neutrality, for example, all implicate this "market versus regulation" fault line, one that has increasingly riven the American polity since the Reagan administration first began to challenge the New Deal consensus.

Scholars have had quite a bit to say about how ideological polarization affects governance, particularly our understandings of Congress (Krehbiel, 1998, Cox and McCubbins, 2005, McCarty, Poole, and Rosenthal, 2006), the parties (Aldrich, 2011), and federalism (Shor, Berry, and McCarty, 2010, Bulman-Pozen, 2014, Gerken, 2014, Metzger, 2015a). This essay reviews a less well-developed literature addressing how polarization affects administrative agencies, and suggests opportunities for new scholarly inquiries that might help us fill in our understanding of the effects of polarization on the bureaucracy. If the modern administrative state is a post–World War II institution, one that has confronted increased partisan polarization only during the last 25 years or so, it follows that the scholarship examining that relationship is necessarily in its infancy. Nonetheless, scholars are beginning to ask interesting questions about the influence of political polarization on agency decision making. Even if this scholarship has not yet generated consensus conclusions about the effects on the bureaucracy of increasingly polarized parties, we can make a few observations about its lessons so far.

The first is that the early evidence suggests that agencies are neither as paralyzed nor as prone to ideologically extreme positions as are their political overseers, even if they sometimes have more ideological room to operate than they once did. Scholars have not yet teased out why this is, though the literature suggests a number of structural explanations. The second observation is that polarization (particularly, congressional gridlock) nevertheless places increasing strain on agencies and courts, as the former face new problems within their jurisdiction without (or with less frequent and helpful) input from Congress, and the latter struggle to review those agency decisions. These struggles have important implications for the place of administrative agencies in the American constitutional design. The final observation is that as of this writing, scholarship has not yet caught up with the Trump administration's right-populist efforts to delegitimize the agency policymaking and the administrative process. It remains to be seen how successful and durable those efforts will be, and how scholars will respond to them. This essay elaborates on each of these observations.

It is important at the outset, however, to note that the task here – tracing the effects of partisan polarization on administrative agencies – implicates age-old debates about the political control of agencies by politicians, and the extent to which agencies can (or should) evade political control. The academic literatures within which those debates are waged have long been fragmented, both substantively and methodologically. Within political science, these questions are taken up by scholars who occupy a variety of subfields, including bureaucratic politics, public administration, Congress, and the presidency. Each frames the problem from the perspective of a different institutional actor, and brings different methodological norms and preferences to the task. Among legal scholars, these questions fall mostly within administrative law scholarship, but administrative law scholars borrow selectively from social scientific analyses, all the while addressing the normative dimensions of this question more directly (and transparently) than most social scientists do.

All of which makes this literature a rich and interesting polyglot, one the constant subtext of which is a tension between two competing visions. One vision is of an executive branch guided by technical expertise and "neutral competence" (e.g., Wilson, 1887, Gulick, 1937, Kaufman, 1967). The other vision is one in which interest-group rent-seeking predominates (e.g., Niskanen, 1971, Stigler, 1971). Scholars wrestle with this tension descriptively and analytically, seeking to discern the extent to which politics affects administrative decision making, and when and whether neutral competence is possible. And they wrestle with this tension normatively as well, either by premising their analyses on the desirability of either political control or neutral competence at the outset, or by engaging the normative question more directly. Thus, Woodrow Wilson's vision of a scientific administration free from politics was a normative one, just as principal-agent models of bureaucratic politics posit the accountability of agencies to their elected principals as normatively desirable or constitutionally necessary.

Of course, these views are archetypes. Today nearly all scholars accept that the "execution of law cannot be meaningfully separated from politics [and that] administration itself is inherently a political action" (Balla, 2012). It is neither the purely technical, apolitical enterprise of Wilson's dreams, nor the purely cynical political exercise in rent-seeking described by public choice scholarship. Administration is instead a much more interesting amalgam of both political and technocratic problem solving: a process of implementing statutory goals, established by politicians, through the delegation of decision power to expert agencies. Those statutory goals necessarily reflect some combination of public and private interests, just as some combination of career technocrats and politically appointed overseers will drive the agency policy choices that implement those statutory goals. Problematically for scholars, however, the extent to which agency decisions reflect private versus public interests (or the priorities of careerists versus political overseers) varies by issue and decision, and depends upon a long list of variables, including (a) the extent to which the decision is salient to Congress or the president (whether each understands and prioritizes the issue), (b) the breadth of the statutory delegation to the agency, (c) whether the agency is an independent commission or an executive agency, and more.

Despite the heterogeneity of both agency decision environments and scholarly approaches to the study of agencies, it is probably safe to say that most scholars of the bureaucracy are interested in understanding the product of agency decision making (policy choices), and the larger implications of agency policymaking discretion.[1] Accordingly, we can reframe our central question this way: what has recent scholarship had to say about how political polarization affects agency *policymaking*? The focus here will be on political science and legal scholarship, and I divide that literature into two overlapping parts: (a) what legal scholars and political scientists have had to say about how polarization influences the ability of politicians – Congress and the president – to steer agency choices, both directly and indirectly; and (b) what scholars have had to say recently about the larger implications of polarization for administration, including the role of courts as the guardians of the constitutional design in a polarized world. This last question necessarily engages (and raises the stakes for) long-standing debates about the normative desirability of agency policymaking discretion. Nor could these debates be more topical: Donald Trump appointed several agency heads who are hostile to the missions of the agencies and departments they will oversee – Rick Perry (Energy), Andrew Puzder (Labor), Scott Pruitt (EPA), and Tom Price (HHS) – and nominated to

---

[1] There is scholarship addressing the effects of politics and polarization on agency behavior that falls outside the boundaries of policy choice, such as ministerial decisions, the work of what bureaucratic politics scholars once called "street level bureaucrats" (Lipsky, 1980) and what Anne Joseph O'Connell more recently described as "bureaucracy at the boundary" (O'Connell, 2014a). This review is confined to an examination of the influence of polarization on agencies as policymakers.

the Supreme Court a judge (Neil Gorsuch) who opposes the delegation of policymaking discretion to administrative agencies.

POLARIZATION, AGENCIES, AND POLITICAL CONTROL

If politics does indeed play some role in administration, we might reasonably infer that ideological polarization and hyper-partisanship influences agency policy choices through any of several possible pathways. One potential avenue of influence is through the actions of elected politicians, who may wish to steer agencies toward the policy choices that they (or favored constituents) prefer. If elected politicians are moving toward the ideological poles, are agencies growing more ideologically extreme as well, either through congressional and presidential oversight or by filling agencies with more ideologically extreme actors? Recognizing that relatively hierarchical agencies face fewer collective action problems when making decisions, does polarization nevertheless paralyze agencies in ways that are analogous to congressional gridlock?

What about the general public? If voters are becoming more ideologically polarized, might they push agency decisions toward the extremes as well, either directly or in partnership with elected politicians? Alternatively, might polarization drive increased opposition to agency policy choices? That is, if the distribution of voters on a single left-right dimension is becoming increasingly bipolar, and the poles are moving farther apart (as in Congress), any agency policy choice (including a choice located at the ideological median) appears to be farther and farther away to increasing numbers of voters. Might this increase the ferocity of opposition to agency policy choices?

The answers to these questions may depend, in part, upon the effectiveness of political control, and how agencies respond to the pull and tug of Congress, the president, and the public. The scholarly literature on political control is well-established and contentious, and its seminal works mostly predate the acceleration of political polarization in Congress and the electorate over the last 25 years. Thus, more recent work of the influence of polarization on agencies can be seen as extensions of these earlier debates.

The Political Control Debate

In the 1960s and 1970s, principal-agent models of political control drawn from economics challenged earlier models of apolitical, scientific administration.[2] These principal-agent models characterized bureaucrats as rational, self-interested actors whose faithfulness to their legislative mandate could be neither assumed nor trusted. Agencies could be expected to use their relative expertise

---

[2] Another challenge came from the behavioral critique of scientific administration, from sociology and psychology (e.g., Simon, 1946, Lindblom, 1959).

and informational advantages to shirk their duty to comply with statutory mandates, or with the wishes of their political overseers; alternatively, they might be "captured" by regulated interests (Niskanen, 1971, Stigler, 1971, Peltzman, 1976). This skeptical view of the possibility of political control, in turn, spawned parallel reactions in the 1980s: theories of congressional and presidential dominance, which teased out more fully the tools of political control available to Congress and the president, respectively.

The congressional dominance thesis emphasized a suite of *ex ante* and *ex post* controls available to Congress to steer administrative agency policy choices in Congress's preferred direction. These controls include the myriad ways Congress can structure agency decision processes by: (a) defining the agency's statutory mission, thereby attracting to the agency people who are dedicated to that mission, and defining the agency's choice set, (b) choosing strategically both the breadth and the executive branch recipient of the statutory delegation, so as to best advance the interests of the winning legislative coalition, and (c) empowering third parties to monitor agency decision making on Congress's behalf by alerting Congress to agency shirking behavior and participating in agency decisions, (so-called police patrols and fire alarms) (Weingast and Moran, 1983, McCubbins and Schwartz, 1984, McCubbins, Noll, and Weingast, 1987, 1989).

Congressional dominance scholars offered the Clean Air Act as an illustrative example. When Congress passed the Clean Air Act of 1970, it granted the Environmental Protection Agency (EPA) fairly broad discretion to determine which pollutants to regulate and how stringently to regulate them, subject to statutory standards that pushed the agency to focus on protection of public health. The EPA thereafter attracted a wide range of environmental professionals dedicated to the improvement of air quality. The 1970 law also included a fire alarm in the form of its citizen suit provision, which empowered environmental groups to enforce the laws requirements directly against polluters when government regulators chose not to do so. These and other fire alarms led Democratic congresses to amend the statute, first in 1977 to plug a regulatory gap for pollution in cleaner air areas, and again in 1990 to force a reluctant EPA (under Republican control) to regulate toxic air pollution more stringently. This, said proponents of the congressional dominance hypothesis, was just the sort of iterative process by which Congress could influence the behavior of administrative agencies.

The presidential control hypothesis, advanced most prominently by Terry Moe, emphasized the president's more flexible and omnipresent tools of influence over agencies, which emanate from the constitutional responsibility to supervise the executive branch within which agencies sit. These tools include the appointment power, the power to review agency rulemakings, the power to influence the public agenda, and a variety of less formal tools of influence over administrative agencies. Presidents face none of the collective action problems inherent in legislative decision making, nor are they handicapped by changing membership every 2 years, making them the more effective influencer of agencies, say proponents of this view (Moe, 1987). Of course, presidents cannot be everywhere at once, nor can they prioritize all of the myriad policy choices made by the executive branch; but, say proponents of the presidential dominance hypothesis, the president can exercise more day-to-day influence over agency policy choices than Congress.

Certainly, Congress can try to weaken the tools of presidential control, most notably by delegating power directly to agencies (rather than to the president), fashioning agencies as independent commissions (limiting the president's removal power and mandating a bipartisan plural executive), and using the power to approve political appointments strategically. Nevertheless, say proponents of presidential dominance, the president's influence is far more flexibly dispensed and informal, and therefore more effective, even with nominally independent agencies. For example, in 1971, President Nixon was able to persuade even the chairman of the Federal Reserve, an institution designed to be apolitical and independent, to take actions that he staunchly opposed (abandonment of the gold standard, and support for a wage and price freeze) (Irwin, 2013). Nor is this an isolated anecdote; the power of the president to influence agencies by informal means finds support elsewhere as well (Cole, 1942, Verkuil, 1980).

These competing congressional and presidential control hypotheses spawned a large cross-disciplinary literature within political science, economics, and legal scholarship. That scholarship challenged and refined each of the two control hypotheses in a variety of ways. Some positive political theorists used formal models to explore in greater detail the logic of delegation (e.g., Epstein and O'Halloran, 1994, Lupia and McCubbins, 1994, Huber and Shipan, 2002, Carpenter, 2004). Other analyses attempted to measure the influence of congressional and presidential controls on agency decisions, reaching conflicting conclusions about their efficacy, depending on the circumstances (e.g., Calvert, Moran, and Weingast, 1987, Wood and Waterman, 1991, Brehm and Gates, 1995, Rinquist, 1995, Balla, 1998, Spence, 1999, Whittington and Carpenter, 2003, MacDonald, 2010). Still others sought to model formally the ways in which agencies could resist political control by playing Congress and the president off against one another (e.g., Hammond and Knott, 1996).

Both formal and empirical models in this literature struggled at times to capture the importance of expertise in the delegation process, particularly the influence of expertise on preference formation. That is, Congress may leave particular policy questions unanswered in enabling legislation because it foresaw the issue at the time of enactment but (a) believed the expert agency was better equipped to address the issue well or (b) could not muster majority support for any particular policy response. Alternatively, Congress might not have foreseen the issue at all, even though the issue is clearly within the class of problems the resolution of which was delegated to the agency by the statute – a circumstance likely to apply to an increasing number of agency policy choices as statutes grow older, unchanged, in the age of congressional gridlock. While a few of the formal models of delegation attempt to model future uncertainty (e.g., Bawn, 1995), most have difficulty capturing all of the reasons why broad delegation might be rational, and likely to yield policy choices that Congress (or the median voter) would have made if it could overcome the information asymmetries and collective action problems that afflict that body. Some of the scholarship responding to the congressional dominance hypothesis raised this point, and questioned whether "Congress" has preferences apart from those expressed in legislation (Shepsle, 1992), and if so, whether they should guide agency decisions (Farber and Frickey, 1992).

For their part, legal scholars tended to focus on the interaction of these various tools of control, and on the normative implications of political control for agency policymaking. Some of this work accepted the strategic assumptions of the congressional and presidential dominance hypotheses (that is, the normative preferability of political control) and sought to refine the dominance hypotheses (Eskridge, 1994, Eskridge and Ferejohn, 1992, 2001, Macey, 1992a, 1992b). Others noted ways in which agencies could retain autonomy nevertheless (Mashaw, 1990, 1997, Spence, 1997), or aimed to nudge thinking about the bureaucracy back toward Wilsonian progressivism (Robinson, 1991, Rose-Ackerman, 1992). Still others articulated a much stronger normative and constitutional case for presidential control, one that challenges some accepted notions of Congress's power to structure or circumscribe the president's supervisory control over executive branch entities (e.g., Yoo, Calabresi, and Colangelo, 2005). This idea, known in legal scholarship as the theory of a "unitary executive," has been embraced by the Trump era GOP as a means of reining in the so-called deep state.[3]

In the end, this debate yielded no consensus but seemed to confirm that because Congress and the president have informational and resource disadvantages vis-à-vis the bureaucracy, Congress, and the president can exercise influence only selectively. But when they can devote their attention to that task, they can each be effective shapers of agency policymaking.

Polarization Via Direct Political Control?

So how does partisan polarization affect these dynamics? We know, of course, that polarized parties in Congress have become more ideologically homogenous, and have grown farther apart ideologically (McCarty, 2004, McCarty, Poole, and Rosenthal, 2006). Scholars ascribe this to a variety of factors, most of which fall within either of two categories: one focusing on the increasing ideological homogeneity in congressional districts (Stonecash, Brewer, and

---

[3] President Trump's lawyer, John Dowd, cited unitary executive theory by name in a confidential memo to Special Counsel Robert Mueller on June 23, 2017, arguing that the constitutional grant of executive power to the president empowers him to fire the special counsel at will (Dowd, 2017).

Mariani, 2003, Carson et al, 2007, Bishop, 2008), and a second focusing on various kinds of institutional factors that affect how parties manage congressional business (Layman, Carsey, and Horowitz, 2006, Pildes, 2011). And scholars have observed that whatever its cause, polarization in Congress begets gridlock (Krehbiel, 1998, Cox and McCubbins, 2005, Binder, 2003), weakening Congress's ability to use legislation to exert political control over agencies.

Throughout most of the history of the modern administrative state Congress has been able to legislate – to fine-tune agencies' enabling statutes – in response to changing circumstances. Indeed, that is exactly what happened in the Clean Air Act example discussed above. But partisan gridlock reduces Congress's ability to steer the agency – to alter the agency's statutory authority when Congress dislikes the agency's policy choices, or when the initial definition of the agency's authority becomes ill-suited to new or changing circumstances. The Dodd-Frank Act, the only major legislation updating an existing regulatory regime during the Obama era, seems the exception that proves the rule, and (given the Trump administration's desire to repeal or weaken it) may well be an illustration of Maltzman and Shipan's (2008) conclusion that laws passed by particularly ideologically diverse coalitions tend to be less durable than those enacted by unified coalitions. Now, more often than not, when voters who are dissatisfied with an agency policy choice try to set off the appropriate fire alarms, there is no response. More accurately, the gridlock interval (defined at its boundaries by the ideal points[+] of the president and Congress) is wider than it once was, so any fire alarm sounded in response to an agency policy choice within that wider interval will fall on deaf ears.

It follows that if Congress cannot mount a credible threat to intervene legislatively to alter the agency decision environment, there is more opportunity for agencies to pursue their own ends, and/or for presidential control of agency choices, at least within the policy discretion afforded by the original delegation.[4] If presidential control is effective, we should expect to see agency decisions moving closer to presidential policy preferences and away from

---

[+] I use here the jargon of spatial modeling, which permeates discussions of partisan polarization. An actor's "ideal point" describes the location of her preferred policy on a single (e.g., left-right) ideological or issue dimension, under specified conditions. The term "gridlock interval" describes the set of policies or policy choices along an issue dimension for which Congress (or Congress and the president, depending upon the model) cannot manage to overturn through legislative action. For a fuller explanation of spatial models of gridlock, see Binder (2003).

[4] Fahrang and Yaver (2015) conclude that during periods of divided government, Congress seeks to impede presidential control by fragmenting its delegations of power among multiple executive branch actors, thereby increasing the transaction costs associated with presidential control efforts. Selin (2015) finds that Congress was able to insulate the Federal Trade Commission (FTC) from presidential influence by imposing statutory limits on appointments and other tools of influence over time. Presumably, since Congress must overcome gridlock in order to legislate in the first place, it finds the creation of these limits on the president increasingly difficult to impose.

congressional preferences during this era of polarization. There is some anec-dotal evidence suggesting as much. Certainly the opposition parties have com-plained loudly about unilateralism during the (George W.) Bush and Obama administrations, and President Obama indicated his preference for "going it alone" in the absence of congressional action in a number of policy areas. A recent analysis of "executive unilateralism" found that presidents are more likely to issue executive orders when Congress is gridlocked (Bolton and Thrower, 2015). The early days of the Trump admininstration saw flurry of executive orders; and the George W. Bush administration seems to have put a particular premium on centralization and ideological loyalty, using signing statements and executive orders, and centralizing review of agency decisions in the White House more effectively than previous administrations had (Moynihan and Roberts, 2010).

Some argue that we can infer increasing presidential influence over agency policymaking from abrupt changes in agency policy direction and enforcement behavior associated with changes in partisan control of the White House. William Kovacic suggests as much from the observation that antitrust enforce-ment priorities and practices vary greatly between Democrat and Republican administrations, as the Obama and (Bill) Clinton administrations opposed more mergers and brought many more enforcement actions than the (George W.) Bush administration did. This back and forth, says Kovacic, is problematic because it reduces the effectiveness of antitrust law and injures the "brand" of the antitrust enforcement agencies (Kovacic, 2014). This phenom-enon seems evident as well in environmental law. As partisan control of the White House shifted from the mid-1990s through the Obama years, the EPA reversed course at each transition on a wide variety of policy decisions relating to air pollution and water pollution, generating a mountain of costly litigation and policy uncertainty. The Obama administration's Clean Power Plan repre-sents the culmination of this process, criticized as overreach by the majority party in each legislative chamber; yet Congress remains unable or unwilling to overrule the program legislatively. And Daniel Ho (2010) found some evidence of increasing politicization within the FCC, associated with the appointment of a strong agency chair willing to use his agenda-setting power to push agency decisions toward the president's preferences. Based on President Trump's executive branch nominees, we might expect a similar sharp change in policy direction for several executive branch agencies in the Trump administration.

Can we infer from these examples that presidents now dominate Congress in the quest to exert control or influence over agencies? Most of the empirical evidence focuses on single-agency examples, which may or may not be repre-sentative of the broader universe of agencies. Nevertheless, when an agency's (or a president's) ideal point on an issue is at or near the edges of a gridlock interval widened by partisan polarization in Congress, then it follows logically that the agency (or the president) can pursue a more extreme position than s/he might otherwise have been able to pursue. Yaver's (2015) empirical analysis of

EPA behavior finds that the agency has had more latitude to pursue its own policy preferences in the era of divided government and polarized parties, demonstrating that agency latitude can be widened by polarization.[5] Among the four presidents who sat atop the modern administrative state in the era that combined mostly divided government and polarized parties, at least two (George H.W. Bush and Bill Clinton) tended to hold relatively centrist policy preferences, and so we might not expect to see their appointees pushing policy toward the boundaries of the gridlock interval. Agency policy choices are further disciplined by the requirement that those choices remain within the boundaries of enabling legislation. Review of agency rules by the White House Office of Information and Regulatory Affairs, which acts as a filter in the rulemaking process, can also push agency decisions away from the extremes. Those centripetal forces may have limited (so far) the opportunities for agency extremism. For example, Freeman and Spence (2014) examination EPA's implementation of the Clean Power Plan and the Federal Energy Regulatory Commission's (FERC) regulation of electricity markets acknowledges the additional latitude afforded agencies in the absence of Congress's involvement in new policy choices, but concludes that both EPA and FERC nevertheless made their choices carefully and iteratively in ways that were sensitive to their political overseers (and the courts), and mostly tempered their bolder instincts.

Importantly, while analyses focusing on contested agency policymaking are illuminating, we do not yet have multiagency empirical studies examining the ideological variance of agency policy choices as a function of ideological polarization in Congress. That kind of quantitative empirical study across agencies poses particularly difficult problems, given the heterogeneity of agency decision-making processes (rulemaking, adjudication, or other informal process), agency cultures (norms of neutral competence vs. politicization), agency jurisdiction (single- vs. multi-industry), and agency structures (independent commissions vs. executive agencies). We might expect more independence from *ex post* congressional control, and from presidential control, among agencies structured as independent commissions, agencies with cultures favoring independence, or with multi-industry jurisdictions, for example. Anecdotally, we see some of this dynamic playing out in the early rounds of the Trump administration's efforts to deregulate (and thereby resurrect) the coal industry. While the Trump appointees who dominate the FERC have resisted the administration's efforts to intervene in energy markets to benefit coal-fired power plants, the EPA administrator has been a much more effective instrument of regulatory

---

[5] Yaver and many other scholars use the language of "bureaucratic drift" to describe situations like this. I avoid that term, in part because it uses Congress's preferences as the anchor from which agency preferences drift; however, it seems more likely that it is Congress's preferences will move more quickly and sharply over time. Congress changes composition every 2 years; agencies preferences seem more likely to be anchored to their (increasingly fixed) statutory missions. Thus, the term "bureaucratic drift" seems misleading.

change, initiating the process of repealing numerous rules and regulations aimed at coal mining and coal combustion in the first few years of the Trump era. However, cross-agency studies focusing on these variables could help us identify any broader trend in the ideological movement of agency policy choices.

Still, if we cannot (yet) detect more systematic movement of agency policy choices toward the extremes, perhaps we can nevertheless detect increasing ideological polarization in the preferences of the individuals that populate agencies. In recent years scholars have developed new and better ways to infer the preferences of bureaucrats, methods that are more granular than merely noting the party of the appointing president. Indeed, some of these methods permit us to infer agency ideal points by bootstrapping from Congressional ideal points, making direct comparisons with members of Congress possible.[6] Interestingly, scholars using these data have mostly concluded that even in the era of gridlock, Congress has the ability to resist the president's attempt to use the appointment power to move agencies toward his policy preferences.

This may be due in part to the Senate's confirmation power, and its ability to simply delay or refuse to approve the president's nominees. The evidence suggests that confirmation delays and executive branch vacancies have grown more common in the era of polarization. (Devins and Lewis, 2008). More to the point, some scholars exploring the ideological implications of this dance between the Senate and the president on political appointments have found that as the ideological distance between the president and Congress grows, presidents are *less* able to secure like-minded appointees (McCarty, 2004, Bertelli and Grose, 2011), and fewer appointees are confirmed (Lewis, 2008). Moreover, we know that Congress engages in more executive branch oversight during periods of divided government (Kriner and Schwartz, 2008); and some research indicates that enhanced oversight can influence agency decisions (MacDonald, 2010, Fong and Krehbiel, 2018). Therefore, if polarization widens the ideological divide between Congress and the president during periods of divided government, perhaps the incentive to engage in adversarial oversight grows as well, further slowing or preventing the agency's movement toward the president's ideal point.[7]

Thus, despite its relative inability to legislate, Congress apparently retains some leverage over agencies, and uses that leverage in ways that may impede movement toward the president's preferences when government is divided. But

---

[6] Clinton and Lewis (2008) used surveys of bureaucrats on legislative issues to compare their ideal points to those of members of Congress. Other scholars look at the behavior of political appointees, such as campaign contributions to members of Congress, to infer the locations of their ideal points (Bertelli, 2011).

[7] Indeed, MacDonald and McGrath (2016) have found that the incentive to engage in *ex post* oversight of agency decisions made by administrations of the opposing party continues during unified government.

the news is not all bad for presidents. Krause and O'Connell (2015) find that presidents place an increasing premium on ideological loyalty in *making* appointments over time, and that this loyalty premium often comes at the expense of the appointee's institutional competence. Hollibaugh and Rothenberg (2018) find that presidents are strategic about appointments, considering both the ideology of the appointee and the independence of the position to which the appointee is nominated in making appointments. Thus, to the extent that these appointees survive Senate confirmation, they ought to move agencies toward the president's preferences. And when the preferences of the president and Congress are relatively closer to one another, presidents may be better able to use the power of appointment to move agencies toward their preferred policies (Devins and Lewis, 2008, Ho, 2010). Consistent with these observations, several Trump administration cabinet officials surived the confirmation process only to be criticized sharply on competency grounds. In sum, though, the extant literature supports the intuition that agency appointees tend to have ideal points that lie somewhere between Congress and the president, and that agency policymaking remains within that ideological space.

Finally, it is worth noting that these kinds of analyses (of political influence over agencies) have difficulty operationalizing the relative influence of careerists versus political appointees over agency policy choices. It is not clear in which direction careerists would push an agency choice. Some proponents of presidential control contend that careerists and their adherence to the norms of their "issue networks" frustrate the president's wishes (Heclo, 1978, Rosenbloom, 2011), but that is not quite the same thing as saying that careerists push policy choices toward the extremes. To the contrary, moderate agency policy choices may appear to be the product of a tug of war between Congress and the president, but those choices may also be pushed toward the center, or toward the agency's view of its statutory mission, by influential careerists within the agency who are dedicated to that mission. Susan Dudley (2012) contends that administration in the era of congressional polarization is more *contested* than it used to be, but not more *polarized* ("hyperventilating, not "hyperpartisan"), in part because of the influence of careerists over agency policymaking. This sort of effect may be particularly difficult to detect in quantitative analyses because the agency decision output and structural variables are visible but the intra-agency process opaque.

In sum, the nascent literature evaluating direct political controls on the modern administrative state in the era of partisan polarization does not suggest that ideological extremism in Congress and the presidency is pushing agency policy choices toward the ideological poles, at least not yet. It may be that regardless of their policy preferences agencies are cautious, and do not wish to attract the adversarial attention of Congress or the president, which keeps their policy choices between the ideal points of those two overseers. Or it may be because agency choices are constrained by statutory mandates created during a period when Congress was more ideologically moderate. As Anthony Bertelli recently noted, "the bulk of the administrative state ... was built with moderates in the congressional party caucuses," during the period stretching from the New Deal through the 1970s (Bertelli, 2011). In other words, agencies may be ideologically moderate because of *ex ante* political controls embedded in their missions by the enacting Congress. The Trump administration's promise of sharp break with the past may represent a departure from this tradition. A populist president may see value in disruption, in pushing agency policy-making beyond statutory boundaries or the congressional gridlock interval. If so, it will be up to courts and Congress to react. If courts discipline agency extremism, will the Republican Congress and president amend agency enabling legislation to authorize the new agency policy? Time will tell.

Voter Polarizaton and Indirect Political Control

Looking beyond Congress's and the president's attempts to influence administrative agencies directly, we might ask what effect the polarization *of the electorate* has on agency decisions? Part of the congressional dominance hypothesis specifies that Congress mobilizes the general public to keep agencies in their respective jurisdictional lanes, and to guard against regulatory capture. Fahrang (2008) found that Congress is more likely to empower citizens to use litigation to control agencies when Congress's preferences diverge from those of the president, consistent with the notion that ideological distance stimulates interbranch contests to influence delegated agency decisions. Proponents of congressional dominance also cite the Administrative Procedures Act of 1946 (APA), which guaranteed the public rights to participate in the administrative process, as an example indirect congressional control.

Might participation in agency proceedings by an increasingly polarized public push agencies toward the extremes? To date there has relatively little scholarship addressing the effects of polarization on agency decisions via this particular pathway. That may be due in part to disagreement among scholars about the degree of polarization in the electorate. Indeed, polarization in Congress need not imply polarization in the electorate (McCarty, Poole, and Rosenthal, 2009, Groser and Palfrey, 2013). Some believe that the ideological polarization seen in Congress is mirrored in the electorate as a whole. (Abramowitz, 2011, Pew Research Center, 2014a). Voters are increasingly consuming their news from ideologically friendly media sources (Iyengar and Hahn, 2009), and disdaining opposing views and information that supports those views (Jamieson and Capella, 2010, Iyengar and Westwood, 2015). However, other scholars believe that polarization along the general electorate is overstated, and that there remains a large group of relatively apolitical voters with either centrist or ideologically ill-defined views; rather, we see more polarization among political and partisan elites than among average voters (Fiorina and Abrams, 2008, Pew Research Center, 2014b).

Levendusky (2009) attempts to reconcile these competing views by distinguishing ideological movement over time from partisan sorting, whereby voters observing ideological polarization among elites are motivated to switch parties in order to eliminate a perceived inconsistency between their ideological identification and their party identification. Other scholars argue that a focus on a single left-right dimension overstates polarization, and that partisans hold much more heterogeneous views when we examine individual issue dimensions (Crespin and Rohde, 2010). This suggests that representatives may be able build majority coalitions across party lines on individual issues (Hillygus and Shields, 2009, Farina, 2015). If so, and agencies are aware of this potential, it may offer yet another explanation for the lack of movement to the ideological poles in agency decision making over time. Additionally, as agency decision making takes place within these individual issue dimensions, if preferences are less spread and/or single-peaked, that may offer another reason why agency decisions have not moved away from the center.

Still, even if average voters have not become more partisan or more ideologically extreme, it may be that partisan elites have. We might hypothesize, then, that if agencies respond more to direct pressure than to their sense of the median voter's opinion, elite polarization ought to make the agency's decision process more contentious (if ideologues at both poles participate). Politically active voters may bolster the participation of pressure groups in agency rulemakings or may exert pressure on elected representatives with influence over agency decisions (the president, state, and local government actors that may have influence on particular agency decisions, or congress via no legislative means). If these partisans are farther from the ideological middle than they once were, a moderate agency policy choice (one near the center of the ideological spectrum) will appear more extreme to them from their positions on the periphery. Consequently, in a polarized environment agencies might expect to receive more comment on proposed rules, and for those comments to be stronger and more negative in tone.

Anecdotal evidence seems to support this hypothesis. The Congressional Research Service speculates that the size of the Federal Register has grown in recent decades, even though the number of rules (and the number of major and economically significant rules) issued by the executive branch has not, because agencies must respond to a larger number of comments (Carey, 2016). For example, recent rulemakings by the Department of Labor on worker overtime and EPA's greenhouse gas regulations generated enormous numbers of comments (250,000 and 4.3 million, respectively). The 400-plus rulemakings through which several agencies continue to implement the various mandates of the Dodd-Frank Act have been slow, and especially contentious.

We might also expect that ideological polarization among interested parties – the perception that an agency decision is extreme because it is farther away from my ideal point – will trigger more legal challenges to final agency rules, all else equal. Moreover, if political polarization is asymmetric between the parties and centered in large part around divide over the role of government, then this increasing antipathy to the administrative state might be expected to generate more opposition (comment and/or litigation) to the decisions made by regulatory agencies, even if those agencies sit near the center of the great ideological divide. Any systematic empirical test of these intuitions will have to overcome difficult specification problems, given the number of important contextual variables that can drive participation in agency proceedings or the decision to litigate.

While participation in agency policymaking is open to citizens across the ideological spectrum, agencies could be moved toward one extreme if that (extreme) view is overrepresented in the agency decision process. Indeed, agency capture posits just such a dynamic. In its insidious form, capture involves the intentional, conscious subversion of the agency's public interest mission through the collusion of bureaucrats, the regulated industry (and Congress or congressional committees). In its innocuous form, agency policy choices move toward the industry's ideal point because the agency is consistently exposed to more information from the industry than from other participants; assuming that industry has the most accurate information about its own business and operations, this version of capture can sometimes be difficult to distinguish from mere informed agency policymaking. The logic of capture has captivated economists, but its insidious version enjoys relatively little support among legal scholars and political scientists (Spence and Cross, 2000, Carpenter and Moss, 2013). Nonetheless, if polarization in the electorate begets more extreme positions among those interest groups that dominate the agency decision process, then this dynamic could push agency policy choices away from the center.

There is another aspect of the relationship between agencies and a polarized citizenry that might be worthy of more scholarly attention: namely, how the rise of populism, as distinguished from small- or anti-government conservatism, influences the work of agencies. The 2016 presidential election cycle put populism on display, in both major parties. The success of the Donald Trump candidacy drove a wedge between populist Trump supporters, on the one hand, and traditional small-government conservatives, on the other, offering some ammunition to Hetherington and Weiler's (2009) thesis ascribing partisan differences in the electorate to citizens' worldview and personality, especially voters' authoritarianism. We might speculate that Republican voters have become more tribal and less *ideological* (as opposed to ideologically homogenous) as the Trump administration pursues protectionism and other market interventions that are inconsistent with traditional conservatism. If so, a populist executive may perceive more leeway to pursue agency policies that deviate from voters' ideological preferences. Alternatively, the Trump GOP may be a coalition of convenience between ideological conservatives and populists alienated from government elites of all ideological stripes – in which case decisions may be a product of intra-coalition bargaining or competition. Future work might examine the presence and effects of these alternative decision rules in agency policymaking. Regardless, whatever divide once existed within the GOP between populists and ideologues seems to have been either papered over or healed, as congressional Republicans have mostly supported the administration's nominees and early initiatives in the common pursuit of a mostly anti-regulatory agenda.

This dynamic seems also to be feeding skepticism toward expertise and experts; it has already spawned news coverage about the "age of distrust" in elites and experts, and of "post-truth politics" (Cohen, 2016). It follows that since agencies are populated with experts and policy "elites," this sort of populism may reduce public trust in agency policymaking, increasing popular opposition to agency decisions, as expressed through comment on rulemakings, litigation, or (perhaps) increasing noncompliance with agency regulations. The rise in right-wing populism is a relatively recent phenomenon, and we do not yet have systematic empirical analyses tying it to agency policy choices. However, we can look to tracking polls for evidence of changes in public trust in agencies. The Pew Research Center asked respondents about their trust in government agencies in 2013 and 2015. It found that despite eroding trust in "government," people continue to hold positive views of most federal agencies (with the exception of the IRS), though Republicans show lower levels of trust than Democrats, and Tea Party Republicans a lower level of trust than other Republicans (Pew Research Center, 2013, 2015). A University of Texas tracking poll on energy issues shows consistently high levels of trust in the "academic/scientific community" across a range of energy issues, but less trust in government regulators, depending on the issue (University of Texas, 2016).

These poll data seem inconsistent with the idea that trust in experts or government agencies is declining precipitously. However, while the number of people who distrust experts or agencies may not be growing, it may nevertheless be that polarization and populism are leading those who distrust to distrust more intensely. Certainly, ideological polarization and populism may exacerbate psychological and cultural biases that lead voters to cling to false beliefs and discount the credibility of experts, something that experimental research has already demonstrated among individuals (e.g., Kahan and Braman, 2006, Nyhan, 2010). Over time, this dynamic could erode trust in regulatory agencies, particularly agencies that are charged with regulating significant risks, such as the Nuclear Regulatory Commission (Slovic et al, 2000). And if populist presidents may be willing to push agencies to pursue policies that please constituents but conflict with enabling legislation, that dynamic may (all else equal) push agency decisions toward extremes.

In sum, scholars have not reached any firm conclusions about how direct participation in agency policymaking by a (potentially) more polarized or alienated electorate is influencing the content of agency policy choices. This may be simply because disentangling the relative influence of public comment from the agency's awareness of congressional and presidential preferences, limits imposed by enabling legislation, and the agency's own policy preferences is a difficult task.

POLARIZATION, JUDICIAL REVIEW, AND CONSTITUTIONAL DESIGN

As a federal appeals court judge once observed, "as night follows day, litigation follows rulemaking" in American regulation (*NWF v. Lujan*, 1991); indeed, judicial review of agency policy choices is the norm. For as long as the administrative state has existed, administrative law scholars have spilled considerable amounts of ink describing, analyzing, and evaluating the judicial review of agency decisions, producing particularly extensive literatures on the question of how, when and why courts defer (and ought to defer) to agency decisions. Since 1946 much of that discussion has been organized around the requirements of the APA, which sought to legitimate agency policymaking by imposing public participation and transparency requirements on that process, and articulating standards by which courts ought to review agency decisions.

Because judicial review of agency decisions often focuses on whether the agency's decision is consistent with its underlying statutory authority, in the era of congressional gridlock that inquiry often involves the application of an old statute to the agency's resolution of a new problem: one that may not have been foreseen by the enacting Congress, but is nevertheless the type of problem that seems to fall within the agency's statutory remit. The courts have devised a series of tests to guide their review of agency decisions in these cases, but the constitutional legitimacy of agency policymaking is always an important subtext to these reviews. Indeed, most judicial review of agency policymaking is colored by the court's assumptions about the proper place of agency policymaking in our constitutional design, as are most scholarly explorations of this same question.

For most scholars, the touchstone of legitimacy in this context is *accountability*: the policy choices of unelected agency decision makers must be "accountable" to the public in some way. Beyond this widely accepted generalization, however, there is disagreement about what accountability means in practice, and how it is, or should be, manifested. Scholars working within administrative law and public administration tend to engage this normative question a little more directly than scholars working within the bureaucratic politics tradition, but almost all undergird their analyses with some sort of normative choice about this issue.

Proponents of congressional control of the bureaucracy suggest that the legitimacy of agency policymaking depends in large part on the ability of Congress to steer agency decisions in some sort of ongoing way, framing the political control problem like this:

A central problem of representative democracy is how to ensure that policy decisions are responsive to the interests or preferences of citizens. ... Because elected officials have limited resources for monitoring [agency decisions], the possibility arises that the bureaucrats will not comply with their policy preferences. (McCubbins, Noll, and Weingast, 1987)

It remains commonplace for social scientists to premise studies of agency behavior on "the responsiveness of government agencies to elected officials" (Selin, 2015). This view is prominent in administrative law scholarship as well, through the influential work of Peter Strauss, who proposed a model of agency legitimation based upon accountability to the political branches. Looking to the Constitution, Strauss referred to Congress, the president, and the judiciary as the "apex institutions" to which agencies *must* be accountable in order for agency policy making to be constitutionally legitimate (Strauss, 1984).

The centrality of accountability to scholarly conceptions of the legitimacy of the administrative state is not surprising. There is no article of the Constitution exclusively devoted to detailing the powers of administrative agencies, the way Articles I through III do for Congress, the president, and the courts. Agencies *are* delegates, whose mandate is specified by legislation, and whose actions are overseen by the president and the courts. However, to frame the relationship between elected politicians and agencies as an *ongoing* principal-agent problem for *both* political principals is too simple. It substitutes a reductivist assumption for a complex, nuanced idea – accountability – and in so doing sidesteps decades of prior scholarship that explores that complexity and nuance.[8] Instead, it might be more productive to explore more closely the various ways in which an agency may be accountable to Congress, the president, and the public.

Legitimacy and Accountability to Congress

One way for an agency to be accountable to Congress is to ensure that its decisions are consistent with the goals of the *enacting* Congress, as articulated in the agency's statutory mandate. Scholars of all stripes agree that the legitimacy of agency action depends upon this kind of accountability to Congress. The more interesting accountability question is the one courts face when reviewing (increasing frequent) agency decisions that are not clearly addressed by that mandate? Should those decisions be guided by the wishes of the *current* Congress? Do agencies owe fealty to the current Congress's preferences, even

---

[8] That literature dates back at least to the 1940s, when public administration scholars Herman Finer and Carl Friedrich engaged in (what was then) a famous debate about the normative desirability of agency policymaking discretion. Finer foreshadowed later principal-agent models when he argued that intervention by elected officials is necessary to hold agencies accountable, because the electoral connection implies that elected officials have a better understanding of the public good than bureaucrats ever could (Finer, 1941). Carl Friedrich, however, saw accountability differently, arguing that bureaucrats' technical expertise and professional norms meant that they make better decisions that served the public better than those made by relatively uninformed, elected politicians (Friedrich, 1940).

if those preferences are not expressed through the passage of legislation or other official actions?

Some scholars would impose on agencies a kind of ongoing fiduciary duty not to stray too far from the wishes of the current Congress, and would ask courts to be less deferential to agency decisions when the current Congress is gridlocked. They argue that congressional responsiveness to police patrols and fire alarms is essential for the legitimacy of agency policymaking. Thus, agencies have a legitimacy problem when gridlock makes it more difficult for Congress to muster legislative majorities to amend agency enabling legislation or cut agency budgets. Scholars premise this idea on Congress's "constitutional responsibility for regulatory oversight" (Farina, 2015), or on a more general notion of legislative supremacy within the constitutional design (Greve and Parish, 2015).

But so what if gridlock *does* impair Congress's ability to intervene? Does it necessarily follow that courts should be less deferential to agencies acting under broad delegations in that case, or that Congress's diminished ability to act poses a constitutional problem for agency policymaking? Legal scholars have begun to devote serious attention to the problem of statutory obsolescence. Several recent papers have worried openly about the mismatch between administrative law in practice and the theory of administrative law, one partly driven by congressional gridlock (Farber and O'Connell, 2014, Sohoni, 2016). Allison Orr Larsen (2015) explores the question of whether statutes can be "unconstitutionally stale," a question she answers mostly in the negative. By contrast, William Eskridge's and John Ferejohn's (2010) idea of "superstatutes" – major, robust, thoroughly deliberated laws addressing important problems through broad delegations to regulators – suggests that courts ought to interpret superstatutes (if not necessarily other statutes) dynamically and flexibly over time.

Other scholars seem less comfortable with agency policymaking that strays from the wishes of the current Congress. Yaver (2015) frames her empirical study of EPA's adherence to the wishes of the current Congress as a compliance problem for Congress, one that goes to the heart of the legitimacy of agency policymaking. Huber and McCarty (2004) describe agency policymaking discretion as a potential usurpation of the politicians' constitutional role, one that is ultimately incompatible with democracy. Legal scholars Michael Greve and Ashley Parish sound similar alarms, in ways that echo earlier administrative law debates over the nondelegation doctrine. They liken judicial deference to agencies to "an ancient royal prerogative ... [and] ... a collection of black and grey holes, where executive power goes unchecked by formal and effective legal constraints," and argue that ultimately "the will of Congress must prevail" (Greve and Parish, 2015).

Several recent Supreme Court opinions have signaled some of this same discomfort with agencies' use of old statutory authority to address important or significant new problems, and suggest that courts should look especially skeptically on agency attempts to address these sorts of "major questions" without new congressional guidance. The major questions rule seems premised, at least in part, on the notion that "Congress is Congress," not merely a succession of (115 and counting) Congresses. Therefore, when asked to review an agency policy choice, courts are presented with two questions: the question of whether the choice was consistent with the wishes of the enacting Congress (expressed in enabling legislation), *and* the question of whether the decision is the kind of decision that ought to be made by the current Congress.

However, it is not self-evident that the legitimacy of agency policymaking depends at all on agency fealty to the will of the current Congress, gridlocked or not. Indeed, what *is* the will of a gridlocked Congress? One could argue that if Congress cannot muster the majority necessary to act, it has no (legally recognizable) will at all. The courts' first task in judicial review of agency action is to hold the agency to its statutory mission, and the will of the enacting Congress that created that mission; the current Congress is an entirely different overseer, one whose authority over the agency is a function of its actions, not its informal or potential opinions. When courts choose to shift decisions about how to implement old statutes to the current (gridlocked) Congress, they merely restore the status quo ante; doing so is no more "democratic" than leaving those decisions with the agency, at least until Congress affirmatively chooses to speak (again) through legislative action. To the contrary, one might argue that by delegating policymaking power to the agency the enacting Congress designated the agency as the statute's custodian, and the agency's claim is arguably the democratically superior one (Freeman and Spence, 2014). Callander and Krehbiel's (2014) recent formal model of delegation arguably supports the notion that courts ought to respect broad delegations to agencies, by demonstrating that such delegations help Congress overcome gridlock and produce decisions that the legislature could not make but for the delegation. Public administration scholar Charles Goodsell (2012) argues that in the face of congressional gridlock bureaucrats should be "stewards of the institutional well-being of the country's administrative assets," which implies a duty not merely "to keep things running smoothly, but also to grapple with the large policy decisions that surround the appropriate allocation of public resources."

One rejoinder to this view is the notion that gridlock is constitutionally preferred, and that the policymaking process was "designed for gridlock" (Burns, 1963). This view fits nicely the Trump GOP's suspicion of the executive branch, and can be used to challenge the legitimacy of exercises of delegated power that involve issues the enacting Congress did not specifically foresee. This view, which may emanate from the lofty position held by Federalist No. 10 in American civics education, might then imply that the use of delegation to overcome gridlock ought to be unconstitutional. However, as many scholars have noted, this view oversimplifies the Framers' intent (Binder, 2003, Gerhardt, 2013). Certainly the Framers wanted a government that works; indeed, they explicitly rejected the kinds of supermajoritarian decision rules that have become the norm in the Senate, and which feed congressional gridlock today (Madison, Federalist No. 58, Hamilton, Federalist No. 22). This ought to be unsurprising given the historical context: the Framers sought to replace a paralyzed and dysfunctional government under the Articles of Confederation with one that could deliberate in order to produce reasoned policy decisions.

In sum, while there is no disagreement about the agency's obligation to remain faithful to the enacting Congress's through its enabling legislation, neither is there agreement among scholars or the courts about whether agency policy choices must be faithful to the wishes of the current Congress, or whether the current Congress's diminished capacity to intervene implies that courts should be more, or less, deferential to agency policy choices.

Accountability and Other Pathways to Legitimacy

Courts troubled by the inability of a gridlocked Congress to exercise ongoing influence over agency policy choices can, if they so choose, seek agency policy-making accountability and/or legitimacy elsewhere, by recognizing: (a) the direct public participation component of most agency policy choices; (b) the power and constitutional basis of presidential oversight; and (c) the argument that agency policymaking more closely resembles the kind of deliberative process envisioned by the original constitutional design than does modern congressional policymaking.

As noted above, in an era of ideological polarization we can expect public participation in the agency policymaking process to be more contentious. Courts reviewing agency action hold the agency to the procedural requirements of the APA, which requires agencies to respond to public comments when engaging in rulemaking, to respect the procedural rights of those individuals who are the object of agency adjudications, to create a record of their decisions, and to follow other APA transparency requirements. These procedural requirements were originally designed to legitimate agency action by mimicking legislative and adjudicative processes endorsed by Articles I and III of the Constitution, respectively. However, some scholars see this idea as a disappearing fiction, and openly lament the disconnect between the APA model of agency decision making and agency decision making in practice (e.g., Farber and O'Connell, 2014). On the other hand, these departures from the APA ideal can also be seen as useful adaptations (e.g., Sohoni, 2016). Gluck, O'Connell, and Po (2015) agree that most policymaking nowadays is accomplished using less transparent, more centralized processes – what they call "unorthodox" lawmaking and rulemaking; however, in their view some of this unorthodoxy helps overcome polarization-induced gridlock. In any case, the APA's procedural requirements, coupled with the other procedural and transparency requirements Congress includes within enabling legislation, collectively provide a public record of agency action according to which courts can review agency decisions. We take this record, and the participation rights it affords, for granted; but it is of no small importance, and is at least a part of how agency policy choices remain accountable to the public.

Proponents of presidential dominance argue that it is presidential oversight that legitimates agency policymaking because it is effective, and because it is constitutionally mandated. Once the initial delegation of authority has been made, presidents seem to have the greater opportunity to influence agencies, particularly executive agencies, and particularly during times of congressional gridlock. Agencies remain subject to the influence of an elected president, even if they are not necessarily continuously influenced by the president. Moreover, proponents of presidential dominance argue that in a time of partisan polarization, that influence is more likely to reflect broad national interests, rather than the narrower interests of a legislative coalition. Indeed, they say, for most of its history Congress has been an ineffective policymaker, one responsive to parochial forces, while presidents represent the national interest because they are elected by a national constituency (Howell and Moe, 2016). Furthermore, when the president exercises supervisory power over administrative agencies, s/he is exercising a constitutional power.[9]

Significantly, Article II not only vests the executive power in the president, it also explicitly authorizes the president to appoint "public ministers and counsels [and] other officers" and to require the heads of executive departments to report to the president on the execution of their duties. And it envisions that when Congress creates additional offices the president will fill those offices with his appointees (Art. II, Sec. 2). It is entirely logical and foreseeable that the executive branch would grow in this way over time, and that delegation of authority would be a necessary and inevitable part of that growth. These Article II admonitions are the rules by which the modern administrative state was built, and they imply a constitutional authority for its construction and operation under presidential oversight (Strauss, 1984, Metzger, 2015b, 2015c). Thus, courts worried about the effects of partisan polarization and congressional gridlock on oversight of the administrative state may instead conclude that presidential oversight can provide agencies with sufficient legitimacy to satisfy the constitutional minima.

Finally, courts worried about deferring to agency policymaking discretion may consider yet another possible argument in favor of its constitutional legitimacy: that modern agency policymaking reflects the kind of deliberative policymaking the Framers sought to encourage. Madison's goal for government resembled that of his contemporary Edmund Burke: that government should decide as the people would decide *if* the people could devote the resources and time necessary to understand the problem. The Madisonian theory government

---

[9] One may wonder whether these conclusions hold up in the face of growing partisan loyalty and reduced salience of ideology in the Trump GOP. Tribal attachment to the leader may give him leeway to pursue less centrist and more extreme positions without risking loss of support.

was (and is) about structuring the delegation of decision authority to a government that will deliberate carefully, and will choose a policy that reflects "the permanent an aggregate interests of the community" (Madison, Federalist No. 52). According to this view, Madison and Hamilton were less interested in congressional dominance, and more interested in designing a system of "institutions [that] would have some level of collective accountability to the people as a whole" (Pope, 2011). The Framers expected much of this careful deliberation to occur in the Senate, insulated as it was from the pressures of factions by the indirect selection of its members (that is, selection by state legislatures). But, as other scholars have noted, the Seventeenth Amendment made the Senate a much less deliberative body. This is a particular problem in today's polarized American polity, where the meaning of the "permanent interests of the community" is particularly hotly contested. Thirty years ago John Rohr (1986) made a persuasive argument that administrative agencies now serve the deliberative function that the Framers envisioned for the Senate. Rohr's argument, that agencies may do a better job of producing policy decisions that correspond to the Burkean ideal of representation, seems more persuasive in light of today's gridlocked, polarized Congress. More recently, Anthony Bertelli (2011) has suggested that polarization has upset the original constitutional design, one that was based on the interaction of deliberation and a strong electoral connection, and that "institutions must adapt to create legitimacy." Might judicial deference to broad delegations of policymaking authority to agencies be one such useful adaptation? Perhaps.

But that deference, however defensible, seems increasingly unlikely in the Trump era. To the contrary, the notion of deference to agency expertise is under attack from the right. Social scientists have not had much to say yet about judicial review of agency action in the Trump era, or about what Gillian Metzger has called a growing "anti-administrativism" among conservative jurists and legal scholars. In particular, Metzger sees a growing sentiment to weaken or undo important precedents calling on courts to defer to agency judgments (Metzger, 2017). Her observation seems accurate, and is partly the product of an economic (public choice) challenge to the very idea that an "aggregate" or "community" interest exists. Despite its success, the normative case for anti-administrativism is not particularly strong. As noted above, delegation is efficient for Congress and the president, and consistent with the constitutional design. Even in an era of partisan polarization, agencies remain accountable to the enacting Congress directly through judicial review. Furthermore, they are directly accountable to the public through the operation of the APA and other procedural controls, and to the president through presidential oversight. Congressional gridlock implies a kind of reduced "accountability" to the current Congress, but as explained above there is (at the very least) room for debate about whether the loss of that kind of accountability poses a legitimacy problem for agencies in the first place. When ongoing gridlock forces agencies to address new problems using old statutory authority, recent scholarship implies that deference to agencies acting under general or broad delegations can overcome gridlock.

CONCLUSION

This essay reviews the ways in which scholars are beginning to tackle the question of how increased partisan polarization affects the modern administrative state. These early scholarly efforts suggest that despite a polarized Congress and (somewhat less clearly or sharply) polarized electorate, agency policy choices do not seem to be moving systematically toward the extremes. Some combination of moderating effects seem to be at work here, including the effect of divided government on appointments, agency preferences driven by moderate statutory mandates and/or the norms of issue networks, and (at times) the influence of ideologically moderate presidents on the size of the gridlock interval. Anecdotally, the Trump administration may represent a departure from these norms: it may be that conservatives in the Trump coalition are freer to pursue policies disfavored by a majority because of the non-ideological nature of populist loyalty to administration policy initiatives. But scholars have not yet been able to confirm or deny whether that is generally true. Regardless, polarization-induced congressional gridlock poses ongoing challenges for the administrative state. Agencies continue to address problems within their regulatory jurisdiction in the absence of input from Congress, using statutes that may have been poorly designed to handle the new problem. And courts reviewing those agency decisions will continue to struggle, case by case, with the implications that sort of agency policymaking for the constitutional legitimacy of agency policymaking.

REFERENCES

Abramowitz, Alan I. 2011. *The Disappearing Center: Engaged Citizens, Polarization and American Democracy.* New Haven, CT: Yale University Press.
Aldrich, John H. 2011. *Why Parties? A Second Look.* Chicago, IL: University of Chicago Press.
Balla, Steven J. 1998. "Administrative Procedures and Political Control of the Bureaucracy." *American Political Science Review* 92: 663–673.
    2012. "The Politicization of Administration." *Georgetown Journal of Law and Public Policy* 10: 357–359.
Bawn, Kathleen. 1995. "Political Control versus Agency Expertise: Congressional choices about Administrative Procedures." *American Political Science Review* 89: 62–73.
Bertelli, Anthony M. 2011. "Federalist No. 41: Does Polarization Inhibit Coordination?" *Public Administration Review (Special Issue)* 71: s62–s71.
Bertelli, Anthony M., and Christian R. Grose. 2011. "The Lengthened Shadow of Another Institution? Ideal Point Estimates for the Executive Branch and Congress." *American Journal of Political Science* 55: 766–780.

Binder, Sarah. 2003. *Stalemate: Causes and Consequences of Legislative Gridlock.* Washington, DC: Brookings Institution Press.

Bishop, Bill. 2008. *The Big Sort: Why the Clustering of Like-Minded America Is Tearing Us Apart.* New York: Houghton-Mifflin.

Bolton, Alexander, and Sharece Thrower. 2015. "Legislative Capacity and Executive Unilateralism." *American Journal of Political Science* 60: 649–663.

Brehm, John, and Scott Gates. 1995. "Donut Shops and Speed Traps: Evaluating Models of Supervision and Police Behavior." *American Journal of Political Science* 37: 555–581.

Bulman-Pozen, Jessica. 2014. "Partisan Federalism." *Harvard Law Review* 127: 1078–1146.

Burns, James MacGregor. 1963. *The Deadlock of Democracy: Four-Party Politics in America Hardcover.* New York: Prentice Hall.

Callander, Steven, and Keith Krehbiel. 2014. "Gridlock and Delegation in a Changing World." *American Journal of Political Science* 58: 819–834.

Calvert, Randall L., Mark J. Moran, and Barry R. Weingast. 1987. "Congressonal Influence over Policymaking: The Cast of the FTC." In Mathew D. McCubbins and Terry Sullivan (eds.), *Congress: Structure and Policy.* Cambridge: Cambridge University Press.

Carey, Maeve P. 2016. "Counting Regulations: An Overview of Rulemaking, Types of Federal Regulations, and Pages in the Federal Register." (Congressional Research Service). Retrieved from https://fas.org/sgp/crs/misc/R43056.pdf (last accessed January 2, 2019).

Carpenter, Daniel. 2004. "Protection without Capture: Dynamic Product Approval by a Politically Responsive, Learning Regulator." *American Political Science Review* 98: 613–631.

Carpenter, Daniel, and David Moss. 2013. "Introduction." In Daniel Carpenter and David Moss (eds.), *Preventing Regulatory Capture: Special Interest Influence and How to Limit It.* Cambridge, UK: Cambridge University Press.

Carson, Jamie L., Michael H. Crespin, Charles J. Finocchiaro, and David W. Rohde. 2007. Redistricting and Party Polarization in the U.S. House of Representative." *American Politics Research* 35: 878–904.

Clinton, Joshua D., and David E. Lewis. 2008. "Expert Opinion, Agency Characteristics and Agency Preferences." *Political Analysis* 16(1): 3–20.

Cohen, Roger. 2016. "The Age of Distrust." *The New York Times* (September 19). Retrieved from www.nytimes.com/2016/09/20/opinion/the-age-of-distrust.html (last accessed January 2, 2019).

Cole, Kenneth C. 1942. "Presidential Influence on Independent Agencies." *The ANNALS of the American Academy of Political and Social Science* 221: 72–77.

Cox, Gary W., and Matthew D. McCubbins. 2005. *Setting the Agenda: Responsible Party Government in the U.S. House of Representatives.* Cambridge: Cambridge University Press.

Crespin, Michael H., and David W. Rohde. 2010. "Dimensions, Issues and Bills: Appropriations Voting on the House Floor." *Journal of Politics* 72: 976–989.

Devins, Neil, and David E. Lewis. 2008. "Not so Independent Agencies: Party Polarization and the Limits of Institutional Design." *William and Mary Law Review* 88: 459–498.

Dowd, John M. 2017. "Letter to Special Counsel Robert Mueller, January 29." *The New York Times* (June 2). Retrieved from www.nytimes.com/interactive/2018/06/02/us/politics/trump-legal-documents.html (last accessed January 2, 2019).

Dudley, Susan. 2012. "Is the Execution of the Law Hyper-Partisan?" *Georgetown Journal of Law & Public Policy 10*: 359–361.

Epstein, David, and Sharyn O'Halloran. 1994. "Administrative Procedures, Information and Agency Discretion." *American Journal of Political Science 38*: 697–722.

Eskridge, William N. 1994. *Dynamic Statutory Interpretation*. Cambridge: Harvard University Press.

Eskridge, William N., and John Ferejohn. 1992. "Making the Deal Stick: Enforcing the Original Constitutional Structure of Lawmaking in the Modern State." *Journal of Law, Economics and Organization 8*: 165–189.

  2001. "Super-Statutes." *Duke Law Journal 50*: 1215–1276.

Fahrang, Sean. 2008. "Public Regulation and Private Lawsuits in the American Separation-of-Powers System." *American Journal of Political Science 52*: 821–839.

Fahrang, Sean, and Miranda Yaver. 2015. "Divided Government and the Fragmentation of American Law." *American Journal of Political Science 60*: 401–417.

Farber, Daniel A., and Anne Joseph O'Connell. 2014. "The Lost World of Administrative Law." *Texas Law Review 92*: 1137–1189.

Farber, Daniel A., and Philip P. Frickey. 1992. *Law and Public Choice: A Critical Introduction*. Chicago, IL: University of Chicago Press.

Farina, Cynthia R. 2015. "Congressional Polarization: Terminal Constitutional Dysfunction." *Columbia Law Review 115*: 1689–1738.

Finer, Herman. 1941. "Administrative Responsibility in Democratic Government." *Public Administration Review 1*: 335–350.

Fiorina, Morris P., and Samuel J. Abrams. 2008. "Political Polarization in the American Public." *Annual Review of Political Science 11*: 563–588.

Fong, Christian, and Keith Krehbiel. 2018. "Limited Obstruction." *American Political Science Review 112*: 1–14.

Freeman, Jody, and David B. Spence. 2014. "Old Statutes, New Problems." *University of Pennsylvania Law Review 163*: 1–93.

Friedrich, Carl J. 1940. "Public Policy and the Nature of Administrative Responsibility." *Public Policy 1*: 3–24.

Gerhardt, Michael J. 2013. "Why Gridlock Matters." *Notre Dame Law Review 88*: 2107–2120.

Gerken, Heather K. 2014. Federalism and the New Nationalism: An Overview. *Yale Law Journal 123*: 1889–1919.

Gluck, Abbe, Anne Joseph O'Connell, and Rosa Po. 2015. "Unorthodox Lawmaking, Unorthodox Rulemaking." *Columbia Law Review 115*: 1789–1865.

Goodsell, Charles T. 2012. "Public Administration as Its Own Steward in Times of Partisan Deadlock and Fiscal Stress." *Public Administration Review 72*: 10–11.

Greve, Michael S., and Ashley C. Parish. 2015 "Administrative Law without Congress." *George Mason Law Review 22*: 501–548.

Groser, Jens, and Thomas R. Palfrey. 2013. "Candidate Entry and Political Polarization: An Antimedian Voter Theorem." *American Journal of Political Science 58*: 127–143.

Gulick, Luther. 1937. "Science, Values and Administration." In Luther Gulick and L. Urwick (eds.), *Papers in the Science of Administration*. New York: Institute of Public Administration.

Hammond, Thomas H., and Jack Knott. 1996. "Who Controls the Bureaucracy?: Presidential Power, Congressional Dominance, Legal Constraints and Bureaucratic Autonomy in a Model of Multi-Institutional Policy-Making." *Journal of Law, Economics and Organization* 12: 119–167.

Heclo, Hugh. 1978. "Issue Networks and the Executive Establishment." In John King (ed.), *The New American Political System*. New York: American Enterprise Institute.

Hetherington, Marc J., and Jonathan D. Weiler. 2009. *Authoritarianism and Polarization in American Politics*. Cambridge: Cambridge University Press.

Ho, Daniel. 2010. "Measuring Agency Preferences: Experts, Voting and the Power of Chairs." *DePaul Law Review* 59: 333–387.

Hillygus, D. Sunshine, and Todd G. Shields. 2009. *The Persuadable Voter: Wedge Issues in Presidential Campaigns*. Princeton, NJ: Princeton University Press.

Hollibaugh, Gary E., and Lawrence Rothenberg. 2018. "The Who, When and Where of Executive Nominations: Integrating Agency Independence and Appointee Ideology." *American Journal of Political Science* 62: 296–311.

Howell, William G., and Terry M. Moe. 2016. *Relic: How Our Constitution Undermines Effective Government—and Why We Need a More Powerful Presidency*. New York: Basic Books.

Huber, John D., and Charles R. Shipan. 2002. *The Institutional Foundations of Bureaucratic Autonomy*. Cambridge: Cambridge University Press.

Huber, John D., and Nolan McCarty. 2004. "Bureaucratic Capacity, Delegation and Political Reform." *American Journal of Political Science* 98: 481–494.

Irwin, Neil. 2013. *The Alchemists: Three Central Bankers and a World on Fire*. New York: Penguin Group.

Iyengar, Shanto, and Kyu S. Hahn. 2009. "Red Media, Blue Media: Evidence of Ideological Selectivity in Media Use." *Journal of Communication* 59: 19–39.

Iyengar, Shanto, and Sean J. Westwood. 2015. "Fear and Loathing across Party Lines: New Evidence on Group Polarization." *American Journal of Political Science* 59: 690–707.

Jamieson, Kathleen Hall, and Joseph N. Capella. 2010. *Echo Chamber: Rush Limbaugh and the Conservative Media Establishment*. Oxford: Oxford University Press.

Kahan, Dan M., and Donald Braman. 2006. "Cultural Cognition and Public Policy." *Yale Law and Policy Review* 24: 147–170.

Kaufman, Herbert. 1967. *The Forest Ranger: A Study in Administrative Behavior*. Baltimore, MD: The Johns Hopkins University Press.

Kovacic, William E. 2014. "Politics and Partisanship in Antitrust Enforcement." *Antitrust Law Journal* 79: 687–711.

Krause, George, and Anne Joseph O'Connell. 2015. "Experiential Learning and Presidential Management of the U.S. Federal Bureaucracy: Logic and Evidence from Agency Leadership Appointments." *American Journal of Political Science* 60: 914–931.

Krehbiel, Keith. 1998. *Pivotal Politics: A Theory of U.S. Lawmaking*. Chicago, IL: University of Chicago Press.

Kriner, Douglas, and Liam Schwarz. 2008. "Divided Government and Congressional Investigations." *Legislative Studies Quarterly* 33: 295–321.

Larsen, Alison Orr. 2015. "Do Laws Have a Constitutional Shelf Life?" *Texas Law Review* 94: 59–114.

Layman, Geoffrey C., Thomas M. Carsey, and Juliana Menasce Horowitz. 2006. "Party Polarization in American Politics: Characteristics, Causes, and Consequences." *Annual Review of Political Science* 9: 83–104.

Levendusky, Matthew. 2009. *The Partisan Sort: How Liberals Became Democrats and Conservatives Became Republicans*. Chicago, IL: University of Chicago Press.

Lewis, Daniel E. 2008. *The Politics of Presidential Appointments: Political Control and Bureaucratic Performance*. Princeton, NJ: Princeton University Press.

Lindblom, Charles E. 1959. "The Science of Muddling Through," *Public Administration Review* 19(2): 79–88.

Lipsky, Michael. 1980. *Street-Level Bureaucracy: Dilemmas of the Individual in Public Services*. New York: Russell Sage.

Lupia, Arthur, and Matthew D. McCubbins. 1994. "Designing Bureaucratic Accountability." *Law and Contemporary Problems* 57(1): 91–126.

MacDonald, Jason A. 2010. "Limitation Riders and Congressional Influence over Bureaucratic Policy Decisions." *American Political Science Review* 104(4): 766–782.

MacDonald, Jason A., and Robert J. McGrath. 2016. "Retrospective Congressional Oversight and the Dynamics of Legislative Influence over the Bureaucracy." *Legislative Studies Quarterly* 41: 899–934.

Macey, Jonathan R. 1992a. "Organizational Design and the Political Control of Administrative Agencies." *Journal of Law, Economics and Organization* 8: 93–110.

1992b. "Separated Powers and Positive Political Theory: The Tug of War over Administrative Agencies." *Georgetown Law Journal* 80: 671–704.

Maltzman, Forest and Charles R. Shipan. 2008. "Change, Continuity and the Evolution of the Law." *American Journal of Political Science* 52: 352–367.

Mashaw, Jerry L. 1990. "Explaining Administrative Process: Normative, Positive and Critical Stories of Legal Development." *Journal of Law, Economics and Organization* 6: 267–298.

1997. *Greed, Chaos and Governance: Using Public Choice to Improve Public Law*. New Haven, CT: Yale University Press.

McCarty, Nolan. 2004. "The Appointments Dilemma." *American Journal of Political Science* 48: 413–428.

McCarty, Nolan, Keith T. Poole, and Howard Rosenthal. 2006. *Polarized America: The Dance of Ideology and Unequal Riches*. Cambridge: MIT Press.

2009. "Does Gerrymandering Cause Polarization?" *American Journal of Political Science* 53: 666–680.

McCubbins, Matthew D., Roger Noll, and Barry R. Weingast. 1987. "Administrative Procedures as Instruments of Political Control." *Journal of Law, Economics and Organization* 3: 243–277.

1989. "Structure and Process, Politics and Policy: Administrative Arrangements and the Political Control of Agencies." *Virginia Law Review* 75: 431–482.

McCubbins, Matthew D. and Thomas Schwartz. 1984. "Congressional Oversight Overlooked: Police Patrols versus Fire Alarms." *American Journal of Political Science* 2: 165–179.

Metzger, Gillian E. 2015a. "Agencies, Polarization and the States." *Columbia Law Review 115*: 1739–1771.

    2015b. "Appointments, Innovation and the Judicial-Political Divide." *Duke Law Journal 64*: 1607–1643.

    2015c. "The Constitutional Duty to Supervise." *Yale Law Journal 124*: 1826–1933.

    2017. "Foreward: 1930s Redux: The Administrative State under Seige." *Harvard Law Review 131*: 2–93.

Moe, Terry M. 1987. "An Assessment of the Positive Theory of 'Congressional Dominance.'" *Legislative Studies Quarterly*, 12(4): 475–520.

Moynihan, Donald P. and Alasdair S. Roberts. 2010. "The Triumph of Loyalty Over Competence: The Bush Administration and the Exhaustion of the Politicized Presidency." *Public Administration Review 70*: 572–581.

Niskanen, William. 1971. *Bureaucracy and Representative Government*. Chicago, IL: Aldine-Atherton.

Nyhan, Brendan. 2010. "When Corrections Fail: The Persistence of Political Misperceptions." *Political Behavior 32*(2): 303–330.

Peltzman, Sam. 1976. "Toward a More General Theory of Regulation." *Journal of Law and Economics 19*: 211–240.

Pew Research Center. 2013. "Trust in Government Nears Record Low, but Most Federal Agencies Are Viewed Favorably." October 18. Retrieved from www.people-press.org/2013/10/18/trust-in-government-nears-record-low-but-most-federal-agencies-are-viewed-favorably/ (last accessed December 11, 2018).

    2014a. "Political Polarization in the American Public: How Increasing Ideological Uniformity and Partisan Antipathy Affect Politics, Compromise and Everyday Life." June 12. Retrieved from www.people-press.org/files/2014/06/6-12-2014-Political-Polarization-Release.pdf (last accessed December 11, 2018).

    2014b. "Beyond Red vs. Blue: The Political Typology—Fragmented Center Poses Election Challenges for Both Parties." June 26. Retrieved from www.people-press.org/files/2014/06/6-26-14-Political-Typology-release1.pdf (last accessed December 11, 2018).

    2015. "Most View the CDC Favorably; VA's Image Slips." January 22. Retrieved from www.people-press.org/2015/01/22/most-view-the-cdc-favorably-vas-image-slips/ (last accessed December 11, 2018).

Pildes, Richard H. 2011. "Why the Center Does Not Hold: The Causes of Hyperpolarized Democracy in America," *California Law Review 99*: 273–333.

Pope, Jeremy C. 2011. "Book Review: Americans, Congress and Democratic Responsiveness: Public Evaluations of Congress and Electoral Consequences (by David R. Jones and Monika L. McDermott)." *Journal of Politics 73*: 287–288.

Rinquist, Evan J. 1995. "Political Control and Policy Impact in EPA's Office of Water Quality." *American Journal of Political Science 39*: 336–363.

Robinson, Glen O. 1991. *American Bureaucracy: Public Choice and Public Law*. Ann Arbor, MI: University of Michigan Press.

Rose-Ackerman, Susan. 1992. *Rethinking the Progressive Agenda: The Reform of the American Regulatory State*. New York: The Free Press.

Rosenbloom, David H. 2011. "Federalist No. 10: How Do Factions Affect the President as Administrator-in-Chief." *Public Administration Review (Special Issue) 71*: s21–s28.

Selin, Jennifer. 2015. "What Makes an Agency Independent?" *American Journal of Political Science* 59: 971–987.

Shepsle, Kenneth A. 1992. "Congress Is a 'They,' Not an 'It': Legislative Intent as Oxymoron." *International Review of Law & Economics* 12: 239–256.

Simon, Herbert A. 1946. "The Proverbs of Administration," *Public Administration Review* 6(1): 53–67.

Shor, Boris, Christopher Berry, and Nolan McCarty. 2010. "A Bridge to Somewhere: Mapping State and Congressional Ideology on a Cross-Institutional Common Space." *Legislative Studies Quarterly,* 35: 417–448.

Sohoni, Mila. 2016. "The Administrative Constitution in Exile." *William & Mary Law Review* 57: 923–974.

Slovic, Paul, James Flynn, C. K. Mertz, Marc Poumadere, and Claire Mays. 2000. "Nuclear Power and the Public." In Ortwin Renn and Rohrman Bernd (eds.), *Cross-Cultural Risk Perception. Technology, Risk, and Society (An International Series in Risk Analysis).* Boston, MA: Springer, pp. 55–102.

Spence, David B. 1997. Administrative Law and Agency Policymaking: Rethinking the Positive Theory of Political Control. *Yale Journal on Regulation* 14: 407–450.

1999. "Managing Delegation Ex Ante: Using Law to Steer Administrative Agencies." *Journal of Legal Studies* 28: 413–459.

Spence, David B., and Frank Cross. 2000. "A Public Choice Case for the Administrative State." *Georgetown Law Journal* 89: 97–147.

Stigler, George J. 1971. "The Theory of Economic Regulation." *Bell Journal of Economics and Management Science* 2: 3–21.

Stonecash, Jeffery M., Mark D. Brewer, and Mack Mariani. 2002. *Diverging Parties: Social Change, Realignment, and Party Polarization.* Boulder, CO: Westview Press.

Strauss, Peter. 1984. "The Place of Agencies in Government: Separation of Powers and the Fourth Branch." *Columbia Law Review* 84: 574–669.

University of Texas. 2016. "Energy Poll: Top Line Wave 10 Results." Retrieved from www.utenergypoll.com/wp-content/uploads/2014/04/Topline-Wave-10.pdf (last accessed December 11, 2018).

Verkuil, Paul R. 1980. "Jawboning Administrative Agencies: Ex Parte Contacts by the White House." *Columbia Law Review* 80: 943–989.

Weingast, Barry R., and Mark J. Moran. 1983. "Bureaucratic Discretion or Congressional Control? Regulatory Policymaking by the Federal Trade Commission." *Journal of Political Economy*: 765–800.

Whittington, Keith E., and Daniel P. Carpenter. 2003. "Executive Power in American Institutional Development." *Perspectives on Politics* 1: 495–513.

Wilson, Woodrow. 1887. "The Study of Administration." *Political Science Quarterly* 2: 197–222.

Wood, B. Dan, and Richard Waterman. 1991. "They Dynamics of Political Control in a Bureaucracy." *American Political Science Review* 85: 801–828.

Yaver, Miranda. 2015. "When Do Agencies Have Agency?: The Limits of Compliance in the EPA." Working Paper. Retrieved from https://pdfs.semanticscholar.org/075d/7745c7356b4dab5b4ce61137f357c264fae3.pdf (last accessed January 2, 2019).

Yoo, Christopher, Steven Calabresi, and Anthony Colangelo. 2005. "The Unitary Executive in the Modern Era, 1945–2004." *Iowa Law Review* 90: 601–731.

12

Polarization and the Changing American Constitutional System

Nolan McCarty

INTRODUCTION

During the first 17 months of his term, President Donald Trump obtained the lowest approval ratings of any president since pollsters began inquiring about such things in the 1940s. In fact, the race for last place was not even close. Second place in this ignominious contest goes to Bill Clinton. But Clinton polled below Trump's 17-month average rating for only 2 weeks in the summer of 1993. No new president has been anywhere close to consistently as unpopular as President Trump. But there was one bright spot for the Trump administration in the polling: he was twice as popular as his coequal branch of government. While the president could count on the support of almost four in ten Americans, Congress was approved by only one in eight.

The upshot of this situation is that our Constitution placed the primary responsibility for checking an unpopular executive in the hands of a much less popular Congress. Even if the GOP-dominated Congress of Trump's first term was truly interested in playing this role against a president of its party, broad public support of the institution is not a resource that it could bring to battle. The situation is further complicated by the fact that the president himself showed little inclination to be constrained by certain constitutional norms pertaining to the separation of power.

But was there anything new going on here? Congress has long been unpopular and almost always less popular than the president. President Trump is not the first president to become frustrated with Congress and attempt to govern around it. All recent presidents have pushed back hard against congressional prerogatives in legislation, appointments, and the war power. But Congress has acquitted itself reasonably well in many of the battles and maintains a formidable set of institutional weapons (Chafetz, 2017).

Despite these successful assertions of legislative authority, there are plenty of reasons to be anxious that Congress's role in the constitutional system has been deteriorating for some time. As I argue in this chapter, Congress not only has lost considerable ground to the executive, its relative weakness has greatly empowered the judiciary and the states. The result is a likely significant change in the balance of de facto constitutional powers.

Scholars have identified many sources of legislative weakness in the American constitutional system. Legislative bodies are beset by collective action problems (Moe and Howell, 1999). Individual electoral motives trump any incentives for institutional maintenance (Mayhew, 1974, Posner and Vermeule, 2011). Legislatures cannot move with the urgency required by the problems of a modern society (Posner and Vermeule, 2011). They lack the required expertise to make good policy (Epstein and O'Halloran, 1999). Legislators are too susceptible to the charms and resources of the special interests (Howell and Moe, 2016). There is a great deal of truth to all of these claims, but many blame fairly constant features of legislative politics and are thus less equipped to explain the slow erosion of legislative capacity we have witnessed over the past few decades.

Consequently, my focus will be on the effects of the rise of ideological polarization and partisan conflict to explain changes in legislative capacity. These trends are often heralded as some of the most dramatic developments in American politics of the past 40 years (McCarty, Poole, and Rosenthal, 2016). The concerns about legislative polarization are so widespread it is difficult to recall that political scientists once lamented the lack of disciplined, distinct congressional parties. Given the centrality of polarization in contemporary congressional politics, a vast literature has developed to explain the rise of polarization and its underlying causes (Barber and McCarty, 2013). But there has been considerably less focus on the consequences of partisan polarization for the performance of our constitutional system.

Concerns about the systemic consequences of polarization arise from the belief that the US Congress is not designed to perform well in highly polarized environments. First, bicameralism and other supermajoritarian institutions make the formation of winning coalitions very difficult even in the best of circumstances (Krehbiel, 1998, Brady and Volden, 2005). Now that polarization has increased the difficulty of building them across party lines, legislating only becomes harder. Second, compounding the problems of legislative partisanship is that each party is heavily factionalized ideologically. Unlike legislative leaders elsewhere who have powers of confidence and dissolution on top of the control of renomination, American party leaders are often unable to manage conflicts within their own ranks (McCarty, 2015a, Pildes, 2015). These conflicts further narrow the needle's eye that legislation must thread. Finally, as legislative partisanship has increased, legislators of the president's party are often forced to act as advocates of the administration rather than as defenders of the prerogatives of a coequal branch.[1] Thus, executive incursions on legislative prerogatives are likely to remain unchecked.

Some of the negative consequences of polarization have been well-documented. Scholars have documented that as polarization has increased (a) legislative output has declined (Binder, 2003, 2015, McCarty, Poole, and Rosenthal, 2016), (b) the appropriations process fails to conclude prior to the beginning of the fiscal year with increasing regularity (Woon and Anderson, 2012, Hanson, 2014, McCarty, 2016), and (c) delays in the confirmation process have increased leading to growing numbers of vacancies in the executive branch and the judiciary (McCarty and Razaghian, 1999, Binder and Maltzman, 2002, O'Connell, 2009, O'Connell, 2015).

But the implications of these reductions of legislative capacity performance on the functioning of the American constitutional system have received far less attention. Thus several important questions are unanswered. How have the other branches of government responded to the decline in legislative capacity occasioned by increased polarization? Have these branches expanded their power, authority, and policy impact at Congress's expense? Or has legislative dysfunction made it more difficult for other actors to carry out their constitutional duties? Moreover, how has political polarization impacted the internal functioning of the executive and judicial branches and the states?

To provide some theoretical clarity to my arguments, consider a very stylized description of policymaking under the separation of powers. I assume that policy outcomes have two components: a quality dimension and a distributive dimension. The quality dimension is one in which higher outcomes benefit the vast majority of citizens and are therefore desirable for all political actors. But citizens and politicians may also have divergent goals about how these benefits are distributed.

I argue that the decline in legislative capacity associated with polarization alters outcomes on both the quality and distributive dimensions. Legislative dysfunction reduces the contribution of Congress to good policymaking. While some of this impact may be offset by a more assertive exercise of executive or judicial power, the central role of Congress in the constitutional system leads to a decline in the quality of governance.

Second, declining legislative capacity can affect the relative influence on Congress over distributive outcomes. The decline in the ability of Congress to reach collective decisions allows more room for other constitutional actors to act without legislative constraint. Moreover, dysfunction enhances the legitimacy of new authority claims by the executive and judicial branches.

---

[1] For a general argument, see Levinson and Pildes (2006). In support of this claim, Kriner and Schickler (2016) find evidence that the effect of divided government on House investigatory activity of the executive has been magnified by polarization, but they find no similar effect for the Senate.

These two effects suggest that legislative dysfunction can affect the balance of constitutional authority in both absolute and relative terms. A poorly performing Congress may allow other actors to expand their influence over policy outcomes at Congress's expense.

The chapter proceeds as follows. In "The Trends in Polarization" section, I provide context for my arguments about polarization by reviewing the historical trends and several arguments about the causes and non-causes of our contemporary partisan divisions. The "Theoretical Perspectives on the Impact of Polarization on Congress" section reviews many of the theoretical arguments that link partisan polarization to congressional performance. These models generally indicate that polarization reduces legislative capacity. I provide some evidence in the "Polarization and Policymaking" section that this is indeed the case. Congress has produced less legislation, managed the budget and appropriations process worse, and has been much slower to confirm executive branch appointees as polarization has grown.[2] In the "Polarization and the Constitution" section, I discuss how polarization has affected the performance of our Constitution through its impacts on the separation of powers and federalism. I argue that the implications for the balance of power within the system are ambiguous. Polarization clearly increases the power of the other branches and the states *relative* to Congress. But because legislative capacity is a complement of the authority of other constitutional actors, the absolute power of the political system to solve pressing social problems has been diminished.

THE TRENDS IN POLARIZATION

To provide some context for my analysis, I begin with a brief review of the history and trends in legislative polarization. Figure 12.1 presents a measure for the United States House and Senate known as DW-NOMINATE (McCarty, 1997). Underlying DW-NOMINATE is a statistical model that estimates the left/right positions of legislators based on observed roll call voting behavior. Larger estimated scores represent more conservative positions. The simplest way to understand the statistical model is that it associates a conservative position for legislators who vote often with conservatives and never with liberals. Liberals are those who vote with other liberals and never with conservatives, whereas moderates are those who votes with both liberals and conservatives.[3] The DW-NOMINATE scores of individual legislators are aggregated into these measures so that the polarization measure is just the average difference in the scores of Republicans and Democrats.[4]

---

[2] While this evidence focuses primarily on Congress's legislative role, there is also evidence of similar problems related to its oversight functions, e.g., Kriner and Schickler (2016).

[3] See McCarty, Poole, and Rosenthal (2016) for a more extensive discussion of the measurement.

[4] An important feature of DW-NOMINATE is that we can use overlapping cohorts of legislators to make inter-temporal comparisons about the degree of polarization. For example, we can establish

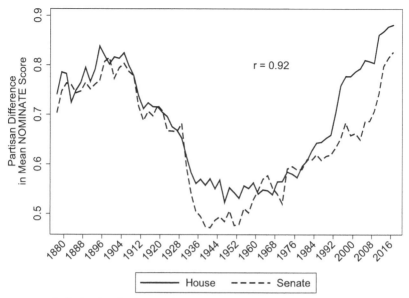

FIGURE 12.1 **Polarization in the US Congress 1877–2014.** Computed from DW-NOMINATE scores. The polarization measure is the difference in the mean score for Republicans and the mean score for Democrats.

The first takeaway of Figure 12.1 is that the level of polarization in Congress has varied dramatically since Reconstruction. Not surprisingly, congressional polarization was quite high following the Civil War and Reconstruction. But it declined markedly from the 1920s to the 1950s where the greatest declines appear to be associated with the Great Depression and World War II. Partisan differences in Congress remained at fairly low levels from the 1950s to the 1970s. During this period, both the Democrats and Republicans were divided ideologically between liberal and conservative wings.[5]

The current trend toward greater and greater polarization began in the late 1970s and was detectable by academics as early as 1982 (Poole and Rosenthal, 1984). This fact lies uncomfortably against any narrative that pivots on a single event or "great person." The trend precedes the election of Ronald Reagan, the unsuccessful nomination of Robert Bork, the impeachment of Bill Clinton, and the election of Barack Obama.

---

that in relative terms Ted Cruz is more conservative than John Tower even though they never served in the Senate together. We can do this by leveraging that John Tower served with Phil Gramm who served with Kay Hutchison who served with John Cornyn who served with Ted Cruz.

[5] Indeed, the *intraparty* divisions were so great that the American Political Science Association commissioned a report arguing for *more* partisan polarization. See American Political Science Association (1950).

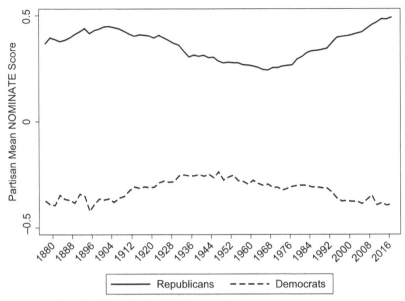

FIGURE 12.2 **Party Positions in the US House, 1877–2014.**

The second takeaway is that the House and the Senate have remarkably similar histories with respect to polarization. The two time series tend to decline together, stabilize together, and increase together. Generally, there is a little less polarization in the Senate, but there are periods in which the Senate was the more polarized body. Although polarization in the Senate leveled off in the early 2000s, it has increased faster than it has in the House over the past half-dozen years.

Figure 12.2 presents a third important historical fact about polarization. Rather than both parties moving toward the extremes, polarization over the past 40 years has been asymmetric. It is overwhelmingly associated with the increased movement of Republican legislators to the right. Each new Republican cohort has compiled a more conservative record than the returning cohort. Importantly this has been the case since the 1970s, it is not a reflection of the emergence of the "Tea Party" movement.[6]

The Democratic party has not followed as extreme a pattern. While some new cohorts are more liberal than the caucus on average, many are more moderate. The slight movement of the Democratic party to the left can be accounted for by the increase of African-American and Latino legislators in

---

[6] At least in the case of the Senate, the Tea Party might have *decreased* polarization through its support of extreme candidates such as Christine McDonnell, Richard Mourdock, and Todd Akin that ultimately cost the Republican party seats that were won by moderate Democrats.

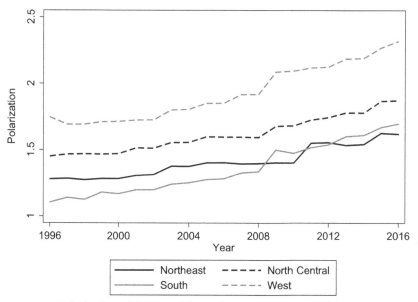

FIGURE 12.3 **Polarization of State Legislators by Region.** Computed from NPAT common space scores (Shor and McCarty, 2011). The polarization measure is the difference in the mean score for Republicans and the mean score for Democrats.

its caucus. Outside of majority-minority districts, the average position of the Democratic party has changed very little.[7]

Explanations specific to Congress and national politics also contradict my findings with Boris Shor based on our measures of state legislative polarization since the 1990s that are comparable to those used for Congress (Shor and McCarty, 2011). We find that on average state legislatures have become more polarized over time (although there is variation across states). Moreover, we find that most state legislatures are more polarized than the US House.

Perhaps the most important takeaway from this section is that our current levels of congressional polarization did not emerge overnight. It has been a 40-year process. These deep roots may explain why political scientists have found very little evidence that electoral reforms would do much to reverse these trends (McCarty, 2015b). Given the deep-seeded nature of polarization and its likely resistance to reform, the focus of the remainder of my essay will be on the ways that the American political system is likely to evolve given a permanently high level of partisan division (Figure 12.3).

---

[7] While there is more variation in the movements of the Democratic and Republican parties at the state level, Republicans have become more extreme on average in state legislatures. Retrieved from http://americanlegislatures.com/2013/07/29/partisan-polarization-in-state-legislatures/ (last accessed December 9, 2018).

THEORETICAL PERSPECTIVES ON THE IMPACT OF
POLARIZATION ON CONGRESS

How does polarization affect the capacity of Congress to fulfill its constitutional functions? A variety of theoretical perspectives and models suggest possible mechanisms through which polarization reduces the ability of Congress to act. At the core of these theories is the fact that Congress is not a majoritarian institution. Constitutional structures such as bicameralism and the separation of powers as well as internal rules such as the Senate's cloture procedures make it difficult for a simple legislative majority to act.

Indeed, if Congress were governed solely by majority rule, legislative outcomes would reflect the preferences of the median legislator.[8] If outcomes were governed by the median legislator, the increasing number of extreme legislators associated with polarization would have no impact on policy outcomes. Moreover, there would be no policy gridlock. If the preferences of the median voter change, there would be a swift policy response moving policy to the new median preferred outcome. Indeed, in a more majoritarian setting the primary policy problem would be policy instability rather than stasis.

If legislative politics were dominated by the majority party as in Westminster parliamentary systems, polarization also would not necessarily imply dysfunction and gridlock. In such a system, the winning party enacts its preferences rather than those of the median voter leaving no gridlock. Polarization should simply lead to wider policy swings upon a change in power.

Thus, any connection between polarization and congressional gridlock should be due to the Madisonian Constitution and the non-majoritarian procedures that Congress has adopted. In the next two subsections, I detail two theories which help to explain why Congress's capacity to govern has been reduced by polarization.

Partisan Politics

Many legislative scholars argue that legislators have strong electoral incentives to delegate substantial powers to partisan leaders to shape the legislative agenda and to discipline wayward members (Cox and McCubbins, 1993, Aldrich and Rohde, 2000, Cox and McCubbins, 2005). To the extent that parties can successfully pursue such strategies, policymaking becomes the interaction of parties.

If control of the House, Senate, and presidency were concentrated in the hands of a single party, the impact of polarization would approximate those of

---

[8] See Black (1948) on the median voter theorem. Technically, the median voter theorem requires that preferences be aligned on a single dimension. Unidimensionality is a reasonably good approximation of the contemporary Congress. See McCarty, Poole, and Rosenthal (2016), Figure 2.2.

the Westminster model described above. But unfortunately, political polarization has occurred in an era of frequent divided government. In situations of divided government with cohesive parties, party theories predict that policy-making represents bilateral bargaining between the parties. Polarization, however, may affect whether a bargain can be struck. Just as a house cannot be sold when the buyer values it less than the seller's reservation price, increased policy differences shrink the set of compromises that both parties are willing to entertain. The increased policy differences have a second effect on bargaining which endangers even feasible compromises. Returning to the analogy of a home buyer, consider the case when the buyer is willing to pay slightly more than the seller is willing to accept. Under such circumstance, the buyer may be more willing to make a "low-ball" offer as her only risk is losing out on a transaction in which she stands to gain little. Returning to the political context, increased policy differences exacerbate the incentives to engage in brinksmanship so that even feasible policy compromises might not be reached. Thus, this perspective predicts that polarization should lead to more gridlock and less policy innovation during periods of divided government.

More sophisticated partisan theories suggest that the legislature may be gridlocked even under unified governments. Gary Cox and Mathew McCubbins argue that the majority party has strong incentives to prevent consideration of issues that divide the party (Cox and McCubbins, 2005). Thus, they argue that the majority party will invoke a version of the so-called Hastert Rule, which requires a majority vote of the majority party before a bill may be considered by the chamber. This form of *negative agenda control* has important implications for legislative gridlock. If we were to assume that legislator preferences were arrayed along a single dimension, any new legislation would require the support of both the median legislator and the median of the majority party. But polarization may reduce this source of gridlock. The preference gap between the party median and the chamber median mainly reflects the lack of homogeneity in the majority party. When the two parties have no ideological overlap, as in recent years, both the majority party median and the House median must be members of the majority party. In this case, minority party preferences have no influence on the gap. As the parties have polarized, they have also become more homogeneous, so the gap today is less than it was in the 1960s (McCarty, Poole, and Rosenthal, 2013). Thus, suggests that other features of our political system are more consequential for linking polarization to gridlock.

The Filibuster and the Presidential Veto

Perhaps the largest deviation from the majoritarian ideal is the institution of cloture in the Senate. Ostensibly to protect its tradition of unfettered and unlimited debate, the Senate requires that three-fifths (i.e., 60) of its members vote for a cloture resolution before debate can be terminated and votes taken on the measure in question. Because opponents of legislation always have the option to keep talking until cloture is successfully invoked, 60 votes has become the *de facto* threshold for passing legislation through the Senate.

We can assess the importance of cloture rules for legislative responsiveness.[9] Again assume that the ideal points of senators can be arrayed from left to right. Given the rules for cloture, we can characterize what a successful coalition must look like. Because 60 votes are required for passage, the senator with the 60th most liberal ideal point must support cloture. Let's call her Senator 60. Suppose the alternative for consideration was too liberal for Senator 60. Then it would also be too liberal for the 40 senators with ideal points to her right. These 40 senators and Senator 60 would vote against cloture and the bill would fail. In a world of liberal-conservative voting Senator 60 is pivotal for policy change. If a policy is too liberal for this senator, it will be too liberal for 40 more conservative senators and no change will occur. But if the policy appeals to the senator, he can push through the policy by voting with the 59 senators who are more liberal. In this sense, Senator 60 is pivotal. Just knowing the vote of this senator will allow us to know if a new policy that is more liberal will pass. Senator 41 (the 41st most liberal) is similarly pivotal. If the bill is too conservative for him, it will also be for the 40 senators to his left and cloture cannot be obtained. For this reason, we refer to senators 41 and 60 as the filibuster pivots.

Since the consent of both pivots is necessary for cloture, the new bill cannot be too liberal for Senator 61 or too conservative for Senator 40, it is easy to see that no bill altering a status quo located between the pivots can be successfully revised. Thus, the ideological distance between Senator 41 and Senator 60's ideal point is a rough gauge of the Senate's propensity to stalemate due to the cloture rule. Because the majority party in the Senate rarely controls 60 seats, the link between polarization and filibuster-induced gridlock is almost immediate.

Internal roadblocks such as bicameralism and the filibuster are not the only impediments to legislative policy change. Bills that survive the legislative process face the presidential veto. Certainly, presidents can from time to time use the bully pulpit to force bills through the barriers posed by partisan agenda control and filibusters. But for the most part, the president's legislative powers are negative (McCarty, 1997, Cameron, 2000, Cameron and McCarty, 2004).

The veto is a tool for blocking change rather than propagating it. A successful bill requires the presidential signature or a two-thirds vote on an override motion. Using logic exactly similar to that for the filibuster, Senator 34 becomes pivotal on the override motion for a leftist president's veto and Senator 66 becomes pivotal on a rightist veto. But because the override motion must carry both chambers, Representatives 148 and 287 are similarly empowered. The most extreme of these two legislators on the president's side

---

[9] For a detailed explication of the underlying theory, see Krehbiel (1998) and Brady and Volden (2005).

of the spectrum is known as the veto pivot. Since adding new pivotal actors can never increase the status quos that can be successfully overturned, the propensity for gridlock expands.

Combing the effects of the filibuster and the veto pivots, we can compute what political scientists call the gridlock interval. This interval is the policy gap between the leftmost pivot and the rightmost pivot. One or the other of these senators could block the change of any status quo in this interval. Therefore, the longer this interval the more likely that policy change can be blocked. Again, the link between the gridlock interval and polarization is quite direct. As the parties' positions diverge, the distance between the pivotal legislative actors will generally move in tandem. Statistics show that a very substantial fraction of the variance in the width of the gridlock interval is due to party polarization.[10]

Strategic Disagreement

Another mechanism which might help transform polarization into legislative paralysis is the increased incentives of politicians to engage in strategic disagreement. Strategic disagreement occurs when a president, party, or other political actor refuses to compromise with the other side in an attempt to gain an electoral advantage by transferring blame for the stalemate to the other side (Gilmour, 1995, Groseclose and McCarty, 2001, Lee, 2009). Classical instances include attempts to bring up controversial legislation near an election in the hopes that a president will cast an unpopular veto such as was done with the Family and Medical Leave Act in 1992 and the so-called Partial-Birth Abortion bill before the 1996 election. Such electoral grandstanding not only lowers legislative capacity by diverting resources into an unproductive endeavor but also because it makes both sides less willing to engage in the compromises required for successful legislation (Lee, 2016).

There are several reasons to believe that polarization may exacerbate these incentives. As the parties have become more extreme relative to voters, making the other side appear to be the more extreme becomes more valuable. Recent examples include the Democrats' engineering of two George W. Bush vetoes of the reauthorization of the Children's Health Insurance Program in 2007.[11] Another example is Republican passage of the Keystone Pipeline Approval Act

---

[10] See McCarty, Poole, and Rosenthal (2016), Table 6.1.

[11] The dynamics of the vetoes suggest the strong role of strategic disagreement. The original bill called for a $35 billion-dollar expansion of the program's budget over 5 years. President Bush vetoed it suggesting that he was willing only to increase the program by $5 billion. Despite this offer, the second bill also provided for a $35 billion increase. While the second bill did contain a few provisions designed to increase Republican support, the number of Republicans supporting a veto override actually fell. Because the Democrats preferred the stalemate to successful legislation, the program would not be permanently reauthorized until President Obama took office. Retrieved from www.congress.gov/bill/110th-congress/house-bill/976/actions, www.congress.gov/bill/110th-congress/house-bill/3963/actions, www.nytimes.com/2008/01/23/washing

to force President Obama into a veto that was not only unpopular but might drive a wedge between the president and the labor unions who supported the pipeline that would connect the Canadian tar sands to the Gulf of Mexico.[12]

Exacerbating things is the contemporary media environment of politics. The media often covers policymaking much as they would a heavyweight boxing match, scoring the winner and loser round-by-round. In such an environment, both sides are loath to make any compromises for fear of having it scored as a losing round. The result is policy stagnation.

POLARIZATION AND POLICYMAKING

The theoretical perspectives described in the previous section suggest that polarization will make it considerably harder for Congress to fulfill its legislative role and other functions. In this section, I focus on three areas, legislative output, budgetary performance, and Senate confirmations, to show empirically that Congress's performance has indeed declined as polarization has risen.

Legislative Output

The approaches described above predict that polarization should make it more difficult for Congress to pass important new legislation. David Mayhew's data on landmark legislative enactments can be used to demonstrate polarization's effects on the legislative process (Mayhew, 1991). Figure 12.4 plots the number of significant legislative enactments by congressional term against the DW-NOMINATE polarization measure. It reveals a striking pattern. Congress enacted the vast majority of its significant measures during the least polarized period. The ten least polarized congressional terms produced almost 16 significant enactments per term, whereas the ten most polarized terms produced slightly more than 10.[13]

To control for other factors that might explain these differences, I developed a multivariate model of legislative output.[14] I attempt to isolate the effect of polarization by controlling for unified party control of government, split party control of Congress, the election cycle, changes in party control of the presidency and Congress, and secular trends. In the preferred specification, there are substantively large and statistically significant negative effects of polarization. To get at the magnitude of these differences, Figure 12.5 presents a counterfactual analysis of Congress's output if polarization had remained at its 1965 level.

---

ton/23cnd-health.html, and www.nytimes.com/2009/01/15/washington/15healthcare.html (last accessed December 9, 2018)
[12] At the time of the veto, a CNN poll showed 57 percent support for the pipeline. Retrieved from www.cnn.com/2015/01/15/politics/poll-majority-of-americans-back-keystone-pipeline/ (last accessed December 9, 2018).
[13] The gap would be even bigger except for the enormous legislative output following the September 11 terrorist attacks during the polarized 2000s.
[14] It is an updated version of that from McCarty (2007).

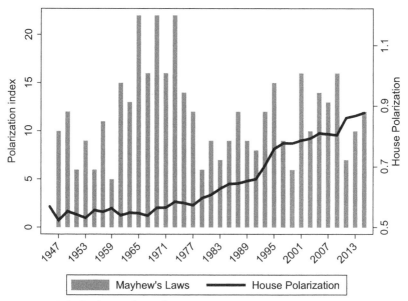

FIGURE 12.4 Polarization and Mayhew Laws.

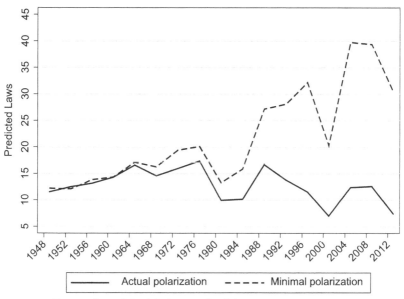

FIGURE 12.5 Counterfactual Legislative Productivity.

Budgetary Disorder

The 1974 Congressional Budget and Impoundment Control Act calls on Congress to pass a budget resolution. Under "regular" order, both chambers pass resolutions and the differences are reconciled by a conference committee. Congressional performance in this stage of the budget process shows clear deterioration over time. Figure 12.6 plots the number of stages successfully reached for each annual budget resolution. These possible stages are House passage, Senate passage, House passage of conference report and Senate passage of conference report. From 1976 to 1998, Congress successfully cleared all four of these hurdles. Since then there has been a completed budget resolution in only 9 of 20 years. In 2011, neither chamber passed its own budget resolution.[15]

Congress is also expected to pass each of its appropriation bills prior to the start of the fiscal year (currently October 1). If it fails to do so Congress and the

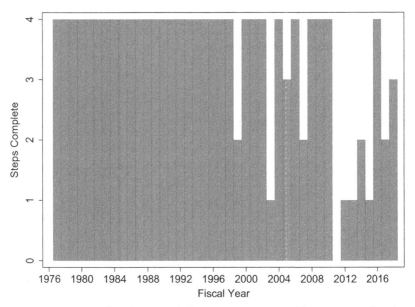

FIGURE 12.6 **Passage of Budget Resolutions, FY1977–2018.** The progress of each annual budget resolution is scored from zero to four. Passage of an initial resolution by either chamber scores one point and the passage of a conference report by either chamber scores one point.

---

[15] The uptick in performance for FY2018 was due to the GOP's desire to use the budget reconciliation process to pass health care reform and tax cuts – thus should not be interpreted as a return to regular order.

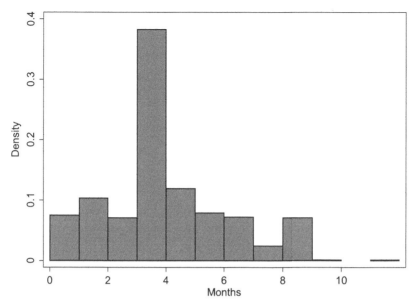

FIGURE 12.7 Distribution of Delays in Successful Appropriation Bills: FY1974–2017.

president must agree to a continuing resolution (CR) or face a government shutdown such as ones that occurred in 1995–1996 and 2013. Generally, CRs continue the funding levels of the previous fiscal year, but many also include some modifications of spending levels. CRs often contain changes to the authorizing statutes, and because they are often "must" pass legislation, unrelated legislation is often attached. Consequently, delays in the passage of appropriation bills and the resulting "governing by CR" has drawn wide concern. Late appropriation bills are said to create budgetary uncertainty for government agencies and private actors, reduce the ability to adjust to new spending priorities, undermine the role of committee expertise, and weaken fiscal governance (Devins, 1988, White, 1988, Hanson, 2013).

To measure the trends in the propensity to begin a fiscal year without completed appropriation bills, I compiled data on each regular appropriation bill for FY1974 to FY2017.[16] To measure delay, I simply compare the date of final passage with the start date of the fiscal year. I consider an appropriation bill to have passed if it is signed by the president as a stand-alone appropriation bill or as a separate title of an omnibus appropriation bill.

Figures 12.7 and 12.8 present the distribution of appropriation delays in months.[17] Figure 12.7 presents the data for the entire sample. Appropriation delays are the norm. Only about 10 percent of all appropriation bills passed

[16] See McCarty (2016) for details.
[17] In both figures, a delay of 0 is assigned to any bill passed prior to the start of the fiscal year.

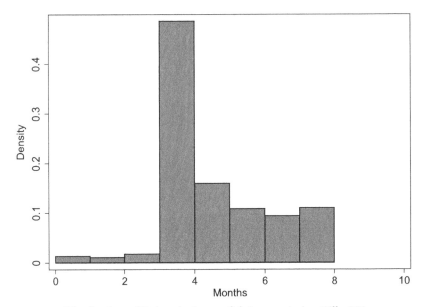

FIGURE 12.8 Distribution of Delays in Successful Appropriation Bills: FY2002–2017.

prior to the beginning of the fiscal year. The modal month of passage is during the third month of the fiscal year (currently December). But a substantial share of bills pass in months 4, 5, and 6.

Figure 12.8 shows the distribution of delays since 2002. Clearly, delays have become much more common. Very few appropriation bills have been completed on time since 2002 and the frequency of delays exceeding 2 months has gone up dramatically.

In a multivariate analysis of the determinant of appropriation delay, I find that delays correlate directly with polarization and with interbranch and interchamber preference differences that themselves are functions of partisan polarization (McCarty, 2016).

Confirmation Delay

The performance of the Senate in the confirmation process is yet another example of deterioration. While battles over the confirmation of Supreme Court nominees and the overt obstruction of other judicial nominees has received much attention, the scope of Senate's problems is often unappreciated. Not only have the confirmations of highly salient appointments succumbed to obstruction and delay, but the Senate is much slower on the hundreds of less important nominations that it must approve each term.

In an earlier study, Rose Razaghian and I collected information about the almost 5,000 nominations to positions in domestic executive branch agencies

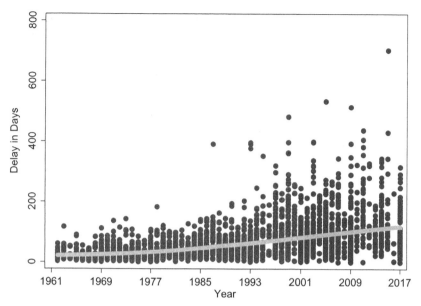

FIGURE 12.9 **Confirmation Delay.**

from the 49th to the 109th Senates (1885–2004). I have updated these data though the end of 2017 to include another approximately 800 confirmations.[18] The main focus of our study was the duration of the confirmation process from the date of the president's official nomination to final action by the Senate.[19]

Using the updated data, Figure 12.9 shows the distribution of confirmation delays from 1961 though the end of 2017 at this writing.[20] A smoothing line is added to show the trends in the expected delay. Two aspects of Figure 12.9 are particularly salient. First, the expected delay in conformations has grown tremendously since the 1960s. In 1961, the average delay was 11 days. In 2017, it had grown to 93 days.[21] Second, the variation in the length of confirmations has grown precipitously. It is now quite common for a nominee to languish hundreds of days without Senate action. Interestingly, the

[18] McCarty and Razaghian (1999). To avoid complications related to senatorial courtesy, we did not collect data on nominees to head regional offices such as United States attorneys or custom officials. Finally, to limit our focus to domestic politics, we did not collect data on the Department of State or Department of Defense.

[19] Thus, we ignore the delay between an announced vacancy and the president's nomination. Clearly, the Senate's performance might also affect the duration of the prenomination selection and vetting process.

[20] Most nominations made in 2018 were still pending as of this writing.

[21] This estimate is subject to substantial censoring as more than 40 of Donald Trump's 2017 nominations to these positions were returned to the president unconfirmed at the end of the session. This happened to only a couple of Kennedy's nominations in 1961.

2013 changes to Senate rules that eliminated the filibuster on nominations appear to have had little effect on the speed of confirmation for these appointees.

In our multivariate analysis, Razaghian and I found a strong correlation between the level of polarization and the duration of the confirmation process. Moreover, we found that the association with polarization was strengthened during periods of divided government. So it seems that polarization has not only affected judicial nominations but all the way to the lowest levels of Senate-confirmed positions.

POLARIZATION AND THE CONSTITUTION

Given the effects of polarization on Congress, how might the other branches respond? How might the balance of power between the legislative, executive, and judicial branches shift? How will our federal balance between the national and state governments be altered?

A Conceptual Framework

To organize my thoughts about the impact of declining legislative capacity on the functioning of our constitutional system, I model constitutional policymaking as a problem of team production (Alchian and Demsetz, 1972). In a model of team production, total output is a function of the contributions and efforts of multiple agents. In the classical team model developed in economics, the level of contribution across players is affected by the incentives for freeriding. Each team member would like to exert less effort while having the others exert more. Unless the team's gains can be divided in such a way to reward effort and penalize freeriders, the team's output will be suboptimal. Thus, suboptimal outcomes generally prevail if individual efforts are not observable or if the team's output is a public good where team members are not excludable from its consumption. Second, the incentives for freeriding are especially severe when the efforts of different agents are substitutes for one another. When efforts are complements, a higher effort outcome can be obtained.[22]

To draw upon this framework, I assume that policy outcomes are the product of team production by a set of actors encompassing the executive, legislature, judiciary, and the states. This reflects the notion that a policy outcome is a combination of legislative deliberation and design, executive administration and implementation, and judicial oversight and enforcement at both the national and state levels.

---

[22] When the efforts of agents 1 and 2 are substitutes, a reduction of the efforts of agent 1 increases the marginal productivity of agent 2's efforts. When efforts are complements, increased effort by agent 1 increases the productivity of agent 2's efforts.

In generating policy outcomes, the actions (or inaction) of these players generate outcomes that vary across two dimensions: a distributive dimension and a quality dimension. The distributive dimension reflects how the divergent policy goals of the agents are reconciled. Thus, each agent will, within the scope of its constitutional authority, try to move policy in such a way that it produces its more preferred outcome. Clearly, the relative policymaking capacities of legislating, administering, and judging will determine whose priorities will be reflected in the ultimate policy outcomes. The quality dimension reflects a set of features that enhance the efficacy, efficiency, or equity of policy outcomes. A non-exhaustive list of quality enhancements might include robust legislative deliberation, clear statutory authority, efficient and equitable implementation, clear legal standards, and political accountability for outcomes. With this broad conception of policy quality, the team production aspect is clear. Quality outcomes are jointly determined by the efforts and capacities of all of the actors.

Within this framework, what are the implications of a decline in legislative capacity? Suppose that there were a decrease in the legislative efforts on both the distributive and quality dimensions. How would we expect the other actors to respond and what are the implications for policy outcomes? Let's begin with the distributive dimension. It is reasonable to think of legislative inputs as primarily substitutes for the inputs of the other actors and vice versa. The extent to which the legislature is a check on executive, judicial, or state policy-making, the judiciary, executives, and states will responded to a weakened legislature by increasing their efforts to move policy in their preferred directions. So on the distributive dimension we should expect to see policymaking move away from Congress into other venues and outcomes will become more reflective of the preferences and goals of those other actors.

The outcomes on the quality dimension are affected somewhat differently. On the quality dimension, legislative inputs are generally complements to the inputs of other institutions. Well-crafted statutes contribute to high quality policies by facilitating predictable and transparent implementation and adjudication. For example, absent renewed statutory authority policies may drift (Hacker, 2004, see also Chapter 10 in this volume). This creates substantial uncertainty about how statutes will be applied in agency rulemaking and court decisions as new policy circumstances arise (see Chapter 11 in this volume). Executive actions and agency rules in the absence of clear statutory guidance are more vulnerable to revision by future administrations. Legislative politics also provides opportunities for deliberation and consensus building.[23] Consensus policies may have a quality advantage in that broader public acceptance will

---

[23] As Curry and Lee show in Chapter 8, consensus policymaking in Congress is not dead. Bipartisan coalitions remain the norm on successful legislation. Thus, it seems better to assume that polarization reduces the level of these legislative inputs rather than transforming them into more partisan versions.

lead to greater compliance (Tyler, 1990, 1998). Statutes passed with large majorities may also be more durable.[24]

The specific consequences of the decline of legislative capacity clearly depend on the extent to which legislative capacity is a substitute or a complement to executive and judicial capacity. But the broad implications are that congressional dysfunction may allow the other branches and the states to increase their *relative* power over Congress, but the *absolute* power of these branches may be declining along with that of Congress.

The total effects of polarization on the constitutional balance of power also depend on the extent to which the other branches are compromised by it. Clearly, polarization is a key contemporary feature of the executive and judicial branches.[25] State legislatures are also very polarized (Shor and McCarty, 2011). Although polarization within these branches may not lessen their decisionmaking capacities as significantly as it does Congress's, such effects may be consequential. Moreover, polarization in these branches may produce significantly more policy oscillation and less durable policy, thus further reducing the quality dimension of policy.

Executive Branch

Recent scholarship has stressed how declining congressional capacity to override presidential and agency decisions allows the executive branch to become relatively more powerful.[26] Consider the conventional models of lawmaking such as pivotal politics (Krehbiel, 1998) or majority party agenda control (Cox and McCubbins, 2005). Each predicts a "gridlock interval" of policies that cannot be overturned by a statutory override. As discussed, these gridlock intervals tend to be larger when congressional parties are more polarized. Therefore, agencies have considerably more leeway to set policy without fear of congressional override when polarization is high (Ferejohn and Shipan, 1990, Howell, 2003).

But this policy setting autonomy may represent a relative gain in power rather than an absolute one. First, many tools of executive policymaking depend on legislative delegation to at least some degree. A less active Congress will give the president much less to work with. Moreover, a more partisan and ideological judiciary may read legislative grants of authority more restrictively. Such constraints are apparent in the judicial responses to recent executive

---

[24] Maltzman and Shipan (2008) find that important statutes go longer before revision if they were passed with large majorities. Adler and Wilkerson (2013), however, do not find statistical evidence for this effect.

[25] See, for example, Clark (2008), Devins and Lewis (2008).

[26] See for example Ferejohn and Shipan (1990), Moe and Howell (1999); Howell (2003), Devins (2008).

actions on immigration.[27] Second, presidents may be charged with implementing and enforcing poorly drafted laws. That sending the bill back to a polarized Congress for technical corrections may not be an option, the administration is opened up to even more judicial scrutiny such as in the recent King v. Burwell case over Obamacare subsidies (*King v. Burwell*, 576 U.S. 2015). Third, congressional delays in confirming presidential appointments and appropriating funds clearly reduce the policymaking capacities of the executive branch. For example, Anne Joseph O'Connell reports that, due in large part to greater confirmation delays, the initial vacancy period at the start of a new administration for all subcabinet officials increased substantially between the Reagan and Bush II administrations (O'Connell, 2009). These vacancies, she argues, foster agency inaction and confusion while undermining agency accountability.

A common presumption is that the executive branch should be less internally affected by polarization in that it is headed by a single individual elected by a national constituency. Putting aside the questionable assumption that a national constituency places meaningful constraints on the partisan or ideological behavior of presidents, there are many reasons to be skeptical that polarization will not undermine the inner workings of the administration. First, polarization would tend to increase the preference differences between political appointees and career civil servants in ways that would undermine political control and performance of agencies (Lewis, 2010). Second, there is considerable ideological heterogeneity across agencies within a single administration (Clinton et al, 2012). Finally, legal restrictions on removal combined with the sluggish confirmation process dramatically limit the ability of presidents to shift the ideological nature of key agencies (Devins and Lewis, 2008).

But even if presidents were able to overcome all of these internal obstacles and govern as a unitary actor with few legislative constraints, executive power would be diminished by polarization in that the outputs of executive policymaking such as orders, memoranda, and rules are far less durable than statutes as they can easily be undone by the next administration.

Courts

Both attitudinalists and those working in the "separation of powers" tradition of judicial decision making predict that courts (especially the Supreme Court) will be able to exercise more policymaking autonomy when Congress is less capable of overriding its statutory interpretations and legislating around its constitutional decisions.[28] The key debate between the two schools is

---

[27] Of course, whether the courts were overly restrictive in enjoining the immigration orders or whether President Obama overreached is a debatable question.

[28] On the attitudinal model, see, for example, Segal and Spaeth (2002). On the separation of powers model, see Ferejohn and Shipan (1990), Gely and Spiller (1990).

the extent to which the Supreme Court tries to strategically avoid legislative overrides and sanctions.

Putting aside that aspect of the debate, there is reasonably good evidence that Congress overrides the Supreme Court less often as polarization has grown. In updating the data from William Eskridge, Richard Hasen finds that the rate at which Congress has overridden Supreme Court statutory decisions has fallen markedly.[29] From 1975 to 1990, Congress overrode an average of 12 Supreme Court decisions in every biennial term. But between 2001 and 2012, the rate was only 2.8 per term.[30] Arguably, the magnitude of this decline may understate the extent to which the Supreme Court has escaped congressional oversight of its statutory decisions. As Deborah Widiss points out, the recent Supreme Court approach to statutory interpretation has been to narrowly construe legislative overrides and to not apply their logic to similar provisions in other statutes (Widiss, 2011). Thus, Congress would have to pass overrides for each statute separately.

But this apparent gain in judicial autonomy may also represent only an increase in relative power. The slowdown of the Senate confirmation process has created large vacancies in the federal judiciary that undermine its capacity. Moreover, the decline in Congress's ability to control the court *ex post* has raised the stakes for *ex ante* control that has deeply politicized the appointment process for federal judges from the Supreme Court on down (Hanson, 2013).

The effects of polarization within the judiciary may also undermine its effectiveness. Key values such as consistency, predictability, and restraint are undermined in a polarized judiciary. Appeals court decisions are increasingly related to the partisan composition of the circuit, which may make circuit splits more common. Small changes in the composition of the courts may lead to large shifts in the balance of political power and create demands for reversing precedents and doctrine. To the extent to which these changes reduce the perceived legitimacy of the courts, the judges may suffer an absolute loss of policymaking capacity.

[29] See Eskridge (1991), Hasen (2012). Some nuance is required when interpreting override rates from the separation of powers perspective. Most separation of powers models assume complete information and therefore predict that the Supreme Court can perfectly anticipate congressional behavior. Consequently, no overrides occur in equilibrium. But if the court were uncertain of the preferences of the closest congressional override pivot, the logic of incomplete information veto models would predict lower override rates when the closest override pivot is more extreme in expectation – the pattern one would expect polarization to produce. See Cameron and McCarty (2004).

[30] Importantly, the decline in overrides cannot be explained by a decline in the number of statutory interpretation cases heard by the court. To the contrary, the number of such cases has been roughly constant since the early 1990s. See Hasen (2012), Figure 5.

States

A third set of actors who may derive some benefits from congressional dysfunction is the states. Federal gridlock may open spaces for states to adopt innovative policies without worries about federal preemption. Consider the liberalization of marijuana laws. Although Congress has not provided statutory authorization for states to legalize medical or recreational marijuana, President Obama's Department of Justice decided not to prosecute certain types of violations of federal marijuana law in those states that have a legal cannabis market.[31] States through their ability to bring lawsuits have also had a very important role in shaping policies related to the environment, tobacco, financial regulation, and immigration in the absence of congressional action.

But legislative gridlock has not only given states the space to pursue their own policy initiatives, but also the enhanced opportunity and incentive to actively resist federal policy. Legal scholars Jessica Bulman-Pozen and Heather Gerken have dubbed this new tendency "uncooperative federalism" (Bulman-Pozen and Gerken, 2009). In their account, states are able to use their sovereign powers in a variety of ways that shape and constrain federal policy. They may shape national policy agendas through legislation or litigation or exploit their role as administrators of federal policies to force the federal government to heed state concerns. The power of the state's role in federal agenda setting is attested to by the increased activity of national interest groups such as the American Legislative Exchange Council (ALEC) in promoting model legislation across states as a way of shaping the national policy agenda.

Polarization clearly enhances the incentives for state contestation of federal policy (Bulman-Pozen, 2014) . This is especially true in the case of unified party control at the federal level. In these situations, states controlled by the national out-party become the locus of opposition to federal policy. Just as Republican states resisted and challenged the Affordable Care Act, Democratic states are challenging Trump administration policies on immigration and the environment. Consequently, states become the primary check on federal executive power when Congress has little incentive to play that role.

Of course, there are other political factors that will shape the role of the states in national politics. An important one is the link between state and national election outcomes. Gubernatorial and state legislative elections are often determined by national-level economic and partisan factors (Rogers, 2016, Hopkins, 2017). On one hand this may militate against state activity on national issues as the political payoffs from pursuing distinctive state-level political agendas may be minimal. But on the other hand, this nationalization of elections may leave state legislators less constrained by the wishes of their constituents (Rogers, 2017).

---

[31] www.justice.gov/iso/opa/resources/3052013829132756857467.pdf

A second factor for state-level policymaking on national issues is that the exercise of the state's powers requires the complicity of the federal executive and judicial branches. As of this writing, it is expected that the Trump administration will reverse the Department of Justice's (DOJ) memorandum on prosecution discretion for marijuana cases. Their ability to set policy as plaintiffs depends on a sympathetic judiciary. Moreover, congressional gridlock leaves the states in a vulnerable position. States can no longer depend on Congress to check executive encroachments or to override unfavorable statutory interpretations by the courts.

Finally, the states may also face their own governance problems as a result of high and increasing levels of polarization in their own legislatures (Shor and McCarty, 2011). Gridlock may not be the primary concern, however. Because states tend to have fewer supermajoritarian rules and rates of divided government are declining, polarization may be more likely to produce more extreme policy outcomes and more variation in policies across states.

CONCLUSION

In recent decades, congressional performance across a number of areas has deteriorated as Congress has polarized. The decline in legislative capacity clearly creates a set of opportunities and challenges for the other branches of our government. In this chapter, I have argued that at least in some cases the executive branch, the judiciary, and the states take advantage of opportunities to move outcomes on the distributive dimension closer to their goals. But power is not zero sum. The proper functioning of the executive, judiciary, and states depends on a functioning Congress. Thus, the quality dimension may suffer, indicating a reduction in the aggregate capacity of government to shape social and economic outcomes. These problems are only reinforced by the fact that each of the non-legislative branches are afflicted to some degree with the same ailments that have infected Congress.

Nevertheless, it is premature to assess the magnitude of these changes. Political scientists and legal scholars will need to focus much more on the impact of polarization on the executive, judiciary, and the states before we state confidently that our constitutional system is likely to be reshaped.

REFERENCES

Adler, E. Scott, and John D. Wilkerson. 2013. *Congress and the Politics of Problem Solving*. Cambridge: Cambridge University Press.
Alchian, Armen A., and Harold Demsetz. 1972. "Production, Information Costs, and Economic Organization." *The American Economic Review* 62(5): 777–795.
Aldrich, John H., and David W. Rohde. 2000. The Logic of Conditional Party Government: Revisiting the Electoral Connection. In Lawrence Dodd and Bruce Oppenheimer (eds.), *Congress Reconsidered, 7th Edition*. Washington, DC: CQ Press.

American Political Science Association. 1950. "Toward a More Responsible Two-Party System: A Report of the Committee on Political Parties." *44(3)*: part 2, Supplement.

Barber, Michael, and Nolan McCarty. 2013. The Causes and Consequences of Polarization. In Cathie Jo Martin and Jane Mansbridge (eds.), *Negotiating Agreement in Politics*. Washington, DC: American Political Science Association.

Binder, Sarah. 2015. "The Dysfunctional Congress." *Annual Review of Political Science 18*: 85–101.

Binder, Sarah A. 2003. *Stalemate: Causes and Consequences of Legislative Gridlock*. New York: Brookings Institution Press.

Binder, Sarah A., and Forrest Maltzman. 2002. "Senatorial Delay in Confirming Federal Judges, 1947–1998." *American Journal of Political Science 46(1)*: 190–199.

Black, Duncan. 1948. "The Decisions of a Committee Using a Special Majority." *Econometrica: Journal of the Econometric Society 16(3)*: 245–261.

Brady, David W., and Craig Volden. 2005. *Revolving Gridlock: Politics and Policy from Jimmy Carter to George W. Bush*. New York: Westview Press.

Bulman-Pozen, Jessica. 2014. "Partisan Federalism." *Harvard Law Review 127(4)*: 1077–1146.

Bulman-Pozen, Jessica, and Heather K. Gerken. 2009. "Uncooperative Federalism." *Yale Law Journal 118*: 1256–1310.

Cameron, Charles M. 2000. *Veto Bargaining: Presidents and the Politics of Negative Power*. Cambridge: Cambridge University Press.

Cameron, Charles M., and Nolan McCarty. 2004. "Models of Vetoes and Veto Bargaining." *Annual Review Political Science 7*: 409–435.

Chafetz, Josh. 2017. *Congress'ss Constitution: Legislative Authority and the Separation of Powers*. New Haven, CT: Yale University Press.

Clark, Tom S. 2008. "Measuring Ideological Polarization on the United States Supreme Court." *Political Research Quarterly 62(1)*: 146–157.

Clinton, Joshua D., Anthony Bertelli, Christian R. Grose, David E. Lewis, and David C. Nixon. 2012. "Separated Powers in the United States: The Ideology of Agencies, Presidents, and Congress." *American Journal of Political Science 56(2)*: 341–354.

Cox, Gary W., and Mathew D. McCubbins. 1993. *Legislative Leviathan: Party Government in the House*. Berkeley, CA: University of California Press.

2005. *Setting the Agenda: Responsible Party Government in the US House of Representatives*. Cambridge: Cambridge University Press.

Devins, Neal. 2008. "Presidential Unilateralism and Political Polarization: Why Today's Congress Lacks the Will and the Way to Stop Presidential Initiatives." *Willamette Law Review 45*: 395.

Devins, Neal, and David E. Lewis. 2008. "Not-So Independent Agencies: Party Polarization and the Limits of Institutional Design." *Boston University Law Review 1988*: 459.

Devins, Neal E. 1988. "Appropriations Redux: A Critical Look at the Fiscal Year 1988 Continuing Resolution." *Duke Law Journal*: 389.

Epstein, David, and Sharyn O'Halloran. 1999. *Delegating Powers: A Transaction Cost Politics Approach to Policy Making under Separate Powers*. New York: Cambridge University Press.

Eskridge, William N. 1991. "Overriding Supreme Court Statutory Interpretation Decisions." *Yale Law Journal 101*: 331–455.

Ferejohn, John, and Charles Shipan. 1990. "Congressional Influence on Bureaucracy." *Journal of Law, Economics, & Organization* 6: 1–20.

Gely, Rafael, and Pablo T. Spiller. 1990. "A Rational Choice Theory of Supreme Court Statutory Decisions with Applications to the State Farm and Grove City Cases." *Journal of Law, Economics, & Organization* 6(2): 263–300.

Gilmour, John B. 1995. *Strategic Disagreement: Stalemate in American Politics.* Pittsburgh, PA: University of Pittsburgh Press.

Groseclose, Tim, and Nolan McCarty. 2001. "The Politics of Blame: Bargaining Before an Audience." *American Journal of Political Science* 45(1):100–119.

Hacker, Jacob S. 2004. "Privatizing Risk Without Privatizing the Welfare State: The Hidden Politics of Social Policy Retrenchment in the United States." *American Political Science Review* 98(2): 243–260.

Hanson, Peter. 2013. "Abandoning the Regular Order: Majority Party Influence on Appropriations in the US Senate." *Political Research Quarterly* 67(3): 519–532.

2014. *Too Weak to Govern: Majority Party Power and Appropriations in the US Senate.* Cambridge: Cambridge University Press.

Hasen, Richard L. 2012. "End of the Dialogue: Political Polarization, the Supreme Court, and Congress." *Southern California Law Review* 86: 205.

Hopkins, Daniel J. 2017. *The Increasingly United States: How and Why American Political Behavior Nationalized.* Chicago, IL: University of Chicago Press.

Howell, William G. 2003. *Power without Persuasion: The Politics of Direct Presidential Action.* Princeton, NJ: Princeton University Press.

Howell, William G., and Terry M. Moe. 2016. *Relic: How Our Constitution Undermines Effective Government–and Why We Need a More Powerful Presidency.* New York: Basic Books.

Krehbiel, Keith. 1998. *Pivotal Politics: A Theory of U.S. Lawmaking.* Chicago, IL: University of Chicago Press.

Kriner, Douglas L., and Eric Schickler. 2016. *Investigating the President: Congressional Checks on Presidential Power.* Princeton, NJ: Princeton University Press.

Lee, Frances E. 2009. *Beyond Ideology: Politics, Principles, and Partisanship in the US Senate.* Chicago, IL: University of Chicago Press.

2016. *Insecure Majorities: Congress and the Perpetual Campaign.* Chicago, IL: University of Chicago Press.

Levinson, Daryl J., and Richard H. Pildes. 2006. "Separation of Parties, Not Powers." *Harvard Law Review* 119: 2311–2386.

Lewis, David E. 2010. *The Politics of Presidential Appointments: Political Control and Bureaucratic Performance.* Princeton, NJ: Princeton University Press.

Maltzman, Forrest, and Charles R. Shipan. 2008. "Change, Continuity, and the Evolution of the Law." *American Journal of Political Science* 52(2):252–267. DOI: 10.1111/j.1540-5907.2008.00311.x

Mayhew, David R. 1974. *Congress: The Electoral Connection.* New Haven, CT: Yale University Press.

1991. *Divided We Govern.* New Haven, CT: Yale University.

McCarty, Nolan. 1997. "Presidential Reputation and the Veto." *Economics & Politics* 9(1): 1–26.

2007. The Policy Effects of Political Polarization. In Paul Pierson and Theda Skocpol (eds.), *Transformations of American Politics*. Princeton, NJ: Princeton University Press.

2015a. "Reducing Polarization by Making Parties Stronger." In Nathaniel Persily (ed.), *Solutions to Political Polarization in America*. New York: Cambridge University Press.

2015b. "Reducing Polarization: Some Facts for Reformers." *University of Chicago Legal Forum* 2015: 243–278.

2016. "The Decline of Regular Order in Appropriations – Does It Matter?" In Jeffrey Jenkins and Eric Patashnik (eds.), *Congress and Policy Making in the 21st Century*. Cambridge: Cambridge University Press, p. 162.

McCarty, Nolan, Keith T. Poole, and Howard Rosenthal. 2013. *Political Bubbles: Financial Crises and the Failure of American Democracy*. Princeton, NJ: Princeton University Press.

2016. *Polarized America: The Dance of Ideology and Unequal Riches*. Cambridge: MIT Press.

McCarty, Nolan, and Rose Razaghian. 1999. "Advice and Consent: Senate Responses to Executive Branch Nominations 1885–1996." *American Journal of Political Science* 43(3): 1122–1143.

Moe, Terry M., and William G. Howell. 1999. "The Presidential Power of Unilateral Action." *The Journal of Law, Economics, and Organization* 15(1): 132–179.

O'Connell, Anne Joseph. 2009. "Vacant Offices: Delays in Staffing Top Agency Positions." *Southern California Law Review* 82: 913.

2015. "Shortening Agency and Judicial Vacancies through Filibuster Reform? An Examination of Confirmation Rates and Delays from 1981 to 2014." *Duke Law Journal*, 64.

Pildes, Richard H. 2015. "Focus on Fragmentation, Not Polarization: Re-Empower Party Leadership." In Nathaniel Persily (ed.), *Solutions to Political Polarization in America*. New York: Cambridge University Press.

Poole, Keith T., and Howard Rosenthal. 1984. "The Polarization of American Politics." *The Journal of Politics* 46(4): 1061–1079.

Posner, Eric A., and Adrian Vermeule. 2011. *The Executive Unbound: After the Madisonian Republic*. New York: Oxford University Press.

Rogers, Steven. 2016. "National Forces in State Legislative Elections." *Annals of the American Academy of Political and Social Science* 667(1): 207–225.

2017. "Electoral Accountability for State Legislative Roll Calls and Ideological Representation." *American Political Science Review* 111(3): 555 571.

Segal, Jeffrey A., and Harold J. Spaeth. 2002. *The Supreme Court and the Attitudinal Model Revisited*. Cambridge: Cambridge University Press.

Shor, Boris, and Nolan McCarty. 2011. "The Ideological Mapping of American Legislatures." *American Political Science Review* 105(3): 530–551.

Tyler, Tom R. 1990. *Why People Obey the Law: Procedural Justice, Legitimacy, and Compliance*. New Haven, CT: Yale University Press.

1998. Trust and Democratic Governance. In Valerie Braithwaite and Maragret Levi (eds.), *Trust and Governance*. New York: Russell Sage Foundation, pp. 269–294.

White, Joe. 1988. "The Continuing Resolution: A Crazy Way to Govern?" *The Brookings Review* 6(3): 28–35.

Widiss, Deborah A. 2011. "Undermining Congressional Overrides: The Hydra Problem in Statutory Interpretation." *Texas Law Review* 90: 859.

Woon, Jonathan, and Sarah Anderson. 2012. "Political Bargaining and the Timing of Congressional Appropriations." *Legislative Studies Quarterly* 37(4): 409–436.

13

Democratic Anxieties

Present and Emergent

Frances E. Lee and Nolan McCarty

This volume grows out of the well-documented psychological impulse to bring information to bear on sources of anxiety. In politics, as in other realms of life, anxiety triggers a quest for information. Perceived threats focus the attention (Marcus, Neuman, and MacKuen, 2000). Anxious citizens take more interest in politics, have more motivation to learn, and weigh the information they collect more judiciously (Marcus and MacKuen, 1993, MacKuen et al, 2010, Albertson and Gadarian, 2015). In these respects, worried citizens are better citizens (Brader, 2005, Valentino et al, 2008).

In this spirit, our purpose for this volume was to assemble the best information social scientists have to address Americans' most pressing anxieties about the performance of their national governing institutions. Under the auspices of the Social Science Research Council (SSRC), we assembled an interdisciplinary working group to first identify the major sources of anxiety about US democratic institutions and then to commission chapters that would synthesize the existing scholarship on the topic and, where possible, bring relevant new data and analysis to bear.

This project was undertaken long before Donald J. Trump descended Trump Tower's golden escalator to launch his presidential campaign on June 16, 2015. No doubt, anxieties about the performance of American democracy are greater in 2019 than they were in early 2015 when then-SSRC president Ira Katznelson asked us to assemble this working group. By 2017, fully 71 percent of Americans in a *Washington Post*–University of Maryland poll said that they thought problems in America's politics had reached a dangerous new high.[1]

---

[1] Wagner, John, and Scott Clement. 2017. "'It's Just Messed up:' Most Think Political Divisions as Bad as Vietnam Era, New Poll Shows," *Washington Post*, October 28. Retrieved from www .washingtonpost.com/graphics/2017/national/democracy-poll/?utm_term=.101c17df4988 (last accessed December 9, 2018).

Even so, anxieties about American democracy were widespread long
before 2016. A sampling of commentary headlines from 2014 offers a sense
for the pre-Trump anxiety level. One asks, "Is American Democracy Dead?"[2]
"American Democracy is Doomed," opined another.[3] "Admit It, Political
Scientists: Politics Really is More Broken than Ever," read a third.[4] When
The Economist ran a cover story in March 2014 entitled "What's Gone Wrong
with Democracy?" it listed the United States among deteriorating democracies
and described its politics as gridlocked, mired in partisan extremism, and
corrupted by lobbyists and moneyed interests.[5] Well before 2016, a sense
of alarm about American governing institutions had also mobilized the philan-
thropic sector. Having concluded that "democracy in America is in trouble,"
the Hewlett Foundation launched the Madison Initiative in the summer of
2014, a $150 million grant-making program aimed at "strengthening the
ability of democratic institutions to find solutions."[6] Also in 2014, eBay
founder Pierre Omidyar established the Democracy Fund, which made
$100 million in grants over the subsequent four years "to organizations aimed
at strengthening U.S. democracy."[7]

Two escalating long-term trends have figured most prominently as sources of
anxiety about American government throughout the twenty-first century thus
far: party polarization and widening economic inequality. The intensification of
party conflict in US national politics over the past four and a half decades raises
profound questions for the Madisonian constitutional system. The Constitution's complex division of power – across coequal, separately elected branches,
a bicameral legislature, and states in a strong federal system – puts a high
premium on negotiation, coalition building, and compromise. Government
action in the United States requires cooperation among many independent
actors, all with their own bases of political power and formal authority. The
need for bipartisanship is particularly acute when the major parties are roughly
evenly matched in electoral support and must therefore share in power.

[2] Zelizer, Julian. 2014. "Is American Democracy Dead," CNN.com, April 27. Retrieved from
    www.cnn.com/2014/04/27/opinion/zelizer-american-democracy-dead/index.html (last accessed
    December 9, 2018).
[3] Yglesias, Matthew. 2015. "American Democracy Is Doomed," Vox.com, October 8. Retrieved
    from www.vox.com/2015/3/2/8120063/american-democracy-doomed (last accessed December
    9, 2018).
[4] Mann, Thomas E. 2014. "Admit It, Political Scientists: Politics Really Is More Broken than Ever,"
    The Atlantic, May 26. Retrieved from www.theatlantic.com/politics/archive/2014/05/dysfunc
    tion/371544/ (last accessed December 9, 2018).
[5] "What's Gone Wrong with Democracy?" 2014. *The Economist,* March 1.
[6] William and Flora Hewlett Foundation. 2014. "Hewlett Foundation Launches $50 Million
    Madison Initiative," July 8. Press release. Retrieved from https://hewlett.org/newsroom/hewlett-
    foundation-launches-50-million-madison-initiative/ (last accessed December 9, 2018).
[7] Goldman, Joe. 2018. "2018 Letter from Our President," Democracy Fund. Retrieved from www
    .democracyfund.org/vision/entry/2018-letter-from-our-president (last accessed December
    9, 2018).

Party polarization undercuts the prospects for successful deal-making and calls into question the Madisonian system's capacity to function.

The hyperconcentration of wealth and income also raises important questions for democratic representation. As gauged by a variety of indicators, economic inequality has been widening since the 1970s. The Gini coefficient of income inequality has been trending upward since the late 1960s. According to the Census Bureau, the Gini index of household income stood at 0.481 in 2016, up from 0.428 in 1990 and 0.397 in 1967.[8] Wealth and national income have also grown much more concentrated in the top 10 percent and even in the top 0.1 percent of the distribution, while the share possessed by the bottom 90 percent has fallen. A central anxiety of American democracy focuses on the extent to which these marked increases in economic inequality translate into widening inequalities of political power and voice.

Neither of these long-term trends toward increasing party polarization and widening economic inequality reversed or decelerated after the 2016 elections. By 2018, the wealthiest households had seen a strong recovery from the 2008 recession, but those in the bottom 90 percent of the distribution were no better off than they were before the financial crisis.[9] Wealth was even more concentrated in 2017 than it had been in 2007.[10] The 2017 tax cuts enacted under President Trump amplified these economic inequalities, with higher income households receiving larger tax cuts as a percentage of their after-tax income than those in lower and middle-income groups.[11]

Party polarization in Congress has also continued to climb in both the House and Senate, even from the extraordinary levels in 2014.[12] Party differences in the mass electorate have further sharpened, as well. Across ten policy issues that the Pew Research Center tracked in surveys over time, the average partisan gap grew from 15 percentage points in 1994 to 36 in 2017.[13] Polarization and

[8] Semega, Jessica L., Kayla R. Fontenot, and Melissa A. Kollar. 2017. "Income and Poverty in the United States," United States Census, Report Number P60–259, September 12. Retrieved from www .census.gov/library/publications/2017/demo/p60-259.html (last accessed December 9, 2018).

[9] O'Brien, Matt. 2018. "The Bottom 90 Percent Are Still Poorer than They Were in 2007," Wonkblog, Washington Post, October 1. Retrieved from www.washingtonpost.com/busi ness/2018/10/01/bottom-percent-are-still-poorer-than-they-were/?noredirect=on&utm_ term=.1acc31d4559d&wpisrc=nl_rainbow&wpmm=1 (last accessed December 9, 2018).

[10] Casselman, Ben. 2017. "Feel that Post-Recession Bounce? The Rich Feel It the Most." *The New York Times*, September 27. Retrieved from www.nytimes.com/2017/09/27/business/economy/ wealth-inequality-study.html (last accessed December 9, 2018).

[11] Tax Policy Center. 2018. Distributional Analysis of the Conference Agreement for the Tax Cuts and Jobs Act, December 18. Retrieved from www.taxpolicycenter.org/publications/distributional- analysis-conference-agreement-tax-cuts-and-jobs-act/full (last accessed December 9, 2018).

[12] Lewis, Jeff. 2018. "Polarization in Congress," Voteview.com, March 11. Retrieved from www .voteview.com/articles/party_polarization (last accessed December 9, 2018).

[13] Pew Research Center. 2017. "The Partisan Divide on Political Values Grows Even Wider," October. Retrieved from www.people-press.org/2017/10/05/the-partisan-divide-on-political- values-grows-even-wider/ (last accessed December 9, 2018).

economic inequality remain salient sources of anxiety about American democracy.

Although the outcome of the 2016 elections surprised most everyone, President Trump's tenure in office has in many respects resulted in a continuation of preexisting trends. It was hardly unexpected when a party-polarized Senate deadlocked over President Trump's first nomination to the Supreme Court. Nor was it surprising that Republicans opted to deploy the "nuclear option" to confirm Judge Neil Gorsuch to the Supreme Court in 2017, given that Democrats had executed the same maneuver in 2013 to allow a simple majority to overcome obstruction of President Obama's lower court and executive branch nominations. There is no question that President Trump is having a transformative effect on the federal judiciary. But that effect largely consists of installing nominees with solid "Federalist Society" bona fides – in other words, hardline but orthodox judicial conservatives who would have been the likely choice of any Republican president elected in 2016. Likewise, the partisan battles in the 115th Congress (2017–2018) over health care, environmental regulation, and tax policy just continued the trench warfare characteristic of congressional politics on these issues across recent decades. One should not exaggerate the extent to which contemporary American politics has departed from the twenty-first-century norm.

But layered on top of these long-standing worries is a new and profound set of anxieties. The 2016 national elections raise questions about how the US system is coping with the pressures of a worldwide "populist zeitgeist" (Mudde, 2004), as voters turn away from mainstream parties and leaders toward charismatic outsiders. Recent developments, including the election of a populist outsider to the US presidency, have even posed the "regime question," meaning the resilience of American institutions to democratic backsliding and autocratic tendencies (Mickey, Levitsky, and Way, 2017, Levitsky and Ziblatt, 2018, Weyland and Madrid, 2019).

Below we weigh what this volume has to say to both long-standing and new sources of anxiety about American democracy and government. Although much more research is needed to bring social science research to bear on the anxieties of American democracy that have emerged since 2016, these chapters offer some insight. We conclude by suggesting a central irony. The very features of the Madisonian system that make party polarization such a worrisome long-term trend may, at the same time, help to impede populist autocracy. With its many veto points, checks, and balances, the constitutional framework has great difficulty functioning under the pressures of pervasive, intractable conflict between two evenly matched parties. Whatever its faults on other dimensions, however, the Madisonian system tends to resist autocratic concentration of power.

LONG-STANDING ANXIETIES

This volume has explored anxieties about American democracy in three areas: (a) the adequacy of political representation, (b) the internal processes of political institutions, and (c) government performance and policy outcomes. It is not easy to summarize a volume covering such a broad and diverse array of topics relating to American government. But it is clear that this volume offers a mixed – and, in some respects, a reassuring – assessment of these three long-standing sources of anxiety about American governing institutions.

Representation

Contributions to this volume do not by any means fully allay anxieties about representational deficiencies, but they also do not validate citizens' worst fears. The research presented and discussed here points to some limits on the potential for governmental capture by the affluent. The chapters also suggest some pathways for broader citizen influence, including even for minority groups disadvantaged in democratic politics.

Brandice Canes-Wrone and Nathan Gibson add to a growing body of scholarship documenting that policy outcomes in American government better reflect the preferences of the well-to-do than those of middle-income and poor voters (Gilens, 2012, Gilens and Page, 2014, Bartels, 2016, Miler, 2018). Canes-Wrone and Gibson show that contemporary senators vote in ways that clearly correspond with their campaign donors, even after controlling for broader public opinion in their states. This pattern is more evident in recent data than in the earlier years of their study. Since 2006, senators' roll call decisions distinctly track the preferences of their campaign contributors, while donor opinion did not have a statistically significant effect on senators' behavior in the 1980s and 1990s. Importantly, however, Canes-Wrone and Gibson find that electoral competition constrains responsiveness to donor opinion. Senators who represent electorates that are not tilted in favor of their party do not exhibit special responsiveness to donor opinion. This finding suggests the potential for vigorous electoral competition to check the influence of campaign contributors on congressional decisions.

Lee Drutman, Matthew Grossman, and Timothy LaPira document the widening inequalities in the universe of interest groups seeking to influence federal policymaking. Even though the lobbying community in Washington, DC has continued to expand at a dramatic rate, lobbying expenditures and resources remain concentrated in a small share of organizations. Out of more than 35,000 unique organizations, the top 100 alone account for at least a third of all in-house lobbyists in Washington and hire about one in five contract lobbyists. Furthermore, the composition of this elite group changes little from year to year. As gauged by both lobbying expenditures and employees, business interests dominate the Washington lobbying community – reconfirming one of America's oldest anxieties (Schattschneider, 1960).

The more pressing question, though, is the extent to which economic inequalities translate into policy distortions. Synthesizing the vast literature on the subject across multiple scholarly disciplines, contributors to this volume do not offer stark conclusions. Social scientists have simply not yet established a consensus on the extent to which economic inequalities drive public policy.

Based on an extraordinarily rich and in-depth look at the literature on business influence in policymaking, Anthony S. Chen concludes that the "evidence still is not clear that business influence distorts the quality of democratic representation." Business influence can be more clearly documented in studies focusing on particular industries and specific policy disputes than in broad, aggregate analyses of policymaking writ large. But researchers have failed to uncover clear evidence that money and lobbying resources succeed in buying policy outcomes. Instead of resources driving policy, the more consistent finding in the literature is a status quo bias (Baumgartner et al, 2009). The complex American system, with its many veto players, tends primarily to advantage whatever side is seeking to maintain the status quo.

Although the effects of economic inequality on American public policy cannot be nailed down precisely, it is also fair to conclude that the scholarly work on these questions does not sustain a thoroughgoing cynicism about corporate or plutocratic control over national policy. Economic inequalities in American society are vast and growing, and those at the top of the income and wealth distribution largely fund political campaigns. These same inequalities are also evident in the universe of groups seeking influence over policymaking. But wealthy donors do not necessarily get their favored outcomes, particularly when officeholders must consider broader electorates. Likewise, business interests are not necessarily able to leverage their resource advantages to obtain their preferred political outcomes. Like other organizations seeking to shape national policy, even well-resourced organizations face high hurdles to success when they seek to alter existing policy. For example, whatever anxieties we may have over recent turns in immigration policy, it is clear that business interests getting their way should not be among them.

Looking beyond the concerns about the outsized influence of well-resourced people and interests, this volume also offers a mixed assessment of the pathways by which ordinary citizens can wield influence over American politics and policymaking. Daniel Schlozman and Sam Rosenfeld take stock of the major political parties as mechanisms to link the governed and the government. They confront the central paradox of contemporary American parties: (a) parties have immense capacity to marshal the loyalties of voters, with partisanship in voting currently at its peak since the start of public polling and (b) parties are weak in performing their essential functions, such as making nominations, developing coherent policy, and mobilizing nonvoters. In their formulation, the parties are "hollow": strong on the exterior, but weak and ineffectual in internal capacity. Even so, Schlozman and Rosenfeld see American parties as capable of renewal. The very strength of American voters' continuing attachment to the major parties is a resource by which US parties may be able to rejuvenate their local organizations and grassroots connections. In this sense, the major parties in the United States may be easier to rehabilitate and revitalize than the mainstream parties in other rich democracies that have fragmented and lost ground to new, insurgent parties on the populist left and right.

One of the most profound and enduring anxieties of democratic representation centers on the role and influence of disadvantaged minority groups. When outcomes are decided on the basis of majority rule, how can minorities have their voices heard and their concerns addressed? Protest has long been an important means by which marginalized citizens express their grievances. Daniel Gillion and Patricia Posey offer empirical evidence documenting the efficacy of minority protest. Based on an extensive dataset of protest events reported in *The New York Times* over decades, Gillion and Posey show that salient minority protests relate to both the subsequent emergence of strong Democratic challengers in congressional districts as well as the outcomes of congressional elections. These findings suggest both direct and indirect lines of accountability. Because minority protest can stimulate electoral challengers and shifts in voter attention, officeholders have incentives to pay attention to protestors and preemptively respond to their demands. Even though minority rights inevitably stand in tension with majority rule, Gillion and Posey point to the capacity for citizen activism to influence policymakers, including activism by disadvantaged minority groups.

Processes

The chapters analyzing sources of anxiety about the processes of American governing institutions are perhaps the most reassuring entries in the volume. On the whole, these contributions tend to tamp down alarm about internal governing procedures.

Peter Hanson and Lee Drutman document that the party-polarized Congress still functions in a bipartisan and deliberative manner when exercising the power of the purse. Despite the ferocious partisanship that characterizes so much congressional activity, House members still often work together across party lines on appropriations. Hanson and Drutman "find ample evidence of bipartisan cooperation and consensus-building," with appropriations bills frequently considered under open amending processes, members of both parties able to offer successful amendments, and many questions decided by lopsided majorities garnering broad support from both parties. At times, partisanship does inhibit members' ability to collaborate on appropriations, particularly when more extreme members exploit open amending processes to offer grandstanding amendments designed to score political points. Likewise, broad member participation and input cannot occur when appropriations are handled via sweeping omnibus or continuing resolutions, as is increasingly common. But even despite these important caveats, the portrait of congressional operations offered here contrasts with broad-brush characterizations of the institution as thoroughly dysfunctional.

Along similar lines, James Curry and Frances Lee argue that Congress retains substantial capacity at conflict resolution, even in the contemporary polarized era. In process terms, today's Congress operates very differently from the "textbook Congress" of the twentieth century. Congressional committees meet less frequently; party leaders play a much bigger role in negotiating policy; and a large share of legislation comes to the floor without a formal committee report. "Regular order" is no longer the order of the day. But none of these changes mean that more laws are passed on narrow party-line votes. In fact, legislative enactments, including landmark laws, still garner roughly the same level of minority party support as they did in the 1970s. In this sense, departures from the open, inclusive "regular order" processes of an earlier era should be viewed as alternative paths to the same ultimate destination. Procedural innovations are more often adaptations to the challenges of legislating in today's environment than a means of ramming through partisan laws. No doubt, congressional action is much more difficult under conditions of intense partisan conflict. But when the contemporary Congress legislates it still usually does so on the basis of support from both parties.

Kenneth Benoit, Kevin Munger, and Arthur Spirling address the long-standing procedural anxiety that democratic discourse is deteriorating. In a world where politicians communicate by tweet and soundbite, the "dumbing down" of debate and deliberation looms as a worrisome prospect, particularly in an increasingly complex, interconnected political world. Examining long-term patterns in the sophistication of political discourse across an array of settings, including presidential speeches, the Congressional Record, executive orders, and Supreme Court decisions, they find little evidence of increased simplification. Although some previous work had pointed to greater simplicity in presidential State of the Union (SOTU) addresses, those changes do not indicate a decline in the sophistication of political discourse more broadly. In fact, their analysis suggests that the changes in SOTU addresses are more cosmetic than substantive, stemming especially from a decrease in sentence length.

Taken together, these analyses of procedural anxieties imply that the more serious problems of American governing institutions center elsewhere – on deficiencies of representation, policymaking, and administration – rather than on institutional processes in themselves. No doubt, the processes of American governing institutions warrant continued study and efforts at improvement. In a world where the values of deliberation and efficiency tend to trade-off against one another, institutional processes will surely continue to prompt critique and fuel anxiety – as they have throughout our history.

Government Performance and Outcomes

Of the three sources of anxiety analyzed in this volume, the chapters focusing on government performance and outcomes offer the least reassuring portrait.

They point to a national government that is frequently unable to address national problems or to update long-standing policies to meet current needs.

Suzanne Mettler and Claire Leavitt examine how polarization-driven gridlock in Congress interacts with the "policyscape," the dense network of policies created in the past. Importantly, the policyscape does not remain static, even when Congress is unable to build sufficient consensus to revise laws. Societal or economic changes can transform the effects of long-standing policy, even when laws remain the same. For example, policies not indexed to the cost of living or inflation, such as the minimum wage or Pell grants, erode in value if the relevant statutes are not updated. Meanwhile, policies that are indexed to increasing costs – such as Social Security, Medicare, and Medicaid – consume an ever-increasing share of the budget, crowding out other priorities. Policies can also foster transformative shifts in private actor behavior, such as the rent-seeking that has driven the rise of a lucrative for-profit educational sector reliant on federal student aid that "leaves students indebted and poorly trained, at taxpayer expense" (Chapter 10 in this volume).

Congress needs to revisit long-standing policies periodically to address dysfunctional or undesirable "policy drift." But a polarized Congress has great difficulty acting. Mettler and Leavitt document Congress's failure to conduct basic policy maintenance, showing that the contemporary Congress was overdue in reauthorizing the major policies in more than half of the public's top priority areas. The result is that existing policies fall into disrepair and no longer fulfill their intended purposes.

David Spence examines how polarization has affected the modern American administrative state. Synthesizing a vast literature across political science, public administration, and administrative law, he argues that polarization has not yet resulted in ideologically extreme agency policymaking. Agencies hew to a middle course in part because Congress and the president usually push them in opposing directions, given that divided government has been the normal condition throughout the polarized era. Instead, the more serious impact of party polarization on the administrative state stems from Congress's deficiencies in conducting basic policy maintenance. As a result, agencies and judges are frequently faced with the difficult, constitutionally fraught task of applying laws to questions and circumstances they were never intended to address. Given how rarely statutes are updated, agencies must also navigate the complexity of handling conflicts between the statute as enacted by a prior (often long prior) congress and the preferences of a current congress. Polarization also fuels skepticism of expertise and experts, the basis of much agency policymaking. In sum, party polarization and its attendant gridlock have imposed new pressures on agencies and courts, straining their capacity.

Nolan McCarty's chapter presents a grim portrait of institutional deterioration under the pressures of rising party polarization. A gridlocked Congress has lost or relinquished power relative to the other institutions of national government, compromising its role in the separation of powers. But the consequences also extend well beyond the balance of institutional power. Congress's reduced ability to legislate, budget, and carry out routine legislative functions weakens the national government's capacity as a whole. Although Congress's inability to act can empower the courts and the executive branch to assert more policymaking autonomy, the unilateral powers possessed by courts and presidents cannot adequately substitute for congressionally enacted legislation. The result is a national government with overall reduced capacity. In short, this is a dynamic account of institutional weakening under the pressures of widening party polarization in American politics.

EMERGENT ANXIETIES

When this project began, our primary focus was on the anxieties that the American public had about the performance of our democratic and liberal institutions. The anxieties that those institutions would be fundamentally subverted were beyond our vision. Sadly, that is no longer true.

The presidential election of Donald Trump – a reality television star with no previous political experience – raises questions about the capacity of American institutions to manage and channel populist pressures. Could the United States follow the path of other democracies that deteriorated into populist autocracy? Since 2016, publishers have churned out an array of titles addressing fears of democratic breakdown: *Fascism: A Warning* (Albright, 2018),*How Democracies Die* (Levitsky and Ziblatt, 2018), *The People vs. Democracy* (Mounk, 2018), *The Road to Unfreedom* (Snyder, 2018), and *Can It Happen Here?* (Sunstein, 2018), among others. Teams of scholars have also organized themselves to monitor the threats of authoritarian populism[14] and democratic erosion in the United States.[15]

No doubt, the range and severity of new democratic anxieties already warrant a sequel to this volume. But here we conclude with a few thoughts on how the contributions to this book can speak to these new anxieties.

Populism has a rich history in the United States (Kazin, 1995) and has long figured prominently in major party platforms and appeals. Widening economic inequalities and increasing racial and ethnic diversity in twenty-first-century America create favorable conditions for populists on both the left and right. Likewise, the tendency of senators to do the bidding of campaign donors (Chapter 4 in this volume) and the concentration of lobbying resources and

---

[14] Miller, Michael, David Szakonyi, and Lee Morgenbesser. 2018. "Expert Survey on American Democracy: May-June 2018," Authoritarian Warning Survey. Retrieved from www.authwarning survey.com/single-post/2018/07/06/Expert-Survey-on-American-Democracy-May-June-2018 (last accessed December 9, 2018).

[15] Carey, John, Gretchen Helmke, Brendan Nyhan, and Susan Stokes. 2018. *Bright Line Watch Survey Report: Wave 5*, May 1. Retrieved from http://brightlinewatch.org/wave5/ (last accessed December 9, 2018).

manpower in a small set of elite organizations (Chapter 3 in this volume) offer plenty of fodder for populist appeals. Set in the context of the transnational rise of populist parties and leaders, the success of the Brexit referendum in the UK, and Trump's election, we hope to see more scholars analyzing populism's effect on the American political system.

This volume does not tackle the topic of populism directly, but Schlozman and Rosenfeld point to our system's key vulnerability – "hollowed out" parties with radically open nominating systems are subject to takeover by populist outsiders. Indeed, populist challengers have been a recurring feature of presidential nomination contests in the post-1968 reformed presidential nominating system. In most cases, the party establishment succeeded in beating back insurgents, as key groups in the party coalition coalesced around a mainstream favorite and starved competitors for financial support in the so-called invisible primary (Cohen et al, 2008). But in a system where party nominations are open to all comers and outcomes and are decided in primaries and caucuses, Trump's nomination and election realized what has long been a latent possibility (Cohen et al, 2016).

Future research should look beyond presidential contests to gauge the extent of populist candidacies at other levels of electoral politics. After 2009, a number of Tea Party candidates successfully challenged the party establishment in the Republican Party, sounding populist themes of "taking our country back." But even in recent years only a handful of congressional incumbents faced any significant primary challenge. On the other hand, populists may be able to win nominations without actually challenging and defeating establishment candidates, given parties' incentives to take a pragmatic attitude toward any candidate who can win the seat. Future work should examine the extent to which populist candidacies and rhetoric figures in US electoral politics and systematically analyze whether or how officeholders elected on such appeals behave differently than others.

The resiliency or porousness of governing institutions to populist pressures can entail high stakes for democracy. Scholars of comparative politics generally view the rise of populist parties and leaders as a "peril" (Müller, 2016, p. 11) because populism "always stands in tension with democracy" (Weyland, 2013, p. 21). Although populist leaders wave the banner of popular sovereignty, once in power they tend to degrade democracy by weakening civil liberties, the rule of law, and the fairness of electoral processes. Recent cases of democratic erosion under populist leaders include Turkey under Recep Tayyip Erdoğan, Venezuela under Hugo Chavez and Nicolás Maduro, Poland under the Law and Justice Party (PiS), Ecuador under Rafael Correa, and Hungary under Viktor Orban.

Levitsky and Ziblatt (2018) make a powerful case that the constitutional system does not inoculate the United States from democratic breakdown. They envision a scenario by which an authoritarian leader, standing at the helm of a party that controls both chambers of Congress and holds a solid majority on the Supreme Court, politicizes election administration and law enforcement to entrench permanent control of the federal government.

Although Levisky and Ziblatt are right to caution against complacency in a world where many democracies have deteriorated (Diamond, 2015), chapters in this volume point more toward continued problems with ungovernability and policy drift than to authoritarian consolidation of power. As documented here, party polarization has not to date empowered presidents or majority parties to enact their sweeping visions for public policy, either through legislation or administration. Legislative enactments overall (Chapter 8 in this volume) and appropriations in particular (Chapter 7 in this volume) remain highly bipartisan. Instead, long-standing policies have languished without either revision or repeal (Chapter 10 in this volume), courts and administrative agencies have endeavored to apply outdated laws to new conditions (Chapter 11 in this volume), and Congress has struggled with both legislation and mundane tasks of governance (Chapter 12 in this volume).

Trump's presidency has seen a continuation of these challenges of governance, rather than a break from the past. Indeed, given his contentious relationship with his own party, Trump has had less success imposing his policy vision than other recent presidents serving under unified party control (Pearson, 2017, Edwards, 2018, Lee, 2018). The administration's top legislative priority, the repeal and replacement of Obamacare, failed outright in Congress, despite the use of budget procedures that would have allowed the legislation to pass with Republican votes alone.

Conflict between the Republican Congress and the Trump administration was often tacit, but nevertheless consequential for policy. In both 2017 and 2018, Congress quietly treated the administration's budget proposals as "dead on arrival." The 2-year spending deal Congress agreed to in February 2018 bore little resemblance to the president's budget and substantially increased rather than cut domestic discretionary spending. By the 2018 midterm elections, congressional Republicans had still shown no interest in acting on a range of issues central to Trump's presidential campaign, including infrastructure and immigration. When Senate Democrats successfully forced a 2018 floor debate on the status of the "Dreamers" (meaning young immigrants brought to the United States illegally as children), the administration's favored immigration bill received fewer votes than any other proposal considered. The 115th Congress appropriated additional money for border fencing, but declined to fund the construction of Trump's proposed southern border wall.

Generally speaking, the only legislative priorities on which the 115th Congress acted were those where Trump's preferences dovetailed with Republican Party orthodoxy. The major legislative achievement of the 115th Congress, the Tax Cuts and Jobs Act, delivered a long-standing Republican wish list of tax reductions for corporations and individuals. It is hard to credit Trump with the achievement, however, as similar legislation would almost certainly have passed under any Republican president elected in 2016.

The legislative record of the 115th Congress reveals a president with only limited ability to drive policy.

President Trump was also not immune to congressional oversight in 2017–2018. Unquestionably, a Congress controlled by Democrats would have been more aggressive in pursuing a wider range of investigations. Normally, the party-polarized contemporary Congress conducts less executive oversight during unified party control than under divided government (Chapter 10 in this volume, see also Mayhew, 2005, pp. 223–226, Kriner and Schickler, 2016). Even though the Republican Congress was hardly eager to launch investigations, congressional oversight and investigations nevertheless broke news and generated media coverage unfavorable to the administration.

Less than 3 months into the Trump presidency, the House and Senate Intelligence Committees launched formal inquiries into Russian involvement in the 2016 US elections and possible collusion with the Trump presidential campaign.[16] After the president fired FBI Director James Comey, the Senate Judiciary Committee opened a third formal inquiry. These congressional probes –encompassing public hearings, closed-door testimony, media interviews with congressional investigators, and numerous leaks – were potent drivers of news coverage throughout 2017 (Kriner and Schickler, 2018). The appointment of Special Counsel Robert Mueller also clearly demonstrates that unified party control of Congress failed to shield Trump and his campaign team from political and legal exposure. The bottom line is that not even unified government fully insulated President Trump from damaging oversight and investigations.

Looking beyond Congress, the Trump presidency faced additional constraints grounded in the constitutional framework. The federal system normally operates so that presidents face a substantial number of states controlled by their party opposition. In light of the stark geographic sorting evident in the outcome of the 2016 elections, the Trump administration quickly encountered strong opposition from Democratic-leaning states across a range of issues. Even as early as 2017, attorneys general in Democratic states had banded together in a number of lawsuits challenging the administration's environmental and health insurance regulations and served as plaintiffs in challenges to his immigration orders. More broadly, President Trump has had no greater success than President Obama in eliciting state and local compliance with his immigration agenda (Reich, 2018). Considering the federal-state collaboration required in most federal policy implementation, presidents usually need willing partners at the state level. When it could not find them, the Trump administration was constrained by "uncooperative federalism" (Bulman-Pozen and Gerken, 2009), as were other recent presidents.

---

[16] The Senate Intelligence Committee launched its investigation on January 13, 2017 and the House Intelligence Committee followed suit on March 3, 2017.

Likewise, the federal courts have bogged down or overturned an array of President Trump's executive orders and administrative actions. The administration's immigration policies faced numerous judicial setbacks, with courts ending the separation of families at the border, disallowing the long-term detention of migrant families, and blocking the administration from ending Temporary Protected Status for migrants from Haiti, El Salvador, Honduras, and Sudan. A federal judge also required the administration to fully restore the Obama-era DACA program protecting "Dreamers." Federal courts blocked the implementation of Trump's January 2017 executive order banning travel to the United States from seven majority-Muslim countries, though a second, scaled-back order was eventually upheld after numerous delays. A series of adverse rulings blocked the Trump administration's Environmental Protection Agency (EPA) from rolling back several health and environmental safety regulations. In addition, lawsuits stymied Trump's short-lived "voter integrity" commission. Despite the administration's significant successes in confirming conservative judges, the federal courts remain an important check on the administration, consistent with past norms.

Taken together, we see more continuities than disjunctures in the operation of the American political system thus far during the Trump presidency. President Trump has broken many norms, including baselessly alleging widespread voter fraud, issuing public demands that the Justice Department prosecute his enemies, declining to divest himself of his extensive financial interests, refusing to condemn neo-Nazi protestors, and labeling the news media the "enemy of the people," among others. Through his continuous use of Twitter and his frequent election-style rallies, President Trump maintains an unusually strong and unmediated connection with his party's base voters in the mass electorate. But despite the many ways in which the Trump presidency shatters the "presidential" mold, his administration's interactions with other institutions of American government have not broken free of the constitution's many constraints.

A New Appreciation of Madison?

The American political system erects high barriers against authoritarianism, populist or otherwise. It is hard to think of a political system in which it is more difficult for any single leader or party to take the reins of power. Far from permitting majority rule, the "American Hybrid" in Dahl's (2001) formulation requires three concurrent, separately elected majorities: majorities of the House and Senate, each resting on a distinct base of apportionment, as well as control of the presidency. To that list, one might also add the need for control of the Supreme Court as well as states across the federal system.

While no political system can be immunized from breakdown, there are numerous institutional obstacles standing in the way of would-be autocrats. Given how extensively the American constitutional system decentralizes and fragments power, ungovernability has long been a more salient worry for the American system than authoritarianism. With perhaps some irony, democratic erosion in American politics is not very likely in great part because the constitutional system makes it so difficult for democratic majorities to govern at all.

Many of the democratic anxieties analyzed in this volume might be seen as the sins of James Madison. Checks, balances, and federalism are enormous impediments to government action. The upshots of these structural features are many failures of legislative problem solving, statutory maintenance, and administrative rationalization, especially those that arise under conditions of tightly competitive, polarized parties. But the very fragmentation of power that makes our system so difficult to manage and mobilize also serves as a bulwark against democratic erosion and executive aggrandizement. In these regards, the Madisonian system tends to defend against our most serious fear: anxiety about the survival of democratic institutions.

REFERENCES

Albright, Madeleine. 2018. *Fascism: A Warning*. New York: Harper.

Albertson, Bethany, and Shana Kushner Gadarian. 2015. *Anxious Politics: Democratic Citizenship in a Threatening World*. New York: Cambridge University Press.

Bartels, Larry M. 2016. *Unequal Democracy: The Political Economy of the New Gilded Age*. 2nd edition. Princeton, NJ: Princeton University Press.

Baumgartner, Frank, Berry, Jeffrey M., Hojnacki, Marie, Kimball, David C., and Beth L. Leech. 2009. *Lobbying and Policy Change*. Chicago, IL: University of Chicago Press.

Brader, Ted. 2005. "Striking a Responsive Chord: How Political Ads Motivate and Persuade Voters by Appealing to Emotions." *American Journal of Political Science* 49(2): 388–405.

Bulman-Pozen, Jessica, and Heather K. Gerken. 2009. "Uncooperative Federalism." *Yale Law Journal (118)*: 1256–1583.

Cohen, Marty, David Karol, Hans Noel, and John Zaller. 2008. *The Party Decides*. Chicago, IL: University of Chicago Press.

Cohen, Marty, David Karol, Hans Noel, and John Zaller. 2016. "Party versus Faction in the Reformed Presidential Nominating System," *P.S.: Political Science and Politics* 49: 701–708.

Dahl, Robert A. 2001. *How Democratic Is the American Constitution?* New Haven, CT: Yale University Press.

Diamond, Larry. 2015. "Facing Up to the Democratic Recession," *Journal of Democracy* 26: 141–155.

Edwards, George C. 2018. "'Closer' or Context? Explaining Donald Trump's Relations with Congress." *Presidential Studies Quarterly 48*: 456–479.

Gilens, Martin. 2012. *Affluence & Influence: Economic Inequality and Political Power in America*. Princeton, NJ: Princeton University Press.

Gilens, Martin, and Benjamin I. Page. 2014. "Testing Theories of American Politics: Elites, Interest Groups, and Average Citizens," *Perspectives on Politics 12*(3): 564–581.

Kazin, Michael, 1995. *The Populist Persuasion: An American History*. Ithaca, NY: Cornell University Press.

Kriner, Douglas L., and Eric Schickler. 2016. *Investigating the President: Congressional Checks on Presidential Power*. Princeton, NJ: Princeton University Press.

Kriner, Douglas, and Eric Schickler. 2018. "The Resilience of Separation of Powers? Congress and the Russia Investigation." *Presidential Studies Quarterly* 48(3): 436–455.

Lee, Frances E. 2018. "The 115th Congress and Questions of Party Unity in a Polarized Era," *Journal of Politics* 80(4): 1464–1473.

Levitsky, Steven, and Daniel Ziblatt. 2018. *How Democracies Die*. New York: Crown Publishing.

MacKuen, Michael, Jennifer Wolak, Luke Keele, and George Marcus. 2010. "Civic Engagements: Resolute Partisanship or Reflective Deliberation." *American Journal of Political Science* 54(2): 440–458.

Marcus, George E., and Michael MacKuen. 1993. "Anxiety, Enthusiasm, and the Vote: The Emotional Underpinnings of Learning and Involvement during Presidential Campaigns," *American Political Science Review* 87(3): 672–685.

Marcus, George E., W. Russell Neuman, and Michael MacKuen. 2000. *Affective Intelligence and Political Judgment*. Chicago, IL: University of Chicago Press.

Mayhew, David R. 2005. *Divided We Govern: Party Control, Lawmaking and Investigations, 1946–2002*, 2nd ed. New Haven, CT: Yale University Press.

Mickey, Robert, Steven Levitsky, and Lucan Ahmad Way. 2017. "Is America Still Safe for Democracy? Why the United States Is in Danger of Backsliding," *Foreign Affairs* 96(May/June): 20–29.

Miler, Kristina C. 2018. *Poor Representation: Congress and the Politics of Poverty in the United States*. New York: Cambridge University Press.

Mounk, Yascha. 2018. *The People vs. Democracy: Why Our Freedom Is in Danger and How to Save It*. Boston: Harvard University Press.

Mudde, Cas. 2004. "The Populist Zeitgeist," *Government and Opposition* 39(4): 541–563.

Müller, Jan-Werne. 2016. *What Is Populism?* Philadelphia: University of Pennsylvania Press.

Pearson, Kathryn. 2017. "President Trump and Congressional Republicans: Uncertain Teamwork in the 115th Congress." *The Forum* 15(3): 513–524.

Reich, Gary. 2018. "Hitting a Wall? The Trump Administration Meets Immigration Federalism." *Publius: The Journal of Federalism* 48(3): 372–395.

Schattschneider, E. E. 1960. *The Semi-Sovereign People: A Realist's View of Democracy*. New York: Holt, Rinehart and Winston.

Snyder, Timothy. 2018. *The Road to Unfreedom: Russia, Europe, America*. New York: Tim Duggan Books.

Sunstein, Cass R., ed. 2018. *Can It Happen Here? Authoritarianism in America*. New York: HarperCollins.

Valentino, Nicholas A., Vincent L. Hutchings, Antoine J. Banks, and Anne I. Davis. 2008. "Is a Worried Citizen a Good Citizen? Emotions, Political Information Seeking, and Learning Via the Internet." *Political Psychology* 29(2): 247–273.

Weyland, Kurt. 2013. "The Threat from the Populist Left," *Journal of Democracy* 24: 18–32.

Weyland, Kurt, and Raúl L. Madrid. 2019. *Trump's Populism: The Mobilization of Nationalist Cleavages and the Future of U.S. Democracy*. New York: Cambridge University Press.

Index

political parties, U.S. (cont.)
  history, 121, 124–125, 133, 135–136, 139, 249
  and media, 142
  mobilization, 128–133, 138, 335
  nominations, 133–134, 141, 339
  organization, 126–128, 139–140
  partisan messaging, 139, 182, 185, 187,
    205–208, 210
  party platforms, 98, 279
  and protest, 106–109, 113
  and public policy, 134–137, 141, 239, 244,
    249
    tax cuts, 245
  theories, 6, 19, 120–126, 128, 339
populism, 63, 87, 136–137, 142, 272,
  285–286, 332, 338–340
Portman, Rob, 76
president
  appointments, 281–282
  executive order, 164, 226, 228, 231–232,
    251, 279, 342
  and federalism, 341
  veto powers, 310–311
Price, Tom, 273
principal-agent model, 272, 274–275, 288
Progressive Caucus, 204
protest. *See* political behavior, protest
Pruitt, Scott, 273
public opinion
  of business, 32, 36
  of Congress, 181, 248, 301
  of government, 32, 87
    trust, 1, 87, 286
  impact on Senate roll call behavior, 79
  influences, 96–97
  of interest groups, 45, 76
  of money in politics, 69, 86
  of partisanship, 121, 208
  of public policy, 240, 250
public policy
  abortion, 81
  and campaign contributors, 86
  and Congress, 185, 188, 196, 250, 337
  economic, 8, 271
  education, 196, 251
  environment, 342
  environmental, 8, 186, 251, 271, 275, 279,
    323, 332
  federal spending, 244–246
  financial, 20, 22, 27–28, 49, 276, 323, 332
  gun control, 93, 98, 163
  health care, 8, 187, 196, 204, 239–240,
    246–247, 332, 340

immigration, 251, 321, 323, 340, 342
infrastructure, 340
intelligence surveillance, 196
as an institution. *See* policyscapes
LGTBQ, 165
marijuana laws, 323
and partisanship, 271–294
and party platforms. *See* parties, U.S.
and polarization, 312–318
policyscape. *See* policyscape
and protest, 95
and regulation. *See* regulation
status quo, 51–60, 242, 251
tax cuts, 245
technology, 271
theories of development, 240–247
  incremental process of change, 242
  policy drift, 243, 337
  policy feedback, 242
  policy maintenance, 250–251
trade, 76, 81
transportation, 163, 196, 243
Puzder, Andrew, 273

Reagan, Ronald, 242, 245, 271, 305, 321
reauthorization, 8, 250–251, 337, *See*
  congressional procedure
Reciprocal Trade Agreements Act, 1953, 16
Recovery Act, 2009, 199
regular order, 6–7, 181, 183, 197, 200, 212,
  336
  appropriations, 155–177
  and legislative environment, 165
  omnibus, 179, 184, 205
regulation
  in business, 20
  of environment, 280–281
  public policy, 240
regulatory capture, 35–38
  future research, 36
representation
  and Congress, 185, 333
    conflict-clarifying representation, 182,
      185, 205–211
  and interest groups, 33
  of minorities, 6, 112, 335
  and polarization, 4, 6, 87, 331
  in the U.S. Senate, 248
  and wealth inequality, 4, 36, 86–87,
    333–334
  wealth inequality, 34
Republican Party. *See* political parties, U.S.
Republican revolution, 73

Index Authors